Manchester Medieval Sources Series

series advisers Rosemary Horrox and Janet L. Nelson

This series aims to meet a growing need among students and teachers of medieval history for translations of key sources that are directly usable in students' own work. It provides texts central to medieval studies courses and focuses upon the diverse cultural and social as well as political conditions that affected the functioning of all levels of medieval society. The basic premise of the series is that translations must be accompanied by sufficient introductory and explanatory material, and each volume, therefore, includes a comprehensive guide to the sources' interpretation, including discussion of critical linguistic problems and an assessment of the most recent research on the topics being covered.

also available in the series

COURT AND CIVIC SOCIETY IN THE BURGUNDIAN LOW COUNTRIES c.1420–1530

MANCHESTER
1824

Manchester University Press

MedievalSources*online*

Complementing the printed editions of the Medieval Sources series, Manchester University Press has developed a web-based learning resource which is now available on a yearly subscription basis.

MedievalSources*online* brings quality history source material to the desktops of students and teachers and allows them open and unrestricted access throughout the entire college or university campus. Designed to be fully integrated with academic courses, this is a one-stop answer for many medieval history students, academics and researchers keeping thousands of pages of source material 'in print' over the Internet for research and teaching.

titles available now at MedievalSources*online include*

Trevor Dean *The towns of Italy in the later Middle Ages*

John Edwards *The Jews in Western Europe, 1400–1600*

Paul Fouracre and Richard A. Gerberding *Late Merovingian France: History and hagiography 640–720*

Chris Given-Wilson *Chronicles of the Revolution 1397–1400: The reign of Richard II*

P. J. P. Goldberg *Women in England, c. 1275–1525*

Janet Hamilton and Bernard Hamilton *Christian dualist heresies in the Byzantine world, c. 650–c. 1450*

Rosemary Horrox *The Black Death*

Graham A. Loud and Thomas Wiedemann *The history of the tyrants of Sicily by 'Hugo Falcandus', 1153–69*

Janet L. Nelson *The Annals of St-Bertin: Ninth-century histories, volume I*

Timothy Reuter *The Annals of Fulda: Ninth-century histories, volume II*

R. N. Swanson *Catholic England: Faith, religion and observance before the Reformation* Elisabeth van Houts *The Normans in Europe*

Jennifer Ward *Women of the English nobility and gentry 1066–1500*

Visit the site at *www.medievalsources.co.uk* for further information and subscription prices.

COURT AND CIVIC SOCIETY IN THE BURGUNDIAN LOW COUNTRIES c.1420–1530

selected sources translated and annotated with an introduction
by Andrew Brown and Graeme Small

Manchester University Press
Manchester and New York

distributed exclusively in the USA by Palgrave

Published by Manchester University Press
Oxford Road, Manchester M13 9NR, UK
and Room 400, 175 Fifth Avenue, New York, NY 10010, USA
www.manchesteruniversitypress.co.uk

Distributed exclusively in the USA by
Palgrave, 175 Fifth Avenue, New York, NY 10010, USA

Distributed exclusively in Canada by
UBC Press, University of British Columbia, 2029 West Mall,
Vancouver, BC, Canada V6T 1Z2

British Library Cataloguing-in-Publication Data
A catalogue record for this book is available from the British Library

Library of Congress Cataloging-in-Publication Data applied for

ISBN   978 0 7190 5619 2 *hardback*
          978 0 7190 5620 8 *paperback*

First published 2007

16 15 14 13 12 11 10 09 08 07   10 9 8 7 6 5 4 3 2 1

Typeset in Monotype Bell
by Koinonia Ltd, Manchester
Printed in Great Britain
by Antony Rowe Ltd, Chippenham, Wiltshire

For George, Imogen and Myrna
and
for Jamie, Louis and George

CONTENTS

ACKNOWLEDGEMENTS

We have incurred a number of debts while working on this book, and would like to express our thanks to Dr Anna Jane Schnitker who went over our translations from Middle Dutch and made a number of very helpful suggestions for the rendering of our material in chapters 4 and 5; Dr Jan Dumolyn, who supplied us with photocopies at short notice during the checking stage; Dr Anne-Laure van Bruaene, who provided valuable advice on our selection of texts in chapter 5; to Dr Mario Damen and Professor Peter Stabel, who allowed us to use forthcoming publications; and to Dr Robert Stein who provided us with photocopies for some of the texts in chapter 5. We would also like to thank Drs Rebecca Reader and Harry Schnitker for their suggestions on translations in chapters 5 and 6; Professor Michael Angold for his help with an identification; and Dr Rosemary Horrox for her painstaking reading of the whole work which spared us many infelicities. Some of the material assembled here was collected during longer periods of research on other projects funded by the Royal Society of Edinburgh and the British Academy, whose support we wish to acknowledge here. Finally, we are particularly grateful to our Honours students at Edinburgh and Glasgow who have used versions of our translations over the past few years, and have made us think a little harder about the material, not least by asking unexpected questions.

NOTE ON COINAGE AND MONEYS OF ACCOUNT

The many systems of money of account used in the Burgundian Low Countries were generally based on pounds (*livres*, abbreviated *£*), shillings (*sous*, abbreviated s) and pence (*deniers*, abbreviated d). The most common in ducal accounts (of the receivers general) was the pound of 40 Flemish groats, the groat being a silver coin in circulation in Flanders. Unless otherwise stated, all references to pounds, shillings and pence relate to this money of account. Receivers also sometimes used a royal money of account known as the pound of Tours (*livre tournois*), which was generally worth 36 Flemish groats. Town accounts used these monies of account and others too. Most important for our purposes is a money of account used in Bruges, the Flemish pound (*pond groot*), made up of 240 Flemish groats (and therefore equivalent to 6 pounds of 40 groats). The Flemish pound of Paris (*Parisis*) also figures as a money of account in Bruges, and was worth 20 Flemish groats.

There were many types of coinage in circulation too, and these were subject to periodic revaluations. The gold coins mentioned in the course of this book were the *écu* (valued at 40 groats), the *philippus* or *ridder* (introduced by Duke Philip in 1433, and valued at 48 groats) and the florin (*c*.40 groats). The standard silver coins in circulation were the Flemish groat and the *stuiver* (valued at 2 groats). *Miten* were small copper coins: 24 made up a groat. After the unification of coinages of the Burgundian Netherlands in 1433, moneys of different regions were tied in fixed relation to each other (such that the pound of 40 groats was equivalent to 1.5 pounds of Brabant).

For further detail on these matters the reader may consult P. Spufford, *Monetary problems and policies in the Burgundian Netherlands (1433–96)* (Leiden, 1977).

ABBREVIATIONS

ADN   Archives départementales du Nord (Lille)
PCEEB   Publications du Centre européen d'études bourguignonnes
RN   Revue du Nord
SAB   Stadsarchief Brugge

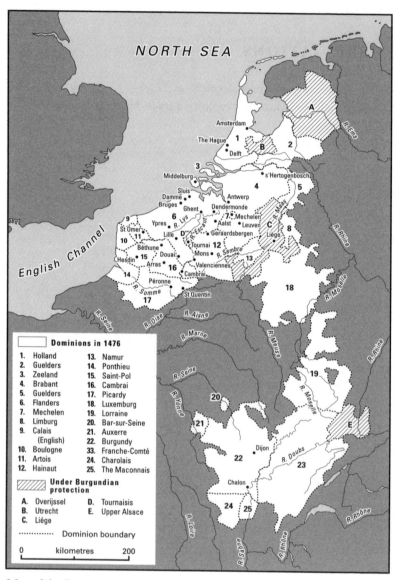

NORTH SEA

Amsterdam

The Hague
1
Delft
B

3
Middelburg
s'Hertogenbosch

Sluis
Antwerp
Damme
Bruges
Ghent
Dendermonde
R. Lys
Mechelen
Aalst
Leuven
C
Liège
9
Ypres
6
7
St Omer
Geraardsbergen
11
Lille
D
R. Escaut
10
Béthune
Tournai
12
Hesdin
15
Douai
Mons
Valenciennes
13
Arras
16
Cambrai
14
Péronne
St Quentin
17

English Channel

2
4
5
8
18
19
E
20
21
22
Dijon
23
Chalon
24
25

R. Ems
R. Rhine
R. Maas
R. Moselle
R. Rhine
R. Somme
R. Seine
R. Oise
R. Aisne
R. Marne
R. Meuse
R. Sambre
R. Seine
R. Yonne
R. Moselle
R. Doubs
R. Loire
R. Saône
R. Rhône
R. Rhône

	Dominions in 1476		
1.	Holland	13.	Namur
2.	Guelders	14.	Ponthieu
3.	Zeeland	15.	Saint-Pol
4.	Brabant	16.	Cambrai
5.	Guelders	17.	Picardy
6.	Flanders	18.	Luxemburg
7.	Mechelen	19.	Lorraine
8.	Limburg	20.	Bar-sur-Seine
9.	Calais	21.	Auxerre
	(English)	22.	Burgundy
10.	Boulogne	33.	Franche-Comté
11.	Artois	24.	Charolais
12.	Hainaut	25.	The Maconnais

Under Burgundian
protection

A. Overijssel   D. Tournaisis
B. Utrecht   E. Upper Alsace
C. Liège

.... Dominion boundary

0   kilometres   200

Map of the Burgundian dominions, 1476

INTRODUCTION

Court and civic society

The terms chosen for the title of this book may still strike some readers as strange bedfellows. The court in our period has been described as 'a closed world', 'an enchanted storehouse for the most precious treasures of its time', 'shielded from the outside ... [and] rigidly organized within by rules designed to preserve proper social distances'.[1] By that reckoning civic society was, if not the polar opposite, then at least a culture apart, physically separated and essentially distinct from a 'courtly universe' which gravitated around the person of the prince. The sense of a gulf between city and court has been perpetuated, in the case of the Burgundian Low Countries, by the long-standing influence of Johan Huizinga's *Herfstij der Middeleeuwen* (variously translated).[2] The 'forms of life, thought and art' in the lands of the Valois dukes and their Habsburg successors represented the glorious autumnal flourish of a declining civilisation, but this was a culture centred around the court, not the great cities of the Low Countries.[3] The contrast with Burckhardt's *Civilisation of the Renaissance in Italy* is marked. In the North, the Burgundian court was the last refuge of a 'high and proud civilisation'; in the south, the city of Florence was the cradle of modernity.

That fifteenth-century Europeans did not subscribe to Huizinga's view of Burgundian civilization has become abundantly clear in recent years. The impact of the cultural forms of the Low Countries in the later Middle Ages has led scholars to 'rethink the Renaissance' as a time when Burgundian arts predominated – in painting, court architecture

---

1 S. Bertelli, 'The courtly universe', in S. Bertelli, F. Cardini and E. Garbero Zorzi (eds), *Italian Renaissance courts* (London, 1986), pp. 7–38, at pp. 17, 19, 35.

2 E. Peters and W.P. Simons, 'The new Huizinga and the old Middle Ages', *Speculum* 74 (1999), pp. 587–620; J. Huizinga, *The autumn of the Middle Ages*, transl. by R.J. Payton and U. Mammitzsch (Chicago, 1996) (all subsequent references are to this edition unless otherwise stated).

3 W. Prevenier, 'Culture et groupes sociaux dans les villes des anciens Pays-Bas au Moyen Âge', in J. Duvosquel et al. (eds), *Les Pays-Bas bourguignons: Mélanges André Uyttebrouck* (Brussels, 1996), pp. 349–59.

or textiles, for instance.[4] It has also become increasingly common to explore how the tastes of the dukes and their entourage were shared by the townsmen of the Low Countries among whom they lived.[5] In music, one can no longer speak of a court style entirely distinct from that of the city, at least in Bruges.[6] Jan van Eyck was a court painter in receipt of an annual pension, but he also worked for Flemish *poorters* (or privileged burghers), perhaps most famously alderman Joos Vijd and his wife Lisbette Borluut from Ghent, for whom he produced his *Adoration of the Mystic Lamb* [14].[7] The accounts of the ducal household record considerable expenditure on the purchase, upkeep and transport of tapestries, but the wills of townsfolk from Tournai and Douai reveal that the ownership of tapestry goods of differing scale and quality was also widespread.[8] The presence of the city in the work of Gérard David, Hans Memling and other artists of the Burgundian Netherlands is hardly surprising given where these men came from and who they commonly worked for.[9] Art production did not – could not – thrive on commissions from the court alone.

The work of Van Eyck emerged, not from some moribund and intro-spective court civilisation severed from its taproot, but in a dynamic world of cultural interactions within court and civic society. The forms which these interactions took, as well as the individuals and corporate bodies who participated in them, will be the subject of the selection of documents translated and annotated in this book.

4 M. Belozerskaya, *Rethinking the Renaissance: Burgundian arts across Europe* (Cambridge, 2002).

5 R. Van Uytven, 'Splendour or wealth? Art and economy in the Burgundian Nether-lands', *Transactions of the Cambridge bibliographical society* 10 (1992), pp. 101–24 (repr. in his *Production and consumption in the Low Countries, 13th–16th centuries* [Aldershot, 2001]); S. Cassagnes, *D'art et d'argent: Les artistes et leurs clients dans l'Europe du Nord (XIVe–XVe siècle)* (Rennes, 2001).

6 R. Strohm, *Music in late medieval Bruges* (Oxford, 1985), p. 93.

7 E. Dhanens, *Van Eyck: the Ghent altarpiece* (London, 1973). The nouns *poorter* (indi-vidual) and *poorterij* (class) derive from Latin *portus* or Dutch *poort* meaning 'gate', and designate the oldest of the bourgeoisie resident within the city gates.

8 Cf. L. de Laborde, *Les ducs de Bourgogne: étude sur les lettres, les arts et l'industrie pendant le XVe siècle*, 3 vols (Paris, 1849–52); E. Soil de Moriamé, *Les tapisseries de Tournai: les tapissiers et les hautlisseurs de cette ville* (Tournai, 1891).

9 P. Stabel, 'Social reality and artistic image', in M. Carlier et al. (eds), *Core and peri-phery in late medieval urban society* (Leuven-Apeldoorn, 1997), pp. 11–32, at p. 19.

The Burgundian lands

The dynasty associated with Burgundian civilisation was French in origin, stemming from the marriage in 1369 of the son of King Charles V of France, Philip the Bold, duke of Burgundy (1363–1404), to Margaret of Male, daughter of Louis of Male Count of Flanders.[10] When Philip became ruler of the lands to which his wife was heiress in 1384, a new group of dominions emerged in two principal blocks: in the north, the counties of Flanders and Artois; in the south, the duchy and county of Burgundy, joined with the counties of Nevers and Charolais. In between lay a few less significant lordships, such as Rethel. Philip the Bold contracted marriage alliances for his many children, a practice which raised the prospect of further expansion into the Low Countries, but both he and his eldest son, John the Fearless (1404–19), devoted much of their energy to expanding their influence in the kingdom of France during the troubled reign of Charles VI. It was not until John's murder in 1419 by his rivals in France and the subsequent alliance of his own son, Philip the Good (1419–67), with the English, that the dukes of Burgundy came to spend the majority of their time in their dominions. It becomes possible to speak of Burgundian court society more convincingly from this period on – hence the starting point for our book.

The itinerary of the court changed markedly as a result of Burgundian expansion into the Low Countries under the third Valois duke. Philip the Good's principal acquisitions were the county of Namur (1420), the duchy of Brabant (1430), the counties of Holland, Zeeland and Hainaut (1433) and the duchy of Luxembourg (1443), all of which lay in the north. Burgundians from the south continued to occupy key positions at court for reasons discussed below, including the chief steward of the household (*maître d'hôtel*) and memoirist Olivier de La Marche cited so often in our texts. But by this period the dukes rarely lived in the south. Charles the Bold was born in the duchy of Burgundy but made only one significant visit to the region during his reign, in 1473–74. Territories which the court rarely visited were certainly not unimportant, nor should we assume that the authority of the regime was weak there. The duchy of Burgundy made substantial contributions to ducal coffers in the form of indirect taxes under Philip the Good and remained fiercely loyal to the dynasty, partly thanks to the role of its elites in the governance of the ducal dominions as a whole. The county of Holland also received relatively few visits from the court, but

---

10 For greater detail see under 'Select Bibliography' the works by R. Vaughan; W. Blockmans and W. Prevenier; A. Brown; and B. Schnerb.

was successfully assimilated thanks to careful handling of indigenous factions, the integration of key figures within the local comital administration, and the deployment of influential courtiers as governors in the county.[11] The relative infrequency of ducal sojourns in these regions nonetheless underlines the fact that the prince and his entourage were habitually drawn not simply to their northern territories in general, but to the southern Netherlands and the north of France in particular. In terms of its customary location the court was Brabantine, Flemish or Artesian, rather than Dutch or Burgundian.

The duke and his extended entourage were thus commonly to be found in one of the most densely urbanised regions in Christendom. The urban network was dominated by Ghent and Bruges, but many other large centres of population lay close by. In 1500, it is estimated, twenty-four of the thirty towns in north-west Europe with populations in excess of 10,000 were to be found in the Low Countries.[12] Between 31 per cent and 45 per cent of the population of the ducal dominions in the north are calculated to have lived in towns or cities, the highest proportion of any European region outside central and northern Italy, and close to the figure of 40–50 per cent which Braudel considered to be the threshold of the modern economy.[13] The dukes of Burgundy had rural residences they could use, such as the ducal castle at Hesdin with its labyrinth and mechanical amusements.[14] But the court was never very far from significant urban centres even when it was to be found in these rural locations, and it was particularly in the cities that the dukes were inclined to reside (at least when they were not on campaign, as Charles the Bold frequently was). Bruges, Lille, Ghent and Saint-Omer (in that order) received regular visits from the court or elements of it, but most of the time spent by Philip the Good and Charles the Bold in cities was spent at Brussels.[15] Similar patterns emerge in the itineraries of the duchesses. Although she eventually withdrew from court life, Isabella of Portugal (married to Philip the Good in 1430) often lived in

11 M. Damen, 'Linking court and counties: the governors and stadholders of Holland and Zeeland in the fifteenth century', *Francia* 29 (2002), pp. 256–68.

12 J. De Vries, *European urbanisation 1500–1800* (Cambridge, 1984), p. 29.

13 *Algemene geschiedenis der Nederlanden: Middeleeuwen*, iv (Haarlem, 1981), pp. 44–6; F. Braudel, *Civilisation matérielle, économie et capitalisme XVe–XVIIIe s. I, les structures du quotidien: le possible et l'impossible* (Paris, 1979), p. 425.

14 B. Franke, 'Gesellschaftsspiele mit Automaten – "Merveilles" in Hesdin', *Marburger Jahrbuch für Kunstwissenschaft* 24 (1997), pp. 135–58.

15 E. Lecuppre-Desjardin, *La Ville des cérémonies: Essai sur la communication politique dans les anciens Pays-Bas bourguignons* (Turnhout, 2004), p. 384.

the capital of Brabant, while her daughter-in-law and granddaughter were to be found in Ghent.[16] Cities were inevitably the location for great court events. The launch of the Order of the Golden Fleece took place in 1430 on the market place at Bruges, where the spectacle was witnessed by an indigenous urban audience and merchants from all over Christendom (chapter 3). Though it occurred in the south, we may also recall that Jacques de Lalaing's *pas d'armes* of the Fountain of Tears was held in 1449–50 on the island of Saint Laurent directly opposite the centre of Chalon-sur-Saône, the second largest commercial centre in Burgundy, its through traffic boosted that year by a papal jubilee.[17]

The unexpected demise of Charles the Bold while fighting the coalition of Swiss and the men of Lorraine at Nancy in 1477 led to a disruptive period of external threat and internal revolt, first under Charles's only child, Mary of Burgundy, who also met an early death due to a hunting accident in 1482, then under Mary's Habsburg husband Maximilian I, who finally secured the position of Philip the Fair, his son by Mary, ten years later. Residence of the court in large cities was more problematic during this period, although it continued in Brussels once the ducal palace was rebuilt in 1480, and recommenced in cities where the worst of the troubles had occurred, notably Ghent.[18] New urban centres of Burgundian power also began to emerge. Charles the Bold's great reforms of the Burgundian state brought several institutions of government to Mechelen in the 1470s, and in the period of Philip the Fair's rule (1492–1506), followed by the regency of his sister Margaret of Austria on behalf of Charles, Philip's son (1507–15, 1519–30), the city began to rival Brussels as a capital of the Burgundian dominions.[19] At the same time Antwerp and Amsterdam were emerging as significant commercial centres in the Low Countries, rivalling and ultimately supplanting Bruges, the decline of which may be attributed to the

16 M. Sommé, 'Les déplacements d'Isabelle de Portugal et la circulation dans les Pays-Bas bourguignons au milieu du XVe siècle', *RN* 52 (1970), pp. 183–97; see also *Het prinselijk Hof ten Walle in Gent* (Ghent, 2000), pp. 79–84.

17 A. Annunziata, 'Teaching the *Pas d'armes*', in H. Chickering and T. Seiler, *The study of chivalry* (Kalamazoo, 1988), pp. 557–82, at pp. 567–74.

18 A. Smolar-Meynart, 'Le palais de Bruxelles: des origines à Charles-Quint', in A. Smolar-Meynart and A. Vanrie (eds), *Le palais de Bruxelles* (Brussels, 1991), pp. 15–90, at p. 46; D. Lievois, 'Het Hof ten Walle in Gent ten tijde van Keizer Karel V', *Handelingen der Maatschappij voor geschiedenis en oudheidkunde te Gent*, New Series 54 (2000), pp. 135–91.

19 W. Prevenier, 'Mechelen: lieu de mémoire de Bourgondische Nederlanden', *Koninklijke Vlaamse Academie van België voor wetenschappen en kunsten. Academiae analecta*, New Series, no 9 (Brussels, 2001).

increasing difficulties of trade and manufacture.[20] Conflict with France ensured that Burgundian power became ever more concentrated on the urbanised Low Countries from 1477 on. Although the counties of Burgundy and Artois were returned to Maximilian by the terms of the treaty of Senlis in May 1493, the duchy of Burgundy itself, and certain other territories in France, were not.

The cry of Burgundy continued to resonate for the dynasty which ruled the Low Countries after 1477. The Valois line survived in Mary, her son Philip the Fair and her grandson Charles V, the last two taking the names of their ducal ancestors. Despite prominent departures for royal service, many important servants of the ducal regime stayed loyal to Mary of Burgundy and Philip.[21] Among other continuities in the post-1477 period, Burgundian institutions such as the Order of the Golden Fleece were upheld and even expanded. Maximilian was at first rejected by both the Flemish cities and members of the highest nobility of Flanders, who had learned to work together and saw themselves as guardians of the Burgundian legacy.[22] Yet the new German ruler was not unreceptive to the Burgundian past himself. The incorporation of the ancient kingdom of Burgundy within the Empire in the eleventh century ensured that the idea of Burgundy was a familiar element of Habsburg political culture, and in 1508 Maximilian even contemplated the resurrection of the title.[23] It is true that Charles V's wider empire kept him occupied far from the Low Countries for much of his adult life: the convenient dynastic date for the end of our volume relates not to the Emperor but to his aunt, Margaret of Austria, regent in the Low Countries until her death in 1530. But Charles remained strongly attached to the idea of Burgundy, establishing the provinces of the Low Countries as a separate part of the empire known as the 'Burgundian circle' in 1548, and famously expressing the wish to be buried with his ancestors the dukes at Dijon.

20 R. Van Uytven, 'Stages of economic decline: late medieval Bruges', in J.-M. Duvosquel and E. Thoen (eds), *Peasants and townsmen in medieval Europe: Studia in honorem Adriaan Verhulst* (Ghent, 1995), pp. 259–69 (repr. in his *Production and consumption in the Low Countries*).

21 H. Cools, *Mannen met macht: Edellieden en de moderne staat in de Bourgondisch-Habsburgse landen (1475–1530)* (Zutphen, 2001).

22 M. Boone, 'Élites urbaines, noblesse d'état: bourgeois et nobles dans la société des Pays-Bas bourguignons', in J. Paviot (ed.), *Liber amicorum Raphaël De Smedt* (Leuven 2001), pp. 61–85, at pp. 81–2.

23 G. Small, 'Of Burgundian dukes, counts, saints and kings, 14 CE–c.1500', in J. Bolton and J. Veenstra (eds), *The ideology of Burgundy* (Leiden, 2006), pp. 151–94.

Urban society

Relations between the Valois and Habsburg rulers of the Burgundian dominions and the great cities in which they commonly resided were stormy at several points between 1420 and 1530, and underlying conflicts and tensions are important in comprehending the significance of many of the documents that follow. The formation of the Burgundian state brought unprecedented fiscal pressure to bear on the towns.[24] The mechanisms used to raise money at Lille to meet ducal demands led to the 'pillaging' of the municipal treasury, particularly under Charles the Bold – a prince who kept nearly 40 per cent of the incomes he permitted the town council to raise in the 1470s.[25] Many of the rights and privileges acquired over the years by municipal authorities could now seem at variance with the interests of the ruler. At Valenciennes, for instance, the town's right to grant asylum to murderers fleeing from other jurisdictions was an unwelcome anomaly to Philip the Good, who abolished it in 1455.[26] Given the numerous potential sources of friction between ruler and municipality, it is unsurprising that several major revolts erupted and were suppressed with varying degrees of difficulty.[27] The most enduring (although not the only) rising of the 1430s occurred at Bruges.[28] In the following decade tension between the ducal regime and Ghent developed from 1447, and led to a bloody war which was not settled in the duke's favour until 1453 [13, 14].[29] Charles the Bold's accession witnessed revolts in a number of towns, including Mechelen and Ghent [15], and on his death many municipalities exploited the weakness of the new dynasty to reassert their privileges.[30] But conflicts

---

24 M. Boone, 'Les Ducs, les villes et l'argent des contribuables: le rêve d'un impôt princier permanent en Flandre à l'époque bourguignonne', in P. Contamine et al. (eds), *L'impôt au Moyen Âge, II. Les espaces fiscaux* (Paris, 2002), pp. 323–41.

25 D. Clauzel, *Finances et politique à Lille pendant la période bourguignonne* (Dunkirk, 1982), pp. 193–7.

26 J.-M. Cauchies, 'Valenciennes et les comtes de Hainaut (milieu XIIIe–milieu XVe siècle): des relations politiques mouvementées', in L. Nys and A. Salamagne (eds), *Valenciennes aux XIVe et XVe siècles* (Valenciennes, 1996), pp. 67–88, esp. pp. 82–4.

27 J. Dumolyn and J. Haemers, 'Patterns of urban rebellion in medieval Flanders', *Journal of Medieval History* 31 (2005), pp. 369–93.

28 J. Dumolyn, *De Brugse opstand van 1436–38* (Kortrijk, 1997).

29 J. Haemers, *De Gentse opstand, 1449–53. De strijd tussen rivaliserende netwerken om het stedelijke kapitaal* (Kortrijk, 2004).

30 W. De Pauw, 'De opstand van 1467 te Mechelen', unpublished *Licentiaat* thesis, University of Ghent 2002–3 (consultable at www.ethesis.net); R. Van Uytven, '1477 in Brabant', in W. Blockmans (ed.), *1477: Marie de Bourgogne* (Kortrijk, 1985), pp. 253–85.

between city and state were most widespread during our period in the
years of Maximilian's regency, from 1482 to 1492. Several urban centres
witnessed major revolts, notably Ghent in 1485 and in 1487–92, and
Bruges in 1485 and 1488–90. It was not until the reign of Philip the
Fair that lengthier periods of peace between the ruling dynasty and its
most important cities were restored, although Ghent's rebellions were
far from over even then.[31]

It would be misleading, nonetheless, to reduce the history of relations
between the ruling regime and the major urban centres of the Burgundian dominions to the story of the origins, course and consequences
of rebellions. The maintenance or re-establishment of peace and prosperity depended on the fostering of mutually advantageous relations
between the prince and his urban subjects, at least the most influential and powerful among them. In most cities, here as elsewhere, the
apex of urban society was occupied by a small elite whose wealth and
dominance of municipal office marked them out from the rest of the
population. In Leuven, the leading group consisted of industrialists
and merchants on the one hand and urban landowners of old standing
on the other, the latter in many respects close to the nobility in lifestyle.[32] Below the elite lay the mass of the population, foremost among
them the heads of the guilds. In some cities, guildsmen aspired to and
attained a substantial role in municipal government, at Brussels and
Tournai in the course of the fifteenth century, for example, and more
enduringly in Ghent where, with the exception of the period from
1454 to 1477, municipal government was divided between 'The Three
Members' of the *poorterij*, the 53 small guilds and the weavers.[33] But
despite wider participation in government in these cases, few would
now concur with Pirenne's vision of the cities of the Low Countries as
early democracies.[34] Some guild deacons led a lifestyle not dissimilar
to that of wealthier social groups, particularly in sectors producing
luxury goods, and the guilds were increasingly becoming a closed

31 J.-M. Cauchies, *Philippe le Beau* (Turnhout, 2003), pp. 79–84; J. Decavele (ed.), *Ghent. In defence of a rebellious city* (Antwerp, 1989).

32 R. Van Uytven, *Stadsfinanciën en stadsekonomie te Leuven van de XIIe tot het einde der XVIe eeuw* (Brussels, 1961), esp. p. 594 et seq.

33 M. Boone, *Gent en de Bourgondische hertogen, ca. 1384–ca. 1453* (Brussels, 1990); G. Small, 'Centre and periphery in late medieval France: Tournai, 1384–1477', in C.T. Allmand (ed.), *War, government and power in late medieval France* (Liverpool, 2000), pp. 145–74.

34 H. Pirenne, *Early democracies in the Low Countries: urban society and political conflict in the Middle Ages and the Renaissance*, trans. J. Saunders (New York/London, 1963).

and hereditary milieu.[35] Governments which incorporated the guilds were scarcely less prone to the problems of nepotism and patronage which outsiders might detect in rule by patriciate.[36] If, as it seems, the description of Philip the Good's dominions as 'the Promised Lands' by the former courtier Philippe de Commynes does indeed hold some truth, the bulk of the city's population in employment benefited less than guild masters, entrepreneurs or urban property owners from favourable economic conditions.[37] Workers in Bruges enjoyed higher salaries than those in some other cities, and within our period the middle third of the fifteenth century was a time of greater prosperity for many living in the Burgundian dominions, but on the whole the lower social orders led a precarious existence.[38] Short of a revolution, the labouring classes were never likely to occupy a role in government, tending instead to swell the ranks of the discontented during periods of revolt discussed above. Close to them but also marginalised was a disparate sector of the population which is hard to quantify, including prostitutes, criminals and beggars.[39]

Urban society thus broadly defined was organised in ways that afforded a large measure of social control to civic elites. Aldermen appointed or at least vetted those responsible for the districts into which all sizeable towns were divided. At Bruges there were six such districts in the city, subdivided into a total of 119 'circles'.[40] Neighbourhood and parish organisations fulfilled a number of important functions: the keeping of the watch and wall-work, fire prevention and fire fighting, the breaking of ice on communal water supplies and the payment of certain taxes,

35 A. Derville, 'Les élites urbaines en Flandre et en Artois', in *Les élites urbaines au Moyen Âge: XXIVe congrès de la Société des historiens médiévistes de l'enseignement supérieur* (Rome, 1996), pp. 119–35.

36 M. Boone and W. Prevenier, 'The " city-state dream" ', in Decavele (ed.), *Ghent*, pp. 81–105, at p. 88.

37 M. Jones (ed. and trans.), *Philippe de Commynes. Mémoires. The reign of Louis XI* (Harmondsworth, 1970); R. Van Uytven, 'La conjoncture commerciale et industrielle aux Pays-Bas bourguignons: une récapitulation', in Duvosquel et al. (eds), *Les Pays-Bas bourguignons*, pp. 435–51.

38 J.-P. Sosson, *Les travaux publics de la ville de Bruges, XIVe–XVe siècles* (Brussels, 1977), and 'Le "petit peuple" des villes: indispensables mesures et mesures impossibles?', in P. Boglioni et al. (eds), *Le petit peuple dans l'Occident médiéval* (Paris, 2002), pp. 191–211.

39 G. Dupont, 'Marginale groepen in de stedelijke samenlevingen in de late Middeleeuwen', in D. Heirbaut and J. Lambrecht (eds), *Van oud en nieuw recht. Handelingen van het XVde Belgisch-Nederlands Rechthistorisch Congres* (Antwerp, 1998), pp. 219–40.

40 R. Van Uytven, 'Scènes de la vie sociale dans les villes des Pays-bas au XVe siècle', *Mémoires de la Société d'agriculture, sciences et arts de Douai*, Fifth Series, 8 (1980–2), pp. 11–31, repr. in his *Production and consumption in the Low Countries*.

but also recreational pursuits, including neighbourhood participation in city-wide festivities (see chapter 4). In some towns, such as Ghent, local neighbourhood officials were responsible for the settlement of minor disputes.[41] The fulfilment of these roles brought city dwellers into routine contact and encouraged the creation and observation of hierarchies among them. Beyond the neighbourhood, many other incorporations defined relations between town dwellers and emphasised the authority of a few. Clearly the professional organisation of the guilds placed the masters in a central position, themselves answerable in certain matters to town councils. Religious confraternities afforded a preponderant role to civic elites, such as the fraternity of the Holy Blood in Bruges in which all but 2 of the 73 recorded members from 1469 to 1500 had served as city magistrates (see chapter 6).[42] Recreational organisations such as the chambers of rhetoric which held poetry and theatrical competitions within and between cities have been characterised in similar fashion [19a–c].[43] Needless to say, jousting fraternities (mainly in the fourteenth century) and archery or crossbow guilds (more widespread in the fifteenth) placed requirements upon their members in the cities of the Burgundian dominions which could only be fulfilled by the relatively well-off [17a–b, 18a–b]. Given the levers of power at the disposal of civic elites, it is tempting to describe the communities in which they lived as 'conformist totalitarian societies based on mutual surveillance'.[44] If this claim appears excessive for such large communities as the cities of the Low Countries, the forms of social organisation outlined here do lend a semblance of credibility to the description of Ghent in one of our sources: 'while the number of people is very great, the multitude itself does not give rise to confusion, for they are all numbered and known in their innermost thoughts by those whose task it is to govern and lead them, such as the deacons and the aldermen, the shopkeepers, the constables and the men responsible for the hundreds and tens in the various parishes and streets, in the member of the small guilds as in that of the weavers' [14]. One can also readily understand

41 Boone, *Gent en de Bourgondische hertogen*, pp. 124–9.

42 A. Brown, 'Ritual and state-building: ceremonies in late medieval Bruges', in J. van Leeuwen (ed.), *Symbolic communication in late medieval towns* (Leuven, 2006), pp. 1–28, at p. 15. There were, though, guilds which included a much wider membership (See chapter 6).

43 H. Pleij, 'Geladen vermaak: Rederijkerstoneel als politiek instrument van een elite-cultuur', *Jaarboek van De Fonteine* 25 (1975), pp. 75–104, at p. 103.

44 Y. Grava, 'La mémoire, une base de l'organisation politique des communautés provençales au XIVe s.', in *Temps, mémoire, tradition au Moyen Âge* (Marseilles, 1983), pp. 69–84, at p. 82.

how popular frustration might accumulate against a civic elite which
monopolised office to its own advantage (or, as the same source has
it, 'the wicked plundering thieves who consume our very entrails, and
in the prince's name ... grow fat on our worldly goods and stuff their
sacks'). Among the principal benefits of office was systematic gift-giving
paid out of public funds for members of the elite on the occasion of great
civic festivities, or at some important point in the life of the office-bearer.
The practice evolved to promote social and political cohesion within
the city.[45] In Ghent, where municipal gift-giving was particularly widespread, one of the greatest beneficiaries in the fifteenth century was
the master carpenter Daneel Van Zeveren, nicknamed 'Liver-eater' by
his enemies because of the monetary gifts amounting to the equivalent of several years' salary for a master guildsman which he received
during a career in municipal government spanning three decades. On
average these networks of sociability consumed between 12 and 15 per
cent of the municipal budget of Ghent in the period 1400–1460. The less
complex political scene of other towns may have reduced the need for
such outlays, but similar gifts at Lille still amounted to more than 7 per
cent of that city's revenues.[46] Social control brought significant material
benefit for the governing elite.

City and state

It was among these groups, and the organisations in which their
members fraternised with kin and friends, that the princely state
found its strongest urban support. Civic elites exercised control over
the wider urban population and were the key to unlocking the fiscal
potential of large urban centres. It is therefore unsurprising that in
many cities the overlap between such groups and princely government
became marked, particularly where organs of ducal government were
based [19b]. Lille was a primary recruiting ground for members of
the ducal *chambre des comptes* which was located in the city.[47] In Dijon,
at least 79 municipal office-bearers (31 of them mayors of the city) held

45 M. Boone, 'Dons et pots-de-vin, aspects de la sociabilité urbaine au bas Moyen Âge:
Le cas gantois pendant la période bourguignonne', *RN* 70 (1988), pp. 471–87, notably
pp. 476–7.

46 Clauzel, *Finances et politique*, p. 153.

47 M. Jean, 'Aux marges du royaume: la chambre des comptes de Lille en 1477', in P.
Contamine and O. Mattéoni (eds), *La France des principautés: Les chambres des comptes
aux XIVe et XVe siècles* (Paris, 1996), pp. 27–41, at pp. 37–8.

a post in the ducal administration between 1300 and 1450.[48] In Ghent, members of the ducal council responsible for justice came in the majority from the patriciate of the city.[49] Official service of the princely state during a period of tenure of municipal office was forbidden or frowned upon for obvious reasons, but this did not prevent former or future magistrates from holding a post in the prince's administration at other times. There are certainly examples of wealthy townsmen who held municipal office and do not seem to have been attracted to the service of the Burgundian state, such as Simon Borluut of Ghent, brother-in-law of Joos Vijd who commissioned Van Eyck's great altarpiece for the church of St John's in Ghent [14].[50] This group of urban notables – if indeed such families really did constitute a recognisable group – is deserving of further study. But historians have emphasised more often the numerous cases of townsmen who rose to high office under the dukes, among them two Brugeois who became chief stewards of the household, Pieter Bladelin under Charles the Bold and Pieter Lanchals under Maximilian I; the Brussels magistrate Jean II Hinckaert, who became master of the ducal forest of Soignes near the capital of Brabant; or the mayor of Leuven Lodewijk II Pynnock, who was a squire in the ducal entourage.[51] The incentives to procure office through the court were considerable. The recipients of financial reward and prestige in the service of the princely state could usually offer greater prospects of advancement to their supporters than other patrons, thereby creating or strengthening local and regional networks which were dependent on the Burgundian court, the public source of patronage, for their prosperity and standing [15].[52] Not all sectors in all civic elites participated fully in this experience, of course. Some of the most vociferous and active opponents of the Valois and Habsburg

48 T. Dutour, 'Les relations de Dijon et du duc de Bourgogne au XIVe siècle', *PCEEB* 33 (1993), pp. 5–19, at pp. 16–17.

49 J. Dumolyn, 'Les conseillers flamands au XVe siècle', in R. Stein (ed.), *Powerbrokers in the late Middle Ages: The Burgundian Low Countries in a European context* (Turnhout, 2001), pp. 67–85, esp. pp. 76–84.

50 Boone, 'Élites urbaines, noblesse d'état', pp. 79–80.

51 G. Milis-Proost, 'Bladelin (Pieter)', *Nationaal Biografisch Woordenboek* 2 (Brussels, 1967), cc. 61–3; M. Boone, 'Biografie en prosopografie, een tegenstelling? Een stand van zaken in het biografisch onderzoek over Pieter Lanchals', *Millennium* 7 (1993), pp. 4–13; P. De Win, 'The lesser nobility of the Burgundian Netherlands', in M. Jones (ed.), *Gentry and lesser nobility in late medieval Europe* (Gloucester/New York, 1986), pp. 95–118, at p. 106; A. Smolar-Meynart, 'Bruxelles face au pouvoir ducal', in Duvosquel et al. (eds), *Les Pays-Bas bourguignons*, pp. 373–84, at pp. 376–7.

52 J. Dumolyn, 'Investeren in sociaal kapitaal: Netwerken en sociale transacties van Bourgondische ambtenaren', *Tijdschrift voor Sociale Geschiedenis* 28 (2002), pp. 417–38.

regimes emerged from among the ranks of leading guildsmen during the fifteenth and sixteenth centuries, for example.[53] The civic elite was the breeding ground for both opponents and supporters of the Burgundian regime. But it is important to recognise that even among the guilds of Flanders, the dukes had their stalwarts [15]. The powerful shippers of Ghent tended to support Valois and Habsburg rulers whose authority extended far beyond the county into the many lands where the haulage industry plied its trade.[54] One such haulier was George Chastelain, the official historian of Philip the Good and Charles the Bold, and the single most-cited source in Huizinga's study of Burgundian court culture.[55] The chronicler's father had contracted a marriage within the lesser nobility, which afforded him access to at least three overlapping networks that help explain George's social ascension: one centred on the governing elite of Ghent and related organs of sociability, such as the prestigious crossbow guild of Saint George; another linking several Flemish aristocrats of the Masmines family, among them local office-holders at the lower end of the scale, and a knight of the Order of the Golden Fleece at the top; and a third gravitating around Chastelain's great-uncle, Jan van Culsbrouc, who was a member of the higher clergy in Ghent with considerable experience as a ducal diplomat. Not everyone enjoyed the opportunities open to George Chastelain, but the example does demonstrate how deep the networks associated with the court might reach to perform an integrative function. Patrons, brokers and clients existed at many social levels: the ultimate patron was the prince.

Service at court: nobles and townsmen

Townsmen might enter court service in a number of ways – as legal or financial specialists, provisioners or simple servants – but it was unusual for them to accede to high office within the household. In this primarily noble milieu, standing was dictated in large measure by one's pedigree:

53 M. Boone, '*Armes, coursses, assemblees et commocions*. Les gens de métiers et l'usage de la violence dans la société urbaine flamande à la fin du Moyen Âge', *RN* 87 (2005), pp. 7–33.

54 D. Nicholas, *The metamorphosis of a medieval city: Ghent in the age of the Van Arteveldes* (Lincoln NE/London, 1987), pp. 224–67.

55 G. Small, *George Chastelain and the shaping of Valois Burgundy* (Woodbridge/Rochester NY, 1997), pp. 9–50, and 'When *indiciaires* meet *rederijkers*: a contribution to the history of the Burgundian "theatre state"', in J. Oosterman (ed.), *Stad van koopmanschap en vrede* (Leuven, 2005), pp. 133–61.

squires 'might rise in estate according to their virtues', acknowledged
La Marche, but 'the house they came from' was also a relevant factor
in their progress (or lack of it) [4]. Some townsmen did indeed attain
noble status, and so could claim to come from a house of noble standing;
but the process was commonly a slow one, and was rarely achieved
within three generations.[56] Proof of nobility over no fewer than four
generations was a membership requirement of the Order of the Golden
Fleece [10], the ultimate expression of the noble's pre-eminence in
the prince's entourage: although the Order was quite distinct from the
court, those members who were recruited from the highest aristocracy
of the ducal dominions played a central role in its affairs, as many of our
texts and the accompanying notes make plain. The primacy of nobility
and its attendant values could result in expressions of disdain for the
non-noble who rose through court service. Arnout van Gouy, who held
high civic office in Ghent when Philip the Good entered the city in 1458
[14], was described in choice terms by the noble chronicler Jacques du
Clercq: 'he was from a lowly background in the town of Douai, bourgeois or merchants, and he conducted himself with such cunning that he
was *bailli* of Douai for a long time, then he became high *bailli* of Ghent,
and he was in Cyprus and elsewhere on several embassies for Philip,
duke of Burgundy, and he profited so much from playing dice and the
exercise of justice and in other ways that he became a rich man, and
he bought several fine lordships and had his eldest son made a knight,
even though at the outset he wasn't worth more than one hundred *écus*,
so they said'.[57] Given the desire of the successful non-noble at court
to assimilate in order to advance, we would do well not to exaggerate
the differences between him and his noble colleagues; nor should we
underestimate the power which the well-placed non-noble might exert
over those deemed by social convention to be his betters [8]. But the
dominant ideology of the court most certainly emerged from the ideals
of the knightly classes. The public weal lay in the hands of a chivalric
elite, albeit one which valued learning as well as prowess.[58]

For the nobility of the Burgundian dominions, the court performed
a more direct integrative function by bringing many of its members

56 Boone, 'Élites urbaines, noblesse d'état', p. 76.

57 Jacques du Clercq, *Mémoires*, ed. F. de Reiffenberg, 4 vols (Brussels, 1835–6), ii,
   p. 341.

58 A. Vanderjagt, 'Classical learning and the building of power at the fifteenth-century
   Burgundian court', in J. Drijvers and A. MacDonald (eds), *Centres of learning* (New
   York/Cologne, 1995), pp. 267–77; J. Hexter, 'The education of the aristocracy in the
   Renaissance', in his *Reappraisals in history* (London, 1961), pp. 45–70.

together to serve and receive reward on a part-time basis.[59] At the hub of the wider court lay the households of the prince, his wife and other members of the family, each with a contingent of attendants who served in the chamber, pantry, cellar and stables [esp. **4, 6**]. The work of these positions was mostly carried out by subordinates, while the office-bearers could find themselves entrusted with tasks of government, such as representing the duke at meetings of the estates or offering counsel. But the ceremonial duties of office were important as we shall see [e.g. **4, 5**], and holders were expected to be present at court during their terms of service, often three or six months at a time, in some instances all year round. The household ordonnances [**6**] which first appeared in the late fourteenth century for the ducal court but became more frequent in the fifteenth and sixteenth centuries identified the office-bearers and defined their conditions of service, notably the number of subalterns and horses assigned to each of them, and whether the latter were to be fed at the duke's expense directly (*a livree*), or whether the officer would receive compensation for their upkeep at a daily rate of 3 *sous* per servant or horse (*a gaiges*).[60] Attendance and payment of wages were noted in a second set of documents, the daily record of household expenses known as the *écroes* (daily rolls of expenditure).[61] Payment of *gaiges* was in reality just one of the many benefits the court office-bearer might expect to obtain from the prince. Gifts in the form of money, cloth, horses or precious objects could be received as a result of some important event in the life of a member of the ruling dynasty, or to meet some need of the servant. In a memorandum written for Philip the Good in 1439, the ducal chamberlain Hue de Lannoy estimated that the prince could allocate around 7.5 per cent of his budget to meeting the cost of such gifts.[62] This figure – which is close, as we have seen, to expenditure on gifts as a proportion of municipal budgets – was matched by recorded expenditure in the accounts of Charles the Bold's household thirty years later.[63]

---

59 W. Paravicini, 'The court of Burgundy: a model for Europe?', in R. Asch and A. Birke (eds), *Princes, patronage and the nobility: the court at the beginning of the modern age* (Oxford, 1991), pp. 70–102.

60 M. Sommé, 'Que représente un gage journalier de 3 sous pour l'officier d'un hôtel ducal à la cour de Bourgogne au XVe siècle?', in J.-P. Sosson et al. (eds), *Les niveaux de vie au Moyen Âge* (Louvain-la-Neuve, 1999), pp. 297–315. See also H. Kruse and W. Paravicini (eds), *Die Hofordnungen der Herzöge von Burgund, I: Herzog Philipp der Gute, 1407–67* (Ostfildern, 2005)..

61 H. Kruse, *Hof, amt und Gagen: Die täglichen Gagenlisten des burgundischen Hofes (1430–67) und der erste Hofstaat Karls des Kühnen (1456)* (Bonn, 1996).

62 R. Vaughan, *Philip the Good* (2nd edn, Woodbridge, 2002), pp. 259–60.

63 M. Damen, 'Gift exchange at the court of Charles the Bold', in M. Boone and M.

'The gift was everywhere' in the Burgundian dominions.[64] Office too was in the gift of the prince, and the court afforded the most direct means of accessing it. A ducal fruiterer could pick up the post of city gate-keeper from the duke, a task he might then delegate to a subordinate, but through which he naturally expected to receive an emolument and additional influence.[65] Princely control over church appointments provided further scope for patronage.[66] The career of the ducal *valet de chambre* Jean Coustain [8] provides an example of the many opportunities that might be seized by someone in close proximity to the prince (although not of the loyal service which the duke expected in return for his gifts). Daily rates of pay were therefore part of a wider picture of integration and reward at court. Although the 3 *sous* per mouth which office-bearers received to meet the living costs of subalterns was adequate, *gaiges* functioned more as a form of retainer and as a calibration of rank than as a salary properly speaking.[67] For the great courtiers, such as Charles the Bold's servant Gui de Brimeu, a man of many income streams, these sums provided a mere trickle of revenue.[68]

Household service recorded in the ordonnances and *escroes* brought the courtier into a wider network in which members of the elite were obligated to the prince and to one another. Sometimes these bonds existed for life. It was common practice for a court servant to solicit a member of the ruling dynasty to act as godparent for his or her offspring. (The count of Charolais fulfilled the role eight times in 1457 alone.) At the very least such relations generated a gift for the child, but sometimes a more enduring relationship developed. Philip the Good's confidant and first chamberlain Philippe Pot was his own godson, and Pot held at least two children over the baptismal fonts in his master's name.[69] Court careers could begin early, particularly if one entered as a page [4]. They might also last a long time, like the career of Isabelle de Moraille

---

Howell (eds), *'In but not of the market': movable goods in late medieval and early modern urban society* (forthcoming).

64 A. Derville, 'Les pots-de-vin dans le dernier tiers du XVe siècle', in Blockmans (ed.), *1477. Marie de Bourgogne*, pp. 449–71, at p. 451.

65 H. Kruse, 'Der burgundische Hof als soziales Netz', *Francia* 29 (2002), pp. 229–55, at p. 249.

66 P. Van Petegem, 'Les Rôles des bénéfices à la collation princière', *PCEEB* 38 (1998), pp. 229–46.

67 H. Kruse, 'Philipp der Gute, der Adel und das Geld', in H. Von Seggern and G. Fouquet (eds), *Adel und Zahl* (Ubstadt-Weiher, 2000), pp. 149–64, at p. 160.

68 W. Paravicini, *Guy de Brimeu* (Bonn, 1975), pp. 421–3.

69 M.-T. Caron, *La Noblesse dans le duché de Bourgogne, 1315–1477* (Lille, 1987), p. 511; Small, *George Chastelain*, p. 77.

who served Philip the Good's mother, third wife and son before finally
receiving – like many who had completed decades of service – a pension
for life in 1447.[70] Long careers encouraged the development of an *esprit
de corps* which helped the dynasty weather the storms of 1477.[71] The
presence of youth encouraged marriages within the court elite which
were brokered by the duke, duchess and other leading courtiers [**5**].[72]
A court marriage might be used to further the fortunes of the bride and
groom in very direct ways: these have left remarkable documentary
traces [**7c**]. Less apparent in the historical record, but no doubt fundamental to the nature of Burgundian power, were the informal bonds
which, one suspects, were constantly forming and reforming between
the politically powerful, their allies and their clients at court. George
Chastelain believed that Guillaume Fillastre, bishop of Toul, 'was
launched by the hand of the lord of Croy and the marshal of Burgundy'
when he rose to become head of the ducal council; 'everything changed
at that point, with new faces and new ways of doing things, all of
them nonetheless for the good'.[73] The threat of factional strife among
competing groups at court was evident and erupted most dramati-
cally in the reign of Philip the Good, notably between the Rolins and
the Croys [**7b**].[74] The problem was easy to anticipate and difficult to
avoid: nevertheless, its importance should not be overestimated in a
court in which a Portuguese lady-in-waiting (Isabella de Souza) could
become the wife of a nobleman from Champagne (Jean de Poitiers) [**5**];
a Burgundian equerry (Olivier de La Marche) the 'singular friend' of a
Ghenter (Chastelain); or a Hainaut lord (Antoine de Croy) the political
patron of a bishop from eastern France (Fillastre).

The diverse attachments generated by court service helped counter-

70 E. Bousmar and M. Sommé, 'Femmes et espaces féminins à la cour de Bourgogne',
   in J. Hirschbiegel and W. Paravicini (eds), *Das Frauenzimmer* (Stuttgart, 2000), pp.
   47–78, at p. 51.

71 M. Sommé, 'Les Jeunes Nobles à la cour de Bourgogne sous Philippe le Bon', in W.
   Paravicini and J. Wettlaufer (eds), *Erziehung und Bildung bei hofe* (Stuttgart, 2002),
   pp. 71–89. A celebrated exception was Philippe de Commynes, who came to court
   'at the end of [his] childhood, at the age when [he] could ride a horse', but who
   abandoned Charles the Bold in 1472: J. Calmette and G. Durville (eds), *Philippe de
   Commynes: Mémoires*, 3 vols (Paris, 1924–5), i, p. 4.

72 Bousmar and Sommé, 'Femmes et espaces féminins', pp. 58–60.

73 George(s) Chastel(l)ain, *Oeuvres*, ed. J.C. Kervyn de Lettenhove, 8 vols (Brussels,
   1863–6), iii, pp. 332–3.

74 W. Paravicini, '*Acquérir sa grâce pour le temps advenir*: les hommes de Charles le
   Téméraire (1433–67)', in A. Marchandisse and J.-L. Kupper (eds), *À l'ombre du
   pouvoir: Les entourages princiers au Moyen Âge* (Geneva, 2003), pp. 361–83, notably pp.
   369–74.

balance some of the shortcomings of the ducal court as a means of integrating the political elites of the Burgundian dominions. The increasing tendency for office-bearers to influence the nomination of their successors encouraged the emergence of service dynasties over several generations, making it harder for families on the outside to break into court service [8]. Lengthy careers of serving office-bearers mentioned above further reduced opportunities for newcomers. Both tendencies contributed to the disproportionate number of posts held by the nobility of certain regions under Philip the Good, notably the two Burgundies, Picardy and Brabant.[75] But although further study is required to prove the point in detail, it is clear that the preponderance of certain geographical groups within court personnel did not remain unchanged throughout our period. The Dutch certainly began to enter court service in greater numbers after 1477, while the place of the Burgundians gradually declined due to the loss of their homeland to the French.[76] At the same time, Picard nobles were placed in greater difficulty due to the long-term warfare between Valois and Hasburg until the early 1490s.[77] Moreover, the court expanded considerably in the first half of our period, permitting ever greater numbers of servants to be retained, albeit with spiralling costs which household ordonnances frequently sought to reduce [6]. In the reign of Philip the Good alone, the personnel of the household more than doubled, increasing still further under Charles the Bold.[78] The number of courtiers declined under Maximilian to levels that were comparable to those of the reign of Philip the Good, and again under Philip the Fair, but as far as possible the Habsburg Burgundians sought to restrict budget cuts to subaltern positions in an effort to retain the integrative capacity of the court at the highest level.[79] Perhaps most importantly of all, the preponderance of certain regional groupings does not appear to have affected the court's ability to engage with wider networks within the

---

75 W. Paravicini, 'Expansion et intégration: La noblesse des Pays-Bas à la cour de Philippe le Bon', *Bijdragen en mededelingen betreffende de geschiedenis der Nederlanden* 95 (1980), pp. 298–314; Bousmar and M. Sommé, 'Femmes et espaces féminins', p. 57.

76 Cools, *Mannen met macht*, esp. pp. 66–83.

77 H. Cools, 'Noblemen on the borderline: the nobility of Picardy, Artois and Walloon Flanders and the Habsburg conflict, 1477–1529', in W. Blockmans et al. (eds), *Secretum scriptorum: Liber alumnorum Walter Prevenier* (Leuven-Apeldoorn, 1996), pp. 371–82.

78 H. Kruse, 'Die Hofordnungen Herzog Philipps des Guten von Burgund', in H. Kruse and W. Paravicini (eds), *Höfe und Hofordnungen 1200–1600* (Sigmaringen, 1999), pp. 141–65, notably pp. 149–51.

79 H. Cools, 'Quelques considérations sur l'attitude des nobles comtois entre 1477 et 1500', *PCEEB* 42 (2002), pp. 167–82, at p. 174–6.

Burgundian dominions. Friends at court permitted individuals, families and corporations to achieve their goals, and while it could help if
the supplicant(s) shared regional associations with the powerbroker in
these informal but fundamental political processes, such as the authorities of Dijon who courted the ducal secretary of the great seal Jean Gros
[**7c**], it was not always necessary that they did. To reduce their share of
regional taxes or to defend some aspect of their privileges, the authorities of Saint-Omer commonly directed their pleas and inducements to
the chancellor of Burgundy Nicolas Rolin or the Hainaut lord Antoine
de Croy, neither of whom came from the region, but both of whom were
profoundly influential at Philip the Good's court.[80] The authorities in
Ghent struck up a relationship with Thibaud de Neufchâtel, marshal
of Burgundy, in their efforts to restore relations after their war with
the same duke [**13**]. Networks of sociability based on gift-giving were
widespread within the cities as we have seen; if the conditions and price
were right, these networks could be extended to incorporate Burgundian courtiers, no matter where they came from.

Such relations between civic authorities and leading courtiers serve
as a reminder that the Burgundian court remained a centre of government. A great many local institutions continued to flourish in the Low
Countries throughout our period, and it was only gradually that central
bodies such as the Great Council (reformed in 1445) and the *Parlement*
of Mechelen (founded in 1473) emerged above them in the sphere of
justice, and the *chambres des comptes* based at Lille, Brussels and the
Hague in matters of finance. As these institutions developed in the
hands of specialists, the court itself became the domain of the generalist.
Charles the Bold did attempt to restore the court as a seat of justice, but
his entourage considered this interest in routine administrative matters
to be unhealthy. (La Marche even dubbed him 'Charles the Tiring'.)[81]
And yet the court was usually able to undo or reverse decisions taken
by the emergent specialised bureaucracies which remained subordinate
to it. From the start of our period it was clearly established that the
ducal council held at court was the centre of government.[82] The situation remained much the same in 1495, when it was stated in Philip the
Fair's household ordonnance that his privy council would consider 'all
matters of any nature not concerning justice' (an exemption which took

80 Derville, 'Pots-de-vin', pp. 348–51.

81 H. Dubois, *Charles le Téméraire* (Paris, 2004), p. 148.

82 Paravicini, 'The court of Burgundy', p. 86.

account of the role of the *Parlement* at Mechelen).[83] The court played a central role in another duty of late medieval government, the conduct of war. Household ordonnances stipulated that each office-bearer would retain fixed numbers of armed men and archers [4, 6], and courtiers had prescribed roles in the event of warfare. Also present at court was a ducal bodyguard consisting of two dozen archers under Philip the Good, rising to more than four times that number under Charles the Bold [4, 15]. The appearance of these armed men and semi-military courtiers inevitably made a considerable impression upon outsiders who witnessed the Burgundian court on parade, such as Antoine de La Taverne, provost of the abbey of Saint Vaast at Arras.[84] Among the accounts of visitors to the Burgundian court which we might have included in our selection are those of the nobleman Schaseck and the Nuremberger Gabriel Tetzel, two servants of the Bohemian nobleman Leo von Rozmital who visited the court in 1466, and who were able to make comparisons with others they had seen; or indeed the famous letter of the Norfolk squire John Paston, who wrote to his mother two years later to describe the splendour of the Burgundian court on the occasion of Charles the Bold's marriage to Margaret of York.[85] Creating a favourable or fearsome impression was one of the governmental functions of the court. For well-travelled Milanese ambassadors, indeed, it seemed that the Burgundian court was more impressive than the French king's, fit even for a pope or an emperor.[86]

The Milanese who made this last observation, Tommaso da Rieti, was particularly taken by the large number of clerics and courtiers who were sent out some distance from the court to welcome him upon his arrival in 1462. 'Sending forth' in appropriate style to receive visiting ambassadors was one of the many acts of protocol which exalted rulers and clarified or transformed relations between them and other powers.[87]

83 Cauchies, *Philippe le Beau*, p. 71.

84 M.-T. Caron, 'La noblesse en représentation dans les annees 1430', *PCEEB* 37 (1997), pp. 157–72, at p. 165.

85 M. Letts (ed.), *The travels of Leo of Rozmital* (Cambridge, 1955); N. Davis (ed.), *The Paston letters and papers of the fifteenth century*, 2 vols (Oxford, 1971–6), ii, pp. 538–40.

86 E. Sestan (ed.), *Carteggi diplomatici fra Milano Sforzesca e la Borgogna*, 2 vols (Rome, 1985–7), ii, p. 148; B. de Mandrot (ed.), *Dépêches des ambassadeurs milanais en France sous Louis XI et François Sforza*, 4 vols (Paris, 1916–23), i, pp. 189–91. For translations of these valuable sources see P. Kendall and V. Ilardi (eds), *Dispatches with related documents of Milanese ambassadors in France and Burgundy*, 2 vols (Athens OH, 1970–1); V. Ilardi and F. Fata (eds), *Dispatches with related documents of Milanese ambassadors in France* (Dekalb IL, 1981).

87 J. Huessmann, 'La procédure et le cérémonial de l'hospitalité à la cour de Philippe le Bon, duc de Bourgogne', *RN* 84 (2002), pp. 295–317.

Virtually every moment of life at court was surrounded by ceremony and ritual, from its defining moments – birth, marriage and death – to the more mundane realities of eating, drinking or sleeping [4–6]. Many other ceremonies were performed outside the confines of the court on city streets and in churches, notably baptisms, marriages and funerals [5]. Rulers and courtiers were involved in urban rituals too, notably civic religious processions [20–27] or princely Entries [13–16] from which participants hoped to gain some betterment of their lot. The Burgundian court developed a reputation as one of the most spectacular in Europe: the presence and function of ceremony in court and civic society require more detailed attention.

Ceremony and ritual

For all the criticism levelled at Huizinga's depiction of Burgundian culture, *Herfstij der Middeleeuwen* remains a remarkably prescient work. The focus, in its early chapters, on the highly developed nature of ceremony at the Burgundian court – the attention devoted to courtesy, etiquette, symbols, colour, precedence and hierarchy in ducal feasts, jousts and diplomatic exchanges – anticipated the profusion of interest in court rituals among historians since the 1980s. None now endorses the conclusion that Huizinga reached: that Burgundian ceremonies, in contrast to the seriousness behind similar cultural forms of play in earlier periods, had become 'empty display',[88] divorced from politics and the everyday. But Huizinga did not argue that all rituals were 'empty' in themselves, and he regarded an element of social play as the basis of all cultures.[89] Nor did he deny that rituals, such as processions, might generate 'powerful emotions', nor yet that they might have 'political effect'.[90] To that extent, modern approaches that analyse the effects of rituals remain in his debt; but it is the effort to remarry what Huizinga had divorced – Burgundian 'rituals' from its 'politics' – that marks interest in Burgundian ceremony today.

This effort is often dominated by another line of historiography to which Huizinga was originally opposed. His contemporary, Henri Pirenne, saw in the politics of the Valois dukes (particularly the last

---

88 Huizinga, *Autumn of the Middle Ages*, p. 45.

89 Ibid., pp. 42, 285; J. Huizinga, *Homo Ludens: A study of the play element in culture* (London, 1970).

90 Huizinga, *Autumn of the Middle Ages*, pp. 8, 54.

two) a seriousness of purpose that formed the beginnings of the early modern state (and ultimately of modern Belgium).[91] What Pirenne also did was to highlight, in the process of state-formation, the struggles of the 'native' (Dutch-speaking) cities of the Low Countries against the 'foreign' (French-speaking) rulers bent on undermining civic independence.[92] Modern historians of the Low Countries are not so teleological in approach, but emphasis on state formation under the Burgundian dukes follows where Pirenne had led. The 'remarriage' of Burgundian politics and ritual in modern historiography is often performed with an acute sense of a conflict between state and city raging in the background. Thus, ceremony was a 'vital idiom in the all-important struggle between city and state'; ducal magnificence grew 'in tandem with the scaling back of civic political rights'. Or, ritual was a 'cheaper way' than repression to curb urban unrest, its forms providing a means of mass communication for princes to tighten their grip on urban society.[93]

However, studies since Pirenne have not ignored the extent to which rulers of the Low Countries were dependent on their towns, or to which the worlds of court and city penetrated one another. Ducal ceremony made use of existing urban traditions: it was constructed, Peter Arnade writes, out of 'urban scaffolding'.[94] Moreover, the urban world was a fragmented one: the different and sometimes competing groups within civic society made this urban scaffolding an unstable structure.[95] The perception of 'state' and 'city' as two monolithic blocs is hardly viable.[96] But for all these qualifications, the relationship between prince and

---

91 H. Pirenne, 'The formation and constitution of the Burgundian state', *American Historical Review* 14 (1908–9), pp. 477–502; and for Huizinga's riposte: J. Huizinga, 'L'état bourguignon, ses rapports avec la France et les origines d'une nationalité néerlandaise', *Le Moyen Âge* 40 (1930), pp. 171–93 and 41 (1931), pp. 11–35, 83–96. For comment on the historiography of this debate, see Small, *Chastelain*, pp. 1–4.

92 Pirenne, *Early democracies*, esp. pp. 29–40. For a critique of these trends in the historiography of the Low Countries see M.G.A. Vale, *The princely court. Medieval courts and culture in North-West Europe* (Oxford, 2001), esp. pp. 295–6.

93 P. Arnade, 'City, state and public ritual in the late medieval Burgundian Netherlands', *Comparative Studies in Society and History* 39 (1997), pp. 309, 317; W. Blockmans and E. Donckers, 'Self-representation of court and city in Flanders and Brabant in the fifteenth and early sixteenth centuries', in W. Blockmans and A. Janse (eds) *Showing status: representations of social positions in the late Middle Ages* (Turnhout, 1999), p. 82.

94 P. Arnade, *Realms of ritual: Burgundian ceremony and civic life in late medieval Ghent* (New York, 1996), p. 7. See also comments in Blockmans and Prevenier, *The Promised lands*, p. 133.

95 Arnade, *Realms of ritual*, p. 7.

96 See the emphasis in Lecuppre-Desjardin, *La ville des cérémonies*, esp. pp. 4, 7, 196, 329.

city is described in most modern accounts as one of antagonism. An opposition remains at the heart of ducal/civic relations: an 'implacable progression of State centralism' confronts the towns; a 'gulf of differences' lay between town and prince which symbolic communication in ceremonies was able to fill only with a 'thick layer of compromise'.[97]

Burgundian ceremony tends to be regarded, then, as a means (or an expression of the attempt) to strengthen ducal authority against rebellious urban subjects. It is firmly connected, in some form or other, to the process of state formation. But the nature of the assumed union between ritual and politics is worth clarifying along two lines of inquiry. First, more generally, how directly can 'ritual' and 'politics' be bound together? The effects of the one on the other may not be characterised with certainty. Neither historians nor anthropologists can agree on what rituals are supposed to do, how they do it, or whether they 'do' anything at all. Secondly, whether specifically Burgundian ceremonies 'did' or 'said' anything may depend on their context, and on who organised or paid for them. Not all were 'urban' or 'courtly' to the same degree.

'Urban' and 'courtly' ceremonies

Certain ceremonies in the Burgundian Low Countries were directly implicated in political conflict. In the aftermath of urban rebellions he had quelled, the duke was able to humiliate a city, financially, politically and through ceremony. Following victory over the Ghenters in 1453, Duke Philip the Good marked his ascendancy symbolically with the removal of three of the city's gates.[98] The Entry that ceremonially witnessed the return of the city to ducal favour in 1458 began outside the city walls with the greeting of the duke by citizens whose posture and garb indicated their repentant subservience [14].

Other kinds of ceremony undoubtedly demonstrated the magnificence of princely authority. The meetings of the Order of the Golden Fleece, the jousts of the *pas d'armes*, the gargantuan feasts (which so repelled Huizinga), or other occasions marking moments of dynastic importance such as princely baptisms, marriages or funerals, were exclusive

---

97 Ibid., pp. 321, 326, 329. See also Arnade, *Realms of ritual*, p. 5.

98 More generally on the forms of ritual humiliation see M. Boone, 'Destroying and reconstructing the city: The inculcation and arrogation of princely power in the Burgundian-Habsburg Netherlands (14th to 16th Centuries)', in M. Gosman, A. Vanderjagt and J. Veenstra (eds) *The propagation of power in the Medieval West* (Groningen, 1997), pp. 1–33.

occasions, largely paid for out of ducal (or high-ranking courtier) coffers [1–12]. But they were invariably held in the major towns of the duke's northern territories, required considerable preparation on the part of citizens, and made a significant impact on the urban landscape [12a, b, d].[99] Olivier de la Marche's prescriptive advice for holding chapters of the Golden Fleece intended that urban church interiors be bedecked with heraldic insignia, and that townsmen witness daily the carefully ordered procession of the Order's knights to church [11].[100] His description of the *pas* of the Golden Tree led by Anthony, Grand Bastard of Burgundy, during the wedding feast in Bruges 1468 has the city's main market place taken over by the jousting event: an enclosure entered through two golden gates, one of them masking the municipal town house, turned commercial space into chivalric arena [2]. While in daylight hours princely magnificence was evident in sumptuous clothes and finery, at night it was made visible by the brilliance of artificial lighting: Eleanor of Poitiers recalled baptismal processions to church lit with a large number of torches [5].

For many of their ceremonial occasions, however, princes required the more active participation of citizens. The Valois dukes had come to rule over northern territories which by the fourteenth century enjoyed a rich tradition of urban ceremonies, secular and sacred – jousting, archery contests, religious processions – which were paid for by townsmen themselves [17–27]. The dukes were swift to engage with them. The nature of this engagement is open to debate. Although the Valois dukes followed precedent set by previous rulers in the region, their involve-ment in urban ceremonies is described by some historians in terms that imply an intent more aggressive than that of their predecessors.[101] Urban traditions were appropriated. Evelyne van den Neste traces a development in which urban jousts such as the Épinette of Lille were transformed from expressions of civic independence in the fourteenth

---

99 For most recent comment on this, see Lecuppre-Desjardin, *La ville des cérémonies*, pp. 159–63, 199–221. Six of the eight Burgundian *pas d'armes* (held between 1443 and 1477) were held within the larger towns of the Low Countries: E. van den Neste, *Tournois, joutes, pas d'armes dans les villes de Flandre à la fin du Moyen Age (1300–1486)* (Paris, 1996), p. 54.

100 And for more permanent symbols of ducal power placed in urban churches, see the gifts of stained glass made by the dukes [26].

101 For the Valois dukes' importing French ideas of sovereignty and mechanisms of government into the Low Countries, see R. Vaughan, *Philip the Bold* (2nd edn, Woodbridge, 2002, with an introduction by M.G. Vale), p. 149; Boone, 'Destroying and Reconstructing', pp. 2, 13; Blockmans and Prevenier, *Promised lands*, p. 18.

century into symbols of civic subservience in the fifteenth.[102] dukes penetrated the event and gave leave for the subsidies requi... for funding it to be collected. According to Arnade, civic traditions in Ghent were made to serve ducal ends. Archery contests and chambers of rhetoric were called upon in the process of strengthening ducal authority and integrating their territories.[103] They might also serve as occasions for extending ducal influence in areas that were not under their direct authority. The archery contest at Tournai in 1455 [**17b**], which brought together representatives from a large number of towns (in Flanders, Artois, Brabant and Hainaut) was honoured by the presence of Anthony the Grand Bastard. For Lecuppre-Desjardin, the dukes gradually appropriated the full range of urban festivals, including annual processions of relics, to create its own 'liturgy of state' and integrate them into a conception of the public weal and a new sense of obedience to the prince.[104]

Entry ceremonies were the occasions when prince most obviously and formally met townsman – and the occasions that have most excited historians, because details recorded by contemporaries offer tantalising possibilities for deconstruction of their symbolic meaning. Not all Entries were alike in scale or function, and their meanings shifted with circumstance. Distinctions must be drawn between, on the one hand, First Entries – and the 'Joyeuses Entrées' specific to Brabant – made by rulers after succession to a particular region (which involved the swearing of oaths by the new ruler and by townsmen) and, on the other hand, subsequent Entries, often on a smaller scale (which usually did not); and between all these Entries on the one hand, and Entries following a rebellion on the other, when the 'contract' between lord and subject had to be symbolically restored (such as at Ghent in 1458).[105] During the period of Valois Burgundian rule, the balance of power exhibited at these events may have shifted decisively in favour of the duke.[106] By 1440, Philip the Good was requiring Flemish townsmen

102 Van den Neste, *Tournois*, pp. 187–206.

103 Arnade, *Realms of ritual*, pp. 65–94, 159–88.

104 Lecuppre-Desjardin refers to ducal engagement with urban traditions at times in more benign terms (as 'assimilation', 'absorption'), and at other times in more aggressive terms ('appropriation', 'usurping', 'assimilation', 'getting hold of', 'overriding'); *La ville des cérémonies*, pp. 197; 131–2, 254, 326.

105 For an overview of Burgundian Entries see J.D. Hurlbut, 'Ceremonial Entries in Burgundy: Philip the Good and Charles the Bold, 1419–1477' (PhD dissertation, Indiana State University, 1990). For further distinctions, see chapter 4 of this volume.

106 For the following see Lecuppre-Desjardin, *La ville des cérémonies*, pp. 135–58, 235–9, 271–91.

to greet him further out from the city gates than his grandfather had done in 1385. By then, ducal pressure on towns apparently prompted townsmen to present more elaborate *tableaux vivants* ('dumb shows') – often bearing flattering allusions to ducal power – along the route taken by the duke from city gate to princely residence. The history of Entries seems to witness a concerted princely effort to turn a ceremony marking the contractual relationship between town and seigneurial lord into an occasion to demonstrate the glorification of state power over loyal subjects.

Nevertheless, the traffic of symbolic power was not all one way. Contemporary descriptions of symbols in Entry *tableaux* may allow us to tease out meanings that were critical of princely power. The programme of Advent liturgical metaphors that, according to Gordon Kipling, underlies the symbolism of the *tableaux* during these Entries was potentially equivocal about princely authority.[107] The ambiguity of the duke's role as avenging lord and loving redeemer (drawn from the liturgy of the Advent of the Second Coming) is a theme that runs through the programme of *tableaux* that greeted Duke Philip through Ghent in 1458: the tenth *tableau* (the famous recreation of Jan van Eyck's *Adoration of the Lamb*) was perhaps intended to confront Philip, as he arrived before it, with the sinfulness of his own humanity in need of merciful redemption [14]. The duke might be entering the city as a kind of Christ-king, but the city he was entering was the New Jerusalem. Throughout the Valois Burgundian period and beyond, Entry ceremonies provided opportunities for townsmen to express their own agenda and remind their rulers of the responsibilities and obligations that came with authority.

The organisation of Entry ceremonies involved collaboration between 'court' and 'city'. Chastelain's account of the build-up to the 1458 Entry suggests a process of delicate and fraught negotiation [13]. Further investigation into the nature of this collaboration is tricky because of the fragmented nature of the evidence; the precise role of urban 'rhetoricians' who may have overseen the event is rarely clear. It may be tempting to regard them as members of an urban 'elite'

---

107 For the following see G. Kipling, *Enter the king. Theatre, liturgy, and ritual in the medieval civic triumph* (Oxford, 1998), esp, pp. 275–6. But for the view that Entries were not so programmatic, see B.A.M. Ramakers, 'Multifaced and ambiguous. The *tableaux vivants* in the Bruges Entry of 1440', in R. Suntrup and J.R. Veenstra (eds) *Medien der Symbolik in Spätmittelater und Früher Neuzeit* (Frankfurt am Main, 2005), pp. 163–94. Also, Lecuppre-Desjardin, *La ville des cérémonies,* (pp. 284–87) for comments on the civic agenda in the 1440 Entry into Bruges.

already committed to the advancement of princely authority – foreign cuckoos, as it were, in the native urban nest. But this interpretation underestimates the potentially decisive role that the city often played in determining the agenda of an Entry programme. Townsmen, after all, paid for the Entry; and the town accounts of Charles V's 1515 Entry into Bruges show that they could buy in 'courtiers' to present an urban view of the Entry to the ruler. The *indiciaire* (official court historiographer) Remy du Puys was paid by the town to write up the event for the court in French [16]. Similar processes may have been at work in earlier Entry ceremonies under the Burgundian dukes.[108] Chastelain himself – court historiographer, but of urban origin – was involved in the events of Charles the Bold's Entry into Ghent in 1469, and may be implicated in the presentation of a case favourable to 'city' rather than to 'state'. It might stretch a metaphor to claim that there were urban cuckoos in the princely nest; but the process of negotiation among groups who had ties to both 'court' and 'city' suggests that Entries were not ceremonies that could be bent without difficulty to a ruler's will.

Some Entry ceremonies went disastrously wrong. Charles the Bold's entry into Ghent in 1467 met with hostile crowds [15]. Chastelain's disgusted observation of 'commoners' rising up against prince and civic authorities reminds us of conflicts other than a straightforward opposition of 'city' to 'state'.[109] But opposition to Charles did not just emerge from social tensions. The timing of his Entry coincided with the return to the city of St Lieven's relics, an annual procession popular in the city since at least the fourteenth century. Indeed Charles's timing reads like a deliberate attempt to override a local tradition with a princely ceremony.[110] The resentment felt by the crowds of returning pilgrims was fuelled with more than the drink that Chastelain believed was liberally consumed on the occasion. Fervent attachment to local cults was not suppressed without difficulty.

Urban traditions were not easy to appropriate for princely purposes. Rulers might often have to engage in subtle ways with the ceremonial events of their civic subjects: becoming members of urban fraternities [24, 27]; involving themselves more circumspectly with local ceremonial events and processions [20, 21, 22, 23]; working with, rather

108 See Small, 'When *indiciaires* meet *rederijkers*', esp. pp. 139–40.

109 For the detailed anatomy of one rebellion against the duke, and for internal conflicts within the town, see Jan Dumolyn's account of the Bruges revolt in 1436 (n. 28 above).

110 Arnade, 'Secular charisma'; see also Lecuppre-Desjardin, *La ville des cérémonies*, pp. 294–300.

than against, the grain of urban tradition.[111] In any case, traditions that involved religious ceremony were never just 'urban' or 'local'. Religious processions, especially those with relics, involved ecclesiastical authorities who had their own traditions to protect.[112] The 'liturgy of the state' could not incorporate all that was sacred. The awesome portents that preceded the arrival of Philip the Good at Ghent in 1458 – the earth tremors and the banging of St Bertoul in his reliquary in the abbey of St Peter – lay beyond human comprehension [13]. In any case, reference in the *tableaux* of Entry ceremonies to biblical themes might suggest flattering comparisons for princely power; ultimately, however, they referred their princely and urban spectators to a spiritual dimension removed in time and place from the earthly matters of the moment. But what, more precisely, did such ceremonies 'say' or 'do'?

Ritual and power

Most historians of Burgundian ceremony agree that ceremonies 'did' something, and that what they did affected political power. Most agree too that the connection between power and ritual is an indirect one: some kind of displacement takes place in the process of transferring from one to the other. Thus Arnade argues that ceremonies allowed conflict to be displaced on to a ritual plane, and to serve as an alternative 'vehicle for negotiation'; for Wim Blockmans and Esther Donckers they 'sublimated real differences' between ruler and ruled, to enclose them in a 'wider symbolic union'.[113]

How ceremonies accomplished this effect on participants is unclear. Arguably they worked at an emotional level: 'collective emotions' generated through ritual cemented ties between lord and subjects.[114] No doubt senses were stimulated during Burgundian ceremonies. The sound of trumpets or the dazzling sight of torches during Entries lifted these events out of the mundane, associating them with liturgical rite and devotional act. But reference to emotional effects alone is an

---

111 See A. Brown, 'Bruges and the 'Burgundian theatre-state': Charles the Bold and Our Lady of the Snow', *History* 84 (1999), pp. 573–89; Brown, 'Ritual and state-building'.

112 Lecuppre-Desjardin also comments that the 'territory of the sacred' was the arena that best resisted 'the centralizing will of the prince' (*La ville des cérémonies*, p. 296).

113 Arnade, *Realms of ritual*, pp. 212–13; Blockmans and Donckers, 'Self-representation', pp, 110–11.

114 Blockmans and Donckers, 'Self-representation', pp. 82, 89, 91. As David Kertzer writes, images of political ritual may be ambiguous in meaning but direct in their emotional effect: see his *Ritual, politics and power* (New Haven CT, 1988), p. 175.

unsatisfactory explanation for the way rituals might work. The assumption that sensory emotion might be separated from rational thought – such that participants in rituals on entering a ceremonial space can be perceived as leaving their reason at the threshold – is reliant on an anthropological tradition that has been subjected to serious criticism.[115] In any case, if Philip the Good was supposed to digest the complex symbolism of Advent in the *tableaux* once he had passed through Ghent's *Walpoort* in 1458, it may be supposed that he was expected to be accompanied en route by his cognitive faculties.

Passage though the threshold of a city gate during Entries has been likened to the 'liminal' experience of a 'rite of passage'.[116] In this model of ritual, emotions still have their part to play but engagement with cerebral reasoning is also implied: an emotionally compelling picture of an alternative, other-worldly society is apparently conjured up at a number of levels. On entering a city prepared for ceremony, the sense of a social limbo, where normal social hierarchies were suspended, was communicated though the symbolism (or 'sacra') of the *tableaux*, and was implied by the cooperation of different guilds and groups within the city who put them together, as well as by the clothing of the civic landscape behind tapestries and drapery and its illumination by a vast number of torches. The end of a liminal event is supposed to return participants to the normal patterns and hierarchies of everyday society, but with their mental outlook transformed.

It may be objected that the suspension of social hierarchies, required in a liminal event, never happened in Burgundian entries: the political order was never abolished during the events, and the duke's right to his title was never in question.[117] A social limbo is much more evident in the jostling suffered and abuse hurled at Charles the Bold during his Entry into Ghent in 1467 – when the ceremony had broken down [15]. An other-worldly limbo is perhaps less evident in First Entries, given that the oaths sworn during the event formed part of the normal political process of accepting a new ruler. And whether these were occasions where anything was 'negotiated' – or even communicated – may also be questioned. We have still to inquire further into the meanings of the event: these might be multiple as well as equivocal. None the

115 C. Bell, *Ritual theory, ritual practice* (Oxford, 1992), pp. 19–32.

116 For the fullest application of Victor Turner's adaption of van Gennep's ideas of liminality to Burgundian Entries, see Hurlbut, 'Ceremonial Entries', *passim*.

117 See the comments made by Lecuppre-Desjardin, *La ville des cérémonies*, p.151; though these objections are partially anticipated by Hurlbut ('Ceremonial Entries', pp. 34–5).

less, the model of 'liminality' has some explicatory value: whether an Entry changed the political process is less relevant than whether it was intended to change attitudes – especially those of the ruler.

The ritual model of liminality is not, however, the model most favoured in studies of Burgundian ceremony. The supernatural symbolism and atmosphere of the Entry ceremony has been interpreted less often as evidence for a 'rite of passage' as for a 'theatre-state'. Clifford Geertz's famous study of nineteenth-century Bali has seemed to offer some enticing comparisons.[118] There, Geertz tells us, rulers who lacked polit-ical power constructed a theatre-state which held up in its rituals, by symbolic reference to the supernatural order, idealized values in which both rulers and ruled could locate themselves. Similarly, in the Low Countries, the dukes came to rule over a patchwork of unruly terri-tories, and indulged in ceremonial spectacles which also incorporated symbolic references to the supernatural and mythical, bringing duke and subject together within a 'wider symbolic union'.

Tempting though the analogies are, the application of the Balinese model to the Burgundian Low Countries is best resisted. The connection in Geertz's theatre-state between ritual and politics is a very indirect one. Ritual did not function as an adjunct of political power: instead, Geertz claimed, the theatre-state created a different kind of power (a sort of inner potency radiating outward from centre to periphery) in which the court ('negara'), through its rituals, became a microcosm of the heavenly order, while the realm, through performance of state rituals, came to resemble the court. This ritualised creation of the heavenly order was an end in itself, not a means to an end: 'pomp served power, not power pomp'.[119] In almost all versions of the Burgundian theatre-state, the relationship between rituals and politics is rather more direct. Pomp does, in the end, serve power: ceremony served the state-building efforts of the dukes.[120]

---

118 C. Geertz, *Negara. The theatre-state in nineteenth-century Bali* (Princeton, 1981). For the first application of the term to the Burgundian context, see W. Prevenier and W. Blockmans, *The Burgundian Netherlands* (Cambridge, 1986), p. 223. For a version of the 'Burgundian theatre-state' which sees it as 'courtly' and not 'urban', see D. Nicholas, 'In the pit of the Burgundian theater state: urban traditions and princely ambitions in Ghent 1360–1420', in B. A. Hanawalt and K. L. Reyerson (eds), *City and spectacle in medieval Europe* (Minneapolis, 1994), pp. 271–95. But other versions tend to stress the incorporation of urban traditions into a courtly theatre-state, and imitation of ducal splendour by urban elites: e.g. Blockmans and Prevenier, *Promised lands*, pp. 132–4; Van den Neste, *Tournois*, esp. pp. 202–6 for 'la politique de l'état-spectacle'.

119 Geertz, *Negara*, esp. pp. 13–14, 102–5.

120 Brown, 'Charles the Bold and Our Lady of the Snow', p. 575.

Kipling's analysis of Entry ceremonies, however, is closer to Geertz's
original model. The connection between state-building and ceremony
is not emphasised: duke and citizens perform their roles in 'microcosmal
drama of the supernatural order'; by acting out the ideal political order
they shape the 'imperfect world into an approximation of the supernatural order'.[121] But a model of ritual that is closer to Geertz's original
harbours its own set of problems. Critics of Geertz have pointed out
that his theatre-state is not quite what it purports to be. The Negaran
theatre-state may well have masked and served political power: Geertz
has little to say about how the Negaran court actually linked with
peripheries; whether peasants accepted court rituals with any relish;
whether the whole notion of a different kind of power served to deflect
attention from its political underpinning by state authority.[122] There is,
thus, an irony here: the Burgundian theatre-state, conceived as a form
of state power, is not the Balinese theatre-state as Geertz defined, but
is closer to what he denied it to be.[123]

The 'theatre-state' – as the ritual expression of state authority – may
continue to be used as a term of convenience to describe Burgundian
ceremony. But whether Burgundian rituals were effective instruments
of power is another question. 'Resistance theory' would suggest that
ritual acts might generate opposition as much as consent; their very
performance may presuppose resistance toward the purpose of ritual
agents.[124] Alternatively, ritual activity was perhaps inherently a gamble
– not just because rituals could go wrong (as they did in the 1467 Entry
into Ghent), but also because they might even require a certain amount
of unpredictability for them to work. The elements of play (or perhaps,
again, 'liminality') involved in the ritual process have been viewed as
generators of their transformative potential.[125] The suddenness with
which Philip the Good was made to confront the sinfulness of his own
humanity before the *'Adoration' tableau* in Ghent in 1458 may have been

121 Kipling, *Enter the King*, esp. pp. 47, 50 note 4, 114.

122 S. J. Tambiah, *Culture, thought and social action. An anthropological perspective* (Harvard,
1985), pp. 316–38; J. Laidlaw, 'On theatre and theory: reflections on ritual in imperial
Chinese politics', in J. L. McDermott (ed.), *State and court ritual in China* (Cambridge,
1999), pp. 399–416; L. Howe, 'Rice, ideology, and the legitimation of hierarchy in
Bali', *Man: the Journal of the Royal Anthropological Institute* 26 (1991), pp. 445–67.

123 For this and the following see Brown, 'Ritual and state-building'.

124 For example J.C. Scott, *Domination and the art of resistance: hidden transcripts* (New
Haven CT, 1990).

125 D. Handelman, *Models and mirrors. Towards an anthropology of public events*, 2nd edn
(Oxford 1999), pp. 63–81; P. Buc, *The dangers of ritual. Between early Medieval texts and
social scientific theory* (Princeton, 2001), p. 8.

part of the programme's dramatic intention. Ultimately, however, whether ceremonies could serve state power was dependent on their ability to communicate a sense of state authority. Here we must turn from what rituals 'do' to what they 'say'.

Symbolic communication and ritual performance

For the importance of symbolism in late medieval culture, we might return to Huizinga once more. His view that symbolic images and gestures in the later Middle Ages had run to excessive extremes, and had become mechanical and disconnected from original meanings and from social life, may be unsustainable. But his emphasis on the medieval need to express the inexpressible through visible signs, and on the 'kaleidoscopic nature of symbolism', and its 'polyphony of thought', is worth recall.[126] Much modern commentary has stressed the indeterminate nature of symbolic communication. Symbols may be carriers of meaning, but meanings can be multiple and hard to pin down. Symbolic communication invariably conveys a message in an indirect way: its meaning escapes immediate recognition.[127]

Thus, the use of symbol in ceremony as an instrument of power would seem a precarious method of state control. This point needs taking further; but it makes an assumption that also requires debate. Emphasis so far has been on what rituals 'did' and how they did it. But did they do anything at all? Lecuppre-Desjardin argues that Burgundian ceremonies did not function as instruments of state formation: they were not real power itself but instruments only in the politics of communication. They 'tell of' the state but do not construct it; they act as 'mirrors' for political intention not tools of power; nor do they function as 'vehicles of negotiation'. They are 'ceremonies' that claim authority through representation rather than 'rituals' that perform functions.[128]

---

126 Huizinga, *Autumn of the Middle Ages*, pp. 234, 239, 242.

127 Gerd Althoff comments that the meaning of a ritual in public communication had to be 'unambiguous and easily understandable' to fulfil its function: see his 'The variability of rituals in the Middle Ages', in G. Althoff, J. Fried and P. Geary (eds), *Medieval concepts of the past: ritual, memory and historiography* (Cambridge, 2003), p.80; but elsewhere he stresses the inherent indeterminacy of symbolic meaning: for example in his 'Zur bedeutung symbolischer kommunikation für das Verständnis des Mittelalters', *Frühmittelalterliche studien: Jahrbuch des Instituts für frühmittelalterforschung der Universität Münster* 31 (1997), pp. 370–89.

128 Lecuppre-Desjardin, *La ville des cérémonies*, pp. 151, 231, 324, 302, 327.

Nevertheless, it is difficult to sustain a distinction between 'ritual' and 'ceremony'[129] or between 'doing' and 'saying'. The transformative power of words and images was at the heart of medieval religious culture – in the words spoken at mass with the elevation of the Host; while processions carrying Host or relics were intended to effect change, emotional and spiritual, within the mind of spectator and performer. That nothing was being 'negotiated' in Entry ceremonies need not mean that they did nothing to participants.

A more fundamental question is whether symbolic communication 'said' anything at all. Any attempt for the historian to interpret a 'society' through its symbols and representations of the 'cosmic order' is bound to be problematic.[130] For medieval contemporaries, interpretation of the cosmic order was troublesome. The meaning to be extracted from the restless behaviour of St Bertoul's remains before Philip the Good's Entry into Ghent in 1458 was unclear: people 'said a thousand ... things, each according to his own thoughts' [13]. Even the meaning of man-manufactured events was not easy to fix. Civic authorities attempted to do so: the production of books about individual Entry ceremonies, for a courtly and perhaps for a wider audience, seems designed to ensure that the event was remembered and in a particular way.[131] But even with an Entry as programmatic as the one designed for Charles V in Bruges in 1515, the civic authorities experienced difficulties in ensuring that their agenda was communicated. The *tableaux* arranged by foreign merchants broke up the chronological sequence of *tableaux* which the city had arranged to chart the long-standing relationship between Bruges and the counts of Flanders.[132] In any case, specific arrangements for most of the city's *tableaux* were delegated to different guilds: as with previous entry ceremonies, these guilds clearly used them as showcases for their

---

129 As Lecuppre-Desjardin acknowledges (ibid., pp. 302–3).

130 For criticism of an anthropological tradition (ultimately Durkheimian) which insists on reading social realities into its symbols see C. Humphreys and J. A. Laidlaw, *The archetypal actions of ritual: a theory of ritual illustrated by the Jain rite of worship* (Oxford, 1994), pp. 261–2.

131 For production of these written accounts, see Blockmans and Donckers, 'Self-representation', pp. 99–107 and Small, 'When *indiciaires* meet *rederijkers*'.

132 Remi de Puys, *La tryumphante entree de Charles prince des Espagnes en Bruges 1515*, ed. S. Anglo (Amsterdam, 1973), *passim*. The civic authorities' concern about the agenda of the foreign merchants (which tended to be more flattering of Charles's wider imperial destiny beyond Flanders) is perhaps best illustrated by de Puys's insistence that the *tableaux* put on by the Hanseatic League – showing Alexander astride Bucephalus – should not be interpreted as justification for further imperial expansion [16].

economic and political presence.[133] When communicating to rulers in Entry ceremonies, the city never spoke with one voice.

Equally, it could not be certain that audiences of events would understand the message in the way intended – if at all. The anonymous English herald witnessing the *tableaux* put on in Sluis for Margaret of York, on her way to marry Charles the Bold in 1468, considered them 'soo obscure, that y fere me to wryte or speke of them, because all was countenance and noo wordes'.[134] Different descriptions of the same event may reveal divergence of interpretation. Chastelain's description of the 1458 Entry into Ghent differs from that of the author of the *Kroniek* [13, 14].[135] Whereas the latter systematically lists the symbolism of all the *tableaux*, Chastelain is more impressionistic, lingering only over the spectacle (absent from the *Kroniek*) of an aquatic contest viewed from a bridge over the River Lys. Writing as 'court historian', he was perhaps recording a courtly perspective rather than the more urban one represented by the author of the *Kroniek*. Perhaps Philip did not want to be troubled with a 'lengthy description' of the *tableaux* which Chastelain deliberately chose to avoid; perhaps Philip's eye was caught by the mermaids by the bridge – 'quite naked with tousled hair' – which Chastelain chose to recall. In the end, Chastelain's account leaves an impression of 'marvels' rather than an understanding of a specific programme of symbolism; the marvellous wealth of the city was perhaps the only message that the civic authorities could hope would make a lasting impact on the duke and his entourage.

Ultimately, perhaps, symbolic communication could not be about the fixing of precise meaning.[136] The shifting of a political problem onto a symbolic plane does not resolve the problem,[137] but may merely defer a solution without ever informing an audience directly on what the

---

133 For a detailed account of the role of guilds in presenting *tableaux* in processions, see B.A.M. Ramakers, *Spelen en figuren: Toneelkunst en processiecultuur in Oudenaarde tussen Middeleeuwen en Moderne Tijd* (Amsterdam, 1996).

134 S. Bentley (ed.), *Excerpta Historica* (London, 1931), pp. 228–9.

135 Compare also Olivier de la Marche's account of the 1468 marriage festivities with de Roovere's [2]; and Molinet's description of the oath Maximilian swore in Bruges in 1488 with the anonymous local chronicler [26].

136 For ritual as the 'consistent displacement of intentional meaning', see Humphreys and Laidlaw, *Archetypal actions*, esp. p. 260.

137 A. Boureau, 'Les cérémonies royales françaises, entre performance juridique et compétence liturgique', *Annales* 46/6 (1991), pp. 1253–64. Lecuppre-Desjardin quotes Boureau and indeed emphasizes at times the ambiguities of message in symbols (*La ville des cérémonies*, pp. 6, 238, 284, 286, 319–20). The implications of this can be taken further.

earthly meaning of the symbolic should be. This process of shifting may cast ritual participants into a world of symbols, a world that refers only to itself. Symbols are perhaps too indeterminate to allow fixed ideas to be imposed on them as forms of social or political control.[138] In certain ways, ceremonies work because meaning is not fixed. A ceremony may produce an effect on participants, who come to it with conflicting agenda, because they are made to 'misrecognise' what is going on: a holistic vision is maintained because different interpretations of it are allowed to stand and are not openly debated outside the ritual context.[139] Prince and townsman saw in symbols what each wanted to see, and it is far from clear that symbolism generated in Burgundian territories inexorably promoted state-formation.

138 See for instance Bell, *Ritual theory*, pp. 104–7, 204–18; P. S. Sangren, *History and magical power in a Chinese community* (Stanford, 1987), esp. pp. 4, 221.

139 M. Bloch, 'The ritual of the royal bath in Madagascar: the dissolution of death, birth and fertility into authority', in D. Cannadine and S. Price (eds), *Rituals of royalty: power and ceremonial in traditional societies* (Cambridge, 1987), esp. p. 295.

I: BURGUNDIAN SPECTACLES

1. The Feast of the Pheasant at Lille, 17 February, 1454

Introduction

Describing the spectacular extravagance on display at the Feast of the Pheasant, held by Duke Philip the Good at Lille, prompted Huizinga to ask the question: 'Are we to take all this seriously?' The answer, he implies, is 'no'. The vows that Duke Philip and more than 100 courtiers made at the sumptuous banquet – to go on crusade and rescue Constantinople which had fallen to the Turks eight months previously – were empty of sincerity, a decadent playing out of chivalric fantasy.[1] Modern historians, however, answer Huizinga's question with an affirmative. The long-standing interest of Philip the Good in the crusading ideal and the practical steps he took before and after the Feast more than suggest a seriousness of purpose (even if a crusading expedition, and a desultory one at that, was not undertaken until 1464).[2] The vows, moreover, were intended to bind; many more were required of nobles in Burgundian lands after the Feast.[3] But the motives behind the event, and meanings to be extracted from the symbolic allusions made during the spectacle, remain the subject of debate.

The Feast itself was an exceptional event in the life of the Burgundian court. Olivier de la Marche's account is first-hand, since he was one of the 'committee' who organised the event and took part as Holy Church (making his dramatic entrance perched on an elephant).[4] The Feast was the culmination of other

---

1 Huizinga, *Autumn of the Middle Ages*, pp. 101–3.

2 On Burgundian crusades generally (and on Anthony of Burgundy's crusade in 1464, which reached no further than Marseilles), see J. Paviot, *Les ducs de Bourgogne, la croisade et l'orient (fin XIVe–XVe siècle)* (Paris, 2003).

3 For the 220 vows collected (107 vows collected at the Feast itself, the rest at Arras, Bruges and Mons shortly after) and their relative practicality of purpose, see M.-T. Caron, *Les voeux du faisan, noblesse en fête, esprit de croisade: Le manuscrit français 11594 de la Bibliothèque Nationale de France* (Turnhout, 2003). For the canonical validity of the vows see G. Orgelfinger, 'The vows of the pheasant and late chivalric ritual', in Chickering and Seiler (eds), *The study of chivalry*, pp. 213–62. For earlier traditions of vows over birds, on secular occasions, in the courts of the Low Countries, see Vale, *Princely court*, pp. 208–20.

4 Although Olivier did not compose his Memoirs until the 1480s, he probably inserted into them an account which he had composed at the time. For the other contemporary account, which differs slightly from de la Marche's, see Mathieu d'Escouchy, *Chronique*, ed. G. du Fresne de Beaucourt (Paris, 1863), ii, pp. 116–237, who may well have borrowed from an 'official' account for which Olivier de la Marche claims

events and jousts that had taken place over the previous eighteen days. Much
of the symbolism of the jousts and *entremets*[5] can be interpreted as referring to
crusading and to the threat of the Turks – notably the figure of Jason whose
chivalric quest to recover the Golden Fleece in Colchis could be symbolically
linked to the recovery of Christian lands in the Eastern Mediterranean.[6] De la
Marche certainly emphasises the seriousness of crusading intent (taking some
trouble to explain the meaning of his elephant). But his conceit of pondering
over the extravagance on display suggests that there was room even for
contemporaries to doubt the piety of intention.[7]

Modern historians are inclined – perhaps over-inclined – to emphasise the
secularity of the event and to detect political motives behind pious vows. The
crusading postures struck by Philip the Good served other purposes. Immediately after the Feast, Philip set out for Regensburg where he might appear
before the Emperor as leader of Christendom against the Turks, and secure
formal recognition of his recent acquisitions within imperial territory.[8] His
vow of dutiful subservience to the king of France in the matter of crusading
might be read as a submissive appeal to the French crusading tradition or as
an anxiety to occupy the armies of *le roi très victorieux*, then on the point of
driving the English out from all France save Calais. Perhaps more important
to Philip was the opportunity such a feast might afford in asserting his control
over the nobility of his disparate territories. The jousts put on by two major
nobles prior to the feast were conceived as subservient to the main event.[9] The

to have had courtly approval. See C. Emerson, 'Who witnessed and narrated the
Banquet of the Pheasant (1454)? A codicological examination of the account's five
versions', *Fifteenth-century studies* 28 (2003), pp. 124–37.

5 An entertainment originally presented between (*entre*) dishes (*mets*) in a banquet, but
more generally as an accompaniment to the festivities.

6 For the symbolism see A. Lafortune-Martel, *Fête noble en Bourgogne au xve siècle:
le banquet du faisan (1454). Aspects politiques, sociaux et culturels* (Paris, 1984). For the
problematic figure of Jason as chivalric hero, see chapter 3 [11a]. For the multiple symbolism of the fleece, see B. Haggh, 'The Virgin Mary and the Order of the
Golden Fleece', in M.-T. Caron and D. Clauzel, (eds), *Le Banquet du Faisan. 1454:
l'Occident face au défi de l'empire ottoman* (Arras, 1997), pp. 273–87.

7 For criticism of crusading within the ducal court, see Caron, *Les voeux du faisan*,
pp. 29–30, 189, 190. And for the need for crusading propaganda at the ducal court,
see A.G. Heron, '"Il fault faire guerre pour paix avoir": crusading propaganda at the
court of Duke Philippe le Bon of Burgundy (1419–1467)' (PhD Thesis, University of
Cambridge, 1992).

8 For the connection between the Feast and acquisition of Luxembourg acquired
during 1441–43 (and for the Feast as a riposte to the jousts organised at Nancy in
1445 by King René of Anjou with Charles VII, who were hostile to Burgundian ambitions in the region), see C. de Mérindol, 'Le banquet du faisan: Jerusalem et l'esprit
de croisade hors de la Bourgogne à la veille de la prise de Constantinople', in Caron
and Clauzel (eds), *Banquet du faisan*, pp. 71–83.

9 Duke Philip also refused to allow members of his household to attend an event held by
the count of St Pol, Louis of Luxembourg, at Cambrai on 18 March, after the Feast of the
Pheasant (which might have trumped his own): M.-T. Caron, '17 février 1454: le banquet
du voeu du faisan; fête de cour et stratégies de pouvoir', *RN* 78 (1996), pp. 269–88.

entremets of the Feast made repeated allusion to symbols and figures associated with ducal authority – St Andrew (one of the duke's patron saints and of the Order of the Golden Fleece), Hercules and Jason. Vows made during and after the Feast expressed submission to the will of the duke. Great care was taken to extract vows from nobles with lands under Burgundian rule (although fewer were acquired from Holland). The crusading symbolism of the Feast drew on the traditions embedded in many of the duke's northern territories, and thus served to create a community of interest among the nobility. The spectacle ultimately affirmed (or hoped to affirm) the existence of a unified Burgundian state.[10]

The Feast was an exclusive event – perhaps the most exclusive of all the major Burgundian spectacles. It took place in the enclosed space of the *palais de la Salle* (the former castle of the counts of Flanders in Lille). Attendance was confined to the great families of ducal lands, arranged at tables in accordance with strict hierarchy. The organising 'committee' was restricted to household personnel close to the person of the duke (unlike the groups who organised Entry ceremonies into towns). But a wider audience for the Feast was clearly intended. D'Escouchy refers to viewing galleries for other spectators in the main banqueting hall;[11] official accounts were produced, letters and descriptions of the event were widely disseminated. Shortly after the Feast, the ducal secretary, Jean de Molesmes, wrote a letter to the mayor and *échevins* of the town of Dijon to the effect that a ceremony had just taken place to which no other previous event was comparable.[12] General processions were ordered in towns to announce the crusading intentions of the duke.[13] The urban world was to be kept informed of high ducal ambition.

But for the rebellion of one town, de la Marche claims, the crusading ambitions of duke Philip would have been realised much earlier. The Ghent uprising from 1447 was finally defeated on 2 July 1453. In some ways, the Feast of the Pheasant, in which Philip surrounded himself with nobles who had fought on the campaign, can be interpreted as ducal celebration of a crushing victory over townsmen.[14] In de la Marche's account there is little left of the urban landscape that provided the setting for the event. Nevertheless, even the exclusive Feast of the Pheasant required more of townsmen than de la Marche chose to present. The jousts certainly needed the wider spaces of market places; the *entremets* demanded the skills of painters and artisans from Lille and many surrounding towns.[15] Perhaps the *entremets* incorporated cultural references

10 M.-T. Caron, "'Monseigneur le duc m'a fait l'honneur de moy eslire'", in Caron and Clauzel (eds), *Banquet du faisan*, p. 241.

11 D'Escouchy, *Chronique*, ii, p. 137.

12 Caron, *Les voeux du faisan*, p. 31.

13 For ones in Douai, see references cited in Lecuppre-Desjardin, *Ville des cérémonies*, p. 220 n. 99. And for the adoption of symbolism used in ducal events in urban culture (such as the story of Gideon presented at Mons 1455), see ibid., pp. 220–1, 274.

14 Caron, *Les voeux du faisan*, pp. 23–8.

15 See Caron, *Les voeux du faisan*, p. 31. For the view that urban 'connivance' with ducal

which extended well beyond an aristocratic elite.[16] The organising of the Feast may not have included townsmen, but the wider dissemination of its message arguably required the active participation of urban festive groups or chambers of rhetoric.[17] In the end, as de la Marche states, the event involved 'all ducal subjects', and if ducal crusades were ever to be launched, they required adroit approaches to estates and towns for financial support[18] – more adroit than Philip's demand for a regular salt tax which had precipitated rebellion in Ghent in 1447.

Olivier de la Marche, *Mémoires*, i, pp. 487–504

Chapter 28

[De la Marche begins by describing how the Pope had sent a knight to Duke Philip to report on the sack of Constantinople in May 1453: how the church of Haghia Sophia was pillaged and how relics and the Eucharist were flung into the streets among the filth, the dung and the swine. The pope's knight asks Duke Philip to prove his willingness to serve the Church. Meanwhile the Emperor has also sent for all the princes of Germany to come to Regensburg, and pointedly reminds Duke Philip of his previously expressed intention of going as far as Asia to serve the Church and the Faith. Duke Philip prepares himself.]

And to stir up the lords and noblemen of his lands and his subjects to serve God in this matter, and to embark on the holy journey out of their willingness and devotion, without constraint, he took advice to publish his enterprise through a great assembly. And because the banquets and festivities followed on from one another, each one grander than the last, and to make sure the conclusion of the banquets was reached under the control of the good duke who would close the Feast, he had preparations made for *entremets* and food. My lord Jehan de Lannoy, a knight of the Order of the Fleece,[19] a wise and inventive man, and a squire called

---

ambitions and ceremony like the Feast of the Pheasant was costly to urban independence, see D. Clauzel, 'Lille, 1454', in Caron and Clauzel (eds), *Banquet du faisan*, pp. 41–52.

16 For the inclusion of popular Flemish images and proverbs in the *entremets* (such as the shooting at the 'pie' as symbolising common enterprise), see Lafortune-Martel, *Fête noble en Bourgogne*, pp. 142–5.

17 M. de Grève, 'Le voeu du faisan et les écrivains, problèmes de reception', in Caron and Clauzel (eds), *Banquet du faisan*, pp. 137–44.

18 See Lecuppre-Desjardin, *Ville des cérémonies*, p. 219 n. 94.

19 Jean de Lannoy (1410–93), son of Jean de Lannoy killed at Agincourt 1415, and of Jeanne de Croÿ, received membership of the Order of the Golden Fleece at Mons in 1451. From 1448 to 1462 he was governor of Holland, Zeeland and Frisia. On him and for most of the following biographical details of those mentioned in La Marche's account, see Caron, *Les voeux du faisan, passim*.

Jehan Boudault,[20] a very honourable and discreet man, arranged this Feast. And the good duke did me so much honour by wanting me to be called; and on this matter several councils met, to which the chancellor and first chamberlain were called, now that they had returned from the war the duke had conducted in Luxembourg ... The greatest and the most privileged were also called to the council; and after deliberations on opinions, conclusions were reached as to what the ceremonies and plays should be. And the duke wanted me to play the character of Holy Church, whom he wanted to help at this assembly; and it was a solemn thing, worth reviewing, and it is relevant to our purposes here. So I have recorded this banquet, as fully as I could, so that it will be remembered.

Chapter 29

[The Feast is held at Lille on 17 February, but the build-up began eighteen days previously, with an announcement made at a banquet given in the town by Adolf of Cleves.[21] The Feast was to begin with a joust on the same day, in which the 'Knight of the Swan' was to take on all comers. The announcement was made during an *entremets*. This took the form of a ship, in which stood an armed knight displaying the arms of Cleves; the ship moved along a river as though pulled by a silver swan. Legend had it that a swan had once miraculously led a knight from Cleves along the Rhine. This knight had married a princess, and from him the present Cleves were descended. After the *entremets*, a chaplet of flowers was presented to the count of Étampes[22] who held another banquet ten days later. At this banquet, the chaplet was then handed to the duke by a young girl, dressed in a robe written on with Greek letters, led by Robert de Miraumont[23] and the lord of Dreuil[24]. The duke then decided to hold his own banquet and began preparations...]

So on the day of this banquet, very early after dinner, my lord Adolf (who had announced the Knight of the Swan), accompanied at the place where he was being armed by my lord the duke, by the count of

20 Jean Boudault, served the household of Jean de Bourgogne, count of Étampes, before entering the service of duke Philip, becoming *bailli* of Château-Chinon.

21 Adolf of Cleves (d. 1492), nephew of Duke of Cleves, servant of Philip the Good and his successors, made a knight of the Golden Fleece in 1459.

22 Jean de Bourgogne (1415–91), count of Étampes and later Nevers, fought in the Ghent war, made knight of the Golden Fleece in 1456.

23 Robert de Miraumont (d.1486), in the service of the count of Étampes and later the duke, and fought in the Ghent war.

24 Gauvain Quiéret, lord of Dreuil (c.1405–62), of the nobility of Artois, militarily active in the service of the count of Étampes and the duke, including in the Ghent war.

Charolais,[25] and by the Bastard of Burgundy,[26] all dressed in robes of black velvet; and each of them had a golden collar, greatly enriched with precious stones, such as diamonds, rubies and pearls. My lord wore on his hat a coronet so rich with precious stones that I do not know how to describe it, except as the garment befitting a powerful prince. My lord Adolf, accompanied (as already said) by my lord, the count of Charolais and my lord the Bastard, and also by the lord of Étampes, left his household with a great company of people who went before him dressed in his robes; after them came drummers; and after them a pursuivant of arms dressed in a coat of arms full of swans; and after him came a large swan, marvellously and skilfully made, with a crown of gold around its neck, from which hung a shield of the full arms of Cleves; and from this crown hung a golden chain on which, from one end, there hung the shield of the knight; and this swan was flanked by two very well made centaurs who had bows and arrows in their hands, and made as though to shoot at anyone who tried to approach the swan.

Holding the golden chain, and armed most richly in all kinds of arms, the knight followed the swan. His horse was covered in a cloth of white damask, bordered with golden fringes, and with a shield decorated in the same way; and to the left, to the right, and behind, were three young page children, dressed in white in the manner of angels, mounted on beautiful coursers, decked out in well-cut white cloth; and after them came a groom, dressed in white, on a little horse, who led by hand a charger covered in white cloth, embroidered with large golden letters with the knight's device; afterward came the duke of Cleves, brother of the said knight, and my lord John of Coïmbra, son of the king of Portugal,[27] with a great number of knights and noblemen, all dressed in white, in the same way as the knight, and carrying lances in fine array.

In such a way and in such company, the knight was led before the ladies; and he was presented by Golden Fleece, king of arms of the very excellent, very high, very powerful princess the duchess of Burgundy,[28] and to other princesses, ladies, and young ladies; and then he was led to the lists, with the centaurs, and was placed on a platform which had been prepared for him …

25 Charles the Bold (1433–77), son of Duke Philip the Good.

26 Anthony, Grand Bastard of Burgundy (1421–1504), son of Duke Philip the Good, made knight during the Ghent war, and member of the Order of the Golden Fleece in 1456.

27 (c. 1435–57), son of Peter duke of Coïmbra, grandson of King John I of Portugal, living at the court of his sister Beatrice, wife of Adolf of Cleves from 1450, and then at the ducal court. Participated in the Ghent war, made knight of the Golden Fleece in 1456. Poisoned at Nicosia after marrying the daughter of the king of Cyprus.

28 Isabella of Portugal (1397–1471), married Duke Philip in 1430.

[The challengers present themselves and perform deeds of arms: Girard de Roussillon,[29] the count of St Pol,[30] Jean de Montfoort[31], the count of Charolais, the Bastard, the lord of the Gruuthuse,[32] lord Chrétien de Digoine,[33] Everard de Digoine,[34] Jean de Ghistelle and Philippe de Lalaing[35] ...]

Then, at a suitable hour, they found themselves in a room in which my lord had prepared a very rich banquet; and my lord arrived accompanied by knights, ladies and young ladies; and finding the banquet ready to be served, he bade them look at the *entremets* which were prepared there. The room in which the banquet was held was a large one, and finely hung with a tapestry in which the life of Hercules was depicted. To enter this room there were five doors guarded by archers dressed in grey and black cloth, and in the hall were several knights and esquires conducting the banquet, dressed respectively in damask cloth and grey and black satin. In this room there were three covered tables, one of an average size, one large, the other small; and on the middle-sized table there was a cruciform church with glass windows, made in a fine way; in it there were a chiming bell and four singers. There was another *entremets* of a little child completely naked on a rock, who pissed rose water continuously. There was another *entremets* of an anchored carrack laden with all sorts of merchandise and with figures of sailors: it seemed to me that not even the largest carrack in the world had more apparatus than this one, or more ropes and sails. Another *entremets* was of a very beautiful fountain, part of which was made of glass and part of lead, with the most original of workmanship; for there were little glass bushes, with leaves and flowers, made with such novelty as to be a marvel; and the space of this artifice was thus like a little meadow, enclosed with rocks of sapphires and other strange stones, and in the

29 Girard de Roussillon or de Rochebarron, cup-bearer at the ducal court, squire pantler to Charles, count of Charolais.

30 Louis de Luxembourg, count of Saint-Pol (1418–75), with lands in Hainaut and Artois, militarily active, fighting in the Ghent war; later mistrusted by both Charles the Bold and King Louis XI of France, executed for *lèse-majesté* in 1475.

31 Jean de Montfoort, lord of Hazerswoorde (Holland), castellan of Montfoort, in the service of the count of Charolais from 1458.

32 Louis of Bruges (1427–92), lord of Gruuthuse, earl of Winchester, served in the Ghent war, made knight of the Golden Fleece in 1461; lieutenant in Holland, Zeeland and Frisia.

33 Chrétien de Digoine, lord of Thianges, made a knight during the Ghent war, counsellor and chamberlain of the duke from 1453.

34 Erart de Digoine, younger brother of Chrétien, lord of Saint-Sornay, counsellor and chamberlain of the duke from 1458.

35 Philippe de Lalaing (c.1430–65), made a knight during the Ghent war; organiser of the *pas* of the *perron fée* at Bruges in 1463, killed at the battle of Montlhéry in 1465.

middle of this was a little upright figure of St Andrew, with his cross before him, and from one of the ends of the cross, the fountain sprang out, to a great height, and fell down into the meadow in such a subtle manner, that no one could tell what became of the water.

The second and longest table had a pastry first of all, which contained twenty-eight live people, playing diverse instruments each in turn. The second *entremets* of this table was a castle made in the manner of Lusignan, and on this castle, at the highest point of the principal tower, was Melusine in the form of a serpent,[36] and from two of the smaller towers orange water issued forth when required, which fell into ditches. The third was a windmill, high up on a hill, and on its highest sail was a pole, on the end of which was a magpie, and around it were men of all estates with bows and crossbows, shooting at the magpie, to show that all men shooting at the magpie are bound in common in the same task. The fourth was a barrel placed in a vineyard, where there were two types of beverage, of which one was good and sweet, the other bitter and bad. On the barrel was a figure of a richly dressed man who held a letter in his hand in which it was written: 'He who wishes it, may take it'. The fifth was a desert, an uninhabited land, on which there was a marvellously lifelike figure of a tiger which fought with a large serpent. The sixth was a wild man mounted on a camel, who pretended to travel from country to country. The seventh was a figure of a man who beat a bush full of small birds with a pole; and near them were a knight and lady seated at a table, who were eating the birds which the other was beating from the bush; and the lady indicated with her finger that he worked in vain, foolishly wasting his time. The eighth was a fool mounted on a bear, between several strange mountains and diverse rocks which were laden with frost and icicles hanging in a fine way. The ninth was a lake surrounded by several towns and castles, on which was a small ship with its sails up, sailing by itself on the water of the lake; and the ship was finely fashioned, and well furnished with things necessary for sailing.

The third table (the smallest) had a marvellous forest on it, as though this was a forest of the Indies; within there were several strange-looking beasts, who moved on their own accord as though they were alive. The second *entremets* of this table was a moving lion, attached to a tree in the middle of a courtyard; and there was a figure beating a dog in front of

36 The figure of Melusine, half-woman, half-serpent, was a widely known legend associated with the house of Lusignan, to which several late medieval dynasties claimed connections. The Lusignans were famed for their crusading efforts.

the lion. The third and last was a merchant passing by a village, carrying around his neck a basket full with all manner of haberdashery.

Now, to describe the manner of service and the dishes would be a marvellous thing to recount; and also I had so many things to do that I cannot truly recount them all; but I do remember, each course was furnished with forty-eight types of food, and the dishes bearing the roasted food were like chariots decorated with gold and azure. In this room, nearest the table, was a tall sideboard laden with gold and silver dishes, and with bowls of crystal, decorated with gold and precious stones; and except for those who served the wine, no one approached this buffet beyond the wooden protection which was placed there.

And so it was that in the middle of the room, lengthways, fairly near the wall, opposite the long table, was a tall pillar, on which there was an image of a naked woman, whose hair was so long that it fell to the small of her back, and on her head was a very rich hat, and she was enveloped in a veil inscribed in several places in Greek lettering, to cover up her modesty; and for as long as the banquet lasted, hippocras flowed from the right breast of this statue. Near her was another wide-based pillar in the manner of a platform on which a live lion was attached by an iron chain, as though guarding and defending the image; and on a shield against this pillar, written in golden letters, were the words 'Do not touch my lady'.

My lord, the duchess, and all their noble company, set about visiting these *entremets* for quite some time. The whole room was full of noble people, and there were few other sorts of people. There were also five well appointed platforms, for those who did not want to sit at table, which soon were filled with men and women, most of whom were in disguise, and as far as is known, there were knights and ladies from great families, who had come from afar, some by sea, others by land, to see the Feast which was greatly renowned. To be brief, after everyone had looked at the *entremets*, the chief stewards, who were taking care of proceedings, came to make the seating arrangements.

The duke was seated in the centre of the middle-sized table, and on his right my lady, daughter of the duke of Bourbon,[37] was seated; after her, my lord of Cleves, my lady of Ravestein, niece of the duchess and wife of my lord Adolf.[38] The duchess was seated to the left of the duke, with my

---

37   Isabelle de Bourbon (1436–65), married to Charles, count of Charolais on 30 October 1454.

38   Beatrice de Coïmbre of Portugal (d.1462), niece of the duchess, brother of Jean, married to Adolf of Cleves in May 1453.

lady of Charny,[39] my lady of Étampes,[40] my lord of Saint-Pol, my lady
of Beures, wife of the Bastard of Burgundy,[41] my lord Pons,[42] and my
lady the chancellor's wife.[43] At the large and second table, were seated
my lord of Charolais, my lord of Étampes, my lord Adolf, my lord of
Fiennes,[44] my lord the Bastard of Burgundy, and my lord of Hornes,[45]
mixed with a great number of ladies and maidens, as well as so many
other knights that the tables were full from one end to the other. Similarly on the third table, squires and damsels were sat together, in such
a way that the tables were full.

When everyone was seated, as described, a very high-pitched bell rang
out from the church (in the first *entremets*); and when the bell had stopped,
three small children and a tenor sang a very sweet song; and after they
had come to an end, a shepherd from the pastry (in the first *entremets* of
the long table) played on a bagpipe in a very original manner. Scarcely
a moment later, by the door at the entrance of the room, entered a horse
walking backward, richly covered in vermilion silk, on which two trumpeters were seated without saddles, back to back, dressed in surcoats of
black and grey silk, with hats on their heads, and with masks over their
faces; and while they played a fanfare from their trumpets the horse
carried them all around the room backward; and leading them, there
were sixteen knights dressed in liveried robes. Once these *entremets* were
over, organs were played; and from the pastry a German cornet was
played in a most peculiar manner; and then a goblin or a very disfigured
monster entered the room, which instead of a body, below the waist had
the legs and feet of a hairy griffin, with long nails; and above the waist
was a body of a man, dressed in a tight jacket made of white silk, with
green stripes, and a hat on his head. He had a strange beard and face;
he carried two spears and a shield in his hands; he had on his head a

39 Mary of Burgundy (d.1475), bastard daughter of Philip the Good, wife of Pierre de Bauffremont, lord of Charny.

40 Isabelle d'Étampes (b.1438/9), daughter of the count of Étampes, married to the duke of Cleves in 1455.

41 Jeanne or Marie de La Viefville, lady of Beveren, wife of Anthony, Grand Bastard of Burgundy since 1446, lady of honour to the duchess in 1447.

42 Jacques lord of Pons (in Poitou) (c.1412–1472/3) had fought the English on the side of Charles VII of France in the 1440s, but had been banished from the kingdom, declared guilty of *lèse-majesté* in 1449.

43 Guigonne de Salins, third wife of the chancellor Nicolas Rolin.

44 Thibaut of Luxembourg, lord of Fiennes (1420–1475/7), brother of Louis of Luxembourg, active in the Ghent war, but withdrew from the world as a Cistercian monk in 1456, and later became bishop of Le Mans.

45 Jacques, first count of Hornes (d. 1488).

man, standing upside down, who held himself up by his hands on the shoulders of the monster; and the monster was mounted on a wild boar covered in costly green silk, and when he had made his tour of the room, he returned whence he had come. When the goblin had left, the people in the church sang out and a flute and another instrument were played from the pastry; and soon after four clarions rang out loudly, and made a joyful fanfare. These clarions were behind a green curtain, hung on a big platform made at the end of the room.

When their fanfare was over, the curtain was suddenly pulled back, and there, on the platform, could be seen the figure of Jason, armed to the teeth, walking about, looking all around him, as if he had arrived in a strange land ...

[Jason proceeds to read a letter that Medea had given him. He then does battle with some enormous oxen with flames coming out of their nostrils. He subdues them with the aid of a phial of liquid which had been given to him by Medea. At this point, the curtain was drawn and the play ended for a while ...]

After the play, the organs in the church played out for the time it took to play a motet; and then a song called 'Saviour of my life' was sung from the pastry by three sweet voices.

Then the door through which the other *entremets* had come in, after those of the church and pastry had played four times, a marvellously large and beautiful stag entered the room, all white with large golden antlers, and covered in a rich covering of green and vermilion silk, as far as I could tell. A young boy twelve years old was mounted on the stag, dressed in a short robe of crimson velvet, wearing a little black slashed hat on his head, and shod in fine shoes. This child held on to the antlers of the stag with both hands. As he entered the room, he began on a song in a very high and clear voice, and the stag seemed to sing the tenor part, without there appearing to be any other person about save the child and artifice of the stag, and the song they sang was called '*Je ne voy onques la pareille etc.*' [I have never seen her like]. While singing in the way I have told, they passed in front of the tables, and then left; and this *entremets* seemed to me to be well and agreeably received. After this fine *entremets* of the white stag and child, the singers from within the church sang a motet, and a lute was plucked from within the pastry accompanied with two good voices; and so in this way, the church and pastry performed something between the *entremets*.

After this, when the players in the pie had done their work, a fanfare rang out, on the stage where the story of Jason was being played out, from the four clarions which had played before. Once their fanfare was over, the same curtain was drawn back …

[This time a terrible serpent sprang out, spewing poison and flames from its jaws. Jason begins to fight the serpent 'so realistically, that it did not resemble a play but all too bitter and mortal battle'. The serpent is defeated with the help of a ring that had been given to Jason by Medea. The serpent's head is cut off and its teeth extracted. Then the curtain was closed, the organs in the church played and four minstrels from the pie played on flutes …]

Then from one end of the room, high up, a dragon breathing fire set off, flying almost the length of the room, and disappeared – no one knew how. The people in the church sang out, and the blind men in the pie played the hurdy-gurdy. Then from high up at one end of the room a heron took flight, to the cry of several voices in the manner of falconers; and soon, from another end of the room a falcon took to the air and circled about and got its bearings; from another end a second falcon took flight and flew with such speed and struck the heron so violently, that it killed the heron in the middle of the room. And when the clamour was over, the heron was presented to my lord the duke; the singers from the church sang once more and the drummers in the pie struck up…

[The curtains are drawn back once more to reveal Jason ploughing the land. He then sows the land with the serpent teeth, from which armed men spring up ready to do battle. Jason kills them all; and the curtains are drawn together again …]

Now that the play had finished, the organs in the church were played, and from the pie issued hunting cries, so that it seemed that there were little yapping dogs, and poachers shouting, and sounds of trumpets, as though they were in a forest. The hunt marked the end of the *entremets*. Such were the worldly *entremets* of this Feast, and I will speak of them no further, and recount a piteous spectacle which seems to me more special than the others.

Through the door where all the other *entremets* had entered and left, came the largest real giant I had ever seen, with a long stride, dressed in a long robe of green silk, striped in several places; on his head was a headdress like a Saracen's from Granada; in his left hand he held a large, thick double-edged axe of an old-fashioned kind, and in his right he led an elephant covered in silk, on which there was a castle containing a lady dressed in a robe of white satin like a nun, and over the robe was a mantle of black cloth; her head was covered up in a white head-cloth like a beguine or a recluse. As soon as she had entered the room and had

surveyed the noble company there, as though caught by necessity, she
said to the giant who led her:

> Giant, I wish to halt here
> for I see a noble company
> to whom I must speak,
> to tell them their will and to teach
> them things which should be truly heard.

When the giant heard the lady speak, he looked at her in great fear,
but he did not stop until he reached the duke's table. There several
people gathered round wondering who this lady could be. As soon as
the elephant had halted, the lady began her lament.

[She explains that she is Holy Church, ruined and in bitter pain; she has
implored help from the Emperor, the 'Christian and most victorious' king of
France, other kings, lords and all good Christians. She is now joyful that she
can bring her lament before the duke of Burgundy, and asks all to reflect on
the shame that has befallen her, appealing in particular to the knights of the
Golden Fleece and other gentlemen for help …]

When the lament of our Mother Church was over, a great number of
heralds entered the room, the last being Golden Fleece, the king of
arms. In his hands he carried a live pheasant, adorned with a costly collar
of gold, very richly decorated with precious stones and pearls. Behind
Golden Fleece came two young ladies, Yolande the bastard daughter
of my lord the duke,[46] and Isabelle of Neufchâtel, daughter of my lord
of Montagu,[47] flanked by two knights of the Golden Fleece, the lord of
Créquy[48] and Simon de Lalaing.[49] In this order, the heralds and Golden
Fleece came up with the pheasant to the table of the duke to whom they
bowed in reverence. Golden Fleece then said: 'Most high and powerful
prince, my renowned lord: here are the ladies who present themselves
to you very humbly. And because it is the custom, and has been since
ancient times, that at great feasts and noble assemblies, the peacock or
some other noble bird is presented to princes, lords, and other noble

---

46 Yolande, Bastard of Burgundy, married Jean d'Ailly, lord of Harnes, vidame of
Amiens, in 1456.

47 Isabelle de Neufchâtel, daughter of Jean lord of Montaigu, lady of honour to the
duchess, married Louis de Vienne, lord of Ruffey in 1457.

48 Jean V de Créquy (Artois) (1400–74), one of the founding members of the Order of
the Golden Fleece in 1430, militarily active in the 1440s, fought in the Ghent war,
went on pilgrimage to the Holy Land in 1448.

49 Simon de Lalaing (c.1405–76), fought against the Mamelukes at Cyprus in 1426, and
the English in the 1430s, and against the Ghenters 1449–53; knight of the Golden
Fleece since 1431; one of the most active in preparing an expedition against the Turks
after 1453, taking part in Anthony of Burgundy's expedition in 1464.

men, on which to make useful and valid vows, they have sent me with these two damsels, to present this noble pheasant to you, praying that you will keep them in memory'. Once these words had been said, my lord the duke (who knew to what end he had held the banquet) looked at the Church, and as if having pity on her, pulled from a breast pocket a letter spelling out that he had vowed to come to the aid of Christianity (as it will be seen later). At this Mother Church made a gesture of joy, and seeing that my lord had handed his vow to Golden Fleece who was now reading it, she cried out aloud ... [She praises God that she will now be served so well by the 'foremost of the peers of France.']

At these words, the giant took hold of his elephant once more, and led it in front of the tables, the way he had come. When I had seen this *entremets* (in other words, the Church) and a castle on such an unusual animal, I wondered to myself what it all could mean. And I could interpret it in no other way than to see the beast she led (a strange and unusual one to us in these parts) as a sign that she worked and laboured under great and diverse trials, on behalf of Constantinople (whose adversities we were aware of); and the castle she was in signified Faith. Moreover, I understood this lady's being conducted and led by this large and armed giant as showing her fear of the arms of the Turks who had driven her out and sought her destruction.

When she had left, all the noblemen, out of pity and compassion, began to make vows, following the lead of my lord the duke, each one in his own fashion, and committed their vows to writing, as it will soon appear. But because so many vows were being made, or seemed about to be made, that it threatened to be too protracted, my lord had Golden Fleece call out that things should stop directly, and all those who wanted to make a vow should hand in their vows to Golden Fleece on the following day, and he would consider them as valid as if they had been made in his presence.

To be brief, as soon as Golden Fleece had made his announcement, the banquet was over, the table-cloths were taken away, and everyone walked about the room. As for me, it seemed that it had all been a dream, for of all the *entremets* and tables, there remained only the fountain of glass. When I saw nothing new to occupy my attention, my thoughts turned to several aspects of this affair. First, I thought of the outrageous excess and vast expense laid out for this banquet which had lasted only a short time; this manner of passing round the chaplets, in which each had tried to outdo the other in receiving the company more nobly, had taken a lot of time; and most of all, my lord had put on such pomp, cost and company, that I called it all an outrageous and unreasonable expense, without finding any virtue in it, save in the *entremets* of the Church, and the vows that followed. And again it seemed to me to have been an enterprise begun too precipitously.

I remained a long time with these thoughts and ruminations, until by chance I found myself next to a lord counsellor and chamberlain who was very intimate with the duke, and with whom I was quite familiar. So I decided to speak with him, and told him of my fanciful thoughts. When I had told him everything, he replied: 'My friend, you should know (and I affirm this on my oath as a knight) that these chaplets, banquets and festivities were arranged and undertaken for a long time past, only under the firm direction and secret will of the duke to accomplish his banquet in the way you have seen, desiring greatly and with all his heart to bring to fruition an old and holy resolution which he had undertaken to serve God our Creator. This resolution is and can be made known through the vow that he has now made public, namely, for the good of Christianity, and to resist the machinations of the enemies of our faith, a desire he has amply demonstrated for a long time now, by hiring and sending ships and troops for the purpose. Indeed, three or so years ago, my lord held a Feast of the Order of the Golden Fleece at Mons in Hainaut, to which a great many lords of the Order were gathered.[50] And at morning mass, the bishop of Chalon, the duke's chancellor, described, in a general sermon, the great desolation and ruin in which the Church Militant lay, and urged the knights of the Order and others to succour our unhappy Mother Church. The knights were seized with noble intentions to increase the service of God and to maintain the faith; and my lord was the principal mover in all this, and the first to offer body and goods. Since then, as it is well known, the rebellion of Ghent overtook him, on which he spent time and money to subdue, and, by the grace of God, as everyone knows, he achieved this well and with honour. Now it was during this time that the Turks made great assaults upon Christianity, gaining Constantinople (no villainy by these evildoers has been greater), killing the Emperor and destroying the Empire. Such things have constantly enflamed the heart and desire of my lord to serve Our Lord Jesus Christ, for it is a duty to serve the needy. So, to conclude, you should be aware that for a long time he

50 The chapter was held at Mons in 1451 (see chapter 3 [**12c**]). For the crusading
   fervour expressed at the meeting (and concern to interest the king of France), see J.
   Paviot, 'Les circonstances historiques du voeu du faisan', in Caron and Clauzel (eds),
   Banquet du faisan, pp. 66–8. The bishop of Chalon-sur-Saône, Jean Germain, who
   delivered the sermon, had long sought to encourage crusading as well as the unity
   of the Church, East and West.

himself has followed through and striven toward this need to have the time to be able to make the vow and to demonstrate the noble will and desire he has for the common good and general profit of Christianity.'

While the knight and I talked and deliberated over the cause and primary intention for which, in his understanding, this Feast and great assembly had been made, there entered, by the main door, a great multitude of torches, and then several players of diverse musical instruments such as drums, lutes and harps. After them came a lady dressed in a robe of white satin, very simply made, in the manner of a nun, and wrapped around her was a large cloak of white damask, and her head was attired very simply with a white head-cloth, all as though she were someone saintly and devout ...

[The lady is called 'Grace Dieu'. She is followed by twelve soldiers, each leading a lady by the hand. When Grace finds herself in front of the duke, she speaks, handing him a letter that promises renown in this world and in paradise for the vow that the duke has made. Further letters are given by the twelve other ladies and read out by Grace-Dieu: these tell of the virtues represented by the twelve ladies: Faith, Charity, Justice, Reason, Prudence, Temperance, Magnanimity, Truth, Largesse, Diligence, Hope and Valour. All these virtues are necessary for the duke's enterprise ...]

After these words, Grace-Dieu left the room, leaving behind her the ladies she had brought in. To complete their act, the letters they carried were taken from their shoulders, and they began to dance like mummers, to make good cheer and to invest the Feast with more joy. They were followed in this dance by knights and ladies; first the lords by name, my lord of Charolais, my lord of Cleves, my lord of Étampes, my lord Adolf of Cleves, my lord John of Coïmbra, my lord the Bastard of Burgundy, my lord of Bouchain,[51] my lord Anthony bastard of Brabant,[52] my lord Philippe bastard of Brabant,[53] my lord Philippe Pot,[54] my lord Philippe de Lalaing,[55] and my lord Chrétien de Digoine; and as for the ladies,

51 Wolfert van Borselen (c.1430–1486), son of Henry van Borselen, one of the wealthiest families in Zeeland, made a knight during the Ghent war, carried the title of marshal of France after 1464, and was made a knight of the Golden Fleece in 1478.

52 Antoine, bastard of Brabant (d.1498), bastard son of Philip the Good, pantler in the ducal household from 1451, chamberlain in 1453.

53 Philippe, bastard of Brabant, bastard son of Duke Philip the Good, ducal chamberlain from 1453.

54 Philippe Pot (1428–94), lord of La Roche-Nolay and Châteauneuf, Grand Seneschal of Burgundy, governor of Lille, Douai and Orchies, godson of the duke and later his chamberlain, took part in the Ghent war, made a crusading vow in 1454, and became a knight of the Golden Fleece in 1461.

55 The text used by M.-T. Caron has Philippe de Lannoy (son of Guillebert lord of Willerval) instead of Philippe de Lalaing (Caron, Les voeux du faisan, p. 131).

my lady of Bourbon, my lady of Étampes, my lady of Ravestein, my lady of Arcis,[56] my lady of Commines,[57] my lady of Santers,[58] my lady of Obeaux,[59] my lady of Chasteler,[60] Marguerite, bastard of Burgundy,[61] Antoinette, wife of Jehan Boudaut,[62] and Ysabeau Coustain.[63] While they danced in this way, the kings of arms and heralds, with the noble men assigned to the task, went about the ladies and maidens, to find out the name of the person to whom the prize for the best jouster and breaker of lances that day should be given and presented. It was found that the lord of Charolais had won and deserved it.

The officers of arms took two young princesses (the lady of Bourbon and the lady of Étampes) to present the prize and they handed it to my lord of Charolais who kissed them as he was accustomed to do and as was the custom; and a loud cry 'Montjoie!' was let out. Soon after the wine and spices were carried out in seven comfit-dishes, most of which were made of precious stones. And then jousts were announced for the following day by the lord of Charolais, accompanied by the lord Bastard Benetru de Chassa.[64] Three companions in arms, wearing shields of violet and black, were named in the announcement. My lord Adolf won the challenger's prize and my lord of Charolais won the home prize. That day my lord the duke threw a banquet for all the ladies in his household.

Two or three hours after midnight, my lord and his company left the banqueting place and retired severally. Now, because I am fully aware that several people have written about the Feast, and that no-one can have seen everything, and because it could be said that I have spoken about it in great detail, so that the manner and record of my account may be true, I have had it inspected by the lord of Lannoy and by Jean

56 Isabella de Souza, married to Jean de Poitiers, lord of Arcis-sur-Aube, from 1431.
57 Jeanne d'Estouteville, lady of honour to the duchess, married the lord of Commines in 1444.
58 Probably Madame de Sambre, wife of Claude de Rochebaron.
59 Antoinette d'Inchy (d.1478), lady of Canteleu, wife of Waleran lord of Aubeaux (near Lille).
60 Wife of Simon lord of Chasteler (chamberlain of the duke who fought in the Ghent war).
61 Margaret, bastard daughter of Philip the Good, serving in the duchess's household.
62 Antoinette de Morale, lady of honour in the duchess' household from 1450.
63 Isabeau Machefoing, married to Jean Coustain in 1449 (on whose execution in 1462, see below, chapter 2); later to Jean de Montferrand, and finally to Olivier de la Marche.
64 Jean de Chassa dit Benetru, counsellor and chamberlain to the duke, took part in the Ghent war (and in the wedding jousts at Bruges in 1468); accused by Charles the Bold in 1470, along with Baudouin, Bastard of Burgundy, of an attempt on the duke's life; thereafter passed into the service of Louis XI.

Boudaut, principal organisers of the events recounted above; and after their inspection had been made and approved of by the lord of Lannoy, I have dared to make public. I beg very humbly of my most redoubtable and sovereign lord the duke, and of all those who read or hear of these things, that they pardon my ignorance and lend their ears to listen to some of the vows which were made at this banquet.

Chapter 30

There follows some of the vows which the very noble and well-renowned prince Philip, by the grace of God, duke of Burgundy, Brabant, etc., and of several other great lords, knights and gentlemen, made in the year 1453. And first of all, the duke's vow:

'I swear first of all to God my Creator and to the glorious Virgin Mary His mother, and then to all the ladies and to the pheasant, that if it is the pleasure of the most Christian and most victorious prince, the king [of France] to take the cross and to endanger his body in defence of the Christian faith, and to resist the damnable enterprise of the Grand Turk and the infidels; and if then I have no legitimate impediment of body, I will serve him personally and with my power in the holy journey, in the best way that God may give me grace to do. And if the affairs of the king prevent him from going personally, and he wants to commit a prince of the blood or some other lord and leader of his army to the task, I will obey and serve at his command on the holy journey to the best of my ability, as if the king himself were there in person. And if, because of his important affairs, he is unable to go or send someone else in his place, and other Christian princes of sufficient power undertake the holy journey, I will accompany them on it, and exert myself with them in the most strenuous way I can for the defence of the Christian faith, provided that this is at the pleasure and permission of my lord the king, and that the lands that God has committed me to govern be peaceful and safe. To this end I will work and set about the task in such a way that God and the world will know that nothing will have held or hold me back. And if during the holy journey I may find out or discover, by whatever means or manner, that the Grand Turk is willing to fight me in single combat, I will, for the Christian faith, fight him with the help of God almighty and of his mother the most sweet Virgin Mary, whom I always invoke to my aid. Made at Lille, 17 February, in the year of the birth of Our Lord 1454, signed by my hand. PHILIPPE.'

[De La Marche then records twenty further vows in his account.[65]]

---

65 For records of the 107 vows known to have been made at the Feast, see Caron, *Les voeux du faisan, passim.*

2. The marriage feast of Charles the Bold and Margaret of York in Bruges, 3–14 July, 1468

Introduction

Charles the Bold and Margaret of York, sister of Edward IV of England, were married on 3 July at Damme, some three miles from Bruges. The marriage was significant as a political alliance from which Charles hoped to strengthen his hand against Louis XI of France.[66] But it is for the extraordinary celebrations in Bruges that followed the wedding that the event is best remembered. The feasts and jousts far surpassed those of the Feast of the Pheasant. There were six grand banquets, not one as in Lille; ten days of jousting, not two. A conservative estimate would put the total cost of the event, for Charles the Bold's household, at a staggering £60,000.[67] Reports of the event exceed those written about the Feast of the Pheasant;[68] memory of it inspired other courts of Europe long after.

66 See R. Vaughan, *Charles the Bold* (2nd edn, Woodbridge, 2002), pp. 41–58; M.A. Ballard, 'Anglo-Burgundian Relations 1464–1472', (D.Phil thesis, University of Oxford, 1992), esp. 150–85; R.J. Walsh, *Charles the Bold and Italy 1467–1477: Politics and Personnel* (Liverpool, 2005), esp. pp. 2–5.

67 There are too many gaps or ambiguities in the accounts to make a precise calculation possible. A separate account for the work preparing the ducal residence and for the painters and image-makers for the banquets and *entremets* was produced by Fastre Hollet, controller of the ordinary expenses of the ducal household. (The controller, or comptroller, was an officer appointed to record a separate account of expenditure to keep a check, and was a feature of the late medieval princely household.) The account gives the total cost at £12,698 (this includes payments for holding the meeting of the Golden Fleece in Our Lady church of Bruges in June 1468): de Laborde, *Les ducs de Bourgogne*, ii, pp. 293–379. Only one detailed account survives for costs at the banquet (the last and most lavish one) which gives the total as £1,496 (the food costing over £1,172 – the expenditure from pantry and kitchen): ADN B3432, no. 118470. See also ibid., nos 118469, 118473, 118478. Tommaso Portinari was paid more than £34,000 for clothes and other materials for the occasion, including £1,488 for a robe of cloth-of-gold which Charles wore at his wedding. In fact the accounts mention a sum of £53,773 that was owed to Portinari in connection with the wedding, though this seems to have included the cost of materials for other purposes: A. Greve, E. Lebailly and W. Paravicini (eds), *Comptes de l'argentier de Charles le Téméraire, Duc de Bourgogne* (*Recueil des historiens de la France: Documents financiers et administratifs*, 10), 2 vols (Paris, 2001), i, pp. 523–77. For other smaller sums connected with the Feast, see ibid., i, pp. 151, 194–5, 236, 241, 331, 349–50, 521; and ii, pp. 359–60. These accounts do not refer to the costs of the joust (the *pas* of the Golden Tree) for which Anthony of Burgundy particularly (according to de la Marche) had to pay heavily; but there are expenses for jousting harnesses for certain individuals (ibid., i, pp. 349–50.)

68 The most extensive accounts of the marriage, apart from Olivier de la Marche's, are those by Jean de Haynin (*Mémoires, 1465–1477*, ed. D.D. Brouwers (Liège, 1905), ii, pp. 17–62); by Anthonis de Roovere (though his authorship has been disputed) in the *Excellente cronike van Vlaenderen* (in A.J. Enschedé, 'Huwelijksplechtigheden van Karel van Bourgondië en Margaretha van York', *Kronijk van het historisch genootschap gevestigd te Utrecht*, 22 [1866], pp. 17–71); and by an anonymous English herald (in *Excerpta historica*, ed. S. Bentley [London, 1931], pp, 223–39). Other reports of it survive in England, Strasbourg and Lübeck: see Vaughan, *Charles the Bold*, p. 49 n. 1.

Like the Feast of the Pheasant, it was an exclusive event. The banquets took place at the *prinsenhof*, the ducal residence in Bruges, within the tennis court, hastily converted to accommodate the guests. Their organisation was in the hands of a small group of courtiers close to the duke: once again, Olivier de la Marche (along with the count of Charny, Michault de Chaugy, lord of Chisse, Jacques de Villers, Jean de Salins)[69] was involved in directing the *entremets*. Anthony of Burgundy, half-brother of Charles the Bold, was the chief organiser of the jousts; participants, besides the Englishmen, were all close associates of the ducal household.[70] The jousts took the form of a *pas d'armes*, a kind of jousting which the Burgundian court had already made its own.[71] This form involved the defence of a passage by an individual knight against all-comers, and adopted episodes or motifs drawn from the pages of romances: the *pas* of the Golden Tree borrowed from the Florimont legend in the Alexander cycle.[72] It differed from the 'joust' and 'tournament', in technical terms, by the use of the sword as well as lance in combat, and by the stipulation that only those with four blood-lines of nobility could take part.

The occasion displayed ducal power – and its virtues – to full effect. The wine that sprung in abundance, and for public consumption, from the arrows of the stone archers outside the *prinsenhof* demonstrated ducal bounty. The labours of Hercules, staged during the banquets, served as models for princely government.[73] Even the food was shaped to represent ducal castles, towns and lordships. The impression of order and plenty within the *entremets* no doubt acted to encourage among the high-ranking guests a sense of common identity under ducal authority.

Olivier de la Marche's account, once again, has little to say about the involvement of the wider urban world in the event: attention is fixed on the *pas d'armes* and on the festivities within the *prinsenhof.* But civic involvement was greater than it had been at the Feast of the Pheasant. Town funds partly subsidised the *pas d'armes*, which was doubtless the spectacle for a wider urban audience.[74]

---

69 Laborde, *Les ducs de Bourgogne*, ii, p. 332.

70 For the literary function that Anthony of Burgundy occupies at these jousts within Olivier de la Marche's *Memoires*, see C. Emerson, '"Tel estat que peust faire le filz aisné légitime de Bourgoinge": Antoine, Great Bastard of Burgundy and Olivier de la Marche', in A. Brown, J.-M. Cauchies and G. Small (eds), *The Burgundian Hero* (Neuchâtel, 2001), pp. 77–88.

71 Eight *pas d'armes* took place within Burgundian territories between 1443 and 1470, more than in any other region. On the different forms of jousting, see Van den Neste, *Tournois*, pp. 50–4; and for the functions of *pas d'armes* (particularly as 'liminal' experiences) see J.-P. Jourdan, 'Le symbolisme du pas dans le royaume de France (Bourgogne et Anjou) à la fin du Moyen Âge', *Journal of Medieval History* 18 (1992), pp. 161–81.

72 G. Kipling, *The Triumph of Honour* (Leiden, 1977), p. 117.

73 See Lecuppré-Desjardin, *Ville des ceremonies*, pp. 215–7. De la Marche was later to claim for the dukes direct ancestry from the legendary hero: see A. Millar, 'Olivier de la Marche and the Herculean origins of the Burgundians', in Brown et al. (eds), *The Burgundian Hero*, pp. 67–76.

74 The town paid more than £17 (Flemish pounds) (£102) for sand, heralds, stages and

A gilded silver image of St Margaret – worth over £79 (Flemish pounds) – was presented to the new duchess. Civic accounts in 1468 show payments for the event exceeding £244 (Flemish pounds) – or £1,464 – considerably less than the expenditure of the ducal household, but significant none the less.[75] Whether this was considered a drain on civic resources is another matter: more than £25 (Flemish pounds) of the total (in the form of a gift of coin) went to the dowager duchess in recognition of the friendship she had shown the town in persuading her son to celebrate his wedding in Bruges.[76]

The arrival of duke and duchess in Bruges was conducted as an Entry ceremony which necessarily required wider participation.[77] De la Marche's account of it is brief, and he concentrates on the pageants put on by foreign merchants in Bruges. He identifies only one figure, Tommaso Portinari, whose financial connections with the Burgundian court were privileged.[78] But the civic authorities of Bruges had gone to some expense to organise the Entry, and had paid Anthonis de Roovere to arrange the *tableaux* which were to align the route of the ducal procession. De Roovere's connections with the court made him an ideal choice as organiser of the *tableaux*.[79] We can speculate that there was liaison with courtiers in their composition, but it is with the urban milieu that he can be chiefly identified. He was associated with the crossbow, archers' and possibly swordsmen's guilds. He devised plays for devotional guilds within Bruges, such as that of Our Lady of the Snow; he was an associate of many members of the guild of the Dry Tree. Both these guilds had dukes and other courtiers as members – another point of contact between 'courtier' and 'townsman'. De Roovere can also be linked with members of the Holy Ghost fraternity, one of the city's chambers of rhetoric,[80] and it may be that it was within this forum that the programme for the Entry's *tableaux* were devised. It is to de Roovere that we may well owe a detailed account of the Entry itself.

---

scaffolding for the jousts (SAB, 216, fos. 38r, 74v). It also rented out stages on the *markt* during the event for £42 3s 5d (Flemish pounds) (more than £252).

75 For receipts and expenses connected with the wedding: SAB, 216, fos. 14v, 37r–38v, 73v–74v, 76v–77v. These expenses do not include gifts of wine. Some of the cost, such as for the *tableaux*, may have been borne (as was often the case) by individual guilds.

76 SAB, 216, fo. 74r.

77 Cost for work on the Cross gate, the cloths hanging over it, the twenty trumpeters, painting, tableaux, and (the largest sum – more than £73) to dress 31 civic dignitaries in black damask cloth, came to more than £100 (Flemish pounds) (i.e., £600).

78 On the career of Tommaso Portinari, see M. Boone, 'Apologie d'un banquier médiéval: Tommaso Portinari et l'état bourguignon', *Le Moyen Âge* 105 (1999), pp. 31–54.

79 Charles the Bold requested the Bruges authorities to pay Anthony a regular emolument in 1466 for his services in Entry ceremonies (SAB, 157: Civiele Sentenciën Vierschaar 1465–9, fo. 26r); For the activities of Anthonis de Roovere (c.1430–1482), see J.B. Oosterman, 'Spelen, goede moraliteit en eerbare esbattementen: Anthonis de Roovere en het toneel in Brugge', in H. van Dijk and B. Ramakers (eds), *Spel en spektakel: middeleeuws toneel in de lage landen* (Amsterdam, 2001), pp. 154–77 and 344–9 and references cited there.

80 De Roovere and two members of the Holy Ghost fraternity, Anthonis Goosens and Pieter van Bouchout, were also paid for their help in the Entry of Philip the Good into Bruges in 1463. For further points about chambers of rhetoric, see *infra*, chapter 5.

The ten *tableaux* each provided representations of marriage drawn mostly from biblical precedent. They might be read as flattering to ducal ambitions or even power. The ninth *tableaux* had King Ahasuerus married off to Esther. The theme was already the subject of a ducal tapestry which according to Jean de Haynin was hung in the banqueting hall before the day of the Feast. King Ahasuerus perhaps commended himself for ducal emulation as a model of princely magnificence (who ruled no fewer than 127 provinces). On the other hand, allusions to females interceding before arbitrary power of male rulers were themes more in line with an urban desire to temper the whims of princes. Esther had persuaded Ahasuerus to save the Jewish people.[81] Perhaps both interpretations were intended. Or are we trying to read too much into symbolic representations which drew from a common stock of images found in a wide variety of festive civic events? In any case, the career and connections of Anthonis de Roovere in the service of town and ducal court make it difficult to determine whether an 'urban' or a 'courtly' programme is detectable in the sequence of *tableaux* that he devised.

The twelve days of jousts and banquets imposed princely celebration on civic space. In Olivier de la Marche's account, the main market place disappears behind the trappings of chivalric romance. The names of sixty towns subject to the duke were placed on the castle-cakes served at the first and second banquets. More pointed references to the submission of city to prince might be discerned: according to Jean de Haynin a tapestry hung in the *prinsenhof* depicted Duke John the Fearless's victory over the Liégeois in 1408. But a different impression emerges from de Roovere's account. Urban power is more evident: from each of the two towers of the Cross gate, the figure of a roaring lion, one bearing the standard of Bruges, the other that of Flanders, greeted the ducal procession as it entered the city. In the end, the staging of such a lavish event was unimaginable without the infrastructure and cooperation of a wealthy city such as Bruges. Courtiers and wedding party spilled over into the houses of Bruges.[82] Even Bruges could not provide all that was required: two messengers had to be sent in haste to Ghent, Brussels and twelve other towns to acquire more workers for making the *entremets*, because not enough of them were available locally, and because the celebrations lasted longer than expected.[83] Between April and July, almost 500 painters, image sculptors, carpenters and other artisans had to be drafted in, many from Tournai, Brussels, Ghent, Oudenaarde, Cambrai, Arras, Douai, Valenciennes, Louvain, Ypres and Sluis.[84] The largest of all Burgundian spectacles was heavily dependent on civic resources.

81 In the Entry of Joanna 'the Mad' of Castile into Brussels in 1496, the accompanying text of a tableau representing Esther and Ahasuerus insists that just as Esther freed the Jewish people from Haman (Ahasuerus's minister), so Joanna will protect her people from the envious (see B. Franke, 'Female role models in tapestries', in D. Eichberger [ed.], *Women of distinction. Margaret of York and Margaret of Austria* [Leuven, 2005], pp. 155–6).

82 Work was done on the Carmelite cloister in the town to provide for the English lords who accompanied Margaret of York (Laborde, *Les ducs de Bourgogne*, ii, pp. 310–11).

83 '… it had been said that the marriage Feast of the duke was to be much shorter than it was': Fastre Hollet's account: Laborde, *Les ducs de Bourgogne*, p. 375.

84 Laborde, *Les ducs de Bourgogne*, pp. 330–81.

Olivier de la Marche, *Mémoires*, ii, pp. 536–69

[La Marche inserts into his memoirs a letter he wrote to Gilles du Mas, steward of the duke of Brittany, concerning 'the most splendid marriage of my time'. He describes how Margaret of York and her company arrived at Sluis[85] on Saturday 25 June; how she was met by the dowager duchess; and how Charles the Bold was betrothed to her by the bishop of Salisbury. A week later she was ferried to Damme. On 13 July she was married to the duke by the bishop of Salisbury; after mass, the duke returned to his residence in Bruges and 'while the other ceremonies were going on, he took the precaution of sleeping, as if he were preparing to spend the whole night on the look-out'.

Soon after, there arrived at Damme, Adolf of Cleves,[86] Jean de Chalon,[87] Louis de Chalon,[88] Jacques de Saint-Pol,[89] Antoine de Luxembourg,[90] Jacques de Luxembourg,[91] Jean de Luxembourg,[92] the count of Nassau, Baudouin, bastard of Burgundy,[93] and 'many others' arrived at Damme. After they had paid their respects, the new duchess stepped into a litter dressed in nuptial clothes, wearing a 'costly crown'. After her came thirteen white palfreys, then five carriages with lady escorts: Lady Scales, the countess of Charny,[94] the vidamesse d'Amiens,[95] in one carriage; and in others, forty to fifty other ladies, including the duchess of Norfolk, secondly the Lady Scales, Lady Willoughby, 'a very beautiful widow',

---

85 Jean de Haynin mentions the great fires lit at 9 pm to the sound of trumpets in Bruges and Sluis during her stay in Sluis: these were made of wooden piles 40 feet high and 30 feet across, each fire costing £120: *Mémoires*, ii, pp. 22–4.

86 Adolf of Cleves was paid £1,200 for clothing and to be well turned out at the festivities (Greve et al., *Comptes de l'argentier*, i, no. 836).

87 Jean II de Chalon, lord of Argueil and Tonnerre, received £800 for his involvement at the wedding festivities, and substantial sums from Charles's treasurer for the provision of soldiers and for his own wedding to Jeanne de Bourbon in 1468 (ibid., i, nos. 839, 1666, 2126).

88 Louis de Chalon, lord of Château-Guion (brother of William, prince of Orange) was paid £48 for a jousting harness at the wedding (ibid., i, no. 1502).

89 Jacques de Luxembourg, lord of Richebourg, 'knight, counsellor and chamberlain' of the duke.

90 Antoine of Luxembourg (d. 1474), count of Roussy, brother of Jean of Luxembourg, paid £600 for clothing at the wedding festivities (ibid., i, no. 838).

91 Jacques I de Luxembourg, lord of Fiennes, nephew of the count of St Pol, constable of France, brother of Jean, supplied soldiers for Charles in 1468 (ibid., i, nos. 1144, 1608). He became a counsellor of Maximilian and was elected to the Order of the Golden Fleece in 1479.

92 This could be Jean de Luxembourg, count of Marle, brother of Jacques (who died at Morat in 1476), but more likely Jean of Luxembourg, lord of Zottegem, paid £48 for a jousting harness probably for the wedding festivities (ibid., i, no. 1502).

93 Baudouin, Bastard of Burgundy, lord of Chorey (in Burgundy), was paid £480 for clothing and to be well turned out at the wedding festivities (*Comptes de l'argentier*, i, no. 840).

94 Mary of Burgundy.

95 Yolande, Bastard of Burgundy.

Lady Clifton, Lady Scrope, Lady Eleanor Roos ...]

In this order, Lady Margaret progressed from Damme to the gate of Bruges called the Holy Cross Gate, and in view of a great number of princes, knights and esquires, noblemen and nations who met the lady that day, richly dressed and in fine order. I pass over this to be brief, because I want to come to the order in which they entered the town. But first I am obliged to call to mind a noble knight from Zeeland, who, at that moment and Entry, had six horses covered in outfits of cloth-of-gold, brocaded with metal threads, of very costly silk cloth and ornamental covering. He was called Adrian van Borselen, lord of Breda,[96] whom I recall in this account for two reasons. The first, because he was the best turned-out in this Entry. The second, because, by the will of God, he died the following Wednesday, through an infected leg. His death was a shame and was greatly regretted by the nobility.

The lining up was done at the Holy Cross gate,[97] and those who accompanied the noble wife processed in the following manner, which I relate omitting nothing.[98] First, all the men of the churches and colleges, accompanying the bishops, abbots and prelates, who were required to carry the relics and lead the processions, and who had waited a long time for my lady at that gate, walked in front, in order and apart, such that the company who followed could march in order by twos.

The first group who walked in order was the *bailli* and *écoutète* of Bruges;[99] after them, two by two, came the gentlemen of the household of princes and lords who were not of the duke's retinue; after them, a gentleman captain of the Bastard of Burgundy, and two archers after him, dressed in overcoats of white metal brocading, with a large golden tree in front and behind them which signified the *pas* of the Golden Tree which my lord the Bastard began the following day and maintained during this Feast, of which mention will be made further on.

After these archers, two by two, came the gentlemen of the duke's household, then the chamberlains, then the lords of the blood who were very

96 Adrian van Borselen was married to Eleanor of Burgundy, bastard daughter of Philip the Good.

97 De Roovere mentions the presence of a roaring lion on each of the two great towers of the Cross gate, holding the standards of Flanders and of Bruges (Enschedé, 'Huwelijksplechtigheden', p. 26).

98 La Marche omits the appearance at the gate of a procession of beguines from the Wijngaard in Bruges who, according to de Roovere, presented Margaret with a circlet of roses (ibid., p. 23).

99 The two ducal officials resident in Bruges, with powers of jurisdiction in civic affairs.

numerous: they were all dressed in the duke's robes and livery, such that the esquires had robes of black damask cloth, and doublets of crimson satin. The chief officers had long black fashioned robes, and doublets of fashioned crimson satin; and the knights and counsellors had long robes of black velvet, and the servants and valets of the household were all dressed in black and violet cloth and camlet doublets. What should I tell you? The duke had given so extensively and lavishly in providing the silk and woollen cloth for these outfits, that the cost came to more than forty thousand francs.[100] And certainly it was a beautiful sight to see the gentlemen dressed in this livery progress in order.

After the noblemen of the blood came a whole range of instruments in order (which had come from many different nations); after them came clarions, minstrels and trumpeters, as many Englishmen as Burgundians, who were very pleasant to listen to. A great number of officers of arms from several countries came after them; twenty-four of them wore tabards. After them came six archers carrying a golden crown on their shoulders: they were archers of the king of England, and each of them had a long arrow in his hand. Then came my lady in her litter, as I described before. At either side of the litter, maintaining plenty of room around it, were the two captains of the duke's archers, that is my lord of Rosimbos[101] and my lord Philippe, Bastard of La Viesville,[102] accompanied by only twenty household archers, and dressed in surcoats brocaded with metal threads. These were on foot, and had their bows, and guarded the litter (as it was said) from the press of people and to make sure the people did not approach the litter. As for the litter, it was splendidly escorted, for the Burgundians on foot were the knights of the Golden Fleece richly dressed and adorned, some dressed in golden cloth, the others very richly brocaded with metal threads. At the head was my lord Adolf of Cleves, first cousin of the duke, then the Bastard of Burgundy, the count of Charny,[103] my lord of Créquy,[104] my lord of

100 See note 67 above for the payments to Tommaso Portinari.

101 Jean de Rosimbos, lord of Fourmelles, (d. 1479) 'knight, counsellor and chamberlain' of the duke (*Comptes de l'argentier*, i, nos 126, 304, 668), who had made an oath at Lille in 1454 to go on crusade, and filled a number of offices in service of the duke.

102 Philip, Bastard of La Viesville, captain of archers in Charles's army, who had escorted the Lord Scales and other lords from England on their journey to the Low Countries (ibid., i, nos 466, 974).

103 Pierre Bauffremont, count of Charny, 'knight, counsellor and chamberlain' of the duke; knight of the Golden Fleece since 1430, often in military service of the duke; took a vow to go on crusade in 1454 in attendance with Simon de Lalaing on the duchess during the wedding festivities (ibid, i, nos. 1375, 2141).

104 Jean de Créquy.

La Vere,[105] my lord of Auxy,[106] my lord Simon de Lalaing,[107] my lord Philippe Pot, lord of La Roche, my lord Philippe de Crèvecoeur, lord of Esquerdes,[108] my lord Jacques de Saint-Pol, lord of Richebourg, and generally all the knights of the Order who were there. On the English side there were many worthy men on foot escorting the litter. As it comes to me exactly, I will recount the names of the gentlemen sent to conduct my lady in this country.

At the head was the Lord Scales, brother of the queen of England,[109] Sir John Woodville his brother, one of the brothers of Lord Talbot, brother of the duchess of Norfolk, Lord Thomas Montgomery, Sir John Howard, Lord Dacre, Sir John Donne, Thomas Vaughan, St Leger, John Parr, and many other knights and gentlemen whose names I do not know. There may have been up to eighty or a hundred nobles, who were in good order and richly dressed throughout the feast, though only ten or twelve of them were on foot around the litter.

After the litter came another six yeomen of the crown, dressed like the first group: they were certainly fine men and well turned-out. After them came the horses and carriages, ladies and damsels, in the state and order I have already said.

The ambassadors, as many prelates as knights, came after the company of ladies, each taking the rank of his master, and the chancellor of Burgundy and the counsel of the household were organised to accompany them. There were the bishops of Salisbury, Metz, Verdun, Cambrai, Utrecht, and Tournai, a knight of the king of Aragon, three or four knights, clerics and gentlemen of the Count Palatine, and many others whose names I cannot remember. After them came the nations in order who processed in the following manner.

---

105 Henry de Borsselen, lord of Veere, was ordered to send ships to the duchess to accompany her from England to Sluis (ibid., i, no. 772).

106 Jean IV, lord of Auxy, knight of the Golden Fleece since 1445. For his role in the matter of Jean Coustain, see [8].

107 Simon de Lalaing, lord of Montigny, knight of the Golden Fleece from 1431, in attendance on the duchess with Pierre Bauffremont during the wedding festivities; and had been in the company of Anthony of Burgundy at the jousts in England in 1467 (ibid., i, no. 2141). He was uncle of the celebrated jouster Jacques de Lalaing.

108 Philippe de Crèvecoeur, lord of Esquerdes, knight, chamberlain and first captain of Charles's household archers (ibid., i, nos 466, 1010). For his trusted role during the Jean Coustain affair, see [8].

109 Anthony Woodville, earl of Rivers.

The Venetians came first,[110] they and their servants on horse, the masters all dressed in crimson velvet, and the valets in vermilion cloth; in front of them there were fifty men on foot dressed in vermilion each with a torch in his hand. Then came the Florentines who had sixty torches, carried by sixty men on foot dressed in blue, and after the torches came four pages, one after the other, who had doublets of cloth-of-silver, and capes of crimson velvet, mounted on four chargers, which were covered in white satin, bordered with blue velvet. Behind the Florentine merchants came Tommaso Portinari, head of their nation, dressed like the councillors of the duke (for he was in his council);[111] and after him came ten merchants, in twos, dressed in decorated black satin; and after them ten factors, dressed in simple black satin: all had crimson doublets. After them were twenty-four valets on horseback, all dressed in blue. Then came the Spaniards, who were thirty-four merchants on horseback, dressed in violet damask; and each merchant had his page on foot in front of him, dressed all the same in doublets of black satin, and jackets of crimson velvet. They had sixty torches carried by sixty men in front of them, dressed in violet and green. The Genoese came after them, with a beautiful girl on horseback in front of them, representing the virgin, the king's daughter, whom St George saved from the dragon, and then St George, armed with all sorts of weapons, his horse covered in white damask, and a cross of crimson velvet; and the girl was dressed in white damask. After this pageant, three pages followed, dressed in white damask, and their horses in violet damask. Afterward came the Genoese merchants, 108 of them, all dressed in violet cloth. And after them came the Germans, 108 on horse, dressed in violet robes, and several in grey fur; and there were six pages dressed in violet satin, and robes of white damask, their horses covered with violet damask; and in front of them were sixty torches, the men carrying them also dressed in violet.

In such an order and array my lady entered her city of Bruges.[112] I

---

110 According to de Roovere, the merchants of the German Hanse came first, with 60 servants on foot; then the Spaniards (26 on horseback); the Venetians (20 on horseback); the Genoese (with 20 men); the Florentines (followed by 150 men). The merchants from Lucca, Portugal and Aragon hung tapestries from the Cross gate and along some of the streets (Enschedé, 'Huwelijksplechtigheden', pp. 23–6). De Haynin has the order as follows: Germans, Genoese, Castilians and Venetians (*Mémoires*, ii, pp. 29–31).

111 See note 76 above on Tommaso Portinari. De Roovere does not single out Portinari in his account of the Florentine merchants (Enschedé, 'Huwelijksplechtigheden', p. 25).

112 De Haynin mentions the large numbers who lined the streets, and those who had to pay an *escu* to have a place at a window (*Mémoires*, ii, p. 33).

must begin by recounting the *tableaux* set up for her joyous Entry. The streets were hung very richly with gold and silk cloth, and with tapestries, and as for the *tableaux*, I have remembered ten of them.[113] The first was of God accompanying Adam and Eve in paradise. The second, how Cleopatra was given in marriage to King Alexander; and in this way appropriate *tableaux* were set up as far as the ducal residence.

In front of the residence was a rich tableau painted in gold and azure,[114] in the middle of which were two lions rampant, holding a shield with the arms of the duke of Burgundy, and around the tableau were twelve blazons of arms of the ducal lands, the duchies and the counties; and on top of the tabernacle on one side was St Andrew,[115] and below it were the flints as devices, and the motto of the duke 'Je l'ay emprins' ('I have undertaken it'). On either side of the tableau were two archers richly painted and in relief. One was a Greek drawing a Turkish bow, and for the duration of the feast, wine from Beaune sprang from the end of his arrow. On the other side was a German firing a crossbow, and from the end of his crossbow sprang Rhenish wine. The wine from both fell into large stone vats, which everyone could fill up from and drink at their pleasure. Within the courtyard, toward the spicery, was a large pelican, which pecked at its breast, and instead of the blood that should have come out, there flowed hippocras, which fell into a wicker basket, subtly done so that nothing was lost; but everyone could partake of it at their pleasure.

Let us return now to the arrival of that beautiful lady. She entered the courtyard around midday: the duke's mother was waiting for her at

113 The memory of De Roovere (as the deviser of the *tableaux*) was rather better. He describes ten of them, their location and the groups within the town who paid for them. They were all, he writes, to signify the good to come to the lands of the duke by the marriage, and took the theme of marriage, nine of them drawing on biblical references: Adam and Eve (put on by the 4 'guilds'); Cleopatra, daughter of King Ptolmy, and Alexander; Mary and Joseph (put on by the butchers and fishmongers); the wedding at Cana (put on by the 17 'guilds'); the bride and bridegroom from the Song of Songs; the Crucifixion (Christ's marriage to his Church); Moses and Tharbis; a woman sitting between a leopard and a lion (i.e., Margaret between the emblems of England and Burgundy), put on by the 'burghers'; King Ahasuerus and Esther (put on by the 'small guilds'); Tobias betrothed to the daughter of Raguel and Gabael, from Tobit: 'Blessing on your wife and parents so that you shall see sons of sons into the third and fourth generation' (put on by the brokers): Enschedé, 'Huwelijksplechtigheden', pp. 26–31. See also the description of the English herald (*Excerpta*, ed. Bentley, pp. 232–4).

114 The tableau or tabernacle was fixed to the wall above the main door (Laborde, *Les ducs de Bourgogne*, ii, pp. 330–1).

115 The accounts also mention an image of St George on the other side from St Andrew (ibid., p. 331).

the entrance of the hall, accompanied by the duke's wife and my lady of Argueil,[116] with a good hundred other ladies and damsels of rank. When the litter drew near, the duke's mother went before it. But soon the yeomen of the crown (who were ordered to do this) took the litter on their shoulders, and carried it away from the horses, in front of my lady, and placed it on the ground. There the litter was uncovered, and the duke's mother helped the beautiful girl out of the litter and, to the sound of trumpets and clarions, led her by the hand to her bedroom. For the moment we will keep silent about the ladies and knights, and return to describe the organisation of the household. To begin with the common offices, in the kitchen there were 300 men, in the saucery twenty-four, in the cup-bearing office and pantry sixty men each, and in the spicery fifteen. Generally all the offices were heavily manned.

In the residence there was a little room set aside in front of the chapel, where the duke alone dined; and next to this room was a large room, where all the chamberlains ate. Further on was a bigger room where the chief stewards and the regular men at court ate, and this one was full several times with the great number of gentlemen, archers, pages, officers of arms, trumpeters, minstrels, and other musicians who were there for the feast. Moreover, there were seven rooms in the house for the entertainment of guests, one of which was occupied by the Bastard, accompanied by my lord of la Roche. In the other rooms were my lord Jacques de Saint-Pol, my lords of Arcis,[117] of the Gruuthuse[118] and of Bergues,[119] and several others who were accompanying them. In each room there was a steward, and men ordered to serve them there. To hold a great court, a room was made in a large courtyard which was called the tennis court.[120]

---

116 Jeanne de Bourbon, countess of Tonnerre, lady of Argueil, wife of Jean II de Chalon, in receipt of gifts from the duke for their marriage (*Comptes de l'argentier*, i, nos 910, 2126, 2293).

117 Jean de Poitiers, lord of Arcis-sur-Aube, counsellor and chamberlain of the duke since 1431, taking the oath to go on crusade in 1454.

118 Louis de Bruges, lord of Gruuthuse.

119 Possibly Jean de Bergues, squire cupbearer of the duke, later given a harness of war (ibid., i, no. 1503), but more likely Philippe de Bergues, lord of Grimberghe (ibid., ii, no. 841).

120 Work on the conversion of the tennis court is described in Fastre Hollet's account: the wooden hall set up in the tennis court was made in Brussels and brought by water to Bruges; the hall was 140 feet long by 70 feet wide, and had to be elevated above the ground with earth and sand to prevent damage from rain; the 20 windows and 9 double windows, 14 feet high were entirely filled with glass, except for a wooden shutter which opened and closed to let the air in and out (Laborde, *Les ducs de Bourgogne*, pp. 296–9). In fact the celebrations involved extensive refurbishment

This room had been hastily made very large, high and spacious, with carpentry. It was illuminated so well and so perfectly through glass windows that everyone said that it was one of the most beautiful rooms they had seen. High up, the room was hung with blue and white woollen cloth, and on its sides were tapestries and hangings showing the story of Jason, by which the beginning of the mystery of the Golden Fleece could be understood.[121] This tapestry was completely made of gold, silver and silk, and I do not believe that such a large and costly tapestry has ever been seen. The room was lit by candelabra made of wood painted white and blue, and from the two ends of the room, there hung two chandeliers which were very subtly made since in each of the structures a man could be hidden. The chandeliers were made up like castles, and their bases were high rocks and mountains which were very subtly made; and on the paths which led around the rocks one could see figures on foot or on horseback, men, women, and an assortment of beasts (which were very well made and subtly done). At the base of each of the chandeliers were seven very large mirrors, so well constructed that one could see everything that was happening in the room through these mirrors. The mountains were covered with trees, grass, leaves and flowers: they were certainly admired and looked at by everyone. They were made by a very ingenious man, called master Jean Skalkin, canon of Saint-Pierre of Lille.[122] For several days Skalkin had

---

of other parts of the *prinsenhof*: the old great hall was re-covered (because it let the rain in everywhere), and was refitted with seats and tables to allow common members of the household to sit, and a large extension to the kitchen was added (which even then was not sufficient, and the covered walkway between the duke's quarters and those of the lord of Dudzele had to be closed off for culinary purposes): ibid., pp. 301–8, 313–4.

121 Jean de Haynin says that the main tapestry depicted the story of Gideon and the Fleece (as does de Roovere: Enschedé, 'Huwelijksplechtigheden', p.33, and the English herald: *Excerpta*, ed. Bentley, pp. 234–5). De Haynin also describes other tapestries: of the battle of Othée (in which Duke John the Fearless had defeated the Liégeois in 1408) in the hall where the sideboard was situated; and of King Clovis in the chamberlains' hall (his coronation, his alliance with King Gundobad of Burgundy, his wedding to Gundobad's niece, his baptism with the Holy Ampule, his conquest of Soissons; how the stag showed him the way across a river; how he acquired the fleurs-de-lys as a coat of arms). In front of the chapel, just before the festivities, were hung tapestries of the history of Duke Begues of Belin, brother of Garin Le Loherant, duke of Lorraine; just before the wedding day, it was replaced by another tapestry of Esther and King Ahasuerus, 'who rules 127 provinces …' (*Mémoires*, ii, pp. 26–7).

122 Skalkin was paid £183 12s 6d (and £123 to cover wages) for his work on the *entremets* including the two great chandeliers or candelabra, both 9 feet across and equipped with 7 mirrors; the mountain-shaped mass rose to a height of 20 feet: Laborde, *Les ducs de Bourgogne*, pp. 375–7, 381.

men placed in the chandeliers who made half of them turn as briskly as windmills; dragons jumped out of the rocks spewing fire and flames in a very strange way, and one could not see at all how the contrivance worked. At the end of the room, in front of the main door, two large platforms, one on top of the other, had been made, decorated with fine tapestries, to seat and install the ladies and damsels who had come to see the feast, and who kept their identities hidden.

In this room three tables had been set up, one of which was at the top end, positioned transversely, as the table of honour.[123] It was higher than the others, reached by steps, and along its length, made of very costly cloth-of-gold, was a costly tester and a hanging so large that it made a cloth covering the seat. Along both lengths of the room ran the other two laid tables, both beautiful and very long, and in the middle of the room was a tall and costly, lozenge-shaped, sideboard.[124] Its lower section was closed up like a tournament list, hung with tapestries showing the arms of the duke; and in front of it began steps and gradations laden with vessels, the lowest of which were the most common, and highest the most costly and delicate. In other words, the lowest of the dishes were of gold-plated silver, and higher up the golden vessels, garnished with precious stones, of which there was a great number. On top of this sideboard was a costly cup garnished with precious stones, and at the corners there were large whole unicorn horns, very large and beautiful.[125] The vessels that decorated that sideboard were not the only ones used that day, for there were other silver vessels, pots and cups, with which the room and chambers were served that day: in truth, the duke could amply furnish his feast with silver vessels; for Duke Philip (whose soul rests with God) had left him more than sixty thousand marks' worth for the purpose, wrought and ready to serve.

The tables were nobly covered and laid out for dinner, and before long, the duke's mother led out her daughter-in-law, the noble wife. Water

123 At the top end of the hall was a double walkway or platform on which was installed the detachable high table (50 feet long by 5 feet wide) covered with a canopy and cloth-of-gold; two platforms, either side of the hall, for two smaller tables; at the end of the hall a high walkway (8 feet wide, 70 feet long) to allow the room to be viewed so that foreign ladies could be installed out of the crowds, with stages for trumpeters and minstrels (Laborde, *Les ducs de Bourgogne*, p. 298).

124 Fastre Hollet's account describes a large lozenge-shaped sideboard in the middle made up of three parts, each 18 feet long, and 20 feet high, with six shelves for flagons and cups ranged according to value. This served only on the day of the great feast (probably the last one held) and for the other days two other sideboards were installed at one of the side walls of the hall (*ibid.*, p. 298).

125 See [4] below on unicorn horns.

was poured and the dishes set down, as will be described. The wife was seated in the middle of the table, and next to her, to her right was the duke's mother; and at the end of the table, on that side was the lady of Burgundy. On the left side had been placed the duchess of Norfolk and my lady of Argueil, but because the duchess was tired, she dined in her room that day, and there was no one next to my lady of Argueil. The countess of Scales and the countess of Charny were placed behind the newly-wed, to help in supporting her, as is the usual custom on these occasions. The other tables were filled with ladies and damsels, very richly attired and dressed.

As for the service, the new duchess was served by the cup-bearer and squire-carver and the pantler, all of them English, knights and men of noble households. The usher of the dining-hall cried out: 'Gentlemen, the food is ready!' And so, we went to the buffet table to look, and around the table, all the ducal relations, and all the knights of the Order as of noble houses, two by two, after the trumpeters, walked up to the food; then a great number of officers of arms, dressed in their tabards, and then came all the household stewards, my lord's as well as my lady's, the last of whom was my lord Guillaume Bische, first chief steward of the household, who had taken the food to the buffet table. The pantler came next, followed by ten or twelve knights and people of noble households, who carried the food. The duke's mother did not wish to be served at all that day with her food covered, but left the honour to her daughter-in-law, as was correct. Now to abridge the account of how the room was organised, there were four gentlemen arranged, and after each one of them, ten gentlemen of rank: these forty-four men served the food to the room, which seemed to be served very attentively. The dinner was served in three stages; and it should not be forgotten that all the rooms, all the chambers, and the large dining room I have talked about, were all served with silver vessels.

The lords in charge of the event led the lords, knights and English gentlemen through the rooms, and in a place called the gallery, the papal legate dined, accompanied by ambassadors of kings and princes who were there, together with all the bishops of this house. The duke dined in the room assigned to him, and all the chamberlains in their correct order. This was a very beautiful thing to see, because they were all dressed the same in the livery of the duke, and all the servants in the correct order, each according to his rank. And one could see no one among them dressed but in velvet and thick gold chains, in great number. So much for my description of the dinner: I return to the joust and *pas* of the Golden Tree which began that day, as you will hear next.

Once the dinner was over, the ladies retired to their chambers to take their ease for a while. It must be recorded that several clothes were changed and replaced; and then they mounted their carriages and palfreys, and in great pomp and triumph they came to their seats. The duke of Burgundy arrived soon after, his horse rigged out with little gold bells, and he himself dressed in a long brocaded robe, with large open sleeves. The robe was lined with very fine sable, and in truth, these clothes seemed to me very important-looking and costly. His knights and gentlemen accompanied him in very great number, and his archers and pages flanked him on foot; and in this way he reached the place that had been prepared for him.

The jousting area was laid out on the market-place of Bruges, and was closed off so that there were only two entrances, though for that day alone, as my lord Adolf of Cleves (who had to open and begin the *pas*), had caused a second entrance to be made to the right of where he had to arm himself. So that the cause of this enterprise might be better understood, the Bastard of Burgundy began his *pas* with a giant whom a dwarf led as a prisoner in chains.[126] The reason for the prison was explained in a letter which a pursuivant called Golden Tree (who was called the servant of the lady of the Hidden Isle) had carried to the duke. It was also explained in a document handed to the duke.

As for the area organized for the joust, at the entrance, in front of the chapel of St Christopher, there was a large gate painted as a golden tree, from which hung a gold hammer. At the opposite end, by the burghers' town house, was a large gate, similarly in the form of a golden tree: this one was fashioned very finely with turrets; and on it were the clarion players of my lord the Bastard of Burgundy, with large banners showing his arms, and dressed in his livery (which for that day were red robes, with little golden trees on the sleeves, as the sign of the *pas*). On each of the two towers of the gate was a white banner with a golden tree. Opposite the ladies, by the side of the great halls, a golden tree had been planted, which was a very beautiful pine tree completely gilded with gold, apart from the leaves. Near the pine tree there was a *perron*[127] with three very finely made pillars, where the dwarf and giant placed themselves, as well as Golden Tree the pursuivant who conducted the

126 De Roovere has Anthony of Burgundy begin the *pas* with a declaration that he has been brought here through a vision granted by the goddess Venus (Enschedé, 'Huwelijksplechtigheden', p. 35).

127 A 'perron' was a kind of platform or column.

pas and the play of the joust. Four lines were written against the *perron*, which ran thus:

> No one should marvel at this *perron*;
> it is an enterprise which wakes noble hearts
> in the service of the most honoured
> lady of honour, and of the Hidden Isle.

Right next to the *perron* was a covered platform where the judges were, commissioned by the duke to keep the *pas* to just and correct procedures. First, there was Thomas de Loraille, lord of Escoville, ambassador and servant of the duke of Normandy,[128] Philippe Pot, lord of La Roche, Claude de Toulongeon,[129] lord of Miraumont, lieutenant of the Marshal of Burgundy. With them were the king of arms of the Order of the Garter, the king of arms of the Golden Fleece, the heralds of Brittany, Constantine and Burgundy, and several others; and on another platform next to the last one were all the kings of arms and heralds (as many foreigners as private ones) who were in this assembly. In front of the judges' platform all the lances were tipped and measured; and there was not a lance broken throughout the *pas* which was not measured as the judges specified, nor any lance run without being measured. But the rights of everyone were very well and faithfully kept; and I accompanied the judges throughout their hard work.

The houses, towers and everything, near and far, around the lists were all so full of people that it was a beautiful sight. But since I have described the jousting area, it is time for me to return to recount the entry of my lord of Ravestein, and that of the Bastard of Burgundy, the knight guarding the Golden Tree who alone ran lances on this day; for in truth, one may easily understand that it was late, since the arrival of the new wife and the dinner took up a long time, and six hours may have elapsed. As stated, my lord of Ravestein, around six o'clock, arrived at the gate of the golden tree which he found shut, and his pursuivant, called Ravestein, dressed in his tabard (showing the blazon of his arms), knocked three times on the door with the gold hammer. Presently the door was opened to him, and the pursuivant Golden Tree, in a white surcoat decorated with large golden trees, came out accompanied by the

---

128 *Bailli* of Caen, counsellor and regular envoy of Charles of France, duke of Normandy and brother of Louis XI.

129 Claude de Toulongeon (1420–1504), son of Antoine (lord of La Bastie and Montrichard, Marshal of Burgundy); took an oath to go on crusade in 1454, 'knight, counsellor and chamberlain' to Duke Charles (*Comptes de l'argentier*, i, no. 1113); militarily active in the service of Charles the Bold; made knight of the Golden Fleece in 1481.

captain of the bastard's archers and six of his archers, who defended the
entrance. Golden Tree said to the pursuivant: 'Noble officer of arms,
what do you want?' And the pursuivant replied: 'The high and powerful
lord Adolf of Cleves has arrived at this gate to carry out the adventure
of the Golden Tree. I present to you the blazon of his arms, and beg
you that he may be admitted and received.' Golden Tree picked up a
tablet, on which he wrote down the name of the knight coming to the
pas; and then took in his hands, with great reverence and on his knees,
the blazon of my lord of Ravestein, and carried it solemnly to Golden
Tree; and passing in front of the judges, showed them the blazon, and
told him of the adventure that he had found at the gate. The blazon was
placed and attached to the golden tree, as was required, and the knight
who guarded the *pas* was given the name of the person who had arrived,
to accomplish his enterprise.

At the same time, Golden Tree (in front), then the dwarf who led the
chained giant, left the *perron* to reach the gate. The dwarf was dressed in
a long robe, half of it white damask cloth, half crimson in-laid with satin,
and with a flat hat on his head; the giant was dressed in a strangely made
long robe of cloth-of-gold, and on his head he wore only a small Provençal
hat. Around his waist was a long dragging chain, held at the end by the
dwarf who led the giant behind him. Thus they arrived at the gate …

[The gate was opened and the lord of Ravestein made his entry in a litter,
flanked by four knights and followed by a footman and a pack horse carrying
two large baskets of surplus armour, between which sat a little jester. The
litter was brought before the ladies; Ravestein emerged to kneel in front of
them. He presented himself as an ancient knight, now weakened with age, but
having heard about the pas of the Golden Tree, could not resist taking up arms
once more. Welcomed by the ladies, he resumed his circuit of the tiltyard, and
presented himself before the judges. The giant was tied to the perron once
more, and the dwarf mounted the perron with his trumpet and clock. Ravestein
left the lists to prepare himself. All of a sudden, there appeared a large yellow
pavilion sown with embroidered golden trees, on top of which was a golden
apple with a banner of the arms of my lord the Bastard. It seemed to move by
itself, guided by the hands of six little pages, until it reached the end of the lists.
Then came seven mounted knights. A lance was chosen for one of these knights
in front of the judges; another lance was taken over to the knight of the Golden
Tree who emerged from his pavilion, carrying a green shield …]

As soon as both knights had their lances upright on their thighs, the
dwarf (who was on the *perron*) prepared his clock (which was made of
glass and full of sand, which took a good half hour to run), and then
blew on his trumpet so that both knights could hear him. They lowered
their lances and began their joust, which was well run and jousted, and

would have been even better done, if the horse of the lord of Ravestein had wanted to charge as well at the end as it had at the beginning. During the half hour, the knight of the Golden tree broke more lances than the challenging knight, and so he won the golden baton as decreed in the articles in the *pas*.

[After half an hour, pikes were selected for another round of combat. Then the two knights came to face each other, to touch before leaving. As soon as this happened, each retired for the day, for it was so late that no other courses could be run …]

I have said enough for now about this day, and must return to the great banquet which was held that night in the great hall. As for the rooms and chambers where several great lords dined that evening, and the service and manner, I pass over to shorten my account, and return to the arrangements made in the hall. First, the tables were laid in the way they had been at dinner, but they were much wider, and on the tables there were thirty ships,[130] each of which carrying the name of one of the lordships of the duke of Burgundy, of which there were five duchies and fourteen counties, and the rest were the other lordships like that of Salins, Malines, Arkel, and Béthune, which are great and noble lordships. The ships were painted in gold and azure, each one showing the arms of the lordship, on banners and shields; and on the topmasts, of which each ship had three, were the banners of the duke; and higher than these there was a large standard of black and violet silk, sown with gold flints, and in large letters the motto of the duke, 'Je l'ay emprins'. The food was inside the ships, forming the dishes. The blazons were of silk, all of gold rope made of fine gold. Soldiers and sailors were placed and raised up among the ships: everything was made as close to real life as possible to create the appearance of a carrack or a large ship.

On the tables were thirty pies covered with different coverings, in the manner of high castles, raised up, and entirely painted in gold and azure, with large banners of the duke of Burgundy. On each castle were the arms and names of the towns of the duke. And so thirty principalities and lordships of the inheritance of the duke, and thirty towns subject to him, were shown, without like in the world. For the decoration of the tables, around each ship there were four very richly decorated little buckets filled with fruits and groceries.[131] There were three moving *entremets* presented that day, of which one, the first, was as follows.

130 The ships were each 7 feet long and were placed on the tables (Laborde, *Les ducs de Bourgogne*, p. 322).
131 'Lemons, capers, olives and similar things' (Laborde, *Les ducs de Bourgogne*, p. 324).

[A unicorn as big as a horse entered the room, covered in a coverlet of silk painted with the arms of England. On top was a lifelike leopard which had a large banner of England in its left paw, and in the right, a marguerite. The unicorn was led in front of the duke; one of the stewards took the marguerite from the leopard's paw, and presented the duke with it. Soon after, a large lion, 'as large as the largest charger in the world', and made of gold, entered the room. On top of it was Madame de Beaugrant (the female dwarf of the lady of Burgundy) dressed in a costly cloth-of-gold, carrying a shepherdess's basket and crook. Two knights, Charles of Ternant[132] and Tristan de Toulongeon,[133] flanked the shepherdess who held a large banner of Burgundy in her hand. When the lion entered the room, it began to open and shut its jaws, and sang a song welcoming the shepherdess as a guarantee against danger. The lion then knelt in front of the new duchess, and presented the shepherdess to her. The third and last *entremets* was a mock dromedary, 'so skilfully made that it seemed to be alive'.[134] It was dressed up in the Saracen manner, and on its back were two large baskets, and between these a man was seated, dressed in a strange way. When the dromedary entered the room, it shook its head wildly; and the man on top opened the baskets, and took out strangely painted birds as though they had come from the Indies, and threw them up into the room and above the tables. Nothing more was done that day, and after supper, the dancing did not last long: before the tables had been cleared, it chimed three hours after midnight.[135] The new wife was led to bed; 'and for the rest of the night, I shall leave to the imagination of the noble minds'[136] ...

The next day was Monday, the second day of the Feast. The duke dined in the large room with the duchess of Norfolk on his right. The jousts followed, not attended by the two duchesses. As soon as the duke was seated, the blazon of the lord of Château Guion, was presented. Twenty-eight lances were run; Château Guion, a novice at the jousts, was awarded the prize. Next in the lists was Charles

132 Charles, lord of Ternant, knight and lieutenant of the duke's first chamberlain (*Comptes de l'argentier*, i, no. 1121); son of Philippe de Ternant (for whose fall from grace in 1451, see chapter 3).

133 Tristan de Toulongeon, knight of the Golden Fleece, counsellor and chamberlain, lord of Soussy, governor of Auxerre, brother of Claude (*Comptes de l'argentier*, i, no. 1115; ii, nos 72, 1696). For his part in the Jean Coustain affair, see [8].

134 The accounts actually include the dromedary as part of the second banquet on the following Monday. The animal was about 9 feet high; the man on top was dressed as a moor. The accounts also mention 30 tents (each with two banners bearing the arms of the great vassals of the duke) and 30 pavilions (each with pennons bearing the ducal arms). The tents contained the roast meats, the pavilions the pastries (Laborde, *Les ducs de Bourgogne*, pp. 325–6). These de la Marche includes in his description of the third banquet.

135 De Haynin says that the whole banquet lasted three to four hours, from 10 pm to around 2 am (*Mémoires*, ii, p. 119).

136 De Haynin relates how Nicolas Binet, the ducal almoner, blessed the bed that the newly-weds slept in, and how on the following day the duchess did not leave her room all day 'following the English custom' (ibid., p. 119).

de Visen;[137] then the lord of Fiennes. Before him were four knights: Jacques de Luxembourg; his uncle the lord of Roussy; his first cousin, Jean de Luxembourg; his brother; and the Marquis of Ferrara.[138] The banquet followed ...]

In order to make the meal more fitting as a banquet, the table which was on the right-hand side was removed, and the table on the other side was made longer, joined to the table of the prince; and on the other side a large buffet dish and vessels for the serving were laid out. The seating and procedure was as follows. That day, the banquet was conducted with twenty-four very large and sumptuous dishes, and there was no other finery on the tables for that evening. Soon after at the end of the table in the room, a curtained platform could be seen, on which trumpets began to sound, and the curtain was drawn back. And there the scenes of the twelve labours of Hercules were shown.

[De la Marche describes the labours in some detail.[139] The first showed Hercules, still dependent on his wet-nurse, killing the serpent which had devoured his twin brother. When the curtains were drawn together once more (and after every subsequent labour) the audience were informed on a linen placard as to the moral of the action. In this case, the vagaries of fortune were emphasised, and how God should be feared since 'it is He who dispenses where He wishes to reward.' For the second labour, Hercules and Theseus are shown stealing the sheep belonging to King Philotes, defeating the giant who guarded them and making the king subject to him. The moral of the story emphasised how princes should exert themselves for the public good ('le bien publique'). The third labour showed Hercules overcoming the monster who wanted to make the daughter of the king of Troy his prey: by this example, noblemen were urged to defend the honour of ladies by their prowess. For the fourth labour, Hercules was shown slaying three lions which represented the earth, the flesh and the devil all of which could devour men: the audience were urged to be soldiers of virtue.

At the end of this play, a large lifelike griffin[140] entered the room; out of its beak

---

137 Charles de Visen, valet of the ducal bedchamber, guard of the lesser jewels; provided with a harness of war to serve in the army in September 1468 (*Comptes de l'argentier*, i, nos 1463, 1505).

138 Francesco d'Este (1429–post 1486), illegitimate son of Leonell d'Este. Marquis of Ferrara, had been at the ducal court since the 1440s (when he had shared the same tutor as Charles the Bold). He was paid £80 for his services at the wedding festivities and the jousts (ibid., i, no. 241). For his career, see Walsh, *Charles the Bold and Italy*, pp. 281–91.

139 De Roovere's comment on the Hercules plays is brief, and makes no mention of the moral of each labour (Enschedé, 'Huwelijksplechtigheden', pp. 45, 53, 61–2). The English herald says that the plays were conducted by 'countenauncyng and noo speche' (*Excerpta*, ed. Bentley, p. 237).

140 The accounts list the griffin as a feature of the third banquet on the Tuesday (Laborde, *Les ducs de Bourgogne*, pp. 326–7).

flew several birds which flew under the tables. Then the dancing began, and there was nothing more to see that day.

The next day, Tuesday, the jousts began again. The Bastard jousted with three other knights in turn. Jean de Luxembourg fought first, but damaged his lance-rest so badly that he was unable to continue. Soon after the lord of Argueil, son of the prince of Orange, and nephew of the duke of Brittany, presented himself; and lastly, Anthoine de Halewin,[141] a Flemish knight, who fought until it was time for the banquet in the great hall …]

That Tuesday the third banquet was held, and the dishes were all covered with great tents of silk, richly painted and decorated diversely with gold and silver; and the pies were similarly covered with pavilions. Underneath the tents and pavilions there were banners and arms of my lord the duke of Burgundy; and along the gutters the mottos of my lord and lady were written in gold and silver, my lord's being 'Je l'ay emprins', and my lady's 'Bien en advienne'. Above each tent and each pavilion, the name of a walled town subject to my lord had been written on a scroll: this time sixty walled towns subject to the duke were shown, besides and above the thirty of the first banquet. On each pie there were two marmosets of gold and azure, dressed in silk, who held the instruments with which the pies would be broken into: some holding pick-axes, others clubs, and others spades; and each one striking various poses. Moreover, the banquet was large, lavish and well supplied; and in the middle of the hall there was a tower as high as the room,[142] made along the lines and in imitation of the large tower that the Duke Charles, as count of Charolais, had begun in his town of Gorinchem, in Holland.

[After the nobility were seated, a watchman on the tower made as if to carry out his watch, and recognising that the tents and pavilions represented towns that were friendly, called for a fanfare of trumpets, which was performed by four boars from the windows in the tower. Then four lifelike goats appeared at the same windows, playing a motet on sackbuts and shawms; followed by four wolves with flutes, then four donkeys singing a song in four parts. For the fifth and last *entremets*, the watchman asked for a 'morisque' dance to entertain the company. Seven lifelike monkeys emerged along a balcony rail from a door in the tower. They found a mercer asleep by his wares and proceeded to play with them. They danced a morisque; then the tables were cleared and the guests danced …]

141 Anthoine de Halewin, 'knight, counsellor and chamberlain' of the duke (for a horse bought from him and given to the king of England in 1469, see *Comptes de l'argentier*, ii, no. 869).

142 It was 46 feet high (Laborde, *Les ducs de Bourgogne*, pp. 326–7). The accounts also include payments for models of elephants carrying soldiers and castles, deer and other wild animals at this banquet.

On Wednesday, the fourth day of the feast, the rooms and chambers, for dinner as well as for the supper, were richly served with fish, as many salt as freshwater ones. That evening no other assembly of dancing or banquet was done on the day, as it was a fish day. But that day the joust continued, and my lord Jean de Chassa, lord of Monnet,[143] a noble Burgundian knight, was the first to present the blazon of his arms and attach them to the golden tree, as was the custom. Before the knight sent his blazon, he had sent some closed letters to the ladies, by way of supplication; and after the ladies had heard the letters spoken and read in their presence, they gave him licence to enter and join the *pas*, which he did in a novel fashion, as you will hear, following the tenor of his letter.

[Appealing to the ladies present, the knight presented himself as an enslaved knight from the kingdom of Enslavement, just arrived in Bruges. He is a love-sick knight who has served his lady faithfully but has been forced by her to wander in the wilderness. He has taken up a quest to forget his melancholy, led by a damsel errant sent by his lady, in order to prove himself. He had been honourably received in France, and he had also heard how honourably strangers were received at the house of Burgundy, and how deeds of arms were continuously practised there more than anywhere else. He hopes he might take part in the *pas* of the Golden Tree.

The lord of Monnet presented himself to fight, but the Knight errant was unable to compete because of inadequate equipment. The next to present himself was Jacques de Luxembourg, accompanied by the Lord Scales and Sir John Woodville, brothers of the queen of England; then the lord of Roussy, the lord of Fiennes, Jean de Luxembourg and all five of Jacques's nephews. The lord of Renty[144] and the marquis of Ferrara accompanied them. The lord Bastard of Burgundy presented himself to Golden Tree to defend him, this time on a horse covered in blue velvet, and on the croup of his horse was a large raised silver plane. Then came Philippe de Poitiers, lord of La Ferté, son of the lord of Arcis,[145] led into the lists by a beautiful girl called the White Lady who presented a letter

143 Jean de Chassa, 'knight, counsellor and chamberlain' of the duke (who took the crusading oath in 1454) was paid £56 for his services at the wedding and jousts (*Comptes de l'argentier*, i, no. 241).

144 Philippe de Croy, lord of Renty and Quiéverain (paid for providing soldiers to Charles in September 1468, *Comptes de l'argentier*, i, no. 1612), eldest son of Antoine de Croy.

145 Philippe de Poitiers, lord of La Ferté, son of Jean, 'knight, counsellor and chamberlain' of the duke, paid £50 for a jousting harness at the wedding festivities, and £40 for clothing and to be well turned out at the wedding (ibid., i, nos. 982, 1502); by 1473 commander of 100 lances in the ducal army.

to the ladies there, asking permission for the knight to perform deeds of
prowess. Last to fight the Bastard was Claude de Vauldrey.[146]

On Thursday, the fifth day of the Feast, after dinner, the jousts were
held: the count of Saulmes, a count from Germany, my lord Baudouin,
Bastard of Burgundy, and my lord of Renty, eldest son of the lord of
Croy, the count of Porcien (attended by five knights) all fought with the
Bastard. De la Marche then returns to describing the banquet …]

First of all there were dishes and courses which were larger and more
sumptuous than there have ever been at any of the other banquets.
On the table there were fifteen peacocks, with their necks, heads and
tail-feathers dressed up, and their bodies all gilded with fine gold; and
mixed up among the peacocks were sixteen silver swans. Each of the
peacocks and swans had a collar of the Fleece, and at their feet there
were little blazons of arms of each of the living knights of the Order;
and on their backs there were little silk surcoats, with the same tabards.
By this *entremets* the thirty living knights of the Fleece were shown.
The peacocks and swans were placed on the tables, each in the order
that the knights they represented went to church on the day of the
solemnities of their feast day.

On the tables were several beasts carrying baggage, such as large
elephants carrying castles, dromedaries with large baskets, unicorns,
stags and does, each carrying different baggage. The beasts were all
bedecked with gold, silver and azure, their coverings made very richly
with gold thread and silk. Their baggages were full and furnished with
diverse spices; and each of them carried the arms of a lord subject to my
lord of Burgundy, with the name of the town or lordship; so that one
carried Condé in Hainaut in the name of Nemours; Avesnes-le-Comte
in Hainaut for the lord of Penthièvre; Saint-Pol and Enghien la Bassée,
for the count of Saint-Pol, constable of France; Dunkirk and Bourbourg,
for the count of Marle; and similarly for the other great lords subject
to my lord of Burgundy and his diverse lands. The banquet was fine
and costly, much admired; and all the lords, ladies and damsels were at
table. After they had begun to eat, on the stage where the labours of
Hercules had been shown, trumpets rang out, and there the fifth labour
of Hercules was seen.

[This showed Hercules rescuing Persephone from Hades, whose gates were
like a large dragon's jaw, and were guarded by the terrible Cerberus. The dog

---

146 Claude de Vauldrey, *bailli* of La Montagne, 'knight and chamberlain' of the duke,
    paid £48 for a jousting harness at the wedding (ibid., i, no. 1502).

was defeated, and Hercules rescued the damsel. The audience was urged to withdraw their souls from damnable vice. The sixth labour saw Hercules pitted against some Amazon women: the moral of the story was a reminder that only God decided the outcome of a battle. For the seventh labour, Hercules killed a half-man and half-serpent creature, whose head, when cut off, sprouted seven more heads. The diners were told that if one vice were encountered, seven more would also be encountered: they were to guard against nourishing vice. For the eighth labour Hercules was armed with shield and club; and he was walking before a city, admiring the beauty of its houses and walls, until several large giants fell upon him. Once he had defeated them two citizens came out of the city and knelt before him: one of them presented the keys to him, and the other placed a crown on his head. And so Hercules was made king of Cremona. 'Against the rabble', the displayed scroll read, 'the chivalrous man shall not be undone' …]

The next Friday, dinner was made and richly served in the chambers and rooms, but quite late, since several people fasted for the Friday; and likewise the English, who strongly follow the custom. They came to the rows of seats to see the joust. My lord the Bastard of Burgundy did not take part because he did not want to run against the Lord Scales with whom he considered himself to be brother-in-arms and who was also supposed to run courses that day and would be fighting in the lists. But my lord Adolf of Cleves took his place to guard the *pas* on that occasion.

[The first to arrive at the seats was Lord Scales who fought with Adolf of Cleves. Misfortune then struck …]

For the lord Bastard of Burgundy caught a heavy kick above his knee from a horse, which greatly injured him, and put him in great danger, were it were not for the good offices of good surgeons; and because of this impediment, he was not able to complete his enterprise. But very injured though he was, he maintained and guarded the *pas*, at his expense, with coverings and all sorts of other things, as he had begun; and no one ran lances in guarding the *pas*, neither the lord of Ravestein nor any other, but with coverings and drapings at the expense of the lord Bastard. This was a great and expensive thing to do, as everyone can plainly see.

[De la Marche continues to describe the rest of the jousts. Next came the count of Roussy, in front of whom was a little dwarf from Constantinople, servant of the king of England, brought by Margaret to the feast. The dwarf was mounted on a little horse, and held a piece of paper (which contained a request to joust), and a key attached to a locket. Afterward came a large castle; inside was the lord of Roussy. It transpired that the dwarf held the knight as prisoner, by the command of a certain lady, and that he wanted to set him free. Once the permission of the ladies present at the joust had been given, the knight leapt from the castle and ran lances for half an hour against Charles de Visen, who was guarding the Golden Tree that day, in the absence of the lord Bastard. De Visen then jousted with Rosquin de Rochefay,[147] both first grooms of the stable of the duke of Burgundy, who presented himself behind two knights of the Golden Fleece, the lord of Auxy and Philippe de Crèvecoeur. No other feast or gathering was held that day 'because most people were fasting, and it was a fish day, which is not a suitable day for banquets and festivities'.

On Saturday, the seventh day of the feast, after dinner, there were further jousts. Two knights were given permission to enter the lists together: Jean de Ligne[148] and Jacques de Harchies,[149] two knights from Hainaut and chamberlains of the duke. Philippe de Poitiers, guarding the *pas* that day, fought with Philippe de Crèvecoeur, lord of Esquerdes, who entered the lists with ten knights of the Golden Fleece before him, followed by the lord of Ternant. As it was a fast day like the previous one, no gathering was made that evening.

On Sunday, the eighth day of the Feast, the dinner in the rooms and chambers was even more lavish than previous ones. The jousts which followed saw Pierre de Bourbon, first cousin of the count of Vendôme,[150] competing. Then came the lord of Contay,[151] a knight from Picardy, on a horse decorated with the cross of St Andrew. Some confusion occurred after de Poitiers was wounded: the judges advised that the marquis of Ferrara who was next in the lists should act as guardian of the *pas*. Unfortunately his horse refused to line up in the lists so he was forced to retire. The last combatant Claude de Waure was disarmed after only one lance had been run.

The banquet followed. On this occasion there were no *entremets*; but the ninth labour of Hercules was shown, in which he defeated Cacus who had stolen his oxen. Princes were encouraged to exert themselves against tyrants and to uphold justice. The tenth labour showed Hercules defeating a large boar which had wreaked havoc among the peasants of Arcadia: the moral urged princes of high birth to destroy falsehood in their lands, for bad custom was to be feared more than marauding boars. In the eleventh labour Hercules defeated several centaurs, whose arrows represented false tongues. The last labour

147 Jean de Rochefay, dit Rosquin, first squire of the stables, paid £48 for a jousting harness probably for the occasion (*Comptes de l'argentier*, i, no. 1502).

148 Jean de Ligne inherited the lordship of Ligne (Hainaut) in 1469, served Charles the Bold militarily, and was to become knight of the Golden Fleece in 1481. He was paid £48 for a jousting harness at the wedding (ibid., i, no. 1502).

149 Jacques, lord of Harchies, 'knight, counsellor and chamberlain' of the duke, paid £48 for a jousting harness at the wedding (ibid.). He had fought in the Ghent war (1449–53), took the oath to go on crusade in 1454; served in Charles's army, died at the battle of Grandson in 1476.

150 Philippe de Bourbon, lord of Carency: for his military service to the duke, see ibid., nos 1142, 1155, 1157, 1620.

151 Louis Le Jeune de Contay, lord of Mourecourt, 'knight, counsellor and chamberlain' of the duke; had taken part in the jousts of Adolf of Cleves and had taken the crusading oath in 1454; killed at the battle of Nancy in 1477.

depicted Hercules planting boundary stones in the 'great sea of Spain'. The final message on the scroll, after the curtain had been drawn to, read:

> Now, all you who read this sign,
> Place limits on your deeds and show prudence;
> In your desires, do as Hercules did;
> Limit your desires in worldly hope.
> For the day is set down (and you must think on it)
> Beyond which we may not pass.
> The tables were cleared and the dancing began.

On Monday, the ninth day of the feast, after dinner 'richly and solemnly done as before', the jousts were watched. The wounded lord Bastard had himself transported about in a litter covered with such pomp that he appeared to be 'heir of one of the richest lordships in the world'. His litter was placed on top of a stage at the end of the lists so that he was out of danger from the press of horses. Soon after came the king of arms of the Golden Fleece, accompanied by two knights of the Order, the lord of Créquy and the lord of Gruuthuse. The duke then arrived on horseback, heralded by trumpets and a large number of knights and noblemen, and armed with all kinds of weapons and a shield covered with plates of Rhenish florins. After him he had nine pages on nine covered horses, then a groom on a horse with a covering embroidered with the duke's motto. All the pages and valets had hats of blue velvet with white ostrich feathers. The duke made his tour around the lists until he came to his seat. Out of the gate of the knight of the Golden Tree came a pavilion, just as a pavilion had emerged on the first day of the *pas*. Inside was Adolf of Cleves who was guarding the *pas* for the lord Bastard …]

To be brief, that half hour was hard run and struck by the two princes, and there were several hard-hitting strikes and broken lances which were not all counted, since the right to decide on how they were broken was reserved; but for lances duly and clearly broken, the lord Bastard broke eight lances and my lord of Ravestein broke eleven, winning the gold baton by so doing. Once the courses had been run, they touched, and at this point the *pas* was ended, and with it the lord Bastard had his helmet off. So the kings of arms and the heralds went toward the judges to find out to whom the prize should be given; the judges sent them before the ladies, to award it as they pleased, but the ladies sent them back to the judges, and referred to the rules of the chapters.

From the books and writings of the kings of arms and heralds, it was reckoned that the prize should go to the person who had broken the most lances during the half hour: and it was found that it had been my lord of Argueil who had broken thirteen lances. The prize was brought to the seats by Golden Tree, accompanied by other officers of arms, with great noise and sound of trumpets and clarions, for it to be handed over. The prize was a charger covered with a covering of fashioned black satin, and white metal brocading was embroidered among the figures, covered and burnished. On the horse were two baskets, in which there was the complete jousting equipment of my lord the Bastard. In truth the armour was one of the most beautiful suits of jousting armour that one could possibly hope to see. And so Golden Tree led his prize around the lists, and then went to find the lord of Argueil, and presented the prize to him, on behalf of the ladies and the judges, for having broken the most lances in the *pas*. And so the prize was presented, and the *pas* completed, as far as the jousting.

Very soon after, the workmen under orders took down the covering and box of the judges and made the square as uniform as possible. And soon the twenty-five blazons of knights and noblemen who were to make up the tournament were sent before the knight of the Golden Tree and his companions, and they were placed and attached to the golden tree in the same way as the others. Once everything had been completed, the twenty-five noblemen arrived, led by Charles de Chalon, count of Joigny, first cousin of the prince of Orange.[152] ... After him came others: my lord Philippe de Commynes,[153] dom Petre, my lord Jacques d'Eymeries,[154] my lord of Monssures, my lord Anthoine de Trapesonde, my lord Hue de Thoisy, my lord of Lens, Drieu de Humières, Robinet de Maneville, Ervé Garlot, Jeromme de Cambray, Anthoine, bastard of Auxy, George bastard of Auxy, John Howard, one of Talbot's sons, the son of Sir John Howard, all three of them English; Charles d'Haplincourt, Pierre Metteneye, Pierre de Salins, Jehan le Tourneur, Frédérik le Palatin, Anthoine d'Usy, and Anthoine d'Oiselet, all richly covered or harnessed, some in silk, others in embroidery or brocaded with metal threads. They were armed and plumed as is fitting on these occasions, and in their hands each carried a blunted sword, and all the swords were presented to the judges to check, as was fitting, whether they were blunted and rounded off.

After the presentation of the count of Joigny and of his companions named above, the Golden Tree gate was opened to the loud sound

---

152 Charles de Chalon, count of Joigny, 'knight, counsellor and chamberlain' of the duke (serving in the ducal army in September 1468) (*Comptes de l'argentier*, i, no. 1215).

153 Philippe de Commynes, lord of La Clite, 'knight and chamberlain' of the duke (*Comptes de l'argentier*, i, no. 328), until his famous 'defection' to Louis XI.

154 All the following Burgundian names appear in the *Comptes de l'argentier* for 1468, listed as knights, chamberlains, squires or valet servants of the duke. Five of them were given jousting harnesses or clothing for the occasion of the marriage Feast; five performed military service for the duke later that year.

of trumpets and clarions; and from there the princes, knights and noblemen came out, those who had jousted against the knight of the Golden Tree, and had run lances in the *pas*, whose names are recorded above, in the order of their arrival at the *pas*. These princes, knights and noblemen accompanied the knight of the Golden Tree, and, in his stead, those who had taken his place. All their horses were covered in costumes similar to that of the knight : they were all coverings of violet velvet embroidered with the Golden Tree. And, with this last covering of the knight of the Golden Tree, you will find that twenty-five coverings and costumes had been used in his *pas*, of which the last was the least costly. Thus they all left the gate of the Golden Tree, and set themselves up in formation along the lists as they arrived. The last to enter was the duke of Burgundy, dressed like the others, and after he had inspected the battle formation, he took up his position and place once more. Their swords were sent to the judges for inspection, like the others, and afterward the judges sent them back, and each had his lance covered, as was fitting. And when they all had their lances on their thighs, you must believe that the square was richly adorned with fifty such people, armed and mounted as they were; and as soon as the trumpet had sounded, they couched their lances, one side then the other. And in this encounter there were many lance blows and many broken lances, and several horses brought to the ground; and some of them became panic-stricken and wounded.

After the course of lances had been run, they drew their swords, and the tourney began on both sides. It was waged and fought so long and with such vigour that the combatants could not be separated; and it was as well that the duke of Burgundy (who that day had tourneyed and jousted, and who in truth had acquitted himself very well on both counts) took off his helmet, so that he could be recognised, and he carried the sword in his hand to separate the *mêlée* which started up again at one end and then at the other. In separating them he spared neither cousin, nor Englishman nor Burgundian, in prising them apart by force.[155] Once the tourney had been broken up, the two sides lined up against each other, and on request, they fought several times one to one, two against two or three against three. But still my lord separated them each time. And so the *pas* was completed, both joust and tournament. Soon my lord was led back to his residence, riding behind the others; and his retinue followed behind him, such that he had ten pages

---

155 The fighting was sufficiently fierce for the new duchess to wave her 'kerchef' with 'dolorous countenauns' (*Excerpta*, ed. Bentley, pp. 239).

behind him, his ten horses all covered similarly in crimson velvet, all their coverings decorated with numerous gold bells. The horse ridden by the valet who led the charger by hand was covered in velvet and embroidery of another kind. The pages were dressed in crimson velvet, each having a large gold sash around his neck. Truth to tell, this pomp was great and rich, for the bells and sashes were worth eight hundred gold marks. And thus for that day, for the joust and for the tournament, my lord had twenty-five coverings. And in this array he went away to his residence, and everyone retired to return for supper, which was as follows.

On that same Monday was the last banquet of the feast, its dishes and courses increased and multiplied more than ever before.[156] On the table were thirty dishes which were made like gardens: the base of these gardens was made of brazil wood inlaid with silver, and the garden hedges were all of gold. In the middle of the enclosures was a large golden tree, and against these trees was the food. The trees had diverse fruits, leaves and flowers: one was an orange tree, another an apple tree, and in fact all other sorts of trees. Their fruits, leaves and flowers were so well done that they seemed to be real trees and fruits, and they made a very beautiful sight. Around each tree was a roll, on which the name of an abbey was written: and so thirty abbeys subject to my lord of Burgundy were shown, of which one was Cluny, another Cîteaux, both mother houses of their Christian orders.

On the table, and around these trees, there were several figurines, as many men as women, decked out in gold, azure and silk, in various poses.[157] Some acted as though throwing sticks against the trees, and others had large poles to knock down the fruits. Some women carried hats to collect the fruit in, others held out their hands with fine gestures.

---

156 The costs of this banquet are given in ADN, B3432, no. 118470. The wine came to £47; the costs of the pantry to £81 2s 10d: 827 dozen small rolls of white bread, 376 dozen other rolls of bread, 20 portions of mustard, 18 dishes of salad and olive oil, salt to serve on table; and the costs of the kitchen to £1,091 1s 5d: 8 whole oxen (£96) and 12 other half oxen (£75), 11 boar, 152 pounds of beef dripping, 385 pounds of lard, 14 calves, 218 sheep, tripe and two ox tongues, 3 portions of veal, 2 dozen pigs trotters, 41 pigs, 13 pheasants, 98 herons (£35 4s), 30 bitterns, 50 little bitterns, 293 goslings, 129 rabbits, 16 dozen quails, 215 large capons, 458 smaller capons, 1569 chickens, 265 pairs of pigeons, 8 dozen cheeses, 2,000 eggs, 76 dozen small cakes, 92 raised pies, 60 large decorated cakes, 80 cakes for chamberlains, 120 cakes for gentlemen (and also flour, ingredients for stuffing, redcurrants, leeks, parsley, onions for soup, salt, and 87 lbs of butter).

157 The accounts mention payments for 60 figures (Laborde, *Les ducs de Bourgogne*, p. 29).

There were also other figures of men and women on the tables, richly decorated: some of them, in twos, carrying a river, others carrying baskets in their hands, others carrying baskets on their backs, and others carrying pedlars' trays around their necks. These baskets were loaded with spices, oranges and other fruits. With these figures the tables were very richly decorated.

Also on these tables were thirty pies, and on top of each one was a wreath of vines full of leaves and red and white grapes which were so well done that they looked like real grapes. At the head of the table, by the duke's place, was a rich edifice, made by master Skalkin, canon of Saint-Pierre of Lille. This edifice was tall and sumptuous, and very skilfully made, for there was a palace and a high mirror in which one could see strange figures. There were moving figures and *morisques*, very well and skilfully made, there were rocks, trees, leaves and flowers; and in front of the palace there was a fountain that poured out from a finger of a little image of St John. This fountain poured out pink water that moved very ingeniously upstream, and it seemed that this fountain was watering the trees and gardens of the banquet; certainly the fountain was very well and skilfully done.[158] After the lords and ladies had surveyed the tables and arrangements long and hard, all went to take their seats according to rank.

Soon after, two giants of marvellous size, richly and strangely dressed and armed, entered the room, equipped with marvellous weapons; and after them they led a whale, the largest and fattest that has ever been seen in any *entremets* and in a single *entremets*. The whale was a good sixty feet long,[159] and of height so tall that two men on horseback would not have been able to see each other if placed on either side of it. Its two eyes were the largest mirrors that one would have thought possible to find. It moved its fins, body and tail so well that it seemed to be alive. In this fashion, it moved around the room, to the sound of trumpets and clarions, until it had completed a tour around the room, and had returned to the table where my lord and the most important lords were eating. Suddenly the whale opened its jaws (which were very large) and two sirens came out, with combs and mirrors in their hands, and began to sing a strange song right in the middle of the room; and at the sound of this song, one after the other, in the manner of *morisque*,

158 Jean Skalkin was paid for the fountain, above which was a mirror so that fish could be seen swimming in the fountain. It was placed in front of the table at which the duke and duchess sat. His chandeliers with mirrors also reappeared at this banquet (Laborde, *Les ducs de Bourgogne*, pp. 329–30, 376–7).

159 The accounts list the whale as featuring in the fifth banquet (ibid., p. 328).

up to twelve knights of the sea came out, some carrying clubs in their hands, others defensive sticks. Soon after a drum began playing from within the whale's belly, at which the sirens stopped singing, and began to dance with the knights of the sea. But an amorous jealousy began to stir within them, such that a quarrel and tournament began among the knights which lasted quite a long time. But the giants, with their large sticks, came to separate them, and chased them and the sirens back into the whale's belly. Then the whale closed its jaws, and leading it, the two giants went on their way, to return whence they had come. And certainly this was a very fine *entremets*, for inside there were more than forty people.

At this point, the tables were cleared and the dances began, and soon after (because it was late) the kings of arms and the heralds began the task of determining to whom the prize should be given. There were great differences of opinion in the matter, for the sword combats had been greatly and well fought, there had been so many great and good people so well shown, that in truth no one knew to whom to give the prize. The ladies, with one accord, said that my lord of Burgundy should have it, for he had proved himself very well at the tournament, and besides they considered that he had jousted with great toughness that day; and so adding tournament and joust together their opinion was as stated. But my lord did not want to accept it, and in the end, it was decided that Sir John Woodville, brother of the queen of England, should have the prize, for three reasons. The first was because he was a foreigner, and honour should be done to foreigners of all noble houses. The second, because he was a fine and young knight, and young men ought to be given the courage to persevere in good deeds; and the third reason, because he had acquitted himself well and honourably in the joust as well as the tournament. So he was presented with the prize by one lady from this region and another from England, from one of the greatest and best houses, as is customary on these occasions.

My lord of Argueil (who had won the prize for the joust) went to ask my lord whether he could hold a joust on the following day, accompanied by several noblemen ready for the task. This joust was marvellously well fought, and with good wooden lances; and the lord of Argueil won the insider's prize, and a young squire, called Billecocq, won the outsider's prize. And because it is a common thing to joust in groups, I won't describe it further.

On Tuesday, the twelfth and last day of this feast, the great hall was decked out in the same way as the first day of the wedding, except for

the large fountain which was in the middle of the room. The three
large tables were laid and covered, and my lord of Burgundy was
seated in the middle of the high table. At his right hand sat the legate,
and then the bishop of Verdun and the bishop of Metz, and after him
the Lord Scales. The right-hand table was full of barons, knights and
English noblemen; the left-hand one was similarly seated with men
from my lord's household. In the middle of the room were three laid
tables, placed lengthwise. On the first ushers and sergeants-at-arms
were seated, on the next, kings of arms and heralds, and on the third
trumpeters and minstrels. As for the service, it was grand and solemn,
and ever multiplying in dishes and food. At the end of the dinner, the
kings of arms and heralds rose, and put on their tabards; and then the
two kings of arms took a stick and placed it on their shoulders, and on
this stick, the two kings of arms carried a large bag full of money, and
went to shout before the lord duke 'Largesse!' as is the custom, and they
did the same at both ends of the high table. Then they went about the
room, the trumpets and clarions rang out, such that everything rever-
berated. After the tables had been cleared and the graces said, and we
had gone to find the spices, the officers of arms of his household came
before him; and there publicly he gave new titles to several men and
turned heralds into kings-of-arms and marshals, and pursuivants into
heralds. As is the custom, he baptised the new pursuivants. Thus it was
that the solemnity and triumph of the feast passed; for, on the following
day, because of business that took my lord to Holland, he left this place,
and took leave of the duchess of Norfolk and other lords and ladies of
England, and gave them gifts, each according to his or her rank, and to
the noblemen and ladies. And with this, I close my account of this noble
feast, and I know of nothing worthy to say to you for the present save
that I am yours.

II: THE COURT

Introduction

With the exception of a very small number of high-status guests and relatives, the many men and fewer women who attended court were there to serve the prince and enjoy his favour.[1] Some attended on a regular basis, the terms of their service set out in the household ordonnances [4, 6]. Others were occasional servants who may have hoped for a regular post [8]. Among them all circulated visitors [3] brought there by a particular mission or simply 'travelling for the sake of travelling', not bound to the prince by an oath of loyalty like ducal servants [8], but certainly obligated by his hospitality.[2] It is impossible to say with any accuracy how many courtiers these various groups added up to at any given time, but calculations can at least be made for the household of the duke on the basis of ordonnances listing officers eligible to serve and the number of subalterns attached to them. In 1426/27 Philip the Good's household numbered around 400 officers and servants.[3] By his son's reign it had increased fourfold. Neither calculation takes account of the officers of other members of the dynasty, occasional servants or visitors, all of whom might increase the size of the court by hundreds of mouths.

Despite the growing size of the court, the Castilian Pero Tafur still found the palace complex at Bruges large enough to accommodate the ducal family and those of leading courtiers during his visit in 1438 [3]. The *Prinsenhof* was indeed substantial, mostly built in brick and Brabant stone and incorporating the principal residence, the chapel, a main keep and a smaller tower for some of the household services, a separate house for the duchess and her ladies and numerous galleries, all situated in close proximity to the great courtyard.[4]

1 W. Paravicini, 'Alltag bei hofe', in idem (ed.), *Alltag bei Hofe: 3. Symposium der Residenzen-Kommission der Akademie der Wissenschaften in Göttingen* (Sigmaringen, 1995), pp. 9–30; C. Woolgar, *The great household in late medieval England* (New Haven/London, 1999), p. 39.

2 W. Paravicini, 'Von der Heidenfahrt zur Kavalierstour', in H. Brunner and N. Wolf (eds), *Wissenliteratur im Mittelalter und in der Frühen Neuzeit* (Wiesbaden, 1993), pp. 91–130; W. Paravicini and B. Schnerb (eds), *Les Étrangers à la cour de Bourgogne* (*RN*, special number, 2002).

3 W. Blockmans, A. Janse, H. Kruse and R. Stein, 'From territorial courts to one residence: the Low Countries in the late Middle Ages', in M. Aymard and M. Romani (eds), *La Cour comme institution économique* (Paris, 1998), pp. 17–28, at p. 21; and Paravicini, 'The court of the dukes of Burgundy', at p. 78.

4 A. Van Zuylen van Nyevelt, *Épisodes de la vie des ducs de Bourgogne à Bruges* (Bruges, 1938), pp. 243–306.

Philip the Good and his successors had many similar residences across the Low Countries.[5] Extensive building work on these palace complexes during our period was often partly funded by municipalities in the hope that the court would be drawn to reside more frequently in the city.[6] At Brussels, work began on the reorganisation of the ducal residence on the Coudenberg within a year of the estates of the duchy accepting Philip the Good as ruler – a lengthy process which required the purchase of more than 100 plots of land around the existing residence, most of which were already built upon.[7] Later, from 1452, a great hall was added at Philip the Good's request, creating an interior space 47m long and 10m wide – ideal for the great occasions of state and vital in a residence which was to become a main base for the ducal court well into the sixteenth century.[8]

The prince could not be present in any one city all the time, with the result that the growth of Burgundian power effectively reduced the number of princely courts within the Low Countries.[9] But even if the ruler were elsewhere, his residence continued to serve and advertise Burgundian power. A minor household which formed part of the court might use a residence during the prince's absence, a notable feature of the history of the Ten Walle palace in Ghent which was rarely used by Valois and Habsburg rulers, but was commonly the principal residence of their sons, daughters and wives, as we have seen.[10] Certain institutions of ducal government occupied princely residences, such as the council of Holland which was based at the Binnenhof at The Hague.[11] The palace was also home to a range of people when the court was not in residence, such as concierges, retired servants, pension holders and other hangers-on.[12]

5 W. Paravicini, 'Die Residenzen der Herzöge von Burgund, 1363–1477', in *Fürstliche Residenzen im spätmittelalterlichen Europa* (Sigmaringen, 1991), pp. 209–63; K. De Jonghe, 'Bourgondische residenties in het graafschap Vlaanderen', *Handelingen der Maatschappij voor geschiedenis en oudheidkunde te Gent*, New Series 54 (2000), pp. 95–109.

6 E. Picard, 'Les hôtels de Monsieur le duc de Bourgogne à Dijon: la tour de Brancion', *Mémoires de la Commission des archives départementales de la Cote-d'Or* 17 (1913–21), pp. 21–51, at p. 37; Small, *George Chastelain*, pp. 87–8 and n. 204.

7 A. Smolar-Meynart, 'Le palais de Bruxelles: des origines à Charles-Quint', in idem and Vanrie (eds), *Le palais de Bruxelles*, at p. 33.

8 Cf. the size of the Bruges hall used for festivities of 1468 wedding [**2**]: around 45m long, 22.4 m wide and 20 m high: B. Franke, '"D'un mets à un autre mets". Tafelspiele am Burgunderhof (1468)', *Aktuelle Tendenzen der Theatergeschichtsforschung: Kleine Schriften der Gesellschaft für Theatergeschichte* 37–8 (1996), pp. 119–37, at p. 121.

9 Blockmans et al., 'From territorial courts to one residence', p. 22.

10 See general introduction to the present volume as well as M. Boone and T. De Hemptinne, 'Espace urbain et ambitions princières: les présences matérielles de l'autorité princière dans le Gand médiéval (12e siècle–1540)', in W. Paravicini (ed.), *Zeremoniell und Raum* (Sigmaringen, 1997), pp. 279–304.

11 M. Damen, *De staat van dienst* (Hilversum, 2000), p. 41.

12 Such as Poncelet, a lowly servant, possibly the man mentioned in [**8**] below, who told one of the stories in the *Cent Nouvelles Nouvelles* and had a house at the Salle-le-Comte in Valenciennes: E. De Blieck, 'The *Cent nouvelles nouvelles*, text and context' (PhD thesis, University of Glasgow, 2004), 2 vols, i, pp. 305–6.

The princely residence thus had a life of its own, albeit one in the shadow of the ruler. Out on the street, its architecture and decoration (at Bruges, a sculpture of the duke's motto and coat of arms accompanying those of twelve of his dominions, surmounted by a bust of Philip the Good with statues of SS. George and Andrew) were visible reminders of his authority, much like the stained-glass windows that bore his image in civic churches [**26**].[13] Even the sounds that came from the palace brought to mind the prince's immanence and majesty: at Ghent, the lions' cage was situated close by the entry of the *Prinsenhof*, its occupants there for passers-by to see and hear.[14]

When the court was resident in a city, its presence was hard to ignore. Hostelries [**3, 12a**], rented housing [**16**][15] and even surrounding towns and villages [**4**] were pressed into service to accommodate the prince's entourage. Hoteliers [**17b**] who regularly came into contact with members of the court were particularly well-placed to gather news and perhaps acquire influence.[16] Regularly confronted by the unseemly rush for good lodgings, wily Milanese ambassadors gave gifts of fine cloth or jewellery to court officials to improve their chances of securing a suitable bed for the night.[17] Courtiers addressed the problem by buying or building substantial permanent residences – one such was Antoine de Croÿ, first chamberlain of Philip the Good, whose home was well placed opposite the gates of the ducal palace in Brussels (cf. [**8**]).[18] The result of these acquisitions was the emergence of districts which might be described as Burgundian 'stamping grounds', such as the Onderstraat in Ghent or the parish of Saint-Médard in Dijon.[19] Other areas in or near the city were given over to the needs of the court, including, at Brussels, the large gardens where more than 1,200 trees were planted in 1440, most of them for fruit; the terrain required for

13 Van Zuylen van Nyevelt, *Épisodes de la vie des ducs de Bourgogne*, pp. 245–6.

14 *Het prinselijk hof ten Walle*, pp. 98–101.

15 M.-T. Caron, D. Clauzel, J. Rauzier and M. Sommé, 'La cour des ducs de Bourgogne (1369–1477): consommation et redistribution', in Aymard and M. Romani (eds), *La Cour comme institution économique*, pp. 31–41, at p. 35.

16 P. Godding, 'Les Aubergistes bruxellois au XVe siècle', *Cahiers bruxellois* 35 (1997), pp. 129–44; A. Greve, 'Gast und Gastgeber: Hansekaufleute und Hostelliers in Brügge im 14. und 15. Jahrhundert', in V. Henn and A. Nedkvitne (eds), *Norwegen und die Hanse* (Frankfurt, 1994), pp. 95–107.

17 G. Soldi-Rondinini, 'Aspects de la vie des cours en France et en Bourgogne par les dépêches des ambassadeurs milanais', in *Adelige Sachkultur des Spätmittelalters* (*Österreichische Akademie der Wissenschaften*, no. 452) (Vienna, 1982), pp. 195–214, at pp. 206–7.

18 A. Smolar-Meynart, 'Un Palais dominant le centre urbain: le Coudenberg (XIIe–XVIIe siècles)', in idem and A. Vanrie (eds), *Le Quartier royal* (Brussels, 1998), pp. 15–41, at pp. 20–1; K. De Jonghe, 'L'Architecture de cour à l'époque de Marguerite d'York: nouvelles tendances', *PCEEB* 44 (2004), pp. 103–12.

19 M. Boone, M.-C. Laleman and D. Lievois, 'Van Simon sRijkensteen tot Hof van Ryhove: Van erfachtige lieden tot dienaren van de centrale Bourgondische staat', *Handelingen der Maatschappij voor geschiedenis en oudheidkunde te Gent*, New Series 44 (1990), pp. 47–85, esp. pp. 69–73; F. Humbert, *Les Finances municipales de Dijon du milieu du XIVe siècle à 1477* (Paris, 1961), p. 24.

looking after the horses, including stables which were 70m long, 8m wide and 5m high; or the hunting grounds which had to be within easy reach of the city walls, such as those which served the ducal residence at Brussels [8]. Given such needs, only the largest cities could accommodate the court on a prolonged basis.[20] For middling cities like Saint-Omer, Arras and possibly Douai, the feat remained possible.[21] For smaller towns like Oudenaarde, Dendermonde or Aalst, putting up the court of Charles the Bold for any length of time would have been very difficult indeed.[22] The court's size and demands might vary according to its activities at any given point in time, but as Tafur noticed on his travels between Brussels and the coast, smaller towns might not even meet the most basic consumption requirement of the courtier – wine [3]. Bruges, by contrast, had everything he could possibly desire. It is clear that the Burgundian court could not survive for long without the city, but to state the reverse would be an exaggeration. At Lille, the presence of the court demonstrably boosted the wine trade, construction sector and market in luxury goods, but indigenous demand was substantial and the contribution of the court is hard to measure in relation to it.[23] Given the short sojourns of the court in many towns, its economic impact was undoubtedly only part of a much wider picture, particularly if luxury items were bought in a regional rather than a local market [7c].[24] But counting only the salaries paid to courtiers – that is to say, setting aside the income from their estates and offices, not to mention the wealth of the prince himself – the daily spending power of the court was equivalent to that of between 1,200 and 1,500 master masons in the 1450s.[25]

The concentration of the prince's entourage at court and the organisation of daily life there necessitated a careful use of available space. While it was possible to distinguish between public and private spheres within the complex of court buildings [6, 8], much of daily life was conducted in public under observation, even under scrutiny.[26] At the centre of it all lay the needs of the prince. Access to the prince's body was possible but carefully regulated [4, 5, 8]. Any object which came into contact with him – his food and drink, his cup

20 P. Stabel, *Dwarfs among giants: The Flemish urban network in the late Middle Ages* (Leuven/Apeldoorn, 1997), pp. 107–13.

21 Populations estimated to be around 10,000–15,000 in the fifteenth century: A. Derville, 'Le Nombre d'habitants des villes de l'Artois et de la Flandre wallonne (1300–1450)', *RN* 65 (1983), 277–99.

22 Respectively estimated to have had 7,300, 5,000 and 4,000 inhabitants in 1469: W. Prevenier, 'La Démographie des villes du comté de Flandre aux XIIIe et XIVe siècles', *RN* 65 (1983), pp. 255–76.

23 Caron et al., 'La Cour des ducs de Bourgogne (1369–1477): consommation et redistribution', pp. 37–9.

24 P. Stabel, 'For mutual benefit? Court and city in the Burgundian Low Countries', in S. Gunn and A. Janse (eds), *The court as a stage* (Woodbridge, 2006), pp. 101–17.

25 Blockmans et al., 'From territorial courts to one residence', p. 24.

26 M. Whitely, 'Public and private space in royal and princely *châteaux* in late medieval France', in A. Renoux (ed.), *Palais royaux et princiers au Moyen Âge* (Le Mans, 1996), pp. 71–5.

and plate, his clothing, saddle or bed linen, for example [4, 5, 6] – was treated
with the utmost care. Proximity to the prince and his needs dictated the hierarchy of the court, for 'the greatest honour is to serve the prince in the most
intimate things' [4]. Serving the prince's food was a responsibility worthy of
only the most senior servants. To dress like the prince or princess was to be
acknowledged as a favourite [8].[27] In many small ways the household represented an extension of the prince's person and was a reflection on his character
[8] – it was 'the first thing the eye beholds, and so it is necessary to arrange
it well and have everything in order'.[28] The household was thus expected to
attain exemplary standards of conduct which the duke himself embodied [4].[29]
Chastelain's account of Jean Coustain's fall from grace [8] suggests that there
may have been a considerable gap between prescribed norms of behaviour and
daily reality, but we should bear in mind that the official chronicler sought
to portray Coustain as the opposite of the courtier in all respects to demonstrate his villainy, and that Coustain's standing appears to have rendered him
oblivious to the judgment of others. Knowing how to conduct oneself in an
environment where the involuntary gesture or utterance might transgress
finely calibrated standards was indeed important. Help was at hand in the form
of advice from experienced courtiers, some of whom set their wisdom down
for contemporaries and posterity. Foremost among these was Olivier de La
Marche [4, 11a], the nobleman from the duchy of Burgundy who worked his
way through the court hierarchy from page to chief steward of the household,
and whose experience over thirty years included the organisation of festivities
as well as daily life. The *Estat de la maison du duc Charles* is the only surviving
work of three which La Marche devoted to the household, and was intended
for Edward IV of England.[30] Eleanor of Poitiers [5] knew the court from a
very young age too, as the daughter of the courtier Jean de Poitiers, lord of
Arcis-sur-Aube, and Isabella de Souza, Portuguese lady-in-waiting to Isabella
of Portugal. From 1458 Eleanor was herself *demoiselle d'honneur* to Charles
the Bold's wife, Isabelle of Bourbon [8]. She later served Mary of Burgundy,
the latter's daughter, and Joanna of Castile, wife (from 1496) of Mary's son,
Philip the Fair. Eleanor lived until 1509, but the record she kept of her experience was set down earlier (July 1484–August 1487), perhaps to advertise her
knowledge during a time spent away from court.[31] Such manuals could not

27 W. Paravicini, 'Soziale Schichtung und soziale Mobilität am Hof der Herzöge von
    Burgund', *Francia* 5 (1977), pp. 127–82, notably pp. 136, 152–3.

28 Chastelain, *Oeuvres*, v, pp. 364–5.

29 W. Paravicini, '"Ordre et règle": Charles le Téméraire en ses ordonnances de l'hôtel',
    Comptes-rendu des séances de l'Académie des inscriptions et belles-lettres (1999), pp. 311–59.

30 W. Paravicini, 'La Cour de Bourgogne selon Olivier de La Marche', *PCEEB* 43
    (2003), pp. 89–124.

31 J. Paviot, 'Les marques de distance dans les *Honneurs de la cour* d'Aliénor de Poitiers',
    in Paravicini (ed.), *Zeremoniell und Raum*, pp. 91–6; B. Sterchi, 'Regel und Ausnahme in
    der burgundischen Hofetikette: Die *Honneurs de la cour* von Éléonore de Poitiers', in
    K. Malettke and C. Grell (eds), *Hofgesellschaft und Höflinge an europäischen Fürstenhöfen
    in der Frühen Neuzeit* (Münster, 2001), pp. 305–23.

predict every awkward situation, but they did contribute – along with visitors' accounts and other correspondence – to the reputation of the Burgundian court across Europe.[32]

The contrast between the princely court in its large civic setting and the other locations where nobles might find themselves was great. The non-princely household away from court was – or at least was expected to be – more simple than that of the prince [5]. The life of the noble who did not serve at court or who was attending to his affairs in the country was a world apart from life in Brussels, as the lesser nobleman Jean de Vy discovered when he arrived there [8]. The abbess who received an unexpected visit from her courtier relative and his exotic Castilian companion [3] was keen to prolong their stay as long as possible. Princes and their servants might enjoy rights of board and lodging in monastic institutions (*droit de gîte*), but the expanding and increasingly demanding court was less likely to find suitable accommodation there than it had in the past.[33]

3. Perceptions of the court: Pero Tafur

Pero Tafur, *Travels and adventures*, ed. and trans. M. Letts (London, 1926).[34]

I departed from Lierre and came to Mechelen, which the Castilians call Mellinas, and although it is small, I have never seen before or since such a charming place. The duke delights greatly to come here to rest, as one retiring to a garden. He has no place in the town, but he lies at the inn, which is so excellent that it is fit to entertain, not him alone, but the greatest prince on earth. I remained in the town two days, and had great pleasure there by reason of its charm and beauty. I then left for Brussels, which is also in Brabant, and there I found the duke of Burgundy and the duchess, his consort, to whom I made my reverence. They received me very graciously, the duke on account of his French

32 For translated Burgundian perceptions of other courts, see Vaughan, *Philip the Good*, pp. 112, 178–84, 299–302; and Vaughan, *Charles the Bold*, pp. 90–1.

33 The contrast between the court and the monastery as places of residence is revealed in other ways in the fictional account of Little John of Saintré's career as a young knight, recounted by Antoine de La Sale (c.1460), tutor of the sons of Louis de Luxembourg, count of Saint Pol: I.S. Gray (ed.), *Little John of Saintré* (London, 1930). For monasteries as residences for servants of the court see M. Vale, 'Provisioning princely households in the Low Countries during the pre-Burgundian period, c.1280–1380', in Paravicini (ed.), *Alltag bei Hofe*, pp. 33–40, at pp. 38–9.

34 Recounting events of 1438, but written c.1453–57. Pero Tafur is thought to have come from Cordova. In 1435, then in his late 20s, he set off with the intention of visiting the Holy Land, but also spent considerable time in Italy, the Empire and the Low Countries: H. Vander Linden, 'Le Voyage de P. Tafur en Brabant, en Flandre et en Artois (1438)', *RN* 19 (1914), pp. 216–31.

descent and the love he bears to the Castilians, and the duchess by reason of her Spanish origin and her relationship with our master, King Juan [II], whose cousin she is. The duke ordered me to be lodged and provided me with everything that was needful for me and mine, and I was soon comfortably bestowed.[35]

The next day I repaired to the palace of the duke whom I found at mass. Afterward I enquired for the Bastard of Saint Pol and I joined myself to him, and greeted him from Gutierre Quixada,[36] who was under obligation to fight a duel with him, and whom I have seen embarking for Jerusalem…

This knight [the Bastard of Saint Pol] showed me the duke's palace as well as the city and everything in it, but nothing could surpass in majesty the persons of the duke and duchess and the state in which they live, which is the most splendid I have ever seen. At that time the following great persons were housed in the palace, to wit, the duke [sic] of Saint Pol,[37] a mighty lord, with his wife and retainers, the count of Estampes,[38] likewise a great lord, with his followers, and the Princess of Navarre, a niece of the duke[39], who keeps a separate establishment, also John of Cleves her brother, and two gentlemen by the name of Charni[40] and Crequi,[41] with their wives, as well as many knights of the duke's household. They say that they are continually in attendance on the duchess, all of whom sleep and eat in the palace, as do also the knights who have no separate establishments, and the duke pays all the expenses as if for his own person. In this he appears to me to be the opposite of the duke of Milan; the one keeps all the men he can in the field and none with him, and the other keeps all with him and none in the field, but the duke of Burgundy can safely retain his knights at court, for he enjoys good peace. The multitude of people and their refinement and splendour can scarcely be described. There is a constant succession of tourneys and everything that makes for pleasure …

35 J. Huessman, 'Hospitality at the court of Philip the Good, Duke of Burgundy (c.1435–67)' (D. Phil. Thesis, University of Oxford, 2001).

36 Gutiere Quixada, lord of Villagarcia jousted with the Bastard of Saint Pol (Jean de Luxembourg, lord of Haubourdin) at the wedding feast of Charles, duke of Orléans and Mary of Cleves in 1440: Enguerran de Monstrelet, *Chronique*, ed. L. Douët-d'Arcq, 6 vols (Paris, 1857–62), iv, pp. 433–44.

37 Louis de Luxembourg, count of Saint Pol.

38 Jean, count of Étampes and Nevers.

39 Agnes of Cleves, married to Charles, Prince of Viana.

40 Pierre de Bauffremont, count of Charny.

41 Jean V de Créquy, lord of Canaples.

While I was there the duke sent for me many times, and enquired as to the places I had visited, and by repeated questions desired to be exactly informed concerning all that I had seen and done ... He asked me whether I desired to continue my journey, or if it pleased me to remain at his court. I replied that having visited his country and Paris, I must speedily return to Castile, for I knew that the king, my master, wished to wage war in person against the Moors, and he took it in good part, and ordered the Bastard of Saint Pol to bear me company and, when I desired to depart, to escort me through his dominions; further, that if it were necessary he would give me letters of recommendation, which pleased me greatly. Afterward we went to see the city [Brussels], which is large and rich, with beautiful houses, and in the centre of a square is the town hall, where the council meets, which has no equal. We went also outside the city to see certain estates belonging to the duke, whither he retires for his pleasure, among which was one with a very fine house and a great enclosed park, about a league in circumference, where there are many deer and other wild creatures.[42]

I departed from Brussels in company with a knight, the captain of Sluis,[43] to whom the Bastard had recommended me, and we arrived that day for dinner at a town where there was not a drop of wine to be had, and I proposed that we should go on to Bruges where we should certainly find some, but the knight informed me that a lady, a kinswoman of his, was abbess of a convent close by, and that he would send to enquire if she had any wine, and this he accordingly did. The abbess sent a message that she had wine aplenty, but that she would not produce it unless he came to dine with her, and brought with him the Spanish knight who was his companion. We therefore presented ourselves and were very pleasantly received.

[Tafur accompanies the Captain of Sluis to Bruges, where they take leave of one another, the captain issuing an invitation to Tafur to come to visit. Tafur lodges at the inn known as the Angel ...]

This city of Bruges is a large and very wealthy city, and one of the greatest markets of the world. It is said that two cities compete with each other for commercial supremacy, Bruges in Flanders in the West, and Venice in the East. It seems to me there is much more commercial

42 Possibly the Zoniënwoud on the outskirts of Brussels, a park around 10,000 hectares in size which had a castle and a summer house for the duchess: C. Niedermann, *Das Jagdwesen am Hofe Herzog Philipps des Guten von Burgund* (Brussels, 1995), pp. 246–50. The palace in Brussels also had its own garden and park, however.
43 Roland van Uutkerke, knight of the Order of the Golden Fleece.

activity in Bruges than in Venice ... The inhabitants are extraordinarily industrious, possibly on account of the barrenness of the soil, since very little corn is grown, and no wine, nor is there water fit for drinking, nor any fruit. On this account the products of the whole world are brought here, so that they have everything in abundance, in exchange for the work of their hands. From this place is sent forth the merchandise of the world, woollen cloths and Arras cloths, all kinds of carpets, and many other things necessary to mankind ... This city of Bruges has a very large revenue, and the inhabitants are very wealthy. Recently they rebelled against the duke, at a time when he was in the city, so that he had to flee with his wife and attendants. He then armed himself, and made war against it and took it by force, and took great vengeance upon it, both in lives and property. I myself saw many high gallows around Bruges, and from there to Sluis, and around Sluis, upon which were fixed the heads of dead men ... [44] Without doubt, the goddess luxury has great power there, but it is not a place for poor men, who would be badly received. But anyone who has money and wishes to spend it will find in this town everything which the whole world produces. I saw there oranges and lemons from Castile, which seemed only just to have been gathered from the trees, fruits and wine from Greece, as abundant as in that country. I saw also confections and spices from Alexandria, and all the Levant, just as if one were there; furs from the Black Sea, as if they had been produced in the district. Here was all Italy with its brocades, silks and armour, and everything which is made there; and, indeed, there is no part of the world whose products are not found here at their best. But there was great famine in the year of my visit ... The famine was the worst which had ever been known, and it was followed by a dreadful plague which devastated many places.

4. A description of the household of Charles the Bold, 1474

Olivier de la Marche, 'L'estat de la maison du duc Charles', in H. Beaune and J. d'Arbaumont (eds), *Olivier de La Marche: Mémoires*, 4 vols (Paris, 1883–88), iv, pp. 1–94.

44 A rebellion which began when the militia of Bruges, mobilised with those of other Flemish towns in 1436 for the abortive siege of Calais, refused to disband. Some attempted to enter Sluis and were refused admission by Uutkerke mentioned above. Revolt erupted in Bruges, during which Uutkerke's wife was hidden in the Duchess Isabella's baggage carts to get her out of the city. When Philip the Good returned in May 1438, he was trapped, and Jean de Villiers, lord of L'Isle-Adam was killed. Bruges came to terms in February 1438 after a blockade, siege and the loss of its commercial rights.

We will begin with the offices of his household, and with divine service and his chapel, which ought to the starting point for everything.

His chapel contains forty men, including a bishop, his confessor, and three other Dominican priests and confessors, other chaplains and officers, organists and stewards. These chaplains, chantrists and officers are governed by the first chaplain. Every day, wherever they are, they sing the hours of the day and solemn high mass. The prince is present at this service and at all hours when they are before him, principally at mass and vespers. It should not be forgotten that the bishop and the Dominicans are important clerics, doctors and preachers, and that they preach very often.[45]

Furthermore, the duke has an almoner and a sub-almoner, men of such authority and trust that they distribute alms for the prince at their own discretion and on their own conscience. These alms are large, amounting to more than £20,000 a year.[46] And to approve these alms, when the duke has to leave a town, his almoner brings him a written account so that the duke may inquire and know where good works have been done and alms have been distributed in that town, such as to old people, poor prisoners, pregnant women, orphans, poor unmarried maidens, people suffering from burns, ruined merchants, and all other necessary causes. And to each one the duke, out of devotion, distributes his alms and signs the paper and sums, which are paid before the almoner leaves the town. The almoner also distributes and hands out money for the offering of the prince who, every day and wherever he is, makes an offering at mass. This offering is made by the most senior prince present in the household. The almoner must also give the blessing at the table of the prince, and the grace afterwards. The chief steward of the household must be present at these prayers ... The almoner should bring the vessel containing the alms before the prince, and then take away the table cloth, starting at the top end of the table (which is the opposite end from where the food is served).

[There follows a description of how justice is arranged and how the finances of the household operate ...]

The duke has a grand chief steward of the household who can attend all his councils, both of justice and of war. The receipts and offerings of the princes and ambassadors must be given to him. He can serve at the four great feasts of the year and when the prince holds estate. He must

45 Cf. A. Vanderjagt, *Laurens Pignon O.P.: confessor of Philip the Good* (Venlo, 1985).
46 See [**27**] for details.

walk in front of the food dishes of the prince, his baton held upright. But he must not do the tasting in the kitchen: the first chief steward of the household should do that or, in his absence, one of the other chief stewards of the household. Once the dishes are set before the prince, the grand chief steward of the household has all the covers of all the dishes from which the prince is served, in the first course, the second and throughout the meal, removed. It should be understood that these things are the right of the grand chief steward of the household in Burgundy: but I do not want to affirm that he has this authority in the other regions and lordships which the duke holds.

[The duties of the other chief stewards of the household, then those of the stewards, are described ...]

For his bedchamber, the duke has sixteen esquires who are men of high birth. They serve the prince by accompanying him wherever he goes, on foot or on horseback, and they take care of his person and his clothes. They sleep near his bedchamber for his security. When the duke has spent the whole day labouring at his affairs, giving audience to everyone, he withdraws to his chamber, where his esquires go to keep him company. Some of them sing, others read romances and new tales, while still others recount tales of love and of arms.

[The duties of the six doctors, four surgeons, forty chamber valets, two spicers and others are described, before introduction of the four offices which serve the body and mouth of the prince ...]

The duke has a first pantler, and fifty esquire pantlers who are led, in war and peace, by the first pantler. They are governed by the five heads of chamber ordained by the prince, of whom each has nine pantlers under him. They ride to the horn of the first pantler in a squadron. I have named the pantlers as the first estate; for according to the rule of the daily lists and ordonnances in the household of Burgundy for more than a century, the pantler must be the first to be named, in honour of the holy sacrament of the altar: the bread is the holy object out of which the precious body of Our Lord Jesus Christ is consecrated ...[47]

I will describe how the pantler should conduct himself in serving the mouth of the prince. When the prince goes to dine and is seated at a set table, the hall usher goes to fetch the pantler whose duty it is to serve that day, and leads him to the pantry. There, the steward of the pantry hands a napkin to the pantler, and kisses it devoutly. The

47 Cf. K.M. Phillips, 'The invisible man: body and ritual in a fifteenth-century noble household', *Journal of Medieval History* 31 (2005), pp. 143–62.

pantler places it on his left shoulder, the two ends hanging in front and behind him. The steward then gives him the covered salt-cellar which the pantler should carry in his fingers between the foot and main body of the receptacle, in contrast to the goblet which should be carried by the foot. The pantler proceeds, bareheaded, behind the hall usher; and after him comes the steward, carrying in his arms the silver vessel which is used for the alms. Within the vessel are the silver trenchers, the small salt-cellar, and another small vessel, together with the baton and unicorn used in the tasting of the prince's food.[48] Once they have reached the room and arrived in front of the table, the steward should put the vessel down in the place shown him by the pantler, and this will be at the lower end of the table.[49] The pantler opens the salt-cellar, and takes salt from the lid, handing it to the butler, who does the tasting in front of the pantler. Afterwards the pantler sets down his salt-cellar and trenchers, the small salt-cellar, the small vessel and taster, and then drapes the napkin over the vessel. When the prince wishes to wash, the pantler hands the napkin to the first chief steward of the household who should serve in this instance. The chief steward of the household should give it to the first chamberlain, who, using his own discretion, gives it to anyone there of higher rank than him, and then returns the napkin to the chief steward of the household. After the prince has wiped his hands, the chief steward returns the napkin to the pantler, who folds it up and puts it back on his shoulder. He then goes back to the kitchen behind the chief steward. When it is time for the dishes to be gathered up, the pantler lifts the covers, and the chief steward tastes the dishes. Once this is done, the pantler covers up the dishes again, and gives out the covered dishes one after the other to the gentlemen of the four offices who have followed on to carry the food of the prince, and to the pages and valets serving the prince. These are assigned to carry, bareheaded, the food of the prince. Once the food is gathered up, the sauce-maker presents the verjuice to the pantler, and the pantler takes one taste of each sauce and returns them to the sauce-maker to perform his act of devotion. The pantler should carry the sauces, and this is why it is the pantler, rather than the chief steward, who

48 The horn of a 'unicorn' (in reality most likely the tooth of a narwhal) was considered to be the most precious of all poison detectors. Mounted in a gold baton, contact with food would reveal the presence of a venom: poisoned bread for instance, would begin to smoke. Salt at table was also thought to act as a dehumidifier, rendering poison detectors more effective: F. Collard, *Le Crime du poison au Moyen Âge* (Paris, 2003), esp. pp. 84–7, 90. Vigilance over food tasting at the Burgundian court was evidently not strict, as the Coustain case [**8**] shows.

49 The opposite end from the board end, where the lord and others of high rank sat.

tastes the sauces, and why he only makes one tasting, while the chief steward makes two, for the pantler only accounts for what he delivers. Neither the chief steward of the household nor the cooks are held to account, but responsibility for the food is placed under the pantler and the esquire who carries it. For this reason, the chief steward makes two tastings of each dish. With the food gathered up, the usher positions himself in front of the chief steward, and after him comes the pantler, then the dishes, and the main dish should be first. The kitchen esquire should come after the food, and the usher should kneel before the prince in making room and clearing the way. Then the chief steward positions himself at the lower end of the table where he should remain until the food is set down and the tasting done. He should always keep an eye on this. The pantler places the food down on the table, then does his tasting, and hands the dishes to the other men one after the other. The pantler returns to the end of the table where the serving vessel is kept, and gives the duke two servings from each of twelve or thirteen dishes. Supper is served once, and the pantler should take one of the knives, place the salt of the large salt-cellar into the small one, make his tasting, and place the salt in front of the prince. He takes the wafers from the side-table, and if there are many people at the banquet, he can place the wafers in front of all those who are seated at the prince's table, but not in front of the others. Then the steward of the pantry takes a short folded white napkin over to the pantler and kisses it, and the pantler wraps it in a napkin which he has draped around his neck over the right side of his chest. It is for this reason that the pantler places the two ends of the napkin in his belt, so that he can better hold on to the napkin which is given to him.[50] Once he has received the napkin, the pantler gives the trenchers, the small vessel and salt-cellars to the steward. As for the large vessel, the almoner should pick it up in the way already described above. With the table-cloth removed, the pantler unwraps his napkin and kisses it and then unfolds it in front of the prince. He takes hold of one end of his napkin, while the esquire-carver takes the other. The reason why the esquire-carver takes the upper end is to respect the order they have taken up at the table before the prince. And when the prince has wiped his hands on the napkin, the pantler should pick it up again and return it to the steward with the first napkin ...

To explain the order of the pantry, I will ... begin with the valet-ser-

---

50 In so doing the pantler's clothes may have resembled the priest's vestments at mass: Phillips, 'The invisible man', p. 147.

vants who deal with the bread. Although they are noblemen, they are called valet-servants because it is the first stage of the estate of nobility. Normally, the prince makes valet-servants from his pages, who then climb to the rank of esquires responsible for serving food, and they continue to rise depending on their virtues and the family to which they belong. The duke has eight valet-servants at any one time.

[The duties of the valet-servants at table are then described in detail, followed by the role of the ushers ...]

The cupbearers, who constitute the second estate, must now be described, following the ancient ordonnance which I find written down. The reason why they are in the second estate is that the cupbearer serves the wine from which the precious blood and body of Our Lord Jesus Christ is consecrated, as we have seen above for the bread. So it is fitting that the service of the bread and wine should be set above all other things. But one thing surprises me, about which I have asked myself many questions: why the cupbearer and his office have a particular name which does not derive from the word for wine or the vine, as the name of the pantler [*panem/pain*] or the esquire-carver does. In truth, I have not found it written down anywhere, and I don't understand or know why. But as a guess, two reasons may be found and no more. The first is that in France and in several great lordships, there are hereditary butlers who receive payment from this title. Although the butler, by his name, has a link with wine, I have never found that he has authority over the cupbearer or over the cup-bearing office, but only over the cellars where the wines of the court reserved for the prince, and not the other supplies, are stored. For that reason, he who is responsible for domestic service and he who serves the prince are named differently ... The second reason is that the prince eats in public and is watched by everyone and should be the mirror of all virtues and respectability, while from another perspective, wine carries with it a meaning of greed, more so than any other form of nourishment. Thus it would not be seemly to call for wine too often for the prince. So the ancient sages chose another name to designate this service ... A third point should be included here: why and for what reason was the name cupbearer (*échanson*) given to this office and not any other? I think that it is a joyful name given to the office after much deliberation, derived from the word to sing (*chanter*), because the Ancients, during banquets, great entertainments and rejoicings, were invigorated and made joyful by wine, and because the main way of showing joy is to sing. I don't know of another explanation. And if anyone knows a better or contrary reason, he should let me know: it will give me great pleasure.[51]

The duke has a first esquire-cupbearer, who has beneath him fifty esquire-cupbearers at any time on the daily household lists. They are led and governed in chambers by chamber chiefs and ride to the horn of the cupbearer in a squadron. The cupbearer has the same authority over them as the pantler over the members of his office. The first cupbearer accounts for the wine which is consumed in the prince's household. The hippocras consumed is also accounted for by the cupbearing office … His office accounts for a great deal of expenditure in the ducal household, for never does a year go by without the duke of Burgundy requiring more than a thousand barrels of wine for his household, and in some years another thousand besides or even more, depending on the gatherings and festivities taking place. The first cupbearer serves in person at the four great feasts of the year. When the chief steward of the household holds estate after the prince's dinner, he must be seated on the bench between the cupbearer and the pantler. The cupbearer should be seated below the chief steward because at the times of the great feasts and important days, the prince asks for wine and spices after his dinner, and the cupbearer has to get up and attend to him. This is why he sits lower down, to be on hand more quickly. To describe this ceremony, the esquire-carver should place in front of the cook who has served the prince, the napkin which he had around his neck and with which he served. No other person should be seated at this table. But I ask myself why the cooks are seated there, rather than the kitchen esquire who is still the head person in the kitchen. To this I reply that there are two reasons. The first is that, according to the royal statutes,[52] one reproaches the cook and not the kitchen esquire. There are, however, great lords who have great cooks holding their office by inheritance, which is an office of great magnificence. The other reason is that the kitchen esquire, who is responsible for the service, should make the first chief steward serve at this table. I am forced to mix up the offices at this point to list the rights of each one.

We will now say how the service of the cupbearers is organised each day. When the table is set, the pantler has arrived and the objects of his office are in place, the hall usher goes to fetch the cupbearer who is serving that day, and leads him to the buttery where the guard of the

---

51 Professor Paravicini has pointed out that the Germans called this office 'Schenck', and that *échanson* shares the same Germanic root: 'La Cour de Bourgogne selon Olivier de La Marche', p. 110.

52 Cf. [5] below on royal precedent for Burgundian practice.

trunk gives him the covered goblet which the cupbearer takes by the foot in his right hand. In his left he holds a cup with the equipment of basins, pots and ewers for the prince, with the help of the steward who washes and cleans them. Then he puts all these things into the hands of the steward who gives the goblet to the cupbearer. The latter positions himself behind the hall usher who should carry the basins in his left hand. After the cupbearer comes the steward of the buttery who should carry two silver pots in his right hand, one containing the prince's wine, the other water. The prince's pot should be recognised by the unicorn pendant which hangs from the pot by a chain. In his left hand the butler should carry a bowl and nothing else, in which one should place a ewer to serve water. The bowl which the butler carries is used by him for the tasting which the cupbearer serves him. Next, the butler goes toward the assistant who should carry the pots and bowls destined for the prince's side-table. These are the rules for dining when the prince holds everyday estate: and this is called serving the prince in simple order.

The cupbearer goes into the hall, places the goblet at the board end of the table and on the side at which the prince is seated. He places the bowl he has brought at the opposite end to the goblet. He should remain there without withdrawing from the table so he can survey what he has brought …

We will now describe what the cupbearer should do, and why he is placed at the board end, above the pantler who is nonetheless first to arrive and the first named among the household services. The reason is that cloths to cover the table come from the pantler's office, and the table needs to be set before anything else is arranged … Secondly, it is done to gain time and to have everything ready when the prince comes, for it often happens that, because of his great affairs, the prince does not arrive at conventional hours: if he arrives late and the goblet has already been brought, the wine would not be cool at all, having lain on the dresser for perhaps two hours. So the time for serving the wine is reduced, so that nothing is spoiled. The reason why the cupbearer is at the board end is to make serving convenient, so that there is only the goblet and bowl at this end. Great princes and ambassadors regularly come to the board end to see the prince at table: the goblet does not prevent them from seeing anything, whereas in contrast the tall vessel and the small one, as well as the salt-cellar and trenchers, would do so at the other end. On this matter, when one speaks of the board end, one usually means the right-hand side, and truthfully it is this side most often. But if one examines the board end as a whole, with all the places set, one should take into account the view one has while sitting there, as well as the entrances and exits in the room. The board end should be placed where the view is best, next to the windows, whether on the left- or right-hand side.

[The serving of water and wine is described …]

At last [the hall usher] dilutes the wine in his goblet, according to his knowledge of the taste and character of the prince. Certainly, in Duke Charles's case, he always tempered his wine so much that I believe there is no prince in existence who drinks so little while spending so much on wine …

The first cupbearer or, in his absence, another cupbearer carries the goblet at all feasts and gatherings of state and honour. Although a prince or great lord may serve the comfit-dish, the cupbearer is the only one allowed to serve the goblet to the prince, for it is not right to take from a gentleman a goblet he has brought and put it into the hands of another. No one should do this, however great he is, unless he be the son of the prince who wishes to serve his father. But it is true that in the bedchamber where the wine is brought by the valets of the bedchamber where the cupbearer is not called, it is the most important prince or the first chamberlain who should serve. For in the bedchamber of the prince, it is the most important pensionary or the chamberlain who should lay out the cap worn at night. So the greatest honour is to serve the prince in the most intimate things.

[The other members of the second office of the kitchen are described – the stewards, guards of the trunk and cellarer …]

On the third office [of the household], I will deal with the esquire-carver and why he should be named third before the esquire of the stable, and what duties he has. The esquire-carver should be named third because he follows the two others in the service of the prince's mouth. He should be named before the esquire of the stable because in battle the pennon with the arms of the prince is placed in the hands of the esquire-carver and should remain under his control for the whole day. He should always follow closely wherever the prince goes, just behind him, holding in his fist the pennon displayed to indicate and make known to everyone where the prince is. As long as the campaign lasts, the esquire-carver should eat like the other chief stewards of the household. And since the pennon bears the arms of the prince like the banner, he should go before the esquire of the stable … The esquire-carver has such rights and such authority that if all the chamberlains were away from the ducal household for whatever reason, the first esquire-carver should take the place of the first chamberlain. I want to justify this with two reasons. The first is that because the chamberlain is someone who is extremely close to the prince and his intimate, it is fitting that he should be replaced by someone on equally intimate terms with the prince. Now it is necessary for the prince to be on terms of greater intimacy with his esquire-carver than with others: if he wishes to be in his bedchamber discreetly, he would be able to eat without the other three offices more easily than he would without the esquire-carver, for the esquire-carver can serve quite easily as a cupbearer and a pantler, whereas the others are not shown how to carve and do not know the prince's tastes, which the esquire-carver should know. The second reason, and the most true, is that the esquire-carver, as described, carries the pennon with the arms of the prince, which is nearer the banner placed in the hands of the chamberlain.

[The duties of the esquire-carver at table are described, including the cleaning and upkeep of knives which are bought by the treasurer, followed by the duties of the kitchen esquire (also linked to this third household service) and the cooks who belong to a 'subtle and sumptuous profession, requiring great trust and profit necessary for the prince'. There are three cooks, each serving for four months of the year. The provisioning of the household is very briefly mentioned (see [6] below), followed by the other kitchen workers, the sauce-makers and their duties at table, and the office of fruiterer. Attached to the latter are six valet-torch-bearers who carry torches at all times, except in the council chambers where secretaries perform this role. A description of the fourth household service, the esquires of the stable, is then given, and mentioned with them are the pages, 'children of a good house', who are instructed by the first esquire of the stables …]

The duke has four foot-valets who should lead the prince's horse to the mounting block, and should fetch it from the stable, leading it by the bridle and not by riding on its back. They should make very sure that no one approaches the horse, and after the groom has delivered the prince's horse into their hands, that no one touches either the saddle or the harness besides the stable-esquire. Each of these foot-valets should have a white baton in his hand, without a point or blade, to push the people back so that they do not approach the prince. For it would not be seemly for the poor people who lovingly run after the prince and come close to see him to be pushed back or struck with a sword or knife; rather, they should be repelled by a baton without a point.[53] The pages,

53 The main courtyard was the most likely spot for the prince to mount his horse; it was

grooms or valets on foot should all be dressed the same. The foot-valets or grooms distribute alms to all the poor people that the prince encounters, and whoever gives out alms renders account on trust for what he has given. The foot-valets go to the exits and entrances of all towns, and go on foot around the prince's horse, as was said.

[After discussing the roles of heralds, trumpeters and archers, La Marche describes arrangements for the household's travels, and how the marshal goes on ahead to arrange lodgings in the town …]

And although the duke of Burgundy is prince and lord of the most beautiful cities of the world, his household is so large that few towns can be found to lodge all its members, and often other towns and villages must be used too.

[De la Marche closes his account of the order of the household by stating that these customs and rules are not to be seen as set above the prince, but that princes arrange them according to their pleasure. He concludes by describing the men-at-arms and artillery.]

5. Etiquette at court: Eleanor of Poitiers

J. Paviot, 'Les *États de France* (*Les Honneurs de la cour*) d'Éléonore de Poitiers', *Annuaire-bulletin de la Société de l'histoire de France* 1996 (publ. 1998), pp. 75–137.

[Of the honours and courtly gestures observed in various meetings and occasions involving princes and princesses …]

I saw the demoiselle [Beatrice] of Coïmbra[54] marry my lord Adolf of Cleves, youngest brother of my lord [John I] duke of Cleves, nephew of my lord Philip the duke. The wedding took place at Lille,[55] but there was no feast because of the Ghent war …

Later my lord of Charolais married my lady of Bourbon[56] on the eve of All Saints at Lille. There was no feast, because Duke Philip was in Germany at that time. A week after the wedding, Lady Isabella held a

also, along with the main public rooms, one of the spaces in the prince's residence to which ordinary people were ordinarily admitted: cf. [14] below. Hence the need for the security measures described by La Marche.

54 A refugee at the Burgundian court since the death of her father in 1449: M. Sommé, *Isabelle de Portugal, duchesse de Bourgogne* (Villeneuve d'Ascq, 1998), pp. 78–80.

55 13 May 1453: W. Paravicini, *Invitations au mariage: Pratique sociale, abus de pouvoir, intérêt de l'État à la cour des ducs de Bourgogne, 1399–1489* (Stuttgart, 2001), p. 88 et seq.

56 Isabella of Bourbon, daughter of John, Duke of Bourbon.

fine banquet where all the ladies of Lille were in attendance – but we all sat together as one usually does at banquets, without the princesses holding estate as befitted such occasions.

Very soon after that I witnessed the visit of my lady of Eu.[57] The count of Eu[58] was the half-brother by blood of my lord of Bourbon through his mother,[59] and the uncle of my lady of Charolais, while my lady of Eu was herself the daughter of [Jean IV de Melun] the lord of Antoing. My lady of Eu conducted herself in a most haughty manner, and would have liked to go hand-in-hand alongside my lady of Charolais, but my lady would not take her; nor did she wash with my lady before the meal …

My lady of Eu and my lady [Marie] of Nevers (who was the daughter of my lord [Charles II] of Albret) were at Lille at that time, visiting Duke Philip. A great quarrel arose over which of them should go in front, but I heard it said that my lord honoured my lady of Nevers more than my lady of Eu, because he always placed my lady of Nevers on his left, and my lady of Eu on his right. And at the time I heard wise people who knew about such things say that whoever was placed on the left of the duke received the greater honour than whoever went on the right. My lord led them in this way whenever they went anywhere with him, but when he went to wash at table neither of them approached him, nor did they approach him at any other time when he was holding estate.

Once my lady of Eu came to see my lady (of Charolais), who was feeling a little ill, at Le Quesnoy. So my lady of Eu ate alone in my lady's great chamber. And on that occasion I saw my lady of Eu permit my lord of Antoing her father to hold her napkin for her, bare-headed, while she washed for supper, and then kneel almost to the ground before her. I heard wise heads say this was folly on the part of the lord of Antoing, and even more so for his daughter to have allowed it …

My lady [Agnes] of Bourbon and my lady [Mary] of Cleves were once at Brussels together visiting my lord Philip [the Good], their brother. But my lord the duke Philip showed greater honour to my lady of Cleves than to my lady of Bourbon, and allowed her to go in front, and he said he did so because she was the older of the two. Otherwise, of course, My lady of Bourbon should have gone in front because my lord of Bourbon was greater than my lord of Cleves, for he is from the royal house of France …

57 Hélène de Melun.
58 Charles, count of Eu, married to Hélène in September 1454.
59 Marie de Berry (d. 1434), daughter of Jean I duke of Berry.

I once saw my lady of Penthièvre[60] (who was the daughter of [Simon IV de Lalaing], lord of Quiévrain in Hainaut, and wife of my lord of Penthièvre, [61] of the lineage, name and arms of the dukes of Brittany) come to visit my lady of Charolais. And I recall that we held council to know what honour my lady of Charolais would show her. It was decided that when my lady of Penthièvre had entered my lady's chamber and had completed the first two honours, my lady would take three steps toward her. And so she did. And in truth she showed great honour to my lady and this was most appropriate, for she was a handsome lady for her age. However, my lady of Penthièvre did not take food or drink, with the result that they remained in the same room. For this reason I did not see my lady of Bourbon or my lady of Ravestein walk with her, so I do not know how this would have been done ...

I heard from my lady my mother that My Lady of Namur[62] used to say that according to the estates of France, all women had to be ranked according to their husbands, however great their own estate was, save for the daughters of kings.

And my lady my mother used to say that at the wedding of King Charles [VII], grandfather of the current King Charles [VIII], my lady of Namur was seated lower than all the other countesses, except one. And when it came to the middle of the dinner, the king came up to her and said that she had sat long enough as the wife of the count of Namur, and that for the rest of the dinner she should sit as his cousin. So he had her seated at the Queen's table. And when grace was said she went back to her place. And my lady of Namur said that there had never been so many princes or great ladies at a royal wedding as there had been there. And on the wedding day, all the ladies dined in one room with the queen, and there were no men seated in that room.

I have heard it said that my Lady of Namur was the most knowledgeable of all the noblewomen of France about the manner in which one should hold estate, and that she had a big book in which everything

---

60 Jeanne de Lalaing.

61 Olivier de Blois-Bretagne, claimant to the title of Duke of Brittany (d. 1433), but who was expelled from the duchy with his brothers and had his lands confiscated after their imprisonment of Duke Jean V in 1420. The awkward social situation which follows arises from the subsequent status of the Penthièvre claim: to fail to respect the rank of the Dame de Penthièvre was, in effect, to reject her family's rights on the ducal title in Brittany.

62 Jeanne de Harcourt, who died at a great age in 1449: G. du Fresne de Beaucourt, *Histoire de Charles VII*, 6 vols (Paris, 1881–91), i, p. 236; iii, pp. 157, 174; Sommé, *Isabelle de Portugal*, pp. 37–8, 52, 207, 403.

was written down. And my mother told me that when Duchess Isabella, wife of the good duke Philip of Burgundy, first came from Portugal, she did nothing in such matters without first taking the counsel and advice of my lady of Namur.

The honour which the queen of France showed to my lady the duchess Isabella when she came before her at Châlons-en-Champagne[63]

My lady the duchess, accompanied by her nephew my lord [Jean II] of Bourbon and several other princes of France came with all her company on horseback and in waggons right into the courtyard of the hostel where the king and queen were residing. My lady the duchess alighted there, and her first lady-in-waiting took the train of her dress. My lord of Bourbon led her by his right hand, and all the other knights and gentlemen went in front. In this manner she came to the room where the queen was residing. There my lady stopped, and sent in the lord [Jean V] of Créquy, her knight of honour,[64] to ask the queen if she would be permitted to enter and pay her respects. Once my lord of Créquy had returned, my lady the duchess approached the door of the queen's room, and all the knights and gentlemen accompanying her entered. Then my lady took the train of her own dress from the lady who was carrying it, and when she entered the room she let the train of her dress fall and knelt right down to the ground herself. Then she walked into the middle of the room, where she repeated the honour. Then she began to walk once more toward the queen, who remained standing upright beside the head of her bed. And when my lady began to perform the honour for a third time, the queen came forward two or three steps, and my lady knelt before her. The queen laid her hand on her shoulder, embraced her, kissed her and raised her up …

Baptism of mademoiselle Mary of Burgundy[65]

My Lady of Charolais gave birth to her in the city of Brussels on the eve of Saint Valentine's day, 1457. The duke was then in another town, but the Duchess Isabella and my lord of Charolais, the father of Mary, were then both in Brussels, as was the dauphin of France as I have said.

On the day of the birth the people of Brussels celebrated with great fires and bell-ringing and other great signs of joy. So did all the other

---

63 The Franco-Burgundian conferences at Châlons were led on the Burgundian side by Isabella on behalf of Philip the Good. Sommé, *Isabelle de Portugal*, pp. 404–8.

64 The leading office in the duchess's household: Sommé, *Isabelle de Portugal*, pp. 292–3.

65 M. Sommé, 'Le Cérémonial de la naissance et de la mort de l'enfant princier à la cour de Bourgogne au XVe siècle', *PCEEB* 34 (1994), pp. 87–103.

subjects of my lord when they heard the news of the birth.

The baptism took place two weeks or so after the birth. The people of Brussels gave 400 torches. My lord of Charolais had 200 made, which gave a total of 600, each of them weighing four or five pounds. The baptism took place at the Coudenberg palace, because the church of Saint Gudule is too far from the residence. Barriers were put up from halfway down the steps of the great hall on both sides up to the door of the church of the palace, far enough apart to permit six or seven people abreast to walk there.

The torches which the city of Brussels had given were carried by their own people, all dressed in the same livery. They stood along the side of the barriers and were placed in such a way that they reached as far as the door of the church. These torches did not process because the distance from the palace to the church is too short. Inside the church there were a hundred torches which my lord had had made, and these were held in the nave of the church by officers of the household who did not process either.

The baptism of Philip [the Fair] of Austria[66]

The baptism of the present lord Philip, son of the duke of Austria and of my lady Mary the duchess of Burgundy, was similar to that of his mother, save that from the duke's palace in Bruges to the church of Saint Donatian, we walked on a platform constructed through the streets and across the market place, roughly at head height, enclosed in wood and cloth. To get onto the platform, we climbed up some steps which were at the palace gate. The whole courtyard of the palace was hung with tapestries, and the streets through which we carried the child to the church were also richly and beautifully hung with cloth, because everyone who had a house on the route had taken great trouble.

The font was constructed on a tall, wide platform so that all the people could see them, and the platform we arrived on was joined to it. And the rest of the ceremony was the same as for the baptism of my lady his mother.

How princesses and others should mourn their husbands, fathers, mothers and relatives

I have heard it said that the Queen of France must remain in mourning for a whole year without leaving the chamber where the news of her

66 Cf. R. Strøm-Olsen, 'Dynastic ritual and politics in early modern Burgundy: the baptism of Charles V', *Past and Present* 175 (2002), pp. 34–64.

husband's death is brought to her. But the mourning robes and gowns are different in France, where they are long, unlike here. The queen's chamber must be hung in black cloth and there must be black floor-coverings too, as is fitting. Madame of Charolais, daughter of the duke of Bourbon, remained in her chamber for six weeks from the moment she heard of the death of her father. She lay throughout on a bed draped in white linen, resting on pillows, but she kept her barbette on,[67] and her gown and her hood which were lined with miniver.[68] The gown had a long train, and the lining of the hood formed a ruff of roughly a hand's width on the outside.

Order to be observed in houses of lower rank

All of these things are not appropriate to houses of lower rank, such as those of countesses, viscountesses and baronesses of whom there is a great number in several kingdoms and other lands. If there is a lady-in-waiting, she should be called a lady companion and not a lady of honour. The young girls of the household should be called damsels or gentle-ladies, and not girls of honour. And the woman who is entrusted with the charge of these girls should be called by her name, such as 'Joan' or 'Margaret', and she should not be called the mother of the girls. And there should be no gentleman in the house to whom the title of cupbearer, pantler or carver is given. Also in such houses, there should be no tasting of wines or dishes of food, nor should any object given to the lord or lady of the house be kissed before it is handed to him or her. There should be no dorser,[69] and the children of the house should not be addressed in the same manner as children in princely houses.[70] Nor should they address their relatives as 'Fair Cousin', but at most they might address them as 'Cousin'.[71] Anyone who behaves in this fashion does so out of vainglory and presumption (as is well known), and he or she amounts to naught: for such actions are wilful, without discipline or reason, and it is not fitting for anyone to take such liberties and make free with ceremonies other than those which suit his or her estate, and which are established by ancient custom …

67 Form of veil which hung from hood or head-dress around the ears and below the chin, thereby covering the neck and framing the face.

68 White or light-grey fur used as a trim on robes.

69 Covering of the back of the seat.

70 An earlier paragraph records how the male children in a princely house 'should be addressed as "My Lord Peter" or "My Lord John", according to their names'. No mention is made of how girls of the same rank should be addressed.

71 Cf. Bousmar and Sommé, 'Femmes et espaces féminins à la cour de Bourgogne', pp. 50–1; Paravicini, 'Soziale Schichtung und soziale Mobilität', p. 135.

These are the honours which have been ordained and which are preserved in the kingdom of France and in the House of Burgundy, approved by kings-at-arms and heralds.

And it is not right to say that this was how things were done in those older times, and that nowadays everything is different. Such allegations are insufficient to break with venerable and well-established ways, which should not be taken as the way things ought not to be done.

6. A household *Ordonnance* for Charles, Prince of Spain, 1515

L.-P. Gachard, *Collection des voyages des souverains des Pays-Bas*, 4 vols (Brussels, 1867–82), ii, pp. 491–501.

Ever since reaching the age of majority and making our joyous entry into the lordship and government of our lands on the other side, we have continually sought to put good order in our affairs and to attend to the disorder there has been in times past due to the wars and divisions which have reigned, and in particular the matter of the running of our household, upon which the well-being, honour and tranquility of ourselves, our servants, lands and subjects depend. So that we are henceforth honourably served and accompanied, we, having received several written submissions from our principal servants, and on the advice of the princes of the blood, the chancellor, the knights of the Order (of the Golden Fleece) and the men of our privy council and our financial officers, have decided upon and order by the present letters the condition of our household and of the persons who are part of the ordonnances as follows. This ordonnance will take effect on 1 January next, when the chamberlains, gentlemen, officers and servants allocated to the first term of service will begin and continue until the last day of June, when those allocated to the second term will enter into service and will continue until the last day of December 1516, and so they will continue year by year.

[A list of 43 named servants follows, consisting of counsellors, masters of the petitions to the prince (*maître des requêtes*), secretaries, a chaplain and ushers of the council.]

Statutes and ordonnances pertaining to our great chapel

First, we order that the chaplains, chanters and other subordinates in the chapel will answer to our first chaplains and display due reverence to them as their superiors, obeying their instructions in matters

concerning our chapel. If any of them should disobey, [his] wages will
be suspended for as many days as seems reasonable and befits [his]
disobedience, and [he] will lose [his] wages for these days.

[High mass was to be sung every day, in honour of the saint whose feast day
it was; so too vespers and compline (depending on whether the following day
was a double feast day); on certain feast days, all the monastic hours of the day
were to be celebrated, viz. Christmas Day, Circumcision, Apparition of our
Lord, Purification of Our Lady, the Annunciation, the Visitation, Assumption,
Nativity and Conception of the Virgin, Easter, Ascension of Our Lord, the Eve
and day of Pentecost, Trinity, Corpus Christi, Nativity of St John the Baptist,
St Peter in June, All Souls, Commemoration of the Dead, SS Catherine, Andrew
and Barbara, and every day from Lent to Advent …]

The said chaplains, chanters and subordinates will be expected to hold
divine service with due reverence and honour wherever we happen to
be or wherever we ask them to do so in full clerical habits, round hats,
surplices on all eves and feast days, and on great double and triple feast
days, and cleanly shaven, on pain of being scored off the household
wages for every day that they are at fault.

When the chaplains, chanters and office-holders enter and leave the
chapel, they will kneel down and honour the Saviour, Virgin Mary and
the patron saint of the chapel.

While celebrating the offices, they will be standing upright; and when
singing the introït of the mass, the Kyrie, Gloria, the Gospel, the *Credo*,
Sanctus, *Pater Noster*, *Agnus Dei* and similarly with the introït of vespers
and compline, at the principal *Magnificat* and *Nunc Dimittis*, at the
prayers, they will have their heads uncovered. And at Advent and Lent,
at holiday offices, they will kneel down at prayers, as they are accustomed to do.

During offices, they will remain silent and abstain from laughing, chat-
ting and other bad behaviour on pain of being scored off the household
wages.[72]

Ordonnances pertaining to the chamberlains

All chamberlains will answer to our first chamberlain in all matters
concerning their office …

The four esquires of the chamber will serve without interruption and
will not absent themselves from the chamber unless there are at least

---

72 On the 'household as a religious community', see K. Mertes, *The English noble household 1250–1600: good governance and politic rule* (Oxford, 1988), pp. 139–60.

one or two of them in attendance at all times. One of those present in the chamber will be responsible for guarding the door without leaving it unattended.

None of the said esquires or any others, whoever they may be, can enter our drawing room when we are on the chamber pot unless our great or second chamberlain or the steward of the body calls for them.

While overseeing the making our bed our first steward of the body will hold a little torch or a lit candle in his hand to check the bed is properly made, and he will not leave until it is ready. And if the said steward is absent he will call for one of the chamberlains who will be deputed to the chamber to hold the torch or candle. No one will come near the bed once it is made.

When we go to bed and when we rise, no officer serving in our chamber, whether he be a barber, dresser, hosier, tailor, shoemaker, robe-maker nor any other shall enter our chamber to carry out his task or for any other reason until he is summoned by the steward in charge.

The water-bearers[73] also may not enter our chamber until we have gone to mass, nor in the night after we have gone to bed, nor can they enter the drawing room unless they are summoned, all on pain of being scored off the household wages and punished at the discretion of our first or second chamberlain, or the steward.

We order that henceforth, outside the entries to our chambers, our pensioners, chamberlains, chief stewards of the household and gentlemen will be arranged as follows.[74] There will be a chamber in front of our bedchamber in which the ushers who guard the entrance to our chamber will lodge, and the aforementioned pensioners, chamberlains, chief stewards and gentlemen will enter into this chamber first. And if it so happens that where we are staying there are two chambers in front of ours, the aforesaid gentlemen will be lodged in the first, and the pensioners, chamberlains and chief stewards will be in the second, which is closest to our own chambers. And if there is only one chamber, they will enter into it and remain there, and will not enter our chambers without being summoned by him or by the first or second chamberlain

---

73 The domestic office for water and vessels for drinking and washing (save for laundry) in the English household was the ewery: Woolgar, *The great household*, p. 235.

74 The assignment of officers to separate chambers was already present in the household ordonnances of Charles the Bold. Some movement between the chambers was permitted, although not into the chamber of the prince himself. As a general rule, the services were expected to respect rank and not mix: Paravicini, "'Ordre et règle'", 334–5.

or their replacement, on pain of incurring our displeasure and being scored off the household wages. Only the grand chief steward of the household, the chancellor and the knights of our Order (of the Golden Fleece) may enter our chambers whenever they wish.

The children of the household[75] may not come and go in our chamber unless they are in twos or threes as ordained each day by the grand chief steward, and called for by the usher of our chamber. The said usher will remain constantly at the door of our chamber and will not let in anyone who is not permitted to enter, unless he is instructed to do so by our first or second chamberlain.

Two of the chamberlains and chief stewards of the household will be waiting outside our chambers henceforward every day before we rise to lead us to mass, and to return with us to breakfast, and they will not leave our company until the first or second chamberlain has arrived, at which time they may leave and take breakfast themselves, after which they will return to the chamber as they have done in the past.

When we are at table no one will approach us from behind to speak, unless we have summoned them or have consented to their approach, with the exception of the princes and the grand chief steward only. Anyone breaking this rule will be scored off the household wages.

We forbid any gentleman or any other, whoever they might be, to approach to speak to us at table or elsewhere, unless their conversation concerns good, honest and praiseworthy matters and is conducted in a seemly manner, and during our meals everyone will be silent in the chamber, without excessive noise and bad language.

Ordonnance for the gentlemen and officers in general

First, all gentlemen and officers will obey the grand and first chief stewards of the household and any other serving chief stewards of the household in all matters pertaining to their role and service, and they will conduct themselves in their office as the said chief stewards will instruct them on pain of being scored off the household wages.

The chamberlains and gentlemen will each be expected to be mounted as follows: chamberlains will be counted at 36 *sous* for six good horses; those counted at 30 *sous* will keep five horses; those at 24 *sous* will keep four horses. All other gentlemen will keep three horses, and will have saddles and other accoutrements appropriate to the man-at-arms to

75 *Enfans d'honneur*, by which is meant the children of the extended princely family and those in their entourage, rather than other children serving at court, such as in a choir or in the kitchens: Mertes, *The English noble household*, esp. pp. 30–1, 174–5.

serve in war and in other ways whenever they are required to do so. On the first day of May each year they will be reviewed by the head of their service or whomever we should designate for that purpose, mounted, armed and fully equipped, on pain of being scored off the household wages.

All officers and servants serving for household wages will be listed in writing on the daily lists for the serving controller and the usher of the hall, and these men will diligently inquire into the absentees and will denounce them to the court office so that the chief stewards of the household can score them off the household wages. We enjoin the chief stewards to attend to this matter without any dissimulation. And if any of the said controllers, ushers of the hall or chief stewards are negligent in this matter, they will be punished and will themselves be scored off the household wages for as long as the absentees were absent.

[Stewards are not to give away anything in their charge without permission, nor cellar wine from another lord in the prince's cellars, nor give away extra rations of wine; chief stewards are not to make gifts of barrels of wine supplied to the household ...]

We also forbid the grand or other chief stewards of the household and the master of the prince's purse[76] from concluding any purchases of wine, wax, spices, meat, fish or other supplies anywhere other than in the office of the court and in the presence of the serving chief steward or controller.

We instruct the said master of the prince's purse to make payments relating to his office only from the monies entrusted to him for that purpose, with the knowledge of the first chamberlain and of the grand and first chief stewards and of no other.

We forbid the esquire of the kitchen to go to the meat or fish market or to buy any other provisions unless in the presence of the said controller and of the master chef or the persons charged with replacing them to record the household expenditure, as has long been the custom.

[The controller is to ensure that no more horses are to be kept in the stables than are required by the great esquire; boatmen and carters are not to be paid until the controller has reached an agreement with them; the spicer is not to count at the end of the month any spices or drugs used to treat the sick;[77] the controller must be in attendance to verify each expenditure list kept by chief

---

76 *Maître de la chambre aux deniers*, the office responsible for keeping overall account of the court's expenses.

77 The spicery was a department of the larger households which, in addition to spices for food and drink, provided medicines and soap for the laundry.

stewards of the household; the clerk of the office will bring the papers of the services every day to the office to be accounted for, and once lists of household expenditure have been checked, he will bring them to the master of the prince's purse or his clerk so he may draw up his own accounts. Chief stewards of the household are not to take delivery of any meat, fish, spices or wax. Subordinates needing to ask anything of the household officers whom they serve must wait at the door. Officers will not set table for anyone whatsoever unless it be for others holding the same office. The quartermaster and the usher of the council will be obliged to swear solemnly in the court office in the presence of the great chief steward of the household to name anyone who has not attended council, whether they be councillors, secretaries or ushers. Absentees will not receive salaries, except for the great and second chamberlains, the great and first chief stewards of the household, the great esquire of the stables, the secretary in charge of the great seal.[78] If any member of the household has to leave to attend to his own affairs, the court office must be informed so he can be scored off household wages ...]

No officer, whoever he may be, will be allowed to lodge at court, except the great, first or second chamberlain or whoever serves in their place; the first steward of the chamber; the great or first chief steward of the household; and the great esquire, so long as there is room for them to lodge.

The officers serving our table and others named hereafter, that is to say of the pantry, the cellar, the fruitery, wardrobe, spicery, the keeper of the jewels or his assistant, the tapestry keeper, the quartermaster, porter and larderer and no others, will also have their lodgings at court. None of these officers will be allowed to keep his wife at court, nor hold his household there, on pain of being scored off immediately ...

Given in our town of Brussels, 25 October, Year of Grace 1515.

7. The court as marriage broker

(a) Jacques du Clercq on court weddings

Jacques du Clercq, *Mémoires*, ed. M. Petitot, in *Collection complète des mémoires relatifs à l'histoire de France*, xi (Paris, 1826), at pp. 51–2.

A furrier named Jean Pinte died on 27 June 1457, and the next day, as he was buried, his wife (who was a young woman of 34 years of age or so) became engaged to a furrier named Willeret de Noeuville aged

---

78 The *audiencier*, principal assistant to the chancellor, chosen from among the secretaries to accept the profits of the great seal: P. Cockshaw, *Le Personnel de la chancellerie de Bourgogne-Flandre sous les ducs de Bourgogne de la maison de Valois* (Kortrijk, 1982), pp. 60–71. See also [7c] below.

20 or thereabouts, and married him on the same day. That very night
they consummated the marriage. I set this in writing because I believe
a woman has never remarried so fast, although in this case she may be
excused for doing so. All over the lands of the duke of Burgundy at this
time, as soon as a merchant or labourer died, or even a bourgeois of one
of the good towns or an office-holder, and if he were rich or if he left a
rich wife, the duke, his son or others of their people sought to marry the
widow to one of their archers or servants. And if the widow wanted to
marry, she had to take the husband these lords gave her, or else a widow
had to pay cash either to the man who would be her husband or to those
who had influence with the lords. Sometimes widows had to give money
to the lords themselves. Even then, only the luckiest were saved with
the help of money and friends, for if widows did wish to marry again,
they had to take the husbands they were given. Likewise, if a rich man
had a daughter to marry, he had to marry her young to avoid being
harassed in this way.[79]

(b) George Chastelain on court weddings

George Chastelain. *Chronique. Les fragments du Livre IV révélés par l'Additional
Manuscript 54156 de la British Library*, ed. J.-C. Delclos (Paris, 1991), pp. 106–7
(*c.*1457).

These two young men (Philippe de Croy, lord of Quiévrain and Antoine
Rolin, lord of Aymeries, courtiers of Philip the Good) were just like
their fathers in nature,[80] and because both of them lived in Hainaut,
each strove to dominate there and to have things their own way. It so
happened that a wealthy young money-changer died in Valenciennes,
leaving behind a pretty young widow who was also rich in inheritance
and money. The lord of Aymeries quickly realised that the widow would
make a fine wife for one of his equerries, a young nobleman from the
duchy of Burgundy named Jehan Pourleing who had served him for a
long time and who was valiant and worthy. Indeed, the lord of Aymeries
spoke to the duke on the matter to achieve his ends, and the duke liberally granted his wish and promised not to grant the widow's hand in
marriage to anyone else, which put the petitioner at his ease. He also
asked for ducal letters for the widow, which he obtained, not so much
because he needed the duke's support to arrange the marriage (for he

79 W. Prevenier, 'La Stratégie et le discours politique des ducs de Bourgogne concernant
    les rapts et les enlèvements de femmes parmi les élites des Pays-Bas au XVe siècle',
    in Hirschbiegel and Paravicini (eds), *Das Frauenzimmer*, pp. 429–37, notably pp.
    434–5.

80 Jean de Croy, ducal chamberlain, and Nicolas Rolin, ducal chancellor.

was sufficiently powerful in Valenciennes to reach his ends), but rather as a precaution, for he wished to prevent anyone else from interfering. He was aware that Philippe de Croy was also attempting to secure the widow for one of his servants, a man who was not of great standing, and he wished to guard against this with letters and to have the duke on his side, as he did. The lord of Aymeries did well, for the woman was his in the end, despite the fact that my lord Philippe [de Croy] tried by means of his friends to get the better of him and to obtain ducal letters against him in this matter – although the duke would never have granted them for anything in the world, because the lord of Aymeries had asked first and had been granted the gift.

Great jealousy grew between the Croys and the family of the chancellor because of this marriage, on top of other long-held grievances which had arisen as a result of the chancellor having his own way in Hainaut.

(c) The marriage of Jehan Gros and Guye de Messey, February 1472

The following documents are gathered and published in Paravicini, *Invitations au mariage*, pp. 132–7.

Jean de Haynin, *Mémoires* 1465–77, ed. D.D. Brouwers, 2 vols (Liège, 1905–6), ii, p. 133.

On 4 February following [1472], on a Tuesday, there took place in Bruges the marriage of Master Jehan Gros,[81] first secretary, secretary of the great seal and controller of the domain and finances of my lord the duke of Burgundy, to Demoiselle Guye de Messey, niece of My Lord of Saillant, knight and chancellor of my lord the duke.[82] On Jean Gros's behalf, letters were written in the duke's name to all the prelates, abbesses, canons, deans, Carthusians, mendicants, barons, knights, towns and notable townsmen in all the lands and lordships of my said lord to request, most amicably, that they come to the wedding, or that they show such honour and favour, and send such representatives, as they could. As a result a great many attended the wedding or sent representatives, and it was calculated that more than 100,000 *écus* were received, which would be £250,000 in Hainaut money.

[Among the towns which received an invitation to the wedding was Dijon. In addition to the letter that follows, the town authorities received a very similar

---

81 Jean III Gros, later treasurer of the Golden Fleece.

82 Guillaume Hugonet, chancellor from 1471 to 1477, executed by the Ghenters on charges of corruption after the death of Charles the Bold (3 April 1477).

request from the bride's powerful uncle, Hugonet, sent on the same day and from the same location.]

Dijon town archives, B450. Letter from Jehan Gros to the aldermen of Dijon, 1 December 1471.

My most redoubted lords, I recommend myself to your good grace most humbly. Since, by the pleasure of my most redoubted lord the duke, a treaty of marriage between myself and Guye de Messey, daughter of Guillaume, esquire and lord of Reins, and niece of my lord of Saillant, chancellor of my lord the duke, has recently been accorded and agreed, and since the wedding will take place (God willing) wherever my lord the duke will be on 4 February next, I (who have always regarded myself as your most humble servant) am taking the liberty of informing you of these events, and beseech you in all humility, since you cannot easily come yourselves without great difficulty, to send someone to represent you and honour the occasion as you see fit. I will be greatly obliged to you and you will find me ready to serve you as well as I can, with the help and grace of Our Lord whom I beseech, most honourable lords, to grant you long life and the fulfilment of your desires. Written at Saint Omer, 1 December 1471. Your small and humble servant Jehan Gros.

Dijon council minutes, 23 December 1471.

It is concluded that because the town has much to do on a daily basis with my lord the chancellor of Burgundy and my lord the secretary of the seal, Master Jehan Gros, we will give on behalf of the town to the secretary of the great seal and the chancellor's niece, his fiancée, a gift of plate to the value of 100 francs or 100 gold florins, and we will send a fitting man to the lands on the other side to present the gift.

[The council resolves to send Nicolas Viard, a bourgeois and alderman of Dijon, who is given the money to take north.]

Receipt from ducal keeper of the jewels, Jacques de Brégilles.[83]

I, Jacques de Brégilles, keeper of the jewels of my lord the duke of Burgundy, certify that Nicolas Viard bought in my presence from Baudoyn Hendric, a merchant residing in Bruges, three silver pots … costing 119 francs 6 gr. 7 eng., which is the best deal the said Nicholas and I were able to strike. And I certify that Nicholas made the payment in gold florins. Witnessed by my signature on 6 February 1471.

83 J. Paviot, 'Jacques de Brégilles, garde-joyaux des ducs de Bourgogne Philippe le Bon et Charles le Téméraire', *RN* 77 (1995), pp. 313–20.

[Nicholas received an undated payment for having the arms of the town of Dijon engraved on the pots, and was reimbursed for his travel costs.]

Letter from Jehan Gros to the aldermen of Dijon, 16 March 1472 (received and opened 6 April).

My most honoured lords, I recommend myself most humbly to you. Please know that I received from Nicolas Viard, alderman of the good town of Dijon and bearer of this letter, your correspondence of 13 January last in reply to my earlier letters. As for the honour and company you accorded me at my wedding in the person of the aforementioned Nicolas, and for the handsome gift of three silver pots presented to me on behalf of you and the inhabitants of Dijon, both to me and to my wife, we thank you most humbly. Concerning the business of the town which you recommend to my attention in the said letters, certainly, my lords, so far as is possible, I am and always will be ready to labour when necessary with good and loyal intent, like the humblest hireling or officer of the town, just as I will attend to your own personal matters should you advise me of them or entrust them to me, with God's help, my most redoubted lords, whose grace I beseech to grant you long life and the fulfilment of your desires. Written at Bruges, 16 March 1472. Your wholly devoted servant, Jehan Gros.

8. Jean Coustain: peasant's son, courtier, poisoner, 1462[84]

Chastelain, *Oeuvres*, ed. Kervyn de Lettenhove, iv, pp. 234–65.

Jean Coustain was a coarse and brutal man, rough in understanding and in deed, a native of Burgundy brought up in service while he was young in the ducal chambers under his uncle Ymbert Coustain, a fine honest man who was also poor and from lowly stock. Ymbert had taught him to the best of his ability everything that had to be done in the duke's chamber. Jean applied himself diligently and followed in his uncle's footsteps, for he could see the road ahead of him was wide open, since his uncle was already old and feeble, and indeed Ymbert Coustain died at Arras and was spoken of after his death with great praise. And so the nephew Jean, who had already had intimate responsibility for the ducal body for some time with his uncle, one as master, the other as valet, was thrust into the post and was enriched by his predecessor's legacy. He quickly married a lady-in-waiting of the court named Isabel,

84 Discussed in Collard, *Le Crime de poison*, pp. 91, 151, 170, 251–2.

daughter of Jean Machefoing of Dijon, who had made his fortune as a
money-lender, and, even more importantly, niece of Philippe Machefoing, mayor of Dijon, a notable.[85] Thanks to this marriage and the
influence he enjoyed over the duke, Jean Coustain became big-headed.
The duke could clearly see what he was like, but he made allowances
and in his kindness let things pass, for there was no one on earth more
benign than he, nor anyone better able to conceal his true feelings from
his servants. This Jean Coustain was acquisitive beyond all measure,
and there was no office or favour he might not have if he could find a
way to ask for it ...

And so this servant became swollen with pride at the familiarity he
enjoyed with the duke, who in his old age locked himself away and was
difficult to approach, so much so that he considered himself the equal
of all the great men, save the duke's own nephews, and spoke to them
without due reverence. He did little to benefit others unless there was
a profit in it for him, and friendship or nobility counted for nought if
money was on offer. There was not a single memorable virtue in him, but
rather vice, coarseness and ingratitude. He was excessively lubricious,
a glutton for wine and food, rough in his innermost thoughts, ignorant
of letters, irreverent to the good and a man who took no account of
the virtue of others; and if he showed favour or friendship to some, he
only advanced wicked sorts like himself. His wife was just as proud
of her good fortune as he, and there was no pretty thing or precious
object that she could not have for herself and wear upon her body if
she dared to covet it, for she had the means. Moreover she enjoyed the
favour of the countess of Charolais[86] who made her her favourite, and
spent all her private rest time with her, even to the point of frequently
dressing in the same clothes as each other like two sisters. None of this
pleased the countess's husband, who for a long time hid his displeasure;
but in the end he grew weary of it, and revealed that he would much
rather that she was kept away from the countess, and that his wife did
not place such trust in her servant. He had noted several things about
[the servant] which displeased him, and more than any other he set as
much store by honour and propriety in his household as he did in his
own conduct. And so this Isabel, a creature of fortune as much as her
husband, noticed that the count of Charolais hated her, and that for a
long time he had been manoeuvring to have her cast out. Troubled, she

85 Isabeau de Machefoing would later take as her third husband Olivier de La Marche:
    see [4] above.
86 Isabelle of Bourbon: see [5] above.

resolved to seek revenge through her husband, or at least find a way through the duke to prevent her from being cast down, and she went to Jean to make her complaints. Seeing the count persisting in his attitude toward him and his wife, Jean Coustain conceived a hidden hatred of the count at the instigation of the Devil. He took the repudiation of his wife – which was now a fact – very hard, and he hated him for it; to which he added a further reason for hating the count, namely that because of this indignation against him and his household, and because the duke himself was very ill and in mortal danger and likely to be succeeded by the son, Coustain feared that his people would be cast out and that he himself would lose all his offices and gains. Rather than let this happen he preferred to settle things once and for all by an irreparable evil: he would dare to plot the count's death ...

While this plot was concealed in his false heart, and to bring the cursed plan to fruition, he sought the means to attain his goal. This Jean Coustain pretended to have important personal affairs to attend to in Burgundy where he came from. Having obtained permission from the duke, he took his leave and was away for the best part of four or five months, which was unusual, so much so that murmurs soon spread, with some saying 'This man is cunning, but he does not serve his sick master well when he stays away so long ...'

[In Burgundy Coustain recruits Jean de Vy, 'a fine squire with a good heart, but poor' to his plot, telling him he wishes to cause the death of a man named Charles without being caught. In return he will make Vy rich and raise his standing. Vy travels to Lombardy where he has a female friend who is expert in necromancy, and returns with the means of achieving Coustain's ends. Coustain returns to court at Brussels, leaving empty promises of rewards to Jean de Vy ...]

The count of Charolais was at Brussels at the time and travelled little because his father was not fully recovered [from illness]. Jean Coustain often went to see the count, dissembling all the while, hoping to reach his ends by gradually winning his confidence. It is said that he had already worked his plan out and had spied his opportunity carefully. In an outrageous and arrogant act, he served the count wine without first tasting from the cup while the count was separated from his own men in a small apartment in the duke's chambers, saying as he did so by way of a joke that the son could trust him because the father had never doubted him. Thinking no ill of it, the count had merely laughed and had taken the wine. But Coustain was not yet ready and was merely trying out his plan for another such occasion when he would make his attempt for real. Luckily the Good Lord prevented him, as you shall hear.

[Jean de Vy comes to Brussels to seek his reward from Coustain, in his possession copies of letters he had earlier received from the courtier which clearly
revealed the latter's guilt …]

When [Jean de Vy] came to Brussels it seemed to him that Coustain
had completely changed, for they were no longer in Burgundy speaking
together man to man, and now there he was in all his glory, full of
pride and scarcely willing to acknowledge him. Jean de Vy bided his
time patiently in the hope that in good time, Coustain would eventually recognise his services and remember what he had done for him.
But the longer he waited, the more time he wasted, for each time they
spoke Coustain gave him empty words at best, or else used a scornful
and haughty tone to be rid of him. And so it happened one day that
Jean de Vy, his heart full of anger against Coustain, saw him passing by
in the outer courtyard while he was himself out walking arm in arm
with another gentleman named Peter Von Hagenbach, an honest and
hearty sort.[87] And Jean de Vy said to Peter 'Do you see that ruffian Jean
Coustain walking past there, full of pride and ingratitude? By heavens
I tell you – and I don't care who knows it – I have it in my power to
dishonour and harm him more than any man has ever been dishonoured
and harmed, and I have his life or death in my hands. I can bring him as
low as he has risen high.' Hearing these words, Peter was taken aback
and fell silent, then said: 'Jean de Vy, what on earth are you saying! You
must be mad to say such unbelievable things! What harm can you do to
Jean Coustain? You're not the man for that, by God, not even a hundred
men like you could harm him. Stop this sort of talk, I beg you, because
you might be overheard by someone who could make you pay for it.'

[Jean de Vy persists, and persuades Hagenbach – a friend of Coustain's – to
arrange a meeting. Coustain tries to persuade Hagenbach that Vy's complaints
are frivolous, but agrees to a meeting which he then fails to attend. Vy complains
furiously to Hagenbach …]

Greatly annoyed, Hagenbach went back to Coustain and reprimanded
him for his conduct. But not wishing to beat about the bush, Coustain
interrupted and asked him, in return for eternal friendship, to kill de Vy
or have him done away with so he could be rid of him. He said he was
an evil wicked felon and that nothing would be lost by his death. But
Peter, who was wise and not easily moved to act in this way, put off the
deed by saying there was no reason to do this, for the gentleman had
not harmed him in anyway. And he left it at that.

87 W. Paravicini, 'Hagenbachs Hochzeit (1474). Ritterlich-höfische Kultur in Frankreich
    und Deutschland im 15. Jahrhundert', in K. Krimm and R. Brüning (eds), *Zwischen
    Burgund und dem Reich* (Oberrheinische Studien, 21: Stuttgart, 2003), pp. 13–60.

[Jean de Vy then solicits the help of Tristan de Toulongeon, ' a gentle knight quick of wit', determined to confess all …]

He sought out Tristan many times to speak to him, so much so that the knight eventually said to him:

'Jean de Vy, you have been pressing me for some time now to have a word with me at your ease and in private, and you lead me to believe the matter you wish to discuss is secret and of great importance. Since you seem in such great need, I am ready to listen to what you have to say. If you do not need to tell me your secret, keep it to yourself. If you have told it to anyone else, and if by any chance it gets out as a result, I have no desire to accept any blame.'

'By God', said Jean de Vy, 'My Lord, rest assured I have not told anyone else my secret, so I have no fear it will be revealed by another. I want to tell it to you, to know whether I should reveal it or not.'

'In that case I am content to listen', said the knight.

Then Jean told the whole story point by point: how Jean Coustain had first approached him and all the dealings between them, which was a dreadful thing to hear. But My Lord Tristan was subtle of mind, and as soon as the matter – most terrible to hear for a good heart – was broached, he interrupted Jean de Vy and asked him:

'Jean, since you have placed your trust in me and you have such a great and serious matter to reveal, would you not like there to be a second person here to listen, since two heads are better than one?'

'By Saint John', said Vy, 'I am happy to agree to that, so long as you choose someone you trust'.

'Indeed, I trust this person'.

At that point the knight had seen Peter von Hagenbach, whom Jean de Vy had first approached, and he hailed him over.

'Peter', said the knight, 'you see Jean de Vy here? He wants to tell us something important. Good sire, let's withdraw to our chambers where we can speak more freely than we can here'.

Once there, they closed themselves off at once and Jean de Vy told them the whole story from beginning to end, right to the last detail of the treasonous act.

[Toulongeon and Hagenbach persuade Vy to write it all down. They fetch him paper and pen and confine him under lock and key in the chamber. To the confession are attached the letters from Coustain to Vy which confirmed the

plot. Toulongeon has to make a decision quickly, for fear that Coustain will
either discover the affair and escape, or carry out his plan. Hagenbach and he
agree to reveal all to the count of Charolais, rather than to the duke. Charolais
admits them on his own to a private dressing chamber where, having heard of
the plot, he thanks the Lord for his lucky escape and promises he will never
forget their deeds or abandon them …]

Immediately after, the count took advice on how he should proceed. It
was deemed expedient to assemble before him as quickly as possible all
the knights of the Order (of the Golden Fleece) who were at court at that
time, along with several of his closest advisers. Once all were present,
the terrible story was revealed and they were all appalled. Coustain's
letter was shown to them, which they all recognised as being from
him. The count then asked what they thought was the right thing to
do, and they all concluded that he should go to his father the duke with
all of them for company, tell him all and seek his advice … So the son
went to the duke his father with some knights of the Order, that is to
say [Antoine] Lord of Croy, his brother Jean the Bastard of Burgundy,
[Jean V] of Créquy, [Jean IV] of Auxy,[88] Adolf of Cleves and My Lord
Simon de Lalaing.

[The count tells the duke he has uncovered a plot against his life without giving
the details. The duke 'with the prudence that comes with age' asks Charles if he
is certain, and how he has come by the news …]

'My Lord,' said the count, 'I have certain proof of the matter and of the
identity of those responsible, so much so that their guilt will be there for
all to behold, and above all for you, My Lord, to see. The principal figure
who has plotted my death and perdition is Jean Coustain, whom you have
raised and who is in your service. Since, my Lord, it is not fitting that
I should punish any of your people, and that this is your prerogative, I
beg you My Lord to give me your advice to find an appropriate way of
resolving this matter. And so that you can be certain of what I say, here
are the lords who have seen and heard how this matter has been dealt
with, and here is the record of it written by noble knights and esquires,
your own servants, along with letters from Jean Coustain written in his
own hand and signed by him which declare his wicked intent.

[The duke is flabbergasted. Before getting to the main point he asks who the
informants were and is told it was his own servants, Toulongeon and Hagenbach …]

88 Appointed mentor to the young count of Charolais by Philip the Good, and therefore
entrusted with his moral and chivalric upbringing.

This news gnawed at the duke's heart and he was angry, not at the fact that the plot had been uncovered, but rather that they had not come to him first before going to his son, for they had sworn their oath to him, he said, and for that reason he should precede the son in the performance of their duties. And the duke had a reason for all this, because had the news come to him first, he might have nipped the wicked valet's plans in the bud without harming or causing a scandal in his household, which he had always managed to avoid. But now he could see his household was stained in the most ugly fashion and that this could not be easily remedied, he was indignant at those who had brought the matter up. Nonetheless wishing to satisfy his son, he told him that punishment was entirely fitting, and that without doubt he would provide justice. But since it was night-time and for his own peace he begged his son to delay arresting the malefactor: he could arrest Coustain at daybreak when he would be made to pay, and the duke was quite happy that Coustain be seized and put in a safe place, and that he, the count, against whom the offence had been planned, could be the judge of the matter.

[The duke has a bad night. The count orders the Lord of Auxy and Philippe de Crèvecoeur to keep a look out with a certain number of the count's own archers. With the duke's agreement Coustain will be taken by these men to the castle at Rupelmonde where he will be questioned. The next day, the duke upbraids Tristan de Toulongeon for going to Charolais first, against the terms of his oath of service ...]

'My most redoubted and sovereign Lord', said the knight, 'I recognise and acknowledge you for what you are to me, as befits your highness. I acted only out of goodwill and in the hope of preventing a greater evil, which I sensed was imminent, and so in my horror I hastened to him around whom the net was closing for fear that this most noble prince, your son, should fall innocently and through the traitor's hands into death's pit, which – had I delayed – would have brought you much bitterness and mischief through my doing, and for which I would never again be worthy of standing in your sight, you whom I must address in complete humility. And if anyone other than you, My Lord, with the exception of the princes of your blood, should wish to accuse me of acting against my honour in this matter or hold me to be at fault, whoever he might be, I am a gentleman, and from such stock as you have seen through my fathers and forefathers who have served you, and I will answer any such charge as befits the case and my honour, and in such a way, I trust, that my honour will not be sullied. Believe me, My Lord, my heart matches my words and more.'

'By Saint John', said the duke, 'if your heart did not match your words you would be worth less, for a gentleman must always love honour more than life itself. Your forefathers have served me loyally, and have died valiantly and honourably in my service. I should therefore place all the more trust in you; by the same token I should be all the more angry when you go against my will'.

'My Lord', said the knight, 'if God himself and you have taken it ill, I swear upon all that I owe you both that I acted only out of good faith and to prevent evil ... My Lord, I recommend myself to your benign nature and to your noble and virtuous courage, of which the earth is full.'

[Toulongeon is forgiven, but the duke 'was never content with Peter von Hagenbach again, or at least for a long time'.]

Sunday morning arrived, when Jean Coustain would have to go to Rupelmonde by consent of the duke. The duke had risen early to hunt in his grounds at Brussels to get away from Coustain, and to give those whose task it was to take him off a chance to do so. The duke himself had told Coustain that he should be ready to depart with the lord of Auxy. So Coustain went to get his boots on, and he told his barber to make ready to accompany him too. Jean feared something bad was about to happen because he had noticed how, all night long, and still at the present time, he was under close watch. So he took his bow and some arrows anyway and pretended nothing was wrong, and went to the hunting grounds with his master to shoot at deer.[89] All the while the Bastard of Burgundy and several others followed him and kept an eye out, never letting him out of their sight. The duke told Jean Coustain again that he should get ready and hear mass, and that after he should depart with the lord of Auxy. Off he went, and again he told his barber to prepare for some sport, just the two of them. The lord of Auxy, who knew just what he had to do, also prepared himself, and in his company were all the count of Charolais's archers who waited only for Coustain's arrival. Given the burden upon him, Coustain was happy to forgo mass. Instead he stood in the door of his chambers and like a hearty fellow invited each person that passed to come and dine with him. But everyone fled from him. Eventually he took a poor valet named Poncelet who used to keep him company, for it may be surmised that Poncelet knew nothing of the case against Coustain. Once the meal was over and

89 By attending, despite having been asked to prepare for another task, Jean Coustain was gate-crashing the hunting party which had its own protocol and procedures, from the assembly to the business of the hunt: Niedermann, *Das Jagdwesen*, pp. 300–6.

the duke had gone to mass, Coustain went back up, thinking he would go to the oratory to see the duke, as was his wont. He knocked but no one answered, for the duke had forbidden anyone to open the door to him. In the end, however, a clerk of the chapel opened the door a little because his knocking was so insistent. Coustain violently, shamelessly and irreverently pushed his way in, puffed up like a boar before the hounds, and without deference he said to the duke:

'Well, look at me. What am I to do? Where will I go?'

'I told you to go with the lord of Auxy, wherever he wants to take you', said the duke.

'Indeed!' said Coustain, 'so that's it? That's what I get for my service? Upon my death, worthy sire, I can see I've spent my time well. I would have been better off serving a swineherd.'

And at that he left the oratory full of spite and rage, without a bow or a word of courtesy, slamming the door behind him so hard that the like had never been seen. Before he did so, however, the duke responded to his last villainous utterance coldly:

'Jean! I have fed you too fat.'

And that was the truth, for never had the body of a villain been so richly fed, nor received such honour beyond its merit. It so happened that the Lord of Croy and his brother Jean were in the oratory too at that time, and they were horrified by such villainous language and misconduct in the presence of a duke. They said that there had never been a worse or more villainous servant.

With only his barber for company, Jean Coustain mounted his horse and went to the lord of Auxy's house, and in the middle of a fine square which was there he found a great many mounted archers, fully equipped. When he saw them he said aloud 'What are you lot doing here? Are you going off to do so some drinking in the tavern? Where do you fancy going?' And then turning upon the lord of Auxy he said 'Ah, there you are, lanky. Aren't you ready today?'

And so he pretended nothing was wrong, although no doubt he imagined there was, because I have heard that the prince had told him something of his predicament. But this wicked man placed such trust in his master that he believed nothing would come of it, and that he would be able to get out of it unscathed. He was powerful and so blinded by his fortune that nothing seemed to scare him.

Brussels was full of rumours at this time, and noblemen did nothing but whisper to one another about this turn of events. They could scarcely have been more surprised than if they had suddenly found they had horns on their head at the news that in the space of a single night, the fortune of such a great man could change so utterly – even to the point that he could be locked up for the crime of treason against God and man.

[Confronted with documentary proof of his crime, Coustain is taken to Rupel-monde.]

The next day the count of Charolais came himself, with the Lord of Croy, the Bastard of Burgundy and the bishop of Tournai to interro-gate Coustain. Without torture or anything else he confessed his crime and wicked enterprise in full, but still did not think he would die for it. Coustain's accuser Jean de Vy was also taken to Rupelmonde, neither aware of the other's presence, and he was also interrogated, but under torture, and he too confessed to a crime worthy of death. The count was afraid that if he tarried too long in meting out justice to this wicked man, by means of his father the duke (who was less prompt in extreme rigour than he) Jean Coustain might escape and reach safety. This was something the count wished to avoid at all costs. So taking counsel from those who had accompanied him, he agreed to have him killed sooner rather than later. The count ordered that Coustain should make his confession to his own confessor, a certain Master Enguerrand, a Dominican.[90]

[Coustain eventually confesses, and confides an even more terrible secret to Master Enguerrand, who advises him to tell this directly to the count ...]

So Master Enguerrand went to the count and told him, not about the confession itself, but that Coustain's salvation required him to speak directly to the prince. So the count went down to see him on a terrace which had a plaster floor, where Jean was already stripped to his under-shirt, ready for the executioner. Jean and the count stood apart from the others, and Coustain told him the secret he had confessed to Master Enguerrand. The count blanched and made the sign of the Cross upon himself several times over when he heard what the sinner had to say; then, full of horror, he withdrew to another chamber from where, behind a trellis, he saw the traitor executed. Once he was in the hands of the executioner and had been blindfolded, Coustain reverted to his rough native Burgundian tongue, the coarsest speech imaginable, mouthing

90 Enguerran Seignart: see [27] below.

his words in his vulgar primitive nature, and he said that there had never been a bigger sinner than him. In the end he turned to words of regret for his wife and children, but Master Enguerrand reprimanded him again, saying 'What on earth is this, Jean? You promised me you would think of no earthly things and that you would only pray to the Lord for mercy. Have you given up on this worthy intention? My friend, turn your heart to God, don't worry about the rest. Give up your soul and your heart, for He who awaits you is nigh.' 'Oh well then, good father, I place myself entirely in His kindness. Please pray to Him for me.' And as he finished, his head flew off, and he died. Immediately after Jean de Vy was brought in to be put to death, for he had been kept secretly in the same place. When de Vy learned of his fate from the confessor he struggled fiercely, saying 'How on earth is this? I raised the accusation of treason and saved my lord of Charolais's life, and now they want to kill me? By what right? What human heart could think this was fair? As long as I live I won't believe this wrong could be done to me by my lord, nor by any other.' 'Heavens,' it was said to him, 'there's no point in struggling against it. You are condemned to death, and the author of your death, Jean Coustain, is dead himself and in two pieces. Think now only of your soul, because that is what you have to do.' 'By Saint John, I will not!' said Jean de Vy, 'Not until I see Coustain's body in the way you describe will I believe he is dead, nor that I myself have to die. Perhaps you just want to scare me for your own ends.' 'Jean, there is no question of simply scaring you. Come and you shall see what you ask for.' And so he went to see, but did not return – for he accepted confession and died by the sword like the other one.

III: THE ORDER OF THE GOLDEN FLEECE

Introduction

The foundation of the Burgundian curial Order of chivalry known as the Golden Fleece was proclaimed on the market place at Bruges on behalf of Philip the Good during the festivities of his wedding to Isabella of Portugal in January 1430.[1] Modelled on the English royal Order of the Garter which the duke had earlier been invited to join [9], for most of our period the membership numbered thirty-one knights (including the sovereign) under the patronage of Saint Andrew.[2] A total of sixteen chapters were held down to 1516.[3] The regulating document of the Order was its statutes [10], promulgated in French in 1431, revised in 1446, and translated into Dutch, German and Latin for the benefit of new members by the end of our period.[4] In 1500, Olivier de La Marche recorded for Philip the Fair the manner in which a chapter of the Order should be held [11]. Recently published minutes of the chapters of the Order to 1468 afford an understanding of how its affairs were conducted in conclave [12c and notes], while those of town councils and the accounts of other institutions [12a, d] reveal something of the impact of chapters on urban life. There is also a valuable account of the 1501 Brussels chapter of the Order

---

1 D'A.J.D. Boulton, *The knights of the crown. The monarchical orders of knighthood in later medieval Europe, 1325–1520* (2nd edn, Woodbridge/New York, 2000), pp. 356–96; R. De Smedt (ed.), *Les Chevaliers de la Toison d'Or: notices bio-bibliographiques* (2nd edn, Frankfurt-am-Main, 2000).

2 The Order originally had 25 members, increased to 31 in 1433, and to 50 by Charles V in 1516. Boulton points out this last increase was to take account of 'the vastly increased number' of Charles V's subjects (p. 374). It is possible Philip the Good increased membership in 1433 for similar reasons: since founding the Order in January 1430, he had become duke of Brabant, and had taken full possession of the counties of Hainaut, Holland and Zeeland.

3 Boulton, *The knights of the crown*, p. 387 n. 124.

4 Although the officer known as the *greffier* had the task of referring to the statutes when it was required, some members had their own copies of the statutes made (of which twenty survive from the fifteenth century alone): J. Lemaire, 'Considérations codicologiques sur les manuscrits des statuts de l'Ordre de la Toison d'Or', in P. Cockshaw and C. Van den Bergen-Pantens (eds), *L'Ordre de la Toison d'or, de Philippe le Bon à Philippe le Beau (1430–1505): idéal ou reflet d'une société?* (Brussels, 1996), pp. 31–8, at pp. 31–2, 37. The central role of the statutes is confirmed in the careful reservations which Alfonso II of Aragon made on accepting them in 1445. S. Dünnebeil (ed.), *Die Protokollbücher des Ordens vom Goldenen Vlies, I (1430–67); II (1468)* (Stuttgart, 2002–3), i, p. 84. In 1461 the Milanese ambassador Prospero da Camogli attempted to obtain a copy of the statutes for his master at the Saint-Omer chapter: *Dispatches* II, p. 350.

by the ambassador of Francesco II Gonzaga, Niccolò Frigio, which may be read in translation elsewhere.[5]

The political value of the Order to the Valois dukes and their Habsburg successors lay in the acceptance on oath of the demanding statutes by a membership of high-ranking noblemen from the Burgundian dominions, and by a smaller but growing number of foreign rulers and dignitaries. The potential of the statutes to promote loyalty, resolve conflict and regulate conduct is clear.[6] In the notes accompanying our texts below, the reader will encounter illustrations of how these prescriptions were applied in practice. In chapter, the conduct of members (those present as well as those represented by proxy) was subject to investigation as a means of upholding the collective responsibility of a chivalric elite to the public weal and to Holy Church. According to Olivier de La Marche, this part of proceedings constituted 'an office in which the knights had to render account, not for their money or expenses or wealth, but for their honour'.[7] The process could be a lengthy one – four days were spent on the matter at Bruges in 1435, for instance.[8] That the exercise was no formality finds ample illustration in the treatment of Philippe de Ternant in 1451 discussed below [12c], and in the breath-taking frankness of the knights' collective critique of Charles the Bold's conduct in 1468 and 1473 (translated by Richard Vaughan elsewhere).[9] Given what was expected of member knights, it is difficult to believe that the Order's political importance was fundamentally undermined by the irregularity of its chapters or by a record of attendance that was far from perfect.[10] The prescription of the daily wearing of the collar

5 W. Prizer, 'Music and ceremonial in the Low Countries: Philip the Fair and the Order of the Golden Fleece', *Early Music History* 5 (1985), pp. 113–53.

6 A potential that was clear, but not always realised. At Bruges in 1468, Adolf of Egmond was reprimanded for making war on a fellow member of the Order: Vaughan, *Charles the Bold*, p. 113. However, the Order failed to mediate between Maximilian and the rebels against his regency – particularly the main cities of Flanders, but also certain knights of the Fleece, among them Louis of Gruuthuse and Adolf of Cleves: W. Blockmans, 'Autocratie ou polyarchie? La lutte pour le pouvoir politique en Flandre de 1482 à 1492, d'après des documents inédits', *Bulletin de la Commission royale d'histoire* 140 (1974), pp. 257–368, at p. 284.

7 La Marche, *Mémoires*, ii, p. 84.

8 Jean Lefèvre de Saint-Rémy, *Chronique*, ed. F. Morand, 2 vols (Paris 1876–81), ii, p. 374.

9 Vaughan, *Charles the Bold*, pp. 172–8; B. Sterchi, *Der Orden vom Goldenen Vlies und die burgundischen Überläufer von 1477* (Bern, 2003), pp. 51–9. This element of the proceedings created an opportunity to express views on political conduct which may not have been readily available in day-to-day business. Prior to the 1461 chapter, the Milanese ambassador Prospero da Camogli learned that Philip the Good's lax conduct of his affairs would be the subject of 'far from gentle mention' in chapter: *Dispatches*, ii, p. 344.

10 An average of fewer than fourteen knights (i.e., less than 50%) attended the chapters which took place between 1431 and 1491. There were never more than 20 knights present (Arras, 1435), and once as few as 5 (Bruges, 1478): J. Paviot, 'Étude préliminaire', in De Smedt, *Les Chevaliers de la Toison d'Or*, pp. xv–xxxii, at p. xxi. Meetings of the Order were also far less regular than every three years as the revised statutes of 1446 envisaged, although they did average at least two per decade up to and including the 1470s.

by men who were often in the presence of the duke was a weighty reminder of the responsibilities of membership.[11] While the latter are manifest in our documents, so too are the benefits which emerge in the statutes. In 1473 Charles the Bold extended the privileges of membership by granting knights access to all councils of ducal government, the prince's protection at all times, a privileged position close to the ruler in church and upon entering or leaving one of his towns, and freedom from taxation on food and drink.[12] Membership clearly added lustre to the reputation of its members and of their lineage: the epitaph of Simon de Lalaing noted that 'First and foremost he bore the Order of the Fleece/ And exalted the honour of his line', while according to the author of the epitaph of Jean de Lannoy, 'He was one of the knights of the Fleece/ a peer and companion of kings and princes'.[13] Each of these points illustrates the importance of the Golden Fleece to the sovereign and knights outside the solemn but infrequent occasions of the chapter. We might add that the office-holders of the Order were generally key figures in the daily business of ducal administration: Guillaume Fillastre, second chancellor, was head of the duke's council; Jean Lefèvre de Saint-Rémy, chief herald of the Order, was one of the most travelled ducal diplomats at court; Martin Steenberghe, *greffier*, was a ducal secretary. The first and last of these men also held positions in two of the most important churches in the Low Countries, Fillastre as bishop of Tournai, Steenberghe as deacon of the church of Sainte-Gudule in Brussels.

There are at least two further political roles that might be ascribed to the Order, one of which has been overemphasised, the other neglected. Careful study of the membership undermines the view that it served as an effective means of integrating the duke's disparate domains.[14] Noblemen from the ducal dominions did indeed constitute the vast majority of members admitted by 1477, but the pattern of recruitment by region was uneven: the representation of some territories was slight (Brabant never having more than two members), while that of others was disproportionately high (Flanders, Artois and Picardy accounting for around half of the membership under the Valois dukes, a proportion which declined somewhat under the Habsburgs). Even the geographical setting of chapters fails to support the integration thesis: of the first fifteen chapters, eight took place in Flanders or Artois, just three in Brabant (and only then if one includes Mechelen, a separate lordship), two in Hainaut, and one

11 Although in 1500, according to the records of the Order, 'A general fault was found among all (the members), that is to say, that they did not wear their collars every day as they should, and for which they were eligible to be fined 8 *sous* for each day they were in default': cited in Sterchi, *Der Orden vom Goldenen Vlies*, p. 17 n. 44.

12 Paviot, 'Étude préliminaire', p. xxi. From 1474 the knights were accorded a place apart in the household ordonnances: Paravicini, 'Ordre et règle', p. 328.

13 C. Thiry, 'L'Ordre et ses chevaliers dans les textes littéraires français', in Cockshaw and Van den Bergen-Pantens (eds), *L'Ordre de la Toison d'or*, pp. 110–14, at p. 114.

14 A view expressed in Vaughan, *Philip the Good*, p. 161, but cf. J. Richard, 'Le Rôle politique de l'ordre sous Philippe le Bon et Charles le Téméraire', in Cockshaw and Van den Bergen-Pantens (eds), *L'Ordre de la Toison d'or*, pp. 67–70, at p. 69; and J. Paviot, 'Le Recrutement des chevaliers de l'Ordre de la Toison d'or (1430–1505)', in ibid., pp. 75–9.

each in the county of Holland and the duchy of Burgundy. None took place in the county of Burgundy. It might be objected that this pattern broadly reflects the itineration of the court, but Brabant, a region which was also very under-represented in terms of membership, hosted far fewer meetings than its impor-tance in ducal itineraries would suggest. To an even greater extent than the court, the Order served as a recruiting ground for members of a select group of families – the Croys and Luxembourgs in the van.[15]

A more neglected dimension of the political importance of the Golden Fleece was its relevance to urban society. The business of the Order was conducted behind closed doors in the chapter properly speaking, but we must not forget that these exclusive proceedings formed part of a wider series of public events which constituted the *fête* of the Golden Fleece. The *fête* included the arrival of the sovereign, knights and their accompanying retinues; the regular formal processions through major thoroughfares between ducal residence and the venue for the chapter; the solemn masses in principal churches; and the street theatre and jousts which took place throughout the event. It is important to note that every one of the feasts in our period took place in a major town or city. Three were held in cosmopolitan Bruges (1432, 1468, 1478), a city which addi-tionally hosted the launch of the Order, and three were also held in the emerging capital, Brussels (1435, 1501, 1517).[16] The strategically located town of Saint-Omer (1440, 1461) hosted two feasts, as did Lille (1431, 1436). A wide range of other ducal towns all hosted one – Dijon (1433), Ghent (1445), Mons (1451), The Hague (1456), Valenciennes (1473), 'sHertogenbosch (1481), Mechelen (1491) and Middelburg (1505).[17] From this list we may conclude that the *fête* of the Order of the Golden Fleece was an exceptional event in the life of individual towns, but that these events were nonetheless essentially urban in nature – even more so than the court which continued to make use of non-urban residences. The presence of a large urban audience for proceedings and the resulting 'perfor-mative ostentation' of the feasts are well-attested in contemporary sources.[18] Spectators came from near and far.[19] Olivier de La Marche relates how, in 1445,

15 Paviot notes the recruitment across six generations of no fewer than 12 members of the Luxembourg clan, and 10 members of the Croy family in its various branches across three generations: Paviot, 'Le Recrutement des chevaliers de l'Ordre de la Toison d'or', p. 76. Vertical and horizontal kin ties between members are discussed further in L. Horowski, '*XXXJ chevaliers sans reproche*. Der Orden vom Goldenen Vlies als Instru-ment burgundischer Elitenpolitik, 1430–77', *Sacra Militia* 1 (2000), pp. 187–234.

16 In 1468 the start of proceedings of the chapter were delayed from 30 April to 4 May to avoid a clash with the procession of the Holy Blood in Bruges, because 'the church-men, magistrates, foreign merchants, ordinary burgesses, guildsmen, inhabitants and governors of the said town are busy': Dünnebeil (ed.), *Die Protokollbücher II*, pp. 40–1.

17 The 1519 chapter was held in Barcelona.

18 G. Meville, 'Rituelle Ostentation und pragmatische Inquisition', in G. Duchhardt and G. Melville (eds), *Im Spannungsfeld von Recht und Ritual* (Cologne, 1997), pp. 215–87, at p. 267.

19 Mathieu d'Escouchy travelled roughly 50 miles in 1451 from Péronne (where he held the office of *prévôt*) to Mons 'to see [the chapter] at my ease, with all the ceremony that was there': *Chroniques*, ed. du Fresne de Beaucourt, i, pp. 346–55. Prospero da

the knights processed 'through the city of Ghent, accompanied by a great many noblemen from home and abroad and by ambassadors, and the streets of the town were full with people'.[20] At the first Habsburg chapter (Bruges, 1478), a Flemish spectator observed the decoration of Sint-Salvators church and described a special stage which was erected in front of the roodscreen for the knights of the Order to take their seats in full view of those assembled for the occasion. The jousts which commonly punctuated proceedings took place on market places in front of urban audiences.

Did civic society merely contemplate the Order of the Golden Fleece when it came to town? To some extent the answer to this question must be yes. Aldermen certainly joined courtiers at Saint-Omer (1461) on specially erected stands to watch the jousts, and were invited to join them at feasts [11]. The court poet Jean Molinet extolled the attributes of the city of Valenciennes when the 1473 chapter took place there, while the city rhetorician Jan Smeken wrote a play in praise of the Order at Brussels in 1516.[21] Despite such interaction, it remains the case that the Golden Fleece was not born of urban traditions and was indeed 'the best example of a festivity artificially embedded in the urban landscape'.[22] But the act of contemplation must not in itself be passed over without further comment. Townsfolk were not simply observing 'a symbol of [ducal] power ... in which the original character of a primitive and sacred game [was] particularly conspicuous'.[23] In the statutes of the Order and in the conduct of its affairs, chivalry was elevated to a principle of government: the public weal itself was the avowed concern.[24] In the midst of the feast, affairs of the highest importance were being deliberated by the governing elite of the duke's lands and by the prince's most valued foreign allies or their representatives. Like all major summits of the day, proceedings were surrounded by religious ritual – masses and processions framed the negotiations at the treaty of Arras, for example, where they were observed and recorded in a journal by Anthoine de la Taverne, native of the town and *prévôt* of the local abbey of Saint-Vaast.[25] The import of this side of proceedings was not lost on a Milanese observer of the 1461 chapter: 'In these [ceremonies] the Duke of Burgundy

Camogli attended the Saint-Omer chapter of 1461 and wrote back fulsomely on the subject to his principal: *Dispatches*, ii, pp. 343–54.

20 *Mémoires*, ed. H. Beaune and J. d'Arbaumont, ii, pp. 87.

21 J. Devaux, 'Molinet dramaturge: une moralité inédite jouée lors du chapitre valenciennois de la Toison d'Or (1473)', *RN* 78 (1996), pp. 35–47; G. Degroote (ed.), *Jan Smeken: Gedicht op de feesten ter eere van het Gulden Vlies in 1516* (Antwerp, 1946).

22 Lecuppre-Desjardin, *Ville des cérémonies*, pp. 114, 161.

23 J. Huizinga, *The waning of the Middle Ages* (7th edn, Harmondsworth, 1979), pp. 84, 86.

24 A. Vanderjagt, 'The princely culture of the Valois dukes of Burgundy', in M. Gosman, A. MacDonald and A. Vanderjagt (eds), *Princes and princely culture, 1450–1650*, 2 vols (Leiden, 2003–5), i, pp. 1–29.

25 A. Bossuat (ed.), *Antoine de la Taverne: Journal de la paix d'Arras faite en l'abbaye de Saint-Vaast entre Charles VII et Philippe le Bon* (Arras, 1936).

exemplified three things: worship, lofty solemnity, ritual'.[26] We can only guess whether civic society felt excluded and intimidated by these ceremonies, or whether its members were left impressed and reassured.

9. The founding of the Order

Chastelain, *Oeuvres*, ed. Kervyn de Lettenhove, ii, pp. 9–14.

How the duke of Bedford sought to have too great an influence over the duke of Burgundy and how he proposed that he become a member of the Order of the Garter

You have already heard how the present duke had given the hand of his sister Anne in marriage to the duke of Bedford,[27] so-called regent of France in the name of his nephew, the young king Henry [VI] of England, and how, because of alliances as binding as this marriage, reinforcing the first general alliance[28] which had been made between the King of England and the duke, there existed between the regent and the duke of Burgundy a particular familiarity, along with frequent and convivial exchanges (at least on the face of it), such as there often are among men who have to do with each other on a daily basis, both because of their fraternal relations and because of the many pressing affairs of this kingdom which each, in his own part of it, sought to deal with, the one as a regent who had entered the land as a conqueror, the other, whose lordship there was natural, in pursuit of his just cause. In this manner they got along well enough for a long time, until pride led the English to show their true colours as usual, and to seek to have the better of their allies, and led this English duke away from his customary good ways. Seeking to dominate his brother-in-law the duke of Burgundy, the duke of Bedford quietly pressurised him by many haughty acts as the regent of the young English king, who at that time called himself the King of France (as indeed the duke of Burgundy then considered Henry to be, because of the just quarrel he had against the true heir to the throne of France).

It is true that some time before relations grew cold between them, the duke regent, thinking how best he might secure durable English rule in France (the strongest part of which he felt he had on his side by

---

26 *Dispatches*, ii, p. 348.

27 Anne of Burgundy was married to John duke of Bedford in 1423.

28 Sealed by the treaty of Troyes (1420).

marriage and sworn alliance, that is to say, the duke of Burgundy), found
himself at a gathering with his ally, and proposed to him that in order
to strengthen and make stable the love and alliance between them, the
duke of Burgundy might like to become a member of the Order of the
Garter, of which so many great princes had been brothers in the past,
and indeed still were. To achieve his aim as quickly as he could, the
duke of Bedford, hoping to win the duke of Burgundy over, asked him
urgently to take the Order for the honour of the English king and all
his line, for this was what the king and his entourage wanted more
than anything in the world, he said, and there was nothing more fine
or fitting for the King or the duke of Burgundy than that they should
always be one and the same, linked in perpetual friendship, for together
they would make all the nations and royal powers in the Christian world
bend before them. The duke of Bedford genuinely meant what he said,
and he hoped that he would be able to achieve his ends. However, the
young wise duke of Burgundy was not about to do anything without
thinking long and hard about it, and noting the gravity of the request,
and how an attempt was being made to turn his freedom into obligation by entreaties which, he felt, he should not be moved by, he found
within himself elegant words which neither refused nor gave hope of
acceptance of the offer, and in this way he hoped to avoid the question by promising to think further on it, and thereby end all talk of it.
However, the duke was so hard pressed by his brother-in-law that in the
end he was going to have to say either yes or no, and he saw no other
way out of it. Then the duke of Burgundy began to reflect on the root of
his extraction, and how he came from a noble house which none of his
predecessors had ever reduced to slavery; and where his nature inclined
him to show his affections, and where more reasonably he was inclined
to offer resistance, even if at the present time he was obliged by doleful
circumstances to pretend otherwise. Not having a cordial love of the
English, the duke thought to himself that he did not wish to become
their perpetual ally, and thereby relinquish his forefathers. Rather, he
prayed to God that he would be permitted life enough to reach his true
goal. He also thought to himself that if he accepted this Order he would
be obliged for the rest of his life by ever stronger bonds, promises and
oaths from which he would never be able to extricate himself. Then,
suddenly, a crafty solution came to him. Thanking his brother-in-law
most graciously for the honour he had offered him – an honour which
he held in great esteem – he said that, for some time now, he had been
thinking of establishing an Order himself, and that he had discussed
the matter in secret with his closest advisers, and had looked into the

arrangements which would be appropriate;[29] and since the proposal had already been mooted, it did not seem honourable to him to not go through with it; and, indeed, he sought his brother-in-law's support in this. The duke of Burgundy then humbly set forth the reasons why he thought he should be excused, pretending that had it not been for this, he would have consented to his brother-in-law's request, for he sought to maintain his own just cause and the duke of Bedford's friendship.

[The duke of Bedford is taken aback at this unexpected reply, but recognising the honesty of the reason, and not thinking as deeply as the duke, did not trouble him further – which was just what the duke wanted.]

All this should be noted by those who in years to come might be led to wonder what led this duke to establish so high and excellent an Order as that of the Golden Fleece, for in searching they will find that he was led to do this by the very special loyalty that he felt toward his mother house, the house of France, from which he had no intention nor desire to be separated for any reason, whether turn of fortune, accident or aching wound, which he fully hoped would be healed.[30]

10. The statutes of the Order

Lefèvre de Saint-Rémy, *Chronique*, i, pp. 210–43

[Copy of the letters founding the noble Order and confraternity of the Golden Fleece, issued at Lille, 27 November 1431.[31]]

Philip, by the grace of God duke of Burgundy, Lotharingia, Brabant and Limburg, count of Flanders, Artois and Burgundy palatine, of Hainaut, Holland, Zeeland and Namur, marquis of the Holy Roman Empire, lord of Frisia, Salins and Malines, let it be known to all, in the present and in times to come, that out of our great and perfect love for the noble estate and order of chivalry – the which, through most ardent and singular affection, we seek to honour and augment, and through which the true Christian faith of Our Lady Holy Church, and the tranquility and prosperity of the public weal are, as they should be, defended and maintained; for the glory and praise of the All Mighty, our Creator and

---

29 A project of the statutes was already in existence in 1429: J. Paviot, 'Du nouveau sur la création de la Toison d'Or', *Journal des Savants* 2002, pp. 279–98.

30 A reference to the event which led Philip the Good to ally with the English in the first place – the murder of his father John the Fearless in 1419 in which the Dauphin, by now King Charles VII, was implicated.

31 Lefèvre gives the revised version of the statutes of 1446.

Redeemer; in reverence to the glorious Virgin Mary and in honour of St Andrew, apostle and martyr; and for the encouragement of virtue and right conduct, we, on the tenth day of January in the year of Our Lord 1430, which was the day of our marriage to our dear and most beloved companion Isabella in our city of Bruges, ordained and created – and, by the present letters, ordain and create – an Order and brotherhood of chivalry or most pleasant company of a certain number of knights which we wish to be called the Order of the Golden Fleece, in the form, condition and manner of the statutes and articles which follow.

First, we decree that in this Order there will be thirty-one knights, gentlemen in name and in arms and without reproach, of whom we, in our lifetime – and after us, our successors the dukes of Burgundy – will be the head and sovereign.

To enter the Order, the brothers and knights must quit all other Orders to which they may belong, either princely or a confraternity, with the exception of emperors, kings or dukes who may be a member of this Order and of any other of which they are the head,[32] but only so long as this is by our consent, by that of our successors as sovereign, and by the brothers of the Order as agreed in chapter and not otherwise.

So that this Order and its members will be known to all, we will give to each of the knights once only a golden collar bearing our device, that is to say a flint striking a firestone from which sparks issue; and at the end of this collar there will be a representation of a golden fleece.[33] The collar, which will always belong to the Order, will be worn every day by us and by our successors, and by each of the knights of the Order, openly around the neck, on pain of having a mass said to the value of 4 *sous*, and of paying 4 *sous* for alms on their conscience for each day they fail to wear it, except when they are in arms, at which times it will suffice to wear the fleece without the collar, should they so wish. Also, if the collar has to be repaired, it can be given to a jeweller and no fine need be paid for the days it is not worn; likewise if a long journey has to be undertaken, or for reasons of illness or personal security. The collar cannot be enriched with precious stones or by other means, nor it can ever be given, sold, pledged or alienated for any reason whatsoever.

So that there should be concord within the Order, all knights are obliged

32 The exception of existing heads of Orders was introduced at the tenth chapter at Saint-Omer in 1440 in advance of the election of Charles of Orléans, member of the Order of the Porcupine founded by his father in 1394: Dünnebeil (ed.), *Protokollbücher I*, 84.

33 For illustrations see Boulton, *The knights of the crown*, p. 368.

on entering to promise to love us and our successors as sovereigns of the Order, and each other, truly and well, and to promote and advance the honour and profit – and to avoid the dishonour and harm – of those who belong to the Order. And if they hear anything said against the honour of any member of the Order, they are obliged to excuse him to the best of their ability.

[The statutes go on to explain that if an accuser continues to make public his charges, knights are obliged to report the matter to the member concerned and to the chapter.]

The knights will promise that if anyone attempts to harm us or our successors by military action, or our lands, vassals and subjects; or if we, or our successors as sovereigns, take up arms for the defence of the Christian faith, or to defend, maintain or reestablish the dignity, state or liberty of Mother Church and the Apostolic See of Rome,[34] then the knights of the said Order are obliged to serve us, the mighty in person, the less strong in return for reasonable wages, unless they have a good reason which prevents them, in which case they are excused.[35]

For this reason, and for our great love of and confidence in our brothers, the knights of the said Order, we and our successors decree that we will not undertake wars or other such weighty matters without first consulting the greater part of the brother knights, to have their opinion and good counsel, except for matters which have to be dealt with secretly or without delay, and in which consultation might be prejudicial to the said undertakings.

In like fashion the knights of our Order, our vassals or subjects, or those

34 While these objectives are commonly linked to Philip the Good's crusading plans, they could be applied to matters closer to home as well. At the Hague chapter (1456) Reinoud van Brederode was charged in a famous case with breaking the statute 'to preserve and defend the Church and obey the Apostolic See'. Brederode's error was to support his own brother's candidacy for the bishopric of Utrecht, despite Calixtus III's approval of Philip the Good's candidate, David, formerly bishop of Thérouanne, one of the duke's bastards. In the course of Brederode's hearing at the Hague chapter, papal letters nominating David to the see, 'corrected in the hand of our Holy Father', were exhibited to the recalcitrant noble 'so he could be certain of them, and so that he might decide whether he would obey the Church and its decrees and support his prince and natural lord the duke in this matter'. He was threatened with expulsion from the Order and other sanctions if he failed to obey: Dünnebeil (ed.), *Protokoll-bücher I*, pp. 118, 121. Brederode promised 'to conduct himself in such away that they [the knights] would have no cause to be discontent with him', although support for his brother persisted in the diocese.

35 John Duke of Cleves was reprimanded at the Bruges chapter of 1468 for having withheld military support from the sovereign of the Order in his wars against Liège: Vaughan, *Charles the Bold*, p. 115.

from lordships under our government, will not make war or undertake distant expeditions without informing us or our successors in advance, or without our permission. We do not intend by this article to prevent the knights of our Order from fulfilling any prior obligations to serve or make war as a result of lands or revenues which they hold from others, nor do we wish to prevent those who are not subject to us from serving in arms and participating in expeditions as they wish, but desire only that they inform us in advance so far as they are able, and that they do so without prejudice to their undertakings or expeditions.

If any dispute arises between knights of the Order from which military action is likely to ensue, the sovereign will forbid both parties from engaging in hostilities once it is brought to his attention, and will enjoin them to submit the matter to him and the Order.

[Their cases were to be brought before the next chapter.]

If anyone should make so bold as to physically harm any knight of the Order, all others present will be expected to remedy the matter ...

Since there are knights in the Order who are not subject to the sovereign, and since the sovereign might find it necessary to make war on the natural lord of these knights, for our part, and that of our successors as sovereigns of the Order, we declare that the knights who are not subjects of the sovereign can preserve their honour and defend their natural lord in the lands which they come from, without incurring a charge of dishonour from the Order. But if the knight's natural lord wishes to make war on the sovereign of the Order, the knight should excuse himself and not serve ...

The knights of the Order are elected for life, unless they commit blameworthy acts which cause them to be deprived of their membership ...

[The charges are heresy, treason and leaving the field of battle once banners have been unfurled.[36]]

To prevent difficulties arising over matters of precedence relating to the status and rank of the knights, and since good and true love and fraternal company should have no regard for such matters, we ordain

---

36 After the creation of the Order but before its first chapter, Burgundian defeat at the battle of Anthon led to the flight from the field of Louis de Chalon, prince of Orange, who had been nominated as a knight of the Order. At the first chapter at Lille, Philip the Good decided not to give the collar to Louis de Chalon on the grounds that he had infringed the statute concerned. The same fate befell Jean I de Chalon, lord of Montaigu, despite the fact that he had already been given the collar of the Order, and that a spirited defence of his conduct at Anthon was offered to the Lille chapter by his proxy, Étienne le Foiant.

that, whether in procession to church, chapter or table, or in naming, speaking or writing, and in all other matters concerning the said order and company, the brothers and companions will be placed in order according to when they were knighted. And if there are some who were all made knights on the same day, we ordain that the oldest among them will be given precedence. And as for those who will be elected in the future to the Order by the sovereign and the knights, we ordain that they will be given precedence according to when they were elected; and if several are elected on the same day, precedence will be given to the oldest, with the exception of emperors, kings and dukes who, because of their high estate, will have their place in the order according to the date when they were knighted, without regard to their noble lineage, their greatness or the extent of their land.[37]

[There then follows the list of the first knights elected.]

We have ordained that the present Order will have four officers, that is to say: chancellor,[38] treasurer,[39] secretary[40] and king-of-arms,[41] who will be known as Golden Fleece.[42] The said officers will serve according to

---

37 Multiple dubbings were common at major engagements, so the clause was valuable. Disputes over precedence arose at the 1435 and 1468 chapters: Dünnebeil (ed.), *Protokollbücher I*, pp. 63–4; *II*, p. 70.

38 Only a 'high prelate of the Church' was to occupy this 'weighty office'. The chancellor was to keep the Order's seal, conduct the ceremony of the chapter, lead inquiries into the conduct of members, and be present for the auditing of the accounts of the Order. The chancellor was not allowed to use the seal without the sovereign's permission: F. de Gruben, 'Les Chapitres de la Toison d'or à l'époque bourguignonne', in Cockshaw and Van den Bergen-Pantens (eds), *L'Ordre de la Toison d'or*, pp. 80–3 at p. 81.

39 Responsible for all documents pertaining to the Order (copies of which were to be kept in the treasury of ducal charters), as well as the vestments, relics, jewels and tapestries used in church, and the ceremonial robes and armorial bearings of the members. He was also to keep account of all monies disbursed and received.

40 The secretary was to 'have a prebend in the church where the foundation of the Order took place'. He was to keep a book (in two copies) recording the statutes, and these copies were to be kept in the church, both chained close to the sovereign's seat. He was also to keep a second book recording the chivalrous deeds of members of the Order as they were reported to him by its king-of-arms. That this book was not kept assiduously is suggested by the fact that in 1473, the new king-at-arms was ordered to find the register which his predecessor, Jean Lefèvre, should have kept: Paviot, 'Étude préliminaire', p. xxii. In a third book the secretary was to keep the minutes of the decisions taken in chapter (the so-called protocol books which do survive).

41 The chief herald, of whom Lefèvre de Saint-Rémy was the first, was to be 'prudent, of good renown, and capable'; he was to wear the emblem of the Order 'every day', carry letters to the members and their replies to the sovereign, and keep an account of their chivalrous deeds.

42 On the occupants of all offices see F. Koller, *Au service de la Toison d'Or: les officiers* (Dijon, 1971).

the instructions set down for them in a book intended for their use. Each will swear the appropriate oath to acquit himself as the office requires, and to keep secret everything that ought to be kept secret pertaining to the Order …

Although it was previously decided that the feast and chapter of the Order would take place every year on St Andrew's day, nevertheless, due to the lack of daylight at that time of year, and the difficulties older knights have in travelling frequently to distant lands in poor weather, we have since taken advice and have decided that the feast, chapter, convention and assembly of the sovereign and all the brother knights will take place every three years, on the second day of May, in whatever place the sovereign designates in advance within a reasonable time, according to distance …[43]

So that the chapter, convention and feast of the Order is held in the aforementioned manner, and is not neglected or prevented as a result of unfavourable events, we wish and ordain that if, for reasons of illness, prison, warfare, dangerous roads or other reasonable and acceptable causes, the sovereign or any of the knights of the Order are prevented from personally attending the chapter, they are required to nominate another knight to act as their procurator.

[There follows a short section on how the chapter should be held [11].]

So that the Order and most pleasant company is maintained in good order; so that the knights and brothers strive to lead virtuous lives, augmenting honour and renown and setting an example to all knights and nobles; and so that the duty of the Order and of the nobility is widely acknowledged and clear to all, the chancellor of the Order will, among other things at the chapter, comment generally on how the members of the Order might correct their vices and amend their lives. This done, the chancellor will enjoin the knights, in the name of the Order, beginning with the most recently elected and in the order listed above, to leave the chapter, and to wait outside until they are summoned.

43 The decision to shift the date was debated at length at the fifth chapter in Brussels (1435): 'On which matter there were varied opinions. Some said that for the following year the feast should be moved three weeks after Easter because the days are longer and the weather more suitable for riding, which would mean more knights could attend and the sovereign could converse and communicate with them about his military campaigns if there were any to arrange, and then begin to carry out his orders. Others proposed two weeks after Easter, others halfway through Lent, while others proposed the feast not be moved at all, so the members of the Order could not be accused of taking matters lightly': Dünnebeil (ed.), *Protokollbücher I*, p. 67.

And once he has left the chapter, the sovereign or his deputy, or the chancellor in the name of the sovereign and the Order, will ask all the knights and the sovereign to swear solemnly, each in turn and beginning with the lowest up to the highest, to say whether they have seen, learned or heard from a person worthy of credence anything which their brother, now absent from the chapter, has done or said against the honour, renown and estate of chivalry, and in particular against the statutes and articles of the present Order and amiable company, by which this order might be blamed or defamed.

If it is found by the report of the brother-knights of the Order, or of a sufficient number of them, that their companion has committed an offence against the honour and estate of chivalry and nobility, in particular against the statutes of the Order in matters other than those which merit removal from the Order, the sovereign, his deputy or the chancellor will censure the brother-knight and will remonstrate with him, and admonish him with good intent to amend his ways, so that all grounds for blame and defamation should cease, and that in the future the companions of the Order should hear better reports of his conduct. And as for punishment, the sovereign and the knights will ordain what is fitting to the case, and the knight who is punished must accept and carry out whatever is decided.

This procedure will apply to the knight in the next seat or to his proxy, up to and including the sovereign of the Order who, in order to maintain love, fraternity and equality, and because the greatest set the best example, will be examined in the same way as the others, and will be corrected and punished on the advice of the knights of the Order if required.

[Conversely, if the absent knight is found to be of good renown, he will be congratulated by the chancellor, so that his good example will encourage others to be good and virtuous. There then follow articles concerning the removal of a member guilty of one of the crimes listed above; the obligation to return the collar in such circumstances; what is to be done if the expelled knight refuses to return the collar; the return of the collar by the heirs of a deceased member; and provisions for remedying the loss of a collar by a serving member ...]

When a place becomes vacant due to the death of a knight or otherwise, another will be elected by the greatest number of votes cast by the sovereign and knights of the Order. In this election, as in all other deliberations concerning the Order's affairs, the sovereign will have two votes and no more, except in the case noted below.

[The manner of holding an election is described; letters of nomination from knights of the Order are presented, and the chancellor asks the knights if they know of any reason why the nominees should not be elected ...⁴⁴]

The chancellor will take all the letters of nomination and will read them aloud, and the names in the letters will be written down and collated to see which has the greatest number of votes. The chancellor will announce the number of votes of each, and the sovereign will announce 'Such and such has the most votes and is therefore elected as a brother and companion of the Order'. And if it should arise that two names have the same number of votes, the sovereign, to conclude the election, may, in addition to his two votes by right, exceptionally add a casting vote to whichever of the names he chooses.

[Articles then follow on the manner of acceptance and on the oath to be sworn by new members: he is to defend the rights of the sovereign; maintain and augment the honour of the Order; return the collar in perfect condition if he is expelled from the Order; attend chapters personally or send a proxy; obey the statutes of the Order; ...]

The knight will swear these oaths in the hands of the sovereign of the Order, upon his good name, and upon the True Cross and the Bible.⁴⁵

This done the said knight will stand reverently before the sovereign, who will take the collar and place it around his neck ... After this, the knight of the first seat will lead the newly received knight before the sovereign, who will kiss him in a sign of perpetual love; and all the other knights will kiss him, in order.

[If a knight turns down the invitation to join, the sovereign will inform the brothers and another election will be prepared ...]

[The obligations of the members are then discussed.]

On entering the Order each knight will pay to the treasurer of the Order the sum of 40 gold *écus* or equivalent to be used for the vestments,

---

44 According to the official ducal chronicler George Chastelain, 'The knights of the Order remained in chapter [in 1468] for a great length of time considering the collars to be awarded ... for there were only seven vacancies, and it was found – after a certified count – that there were fifty valiant knights who were all worthy': *Oeuvres*, v, p. 379.

45 The binding nature of the oath to uphold statutes led a group of knights to seek the advice of Jean Chevrot, bishop of Tournai, and Nicolas Rolin, chancellor of Burgundy, in full chapter at Saint-Omer (1440) on whether amendments could be made to the statutes without formal dispensation. Their answer was that amendments could be made, just as a church or chapter would uphold its own statutes only so long as it seemed profitable for Holy Church to do so: Dünnebeil (ed.), *Protokollbücher I*, pp. 85–6.

jewels and adornments used in divine service in the chapel of the Order. However, if he wishes to present vestments and jewels himself of the same value, he may do so.

When any knight of the Order dies, each brother is bound to send money to the treasurer for the singing of 15 masses, and 15 *sous* for alms, for the soul of the deceased knight ...

The sovereign of the Order will give an annual pension of 50 nobles to the king-of-arms, and the sum of £50 for the robes and garments of the Order. And each knight will give the sovereign one noble at each chapter for these purposes.

[If the sovereign is succeeded by a minor, the knights will elect one of their number to conduct the affairs until the minor has reached his majority; if the heir is an unmarried girl, a knight will conduct the Order's affairs until the girl is married to a knight suitable to become sovereign ...[46]]

And because this Order is a confraternity and amiable company to which the brothers and knights are prepared to submit themselves in the ways stated above, and which they have sworn to uphold, we ordain, wish and decree that the said Order will be the sovereign court in cases pertaining to the Order and the brother and knights who belong to it; and that all summonses and punishments, penalties, settlements, sentences, judgments and arrests which are carried out pertaining to the Order and to the brothers and knights will be held to be as binding and valid as those of a sovereign court, without impediment and without recourse to appeals, complaints, supplications or other means whatsoever addressed to any other lord, prince, court of law or association of any kind, to which the sovereign and brother knights need not respond, given the voluntary and free submission they have solemnly sworn.[47]

We have laid down all of the statutes, conditions and articles mentioned above, and as sovereign of the Order, and on behalf of our successors, dukes of Burgundy and sovereigns of the present Order and amiable company of the Golden Fleece, we promise to uphold and accomplish them fully and to the best of our ability at all times.

---

46 A remarkably prescient statute given the events of 1477, when Charles the Bold died leaving an unmarried female heir.

47 At the Bruges chapter of 1468, Charles the Bold clarified that the chapter's jurisdiction as a court sitting in judgment on its members was limited to cases of honour, reserving criminal cases for his jurisdiction as prince: Paviot, 'Étude préliminaire', p. xxii. That criminal cases were subject to the duke's ordinary justice is made clear in the case of Philippe de Ternant below [12c].

11. Organisation of a chapter, *c.* 1500[48]

Olivier de la Marche, *Epistle on how to celebrate the noble feast of the Golden Fleece*, in *Mémoires*, ed. Beaune and d'Arbaumont, iv, pp. 158–89.

My sovereign lord,[49] my prince and master, I, Olivier, lord of la Marche, unworthy first chief steward of your noble household, place in your noble hand, as chief of the Order of the Golden Fleece, this epistle which I have written for the reasons set out below.

It is well known that I am in my seventy-sixth year, with nothing but goodwill left in my body, and can no longer serve you as I would like; and it is possible that through death or incapacity, I may no longer be able to accompany you to wherever you will celebrate the solemnity of the noble feast of the Fleece. In my long life, and by God's grace, I have been able to serve as chief steward of the household under the late Duke Charles (God rest his soul), under your father, and under you; and I have seen the feast celebrated several times by your ancestor and the founder of the Order, Duke Philip. The Order is the principal adornment of your house, and the source of honour which you must maintain and exalt, and you rebut those who would diminish or extinguish it, for by means of the Order you and your fellow members will have – and, indeed, already enjoy – many great fraternal alliances with emperors, kings, dukes, counts, barons and knights of great renown. It is therefore with pleasure that I set about writing how, as I understand it, this great solemnity should be conducted, and the order which is appropriate, in church, within the household, and in the public meeting and dining rooms …

[It] is only fitting that I should remind you what your predecessor, Duke Philip, your ancestor, took as his inspiration when he established the noble Golden Fleece. In the first instance he was inspired by the fable of Jason, which tells how, on the isle of Colchis, there was a sheep of immense size whose skin and fleece were entirely made of gold; and the story, which I will abridge to the best of my ability, relates that the sheep was guarded by dragons, serpents and wild bulls which spewed forth flames and other magical spells. Jason, a most valiant knight, went to Colchis to win the sheep, but he would never have succeeded without Medea, daughter of the king of the island, who had many spells and charms. Medea fell in love with Jason, and they had so much to do

48 Written at the end of the fifteenth century.
49 The text was written for Philip the Fair.

with one another that he promised to take her away and marry her. She taught him the spells he would need against the dragons and the bulls, and other spells which were quite unsuited to a knight who wished to capture the sheep. Jason believed Medea and did what she had told him to do, so much so that he prevailed against all the magical things I have mentioned, and he got to the sheep and killed it. But because the sheep was too large and heavy to be carried, Jason skinned it and carried away its golden fleece. From this fleece there hung the sheep's head, horns, four feet and tail. And this is why it is said Jason won the Golden Fleece, and why nothing is said of the sheep, for it was with the fleece that he returned. However, Jason cheated Medea: he did not take her away to be his bride. And there, my lord, you have the abridgement of what the good duke Philip, your ancestor, based himself on when he first founded the Order.

Since then, however, one chancellor of the Order, a bishop of Chalon in Burgundy by the name of Jean Germain, a most worthy cleric and great orator, changed the meaning of the foundation, and alighted upon the story of Gideon, which is a story from the Bible and is approved.[50] And it is worth recalling something of that here. This story tells how the Philistines greatly persecuted the Jews, the people of God, and how Our Lord could no longer bear the misery of His people, and how He raised up a labourer named Gideon, whom He told through an angel to take up arms against the Philistines and raise as many of the Jews as he could, and how He gave him hope that he would be victorious in battle against the Philistines. Although he was strong and is counted among the three strongest men, Gideon was fearful of the outcome of his venture and asked the Lord to assuage his fears. Twice he tried, as devoutly as he could: the first time he spread out a sheep's fleece on the ground and asked the Lord to let rain fall all night on the ground without wetting the fleece. And so it happened. But still Gideon was not reassured, so he asked the Lord in His goodness for another sign

---

50 Jason's disloyal treatment afforded him a bad reputation in later treatments of his legend (reflected for instance in the work of Christine de Pisan); this, and his pagan status, are thought to have motivated Germain's support for Gideon which Germain first voiced at the Dijon chapter of 1433. The continuing association of Jason with the Order may be explained by his partial rehabilitation as a successful and brave adventurer in certain texts (e.g. the anonymous *Ovide moralisé*). This more positive view was also maintained in the fifteenth century in works such as *Le Premier et second volume de la Toison d'Or* by Guillaume Fillastre, second chancellor of the Order. See D. Queruel, 'La Toison d'or, sa légende, ses symboles, son influence sur l'histoire littéraire', in Cockshaw and Van den Bergen-Pantens (eds), *L'ordre de la Toison d'or*, pp. 91–8; A. Van Buren-Hagopian, 'La Toison d'or dans les manuscrits de Philippe le Bon', in *ibid*, pp. 189–93.

to set his mind at rest. He spread another fleece on the ground, and he asked the Lord to let rain fall all night on the fleece without wetting the ground, which the Lord duly granted. Gideon was reassured, and he asked the Lord's forgiveness. Then he made his tunic from the fleeces, front and back. The story goes that under his leadership six hundred thousand Philistines were defeated and killed, and with so few losses that it was clear the hand of God had been at work. And this is how My Lord Jean Germain changed the thinking behind the choice of the fleece, from Jason to Gideon ...

Duke Philip established two divine services for this solemnity.[51] For the first, the knights went to vespers, and the following day to mass; they wore scarlet robes with great cloaks of the same colour, the orphrey of which was at least a foot deep, with flints and the fleece richly embroidered in gold thread.[52] The second service was in the evening when the knights attended vigils, dressed in black robes with black cloaks which had no orphrey. The following day they came to mass dressed in the same manner. This second service was for prayers for the souls of the dead and especially for those of the Order. Duke Philip instructed the four officers of the Order to process before the members dressed in the same clothes without the orphreys ...

Since then Duke Charles, who was most lavish in pomp and dress, in war as in peace, augmented the gowns of the Fleece, and made the scarlet of the first foundation a dark red velour for the robes, gowns and hoods. And he had the orphreys made as richly as the first. He also augmented the feast by adding two services, one in the name of the Holy Spirit, the other in the name of the glorious Virgin Mary ...

51 Mass in the principal church of a town was a public occasion. At Dijon in 1433, mass in the chapel of the dukes was attended by 'several prelates, nobles and a great multitude of people of all estates': Dünnebeil (ed.), *Protokollbücher I*, p. 45. At Valenciennes in 1473, according to the chapter acts of the Golden Fleece, the audience outside the church was even wider: 'the people watched, crying with joy at seeing their lord in the flesh and looking so noble and powerful, and the children cried out "Noel, long live Burgundy"': translated in B. Haggh, 'The archives of the Order of the Golden Fleece and music', *Journal of the Royal Musical Association* 120 (1995), pp. 1–43, at p. 11.

52 In addition to the ostentatious quality of scarlet robes (among the most expensive colours of dye), this was one of the main colours of the Burgundian party in the conflict with the Armagnac party in the generation prior to the foundation of the Order: J.H. Munro, 'The medieval scarlet and the economics of sartorial splendour', in N. Hart and K. Pontin (eds), *Cloth and clothing in medieval Europe: Essays in memory of Professor E.M. Carus-Wilson* (London, 1983), pp. 13–70; M. Pastoureau, 'La Toison d'or, sa légende, ses symboles, son influence sur l'histoire littéraire', in Cockshaw and Van den Bergen-Pantens (eds), *L'ordre de la Toison d'or*, pp. 99–105, at p. 103.

And since on several occasions it has been suggested that the number of knights of this noble confraternity of the Fleece should be increased, I offer my opinion that if the Order is to continue to enjoy the great esteem it has had in the past, as I desire, it should remain just as Duke Philip founded it, with thirty-one knights as stated above. For the greater the number of knights, the greater the possibility of unfortunate occurrences between them, which would not be to the benefit of the union among them, nor to the profit of the Head of the Order ...

And now it is time to discuss how the feast is to be celebrated at church, for our Lord and Holy Church should precede all other matters.

The treasurer and the officer-at-arms, who must be Golden Fleece, are to see to it that the church is prepared for the devotions which accompany this solemnity, and that the painter who is entrusted with the task is provided with the panels which represent the knights, living and dead. A levy is charged for each painted panel, which the head of the Order pays for foreign knights and the deceased, and the other knights, those of the household, must pay for their own. The panels for the living must be properly emblazoned and bearing the appropriate helm so that they are recognisable, and those for the dead must be painted on a flat shield, emblazoned only with the arms of the deceased and without helm. These panels must be hung under the instructions of the king-of-arms, that is to say, the knights according to when they first entered the Order, and when two or more knights entered on the same day, their panels will be hung according to the date they were dubbed to knighthood. This is the order which knights must process in and respect, as is fitting. Above them all on this same row must be the panels of the dukes, according to their nobility and lordships, and above the dukes must come the kings, according to their rank. The king-of-arms must take care to see that over the panels of the kings, living or dead, a pall is hung to show that kings are above all others. The panels of the kings must be bigger and more lavish than those of the others. These panels for the knights must be placed on both sides of the choir, fifteen on each.

As for the chair of the head of the Order, it must be raised higher than those of the knights, and the panel hung above bearing his arms. The father and the son must be seated on the same chair, and must each have his panel with his own arms and titles, and a baldachin above both or one of them, and it must be understood that the place for the sovereign must accommodate both the father and the son, and the panels the same. As for the four officers, they must sit on a low bench at the chief's feet, dressed in the appropriate garb ...

At this point I must enter into a point of controversy concerning the panel of the Emperor, your deceased grandfather (God rest his soul).[53] I am of the opinion that since an Emperor accepted membership of the Order, consideration must be shown for the fact that he was sovereign of several of the lordships which you hold, and for this reason you must accord him greater honour than you would to another king. And so the Emperor's panel should be placed on the other side of the door opposite the chair and panel of the head of the Order, and at the same height, and it should be decorated above with a rich baldachin. If a king of France were to become member of the Order, the same honour would have to be shown to him because he is the sovereign lord of some of your lands. One must accord the greater honour to those who are your sovereign lords than one does to those from whom you hold nothing, if not the brotherly love and alliance of the Order ...

And to further enlighten the matter of how this noble feast should be held, an account of the disposition of the chambers and dining arrangements follows. At least six of the knights must meet in conclave with the officers of the Order and the sovereign to fix the date of the meeting, so that the kings, dukes and knights of the Order can be written to in order that they might attend in the town agreed upon. This meeting must occur six months before the date agreed so that those far away might prepare themselves to come in person, or arrange a proxy; and proxies may only be other knights of the Order whose attendance of the chapter is certain. And at the offertory the king-at-arms will come before the panels of those unable to attend as if those absent members were there in person, and will place the candle before each panel and invite the absent member to make the offering; and the proxy charged with representing the absent knight will take the candle and make the offering on the absent knight's behalf.

As for the knights in attendance, each will be called in order and will be given the candle to make his offering. It should be understood that the knights who are present and absent, the latter by proxy, will go the offertory two-by-two, as and when they are called. As for the deceased knights, no one will go on their behalf save the king-at-arms, unless the deceased knight in question is the sovereign of the Order. In this case the heir, as upholder of the Order, will go to the offertory for the deceased, accompanied by all the brother knights who are present. And

---

53 Frederick III, elected at Mechelen in 1491.

thus the solemnity of the offertory will be held. After the mass the officers, knights and sovereign will go in the order in which they came to the residence, and there they will enter their conclave to attend to their affairs. In the meantime, the dinner and the measures required for its service will be prepared. Once the dinner is ready, the chief stewards of the household must advise the sovereign and the knights and the others who are to be summoned to come to this noble gathering.[54] The officers, knights and sovereign will come in the customary manner, dressed in the clothes they wore to church, and they will withdraw to the high bench near the table on the right-hand side, and there the first butler will bring water to the sovereign to wash his hands, and a napkin will be brought to him by one of the high princes in attendance who is not a member of the Order. Then the esquires will bring several basins and all the knights and officers will wash. The chancellor of the Order must wash separately, and the three other officers of the Order together. At this time too, water will be brought for the ambassadors to wash themselves. Once the water has been given, the sovereign must take his seat in the middle seat at table, and all the other knights of the Order must take their seats up and down from him. The king-at-arms must take care to ensure that each knight takes the correct seat. Then the officers of the Order and the ambassadors present will sit at their own tables, and the chief stewards of the household must ensure that each ambassador takes the seat befitting his rank. Once the knights, ambassadors and officers of the Order are all seated, the household officers will serve what the prince has ordered according to season; that is to say, fresh butter in May,[55] strawberries or cherries in June, and grapes in August or September. In this way, depending on the season, each will have his fruit for that day. And if it is a fish day, each will have white hippocras and canapés for a starter. And while these are being served the ushers will call to named chamberlains to bring forth the meat dishes, and these chamberlains must have been selected and advised of their duty beforehand. The first pantler will take the napkin, and the chief stewards of the household will process in front of the meat dishes. Each noble man instructed to serve the meat will be provided with men

---

54 At Saint-Omer in 1461 the acts of the Order record that after mass the knights 'returned from the church to dine in a great hall, richly adorned with cloth of gold, and a canopy, and backing above and around the great table all hung with rich tapestries, and there was also a dresser richly arrayed with jewel-encrusted silver and gold plate...': Dünnebeil (ed.), *Protokollbücher I*, pp. 127–8.

55 'bure fretz', which the editors give as (fresh) butter. This is not a fruit as the following clause leads one to expect, but 'beurre de May' was a butter prepared for medical purposes, so the identification may be accurate.

to carry the meat before him, as I say. And once the meat is plattered, the trumpeters, minstrels and musicians will enter the hall first, then the heralds dressed in their coats-of-arms, and after them, two-by-two, will come the great lords of the household who are not members of the Order. After them will come the chief stewards of the household, then the grand and first chief stewards, then the first pantler and his suite of platters, then the noble men and the dishes entrusted to them. This order must be respected, and each esquire must know which knight he is to give his platter to.

And continuing the order of service, the servants of my Lady will serve the ladies in the gallery, and those who are in the second chamber will be served with two meat dishes. And the same must be provided for the worthy aldermen of the town in which the chapter is held, all of whom will be men of good renown, eight or ten in number. Good care must be taken of these men, for the towns commonly grant gifts and subsidies toward the cost of the chapter. These men must be invited to the feast and notified of the date beforehand by one of the chief stewards of the household. And after these sittings the heralds and other officers-at-arms must be served in lesser fashion.

The first serving will be organised in this way. The first serving must be cleared away to bring the second, and the almoner and the almoner's valet, acting under instruction from the esquire of the kitchen, must have prepared a place for the meat to be taken to once it has been cleared away.[56] With the first serving cleared away, the second will be brought forth and served to the prince, the knights and all the other tables in the hall and in other rooms in the same manner as the first. The knights will be served wine by their own gentlemen, and the sovereign of the Order by his own first cupbearer, and his first carver will carve for him, for on this solemn occasion the heads of the household services must serve above all others. And from the first serving there will be three others. If there are any entertainments between courses, they should be brought out with the third serving, and they should be devised by the chief steward of the household to adorn the feast.

With the four courses finished and cleared away, each guest will be served hippocras and light pastries. The esquires must bring the hippocras, and the first pantler must serve the pastries to the prince's table. No one should place pastries on the prince's table without the first pantler's permission, and the rest of the hall will be served there-

56 The almoner was responsible for distributing leftovers to the poor.

after. The gallery for the officers and heralds is not usually served with hippocras or pastries, so they should rise from their places at this point, and their tables are to be folded away by the quartermasters so that the hall appears larger and more balanced. Once this service is finished, the four officers of the Order and the ambassadors will rise from their places at the same time, and their table will be folded away by the quartermasters; then the quartermasters will fold away the great table and the knights will rise while showing reverence to their sovereign, and on this occasion grace will be said by the almoner or by the first chaplain. Immediately thereafter the chief stewards will have the spices brought forth for the sovereign in a bowl with a lid, and without lid for the others. Several bowls should be available for this purpose. The first cupbearer must bring the sovereign's wine and serve him before anyone else, unless the sovereign's son and heir should be present, in which case he will serve the sovereign. The most senior prince who is not a member of the Order will serve the sovereign from his bowl, and then he will return it to the spicer; the chief stewards of the household will then serve the other lords from the bowls and pour their wine. Then the four officers of the Order and the ambassadors will be served. Wine and spices will only be served in the main hall. It should not be forgotten that at such a grand occasion largesse should be shown to the heralds, and this ought to be called when the hippocras and pastries are served, with all officers at arms and Golden Fleece in attendance.

With the service of the meal over, the knights will withdraw into their conclave while vigils in the great church are prepared. The knights will attend vigils in the customary order, but they will be dressed in their great cloaks, robes and black hoods, for on this second day of the chapter vigils are held for the souls of the deceased members of the Order. Each will sit below his panel as before.

The chief stewards of the household must see to it that those who served the dinner and who might want to dine themselves, especially the noblemen, should have a table set in the great hall, and the esquire of the kitchen will serve them the best remaining meat. Likewise, pantlers, cupbearers and other officers of the household will serve this table as required.

And that will be the end of the first day of the chapter. The second will begin with the vigils in the manner I have described.

On the second day the knights will go to mass in the usual manner, dressed in black, each taking his place, and high mass will be said for the souls of the deceased. Before the Offertory the clerk of the Order will make a brief speech recalling all the deceased brothers of the Order and will speak of their noble conduct and deeds, at which point the offering will be made as on the first day. Once high mass is over, the knights will return to the residence in the customary manner and will withdraw into their conclave. Meanwhile, the second dinner will be prepared, and the tables will be set as I will now describe.

The quartermasters will set the prince's table, which should be long enough to seat just three people – that is to say, the prince in the middle, the prelate who has performed the mass on his right, and a prince or ambassador on his left. As for the other knights of the Order, they will be seated at another table in the middle of the hall, where the ambassadors had sat the day before. The knights will all be seated on one side of the table and they will be served with three or four dishes, each with eight or ten accompaniments, like the prince's table. The officers of the Order will have their customary place and will be served with two meat dishes, each dish with as many accompaniments as the others. As for the assembly, the same service as the previous day will apply, and the ladies in the gallery watching the feast will be served as many dishes as the prince. The prelates attending the chapter will be served on this second day in the chamber used for the good men of the town on the first day, and they should be invited to attend by the chief steward of the household during vigils. On this second day, fourteen dishes furnished with eight or ten accompaniments will be required, as I have said, and these dishes will be served three times, each time with the accompaniments I have mentioned. After the third serving, hippocras and pastries will be served, as on the first day. The prelates must come back into the hall to say grace. Once the tables have been folded away, wine and spices will be served as on the previous day ...

And to move on to the third day, the knights will go to vespers on the feast of the Holy Spirit dressed and coiffed in garments of red velour, and they will process in the customary order for going to church. Each day there will be an offering like that of the first. And if an election of a new knight should have occurred in the interim, and he is present and bearing the collar, he may enter into the conclave with the others, so long as he is dressed like them. However, such knights are not to go to church during the present chapter because they would not know the correct order and would not have painted panels bearing their arms like the others.

On this third day the knights will go in the customary manner to hear the mass of the Holy Spirit, and they will be dressed in red velour as they were the previous evening for vespers. In this great mass the offering will be made as before, but there will be no sermon or remembrance. Once mass is over the knights will return to their conclave in order, and will then return to the hall which will have been prepared as it was on the previous days. To entertain the foreigners, new guests will be invited to dinner that evening in the chamber where the townsmen and prelates had previously dined. A different prelate must sit at the prince's table on this occasion, likewise a different prince or ambassador to better adorn the feast. They must all be served three times as on the previous day, each time with eight or ten accompaniments. Each day the chief stewards of the household, the esquire of the kitchen and the cook must meet to devise the dishes and meats which are to be served, each of which must be as different as possible. The prelate will say grace and the knights will return to their conclave. And one must remember to entertain the ambassadors appropriately each day in their chambers.

For the fourth vespers, the knights will go to church dressed in white damask and coiffed in red velour. They will return to their customary seats, and after vespers will enter into their conclave. The following day they will hear mass in honour of Our Lady, for it is in her name that this fourth day of the chapter is held ...

The expenses of the four days must be accounted for by the chief stewards of the household, the controller of the household accounts and the clerk of the four household offices in the presence of those deputed to the task by the duke's accounting office and, once the account has been agreed, it must be written down in the daily rolls of the ordinary expenditure.

And so I bring to an end this present mémoire, my most redoubted and sovereign lord, which I submit to you and to those of the Order for approval, and if I have spoken of any matter more than I should have, I most humbly seek your grace.

12. The Mons chapter, 1451[57]

(a) A town council prepares

Mons town council minutes, published in L. Devillers, 'Les séjours des ducs de Bourgogne en Hainaut: 1427–82', *Bulletin de la Commission royale d'histoire* Fourth Series, vi (1879), pp. 323–468, at pp. 408–10.

On Saturday 17 April 1451 the consuls of the town met in the hall to discuss the safety of the town during holy week, at Easter, and the arrival of our most redoubted lord and prince and the feast of the Golden Fleece which is meant to be held in this town in the coming month of May ...

It is decided that a party will go forth from the town to meet the prince and welcome him, and to present him with two barrels of wine, along with one barrel to my lord of Orléans if he comes, in place of the one intended for my lord of Alençon ...

And since it has become known that our most redoubted lord and prince intends this coming month of May to hold his feast of the Fleece in this town, and that a great number of gentlemen and others might come, it is decreed that the aldermen shall inspect the inns and the houses of the burgesses in the town where our most redoubted lord's quartermasters have placed banners to indicate where gentlemen, and others if necessary, will be lodged. This is to be done because there is some doubt the said inns will be able to accommodate everyone. A written report on the number of people who can be put up in each place will be submitted. In addition, those who are putting up the visitors will be told to speak to their paying lodgers graciously and courteously, so that no complaint is raised against them. Those providing accommodation will be told that should they notice any trouble or commotion among their own people, they will come and inform the aldermen immediately so that a remedy might be sought. And every night the hoteliers will send a note to the town hall of the number of people lodged on their premises. Everyone must keep a close lookout for fire.

---

57 In addition to the documents translated here, entries in the ducal accounts for expenses incurred in preparation for the Mons chapter are published in F. de Gruben, *Les Chapitres de la Toison d'Or à l'époque bourguignonne* (Leuven, 1997), pp. 495–506. The costs included the purchase of cloth and the making of clothes, wax, paintings and hangings, offerings made at church, transport, the copying of correspondence and the preparation of a copy of the Order's statutes for the host church. A separate role of expenditure amounting to £553 4s was drawn up by Pierre Bladelin, but this figure does not include the many other payments made to officers of the Order or foreign princes or their representatives.

Watch will be kept every night in the town hall, consisting of one alderman, two councillors, one sergeant, one crossbowman, one archer and one gunner, and there will be two men from each constabulary.

Those responsible for hanging the town chains will do so in the event of any commotion, but they will not hang the town's chains by night as is the custom because the lords lodged in different places in the town will need to come and go to court often and outside normal hours.[58]

My lord the *bailli* of Hainaut will be asked to announce on behalf of our most redoubted prince that all those with oats and other foodstuffs within a radius of four leagues of the city should bring their goods for sale during the time our redoubted lord and his people are in the town so that there are enough supplies and prices do not increase.

Also, that it be decreed that all butchers, innkeepers and others selling produce are not to increase their prices during the time my lord the prince and his people are in the town.

(b) A church prepares

Accounts of the chapter St Waudru at Mons, published in Devillers, 'Les séjours des ducs de Bourgogne en Hainaut', at pp. 411–12.

The receiver reports that at the feast of the Order of the Golden Fleece which my lord the duke held in the said church on the second day of May 1451, my lord and the knights of the Order made an offering of 25 golden florins which were received on the church's behalf by Henry de Jausse, which he delivered into the hands of canonesses de Boulers, d'Espagne and de Marbaix, then governors of the fabric of the said church.

The receiver also reported that at the said feast of the Fleece 24 torches made of 38 lbs of wax were arrayed on the great altar on the Saturday, Sunday, Monday and Tuesday, and on the Sunday, for the mass of the dead, a wooden chandelier was hung above the choir bearing 31 torches, each weighing 2lbs ...[59]

58 Use of chains across city streets was a common defence to impede large crowds or mounted men in the event of disorder or attack: P. Contamine, 'Les Chaînes dans les bonnes villes de France (spécialement Paris), XIVe–XVIe siècle', in C. Giry-Deloison and M. Keen (eds), *Guerre et société en France, en Angleterre et en Bourgogne XIVe–XVe siècle* (Villeneuve d'Ascq, 1989), pp. 293–314.

59 The canonesses sought to gain a spiritual benefit from the chapter of the Golden Fleece. One of the exotic dignitaries drawn to Mons by the event was Jean II Juvenal des Ursins, archbishop of Reims. The canonesses met with the canons (including the composer Guillaume Dufay) on Tuesday 4 May to discuss what pardons and indulgences they might solicit from the archbishop: Devillers, 'Séjours', p. 412.

(c) The business of the chapter

Register of the capitulary acts of the Most Noble Order of the Golden Fleece, from the founding of the Order to the eighteenth chapter held at Saint-Omer in May 1461 (Archive of the Order of the Golden Fleece, Vienna), ff. 33v–36 (Dünnebeil (ed.), *Protokollbücher I*, p. 104 et seq.)

The sixteenth feast and solemnity of the Order of the Golden Fleece was held at Mons in Hainaut on the second day of May 1451, where the knights of the Order presented themselves at the church of Saint Waudru, namely:

My lord the duke, sovereign of the Order, my lord of Charolais and many others who appeared in person, others by proxy.

On Saturday 1 May, the eve of the Feast of Quasimodo, vespers were said most solemnly before a great assembly of prelates, lords, nobles and others of all estates. The following day, the great mass was said and a sermon preached by my lord the bishop of Chalon-sur-Saône, chancellor of the Order.[60] On the Monday the mass for the dead was said by my lord the archbishop of Besançon.[61]

On the same Monday after dinner, when my lord the sovereign was in his chambers with my lords the knights of the Order wearing the requisite garments, along with my lord the bishop of Tournai[62] and my lord of Autun, chancellor of Burgundy,[63] my lord the bishop of Chalon-sur-Saône presented to the sovereign a large volume containing five extracts from books which he had compiled for the purpose of exulting and elucidating the Christian faith, and refuting the erroneous sect of Mohammed.[64] He

60 Jean Germain. The sermon was on the theme of the desolation of Holy Church and a new crusade, and was copied by Germain himself into his *Book of the virtues of Philip, duke of Burgundy and Brabant* which he dedicated to Charles count of Charolais: J. Paviot, 'L'Ordre de la Toison d'or et la croisade', in Cockshaw and Van den Bergen-Pantens (eds), *L'Ordre de la Toison d'or,* pp. 1–4, at p. 72; Dünnebeil (ed.), *Protokoll-bücher I,* p. 104 n. The *acta* of the Order occasionally record the topics of the sermons preached, 'usually on one or more of the fleeces' (such as Guillaume Fillastre, bishop of Tournai, at Valenciennes in 1473, based on Judges 6:39): Haggh, 'The archives of the Order of the Golden Fleece', pp. 15–16. According to Olivier de La Marche, the decision to hold a feast for the purposes of taking the cross, ultimately the Feast of the Pheasant at Lille in February 1454 [1], was taken at this chapter.

61 Quentin Menart, also provost of Saint-Omer and ducal ambassador, notably to the council of Basel.

62 Jean Chevrot, bishop of Tournai, also head of the ducal council.

63 Nicolas Rolin, the duke's senior administrator until his disgrace in 1457.

64 Jean Germain completed his *Débat du Chrétien et du Sarrasin,* aka *Trésor des simples,* in 1451: H. Müller, *Kreuzzugspläne und Kreuzzugspolitik des Herzogs Philipp des Guten von Burgund* (Göttingen, 1993), pp. 25, 49; Paviot, *Les Ducs de Bourgogne,* pp. 227–9.

also gave my lord the duke some other books, and a map of the world in French representing all the inhabited regions, provinces and places.[65] In addition he presented my lord of Charolais with a book in Latin which he had written for him on the instruction and encouragement of virtues. The bishop also gave certain books on the miraculous conception of Our Lady to the chancellor of Burgundy,[66] and to the bishop of Tournai he gave a copy of the map of the world he had given to the duke, written in Latin.

On the same day and in the same place it was declared by Pierre Bladelin, counsellor and chief steward of the household of my said lord the duke and treasurer of the Order, that in the accounts sent to him by the heirs of his predecessor in this last office, the late Gui Guilbaut, it was stated that some of the living and deceased knights of the Order and their heirs owed monies which should have been given to him for the purposes stated in the statutes. He therefore asked how he should proceed in the matter. Opinions were given and it was concluded that the accounts of the receipts and expenses submitted by the heirs of Gui Guilbaut would be audited by a commission appointed for the task, and that whatever was owed should be asked for and collected from those who owed it. If any subject of my lord the duke were to refuse, they would be sent an official mandate to force them to pay, as would be the case in any ordinary debt owed to my lord. Those not subject to my said lord would be written to and asked to pay, as indeed they were obliged to do.

On Tuesday 4 May after mass was said for Our Lady and before dinner, when my lord the sovereign, the knights and the officers of the Order were in the chamber of my said lord the duke, my lord the count of Charolais, Reinoud lord of Brederode and my lord of Humières, knights of the Order, took the oath pertaining to the points and articles in the statutes in plenary chapter. Pierre Bladelin, treasurer of the said Order, took the requisite oath for his office. Once this was done my lord the sovereign and the knights of the Order swore that they would loyally proceed to the election of new members in place of the six knights who had died.

---

65 Jean Germain composed his *Mappemonde spirituelle* in 1449: Paviot, 'L'Ordre de la Toison d'Or et la croisade', p. 72.

66 In the fifteenth century, the fleece moistened with dew was interpreted as a symbol of Mary's immaculate conception. The fleece of Gideon may have been the subject of the two volumes presented at the meeting of the Order in 1451: Haggh, 'The archives of the Order of the Golden Fleece', pp. 17–20.

And on the same day after dinner, when my lord the sovereign and the knights were in the duke's chamber wearing the aforementioned garments, the elections were held in the customary manner. The following knights were elected, in this order:

My lord the duke of Cleves[67] in place of Florimont de Brimeu[68]

My lord the count of Ariane[69] in place of my lord the count of Mörs[70]

My lord the count of Goliane[71] in place of Jacques de Brimeu[72]

My lord of Lannoy[73] in place of my lord David de Brimeu[74]

My lord Jacques de Lalaing, lord of Buignicourt,[75] in place of my lord of Jonvelle[76]

My lord of Montagu[77] in place of my lord of Roubaix.[78]

Afterward my lord Philippe de Ternant declared to the sovereign and the knights of the Order that he had received a summons to appear in person before them, in letters sealed with the duke's seal and written by public notary, and so he now presented himself, ready to do whatever might be reasonably expected of him. He asked for a hearing and for an

67 John I duke of Cleves.

68 Colart, a.k.a. Florimond III, of Brimeu, lord of Maizicourt. Knight and ducal chamberlain from the region of Artois. Nephew of David and Jacques below.

69 Iñigo of Guevara, count of Ariano (Puglia), leading servant of ducal ally Alfonso V of Aragon (elected Ghent, 1445).

70 Frederick V count of Mörs.

71 Pedro de Cardona, count of Golisano, leading servant of Alfonso V of Aragon. In fact, Cardona predeceased his election to the Order.

72 Jacques de Brimeu, lord of Grigny. Uncle of Colard above and younger brother of David below.

73 Jean de Lannoy, lord of Lys, Wattignies and Yser. An orphan, Jean was raised by his uncles, both knights of the Order, Jean and Antoine of the powerful Croy family of courtiers.

74 David de Brimeu, lord of Ligny-sur-Cauche. Uncle of Colard and elder brother of Jacques above.

75 Jacques de Lalaing, 'knight without reproach', was the most celebrated jouster of his day. Formerly a servant of John I duke of Cleves above, he was killed in the Ghent war two years after his election. Jacques de Lalaing was nephew of two other knights of the Order, Jean V de Créquy and Simon de Lalaing.

76 Jean de La Trémoïlle, lord of Jonvelle, knight and holder of the hereditary office of first chamberlain in the duchy of Burgundy.

77 Jean II de Neufchâtel, lord of Montaigu, son of Thibaud (himself elected at Dijon in 1433).

78 Jean, lord of Roubaix and Herzele, knight and ducal chamberlain, brother-in-law to three other knights of the Order from the Lannoy family, and father-in-law of another member, Antoine de Croy.

acknowledgement that he had appeared as required, which was granted to him.[79]

This done, my lord Jacques de Lalaing entered the chapter. After he was informed of his election he accepted it reverently and with thanks, and took the required oaths. He was given the collar and mantle of the Order with the customary ceremonies and solemnities.

On Friday 7 May after dinner, when my lord the sovereign was in the chapter of his Order in his residence at Mons along with the knights and officers in the customary garments, following an opening sermon preached by the bishop of Chalon-sur-Saône, chancellor of the Order, there began the examination and correction of the conduct and way of life of each of the knights of the Order present, as well as of the absent represented by their proxies. The most recently elected were examined first, proceeding by order in the customary manner. No vice, great blame or charge was found among them which required correction, except the following case.

When it came to the examination of my lord of Ternant, the knights of the Order commended him and praised his valour, wisdom and virtues. However, they were compelled by their oaths to note with great regret and much difficulty how they had heard it charged against him that, some time before, while serving my lord the sovereign as first chamberlain, and fully cognisant of the truces which had been agreed with the English for the well-being of the lands and subjects of my said lord and for the pursuit of trade, he had had an English merchant arrested and imprisoned by some of his men, in contravention of the truces and against the wishes, guarantees and promises of my lord the duke, greatly to my lord's dishonour. And when my lord the duke had first kindly asked him in private if he had made this arrest and was responsible for it, he had denied it and had said that he was not. When the truth of the matter was later uncovered, my lord the duke had him arrested and imprisoned in his castle at Courtrai for eight months or thereabouts. And when speaking to several knights of the Order and other leading men of the council whom my lord had sent to him, he had used arrogant and angry words, and had made dishonourable accusations, such as: 'There is no one here whose affairs, if subjected to the

---

79 M.-T. Caron, 'Olivier de La Marche, Philippe de Ternant, ses protecteurs et ses amis', *PCEEB* 43 (2003), pp. 55–77; M. Sommé, 'Les Conseillers et collaborateurs d'Isabelle de Portugal', in A. Marchandisse and J.-L. Kupper (eds), *À l'ombre du pouvoir: Les entourages princiers à la fin du Moyen Âge* (Geneva, 2003), pp. 343–59, notably pp. 354–5.

same scrutiny as mine, would not be found just as guilty as me', among other things. It was also said that when my lord the duke had given him the task of taking a great sum of money amounting to 29,000 gold *écus* to give to the Dauphin and his main advisers, who were then near Montbéliard on the marches of Germany, he had not acted according to the mandate he had been given and had not delivered all the monies, and that those which he had delivered were not of the gold coin that had been given to him. This charge was laid against him, and it was noted that my lord the duke had received several complaints and inquiries about the matter. Moreover, it was said that he had kept back a great sum of wages, amounting to £2,800 or thereabouts, intended for the poor soldiers of the castle at Sluis, where he was captain, much to their detriment, and my lord the duke had received many complaints and inquiries on the subject. Also in the matter of his captaincy at Sluis, he was said to have conducted himself very poorly and in a disorderly fashion. Several similar charges were made against him.[80]

Thereupon, after raising several excuses, my lord of Ternant finally acknowledged that he had been at fault in the arrest of the English merchant, but he said that he had paid the penalty through his imprisonment and losses, and that he had asked for – and received – the duke's pardon. To this it was answered that the duke had pardoned the offence to his majesty and his common justice as prince, but that the offence to my lord the duke as head of his Order, and to the knights and brothers of the same who had been outraged and angered at his words, had still not been made good. My lord of Ternant submitted and offered to accept any punishment which might await him. After deliberation it was decreed that he should immediately seek the pardon of my lord as sovereign of the Order, and of my lords the knights and brothers of the same, which he did without delay. My lords the sovereign and knights pardoned him amiably and with good heart. For a punishment he was then enjoined to go on pilgrimage to Santiago de Compostela before the following Easter, which he agreed to do.

In the said place and chapter it was concluded that henceforth and for all time, the monies owed by the knights for the fifteen masses for each of the deceased members and the distribution of alms would be paid, in accordance with the statutes of the Order, to the treasurer, who would send them to the canons of the chapter of the chapel at Dijon where

80 The extent of Ternant's fall from grace is underlined by the fact that he had been one of a select group of four knights appointed to reform the Order's statutes at the Ghent chapter of 1445: Dünnebeil (ed.), *Protokollbücher I*, pp. 95–6.

they would be used for the masses and alms. It will be certified by the deacon of the chapel and the *bailli* of Dijon, guardian of the Order, that the monies have been received and used for the said masses and alms. The certification will be delivered to the treasurer of the Order for his accounts. And as for the fact that knights had previously paid for the holding of the masses and distribution of the alms elsewhere and by other means, they were held to have acquitted themselves of their dues.

It was also decided that the monies owed to the Order should be used in the first instance by the treasurer to buy cloth of gold and silk to make four gowns and other vestments – one blue, one red, one black and one white – to be sent to the chapel at Dijon for use in the masses and divine service of the Order of my lord the duke.

The knights of the Order also asked my lord the duke to give four pairs of large embroidered orphreys which he had recently had made for four sets of liturgical vestments for use in the chapel ... My lord the duke responded to the request most generously and with good heart, and declared he would have the orphreys delivered to my lords of the chapter of the chapel at Dijon for divine service. My lords the knights and brothers of the Order thanked the duke profusely.

(d) After the chapter

Second register of the *Consaux* (town council minutes), published in Devillers, 'Les séjours des ducs de Bourgogne en Hainaut', at pp. 412–13.

[At the meeting of the town council on 18 May] the matter of the request received from our most redoubted lord the duke was discussed, in which he let it be known that, for the love and affection he held for this town, he had come here to hold the feast of his Order of the Golden Fleece, even though several other towns had asked him to come and had offered him great sums of money if he did so, which he had refused. Nonetheless, the duke did not wish the town of Mons to give him any such gifts. But to help him defray the great expenses he had incurred in this matter, he requested that the town lend him – and pay to those who had extended him credit for his expenses – the sum of £2,400 which could be deducted from the first instalment the town was due to make to him on the tax recently granted to him by the three estates of Hainaut under certain conditions which my said lord the duke was not happy about. It was decided that the duke should be told that the grant of taxation was not made for this purpose, and because the town was only a part of the said three estates, and because the town did not want to dissociate itself from the three estates in any way, it did not wish to make the loan, and it beseeched the duke to be content with this reply, for the town was poor and heavily burdened. And if the duke was not happy with this reply, the matter would be brought back to the council for further consideration ...

[The ducal reply to this proposal was 'sharp'. The town council resolved to enter into negotiations to reduce the sum owed. If this proved unsuccessful they would meet the whole cost, but on the understanding that the money would be reclaimed from the tax levy as the duke originally proposed. As the following entry from the town accounts makes clear, the worst-case scenario materialised ...]

To several bourgeois and residents of the said town, to whom money was owed for the expenses incurred by our most redoubted lord and prince and his people when the feast of the Golden Fleece was held in the month of May 1451, has been paid, from monies lent by the town to our prince, and which will be recouped from the first tax levy, the sum of £2,400.

IV: ENTRY CEREMONIES

Introduction

The ceremonies accompanying the formal Entry of a dynast into a subject city in later medieval Europe have generated a rich and varied literature in the last generation, particularly in the case of the Burgundian Netherlands.[1] Relatively infrequent at the start of Philip the Good's reign, such ceremonies grew steadily in number and complexity in the ducal dominions in the course of the fifteenth century: perhaps as many as 200 occurred in the fifteenth century, with a marked concentration in Flanders and Brabant and a relative absence in the county of Holland. The Entry ceremony was quite distinct from the normal pattern of ducal itineration, occasioned as it was by a significant event, usually an inauguration of some kind. The accession of a new ruler was the most obvious occasion for an Entry, and it was usually by such means that the prince took possession of the city and the territory of which it was the capital. A dynastic marriage might result in a tour of cities by the new bride or groom [2], while a military victory, the need to bolster loyalties in the face of a military threat [13], the attainment of the age of majority by a prince or princess [16] or the taking of the cross were also seen as important moments which could give rise to Entry ceremonies. Least common but in some ways most problematic was the Entry of reconciliation [13, 14], the ceremony by which a rebellious city sought to make a new peace with the ruler.

In all Entry ceremonies a set of 'formal observances' may be identified which, when fully respected, made the event an elaborate and costly undertaking for its organisers. The prince and his party were commonly met a few kilometres from the host city by a substantial group of notables [14]. Here a formal address of welcome might be made on behalf of the municipality [14]. In the event of an inaugural Entry the ruler could exercise the right of clemency by pardoning exiles at this stage [15]; if the Entry were one of reconciliation, the first meeting beyond the city gates might also incorporate some form of ritual submission. Once inside the gates the ruler and his entourage proceeded along a carefully planned route which took in important sites, including the principal church or public square where oaths and gifts were exchanged between ruler and municipality during an inaugural Entry [15]. Events usually ended with the arrival of the procession at the ruler's residence, but several hours would commonly elapse [14] before he and his party had completed their journey.[2] Their route was lined with a great number of spectators, hemmed in by cloth hangings on erected scaffolds and buildings, lit by torches (for many

---

1 See most recently, with a full bibliography, Lecuppre-Desjardin, *La ville des cérémonies.*
2 Hurlbut, 'Ceremonial Entries', Table 3.1.

ceremonies took place at night or in the afternoon), bathed in the sound of trumpets and the ringing of the city's bells, and – increasingly – interspersed with stages upon which actors and/or mechanical devices represented 'stories' or 'mysteries' judged fitting to the occasion by the organisers of the event [**14, 16**].[3] The staged performances were sometimes accompanied by written scrolls or by an actor to communicate the content and meaning of the story depicted [**16**]. The organisers of the Entry ceremony included men attached to the court, such as the ducal chaplain consulted by the Dijon authorities in 1474 on the content of the plays accompanying the Entry ceremony of Charles the Bold, but on the whole the conception and planning of the Entry ceremony were the responsibility of the town council (although they too may have included men with links to the court).[4] The municipality delegated the many tasks involved to a wide variety of groups: parish, confraternity or neighbourhood associations [**16**] and, increasingly, the rhetoricians of the city [**19a–c**].[5] It was from among civic rhetoricians that the small committee [**16**] or single 'factor' responsible for devising the 'stories' and 'mysteries' represented on stages began to emerge during our period. Salaries for the organisers, along with many of the other costs of Entry ceremonies, were met by the municipality rather than by the prince [**16**], and further or alternative remuneration might be received by participating groups in the form of prizes awarded by the town for the best displays in the course of the Entry. These monies aside, the time spent, skills deployed and personal possessions pressed into use by many of the participants in an Entry ceremony appear to have gone unrewarded by the municipality. In such cases we must assume that the many who participated did so to advertise their support for the values enshrined in the ceremony, and to defend or augment their status and prestige by means of their performance. It seems important to bear such considerations in mind when assessing whether the 'pit of the Burgundian theater state' was princely or urban in nature.[6]

Interpretations of Entry ceremonies are commonly grounded on the notion that they witnessed a dialogue between prince and subjects, the former communicating his authority, qualities and intentions as a good ruler, the latter advertising their loyalty and stating their corporate aspirations [**14, 16**].[7] If the ruler himself was silent for much of the ceremony, his presence and that of his family and entourage could of course be withheld, rendering the ceremony redundant

3 D. Eichberger, 'The *tableau vivant*: an ephemeral art form in Burgundian festivities', *Parergon* 6 (1988), pp. 37–64.

4 P. Quarré, 'La "Joyeuse entrée" de Charles le Téméraire à Dijon en 1474', *Académie royale de Belgique: Bulletin de la Classe des Beaux-Arts* 51 (1969), pp. 326–40, at pp. 328–9; J.-M. Cauchies, 'La Signification politique des entrées princières dans les Pays-Bas: Maximilien d'Autriche et Philippe le Beau', *PCEEB* 24 (1994), pp. 19–35.

5 A. de La Grange, 'Les Entrées des souverains à Tournai', *Mémoires de la Société historique et littéraire de Tournai* 19 (1885), pp. 5–321, at pp. 32–69.

6 Cf. Nicholas, 'In the pit of the Burgundian theatre state' pp. 271–95; Arnade, *Realms of ritual*, pp. 49, 177.

7 W. Blockmans, 'Le Dialogue imaginaire entre prince et sujets: les joyeuses entrées en Brabant en 1494 et en 1496', *PCEEB* 34 (1994), pp. 37–53.

[**13**]. His deportment could also have a dramatic bearing on the outcome of proceedings [**15**]. As the ruler and his party moved through the route laid out for them, the organisers and performers had the opportunity to impress corporate messages upon the ruler. The repertory of sacred, classical and more recent history was deployed to achieve this end, articulating the wishes of organisers and participants for good governance, forgiveness [**14**] or favour [**16**]. Whether any of these objectives was demonstrably achieved is very hard to say: municipal authorities could draw up a balance sheet of the financial costs of an Entry ceremony [**16**] but could rarely measure the goodwill or even the material benefits won. For all the planning, costs and rehearsals beforehand, the time and effort spent during the event and the inevitable reflections that followed, the result of an Entry ceremony was therefore uncertain. The ceremony might even fail to perform its function of reconciliation, congratulation or introduction with disappointing or even disastrous results [**13, 15**]. The Entry ceremony was thus not an event the municipal authorities could afford to take lightly. With each successful performance the benchmark for future success was set a little higher. Through these pressures, the future of 'splendid ceremonies' in the Netherlands was assured.[8]

13. Preparing for the prince, Ghent, 1458[9]

Chastelain, *Oeuvres*, ed. Kervyn de Lettenhove, iii, pp. 396–416.

How the Ghenters most humbly requested the duke of Burgundy to visit their city

[T]hrough long and varied efforts, [the Ghenters] had laboured to attract their prince the duke of Burgundy to their city to see his people who languished in sorrow, for while he visited all his towns elsewhere, he seemed to hold the chief city of all in contempt and shunned it.[10] The people of Ghent were deeply saddened by this; on top of the pain of their past wound and ruin, this rejection was a new source of grief and they did not know how to remedy it. And so several of the city's notables were sent many times and on different occasions to the duke to beg him most humbly, for pity's sake and overlooking old faults, to come among them out of kindness and visit his town, for although his

8 J. Landwehr, *Splendid ceremonies: state Entries and royal funerals in the Low Countries: a bibliography* (Leiden, 1971).

9 J. Chipps-Smith, '*Venit nobis pacificus Dominus*: Philip the Good's triumphal Entry into Ghent in 1458', in B. Wisch and S. Munshower (ed.), *All the world's a stage … Art and pageantry in the Renaissance and Baroque* (Pennsylvania, 1990), pp. 258–90; Hurlbut, 'Ceremonial Entries', p. 222 et seq.; Arnade, *Realms of ritual*, pp. 128–42.

10 Following the conclusion of the Ghent War at the Battle of Gavere on 23 July 1453, Philip the Good did not return to Ghent until his Entry in April 1458.

peace and forgiveness had been granted to them, it seemed that because
he avoided the city and visited others instead, he still harboured some
feelings of resentment against it, which troubled them greatly.[11] Many
times the Ghenters had expressed their sadness to the duke and humbly
entreated him to win him over, and the duke had shown himself cold,
harsh and slow to respond to their urgings. Now, however, with the
duke at Bruges and the Ghenters thinking that by importunate and
incessant requests they would vanquish and soften his resolve, and that
by so much banging and ramming the gates of fulfilment would be
opened to their wishes, they returned once more in fine and worthy
array to Bruges and, taking as their advocate the heir to the throne
of France,[12] who was joined by [Guillaume Fillastre] the bishop of
Toul (his influence was then supreme),[13] [Thibaud de Neufchâtel] the
marshal of Burgundy and [Charles] lord of Rochefort, the Ghenters
renewed and reinforced their pleas and, distributing great sums of
money here and there to secure advocates, they also promised an abundance of wealth to their prince to reach the desired end.[14] This marshal
of Burgundy was once the most hated man in Ghent,[15] but now, by
subtle means, he had found allies within the city and he kept all matters
relating to it in his own hands, and he played with the town as a child
might with a ball. The governors of Ghent put such faith in him and
gave him such authority that they wanted to do nothing without him
and everything through him, and to use his services first and foremost.
And so he acquired more wealth than he did praise for public service.
This marshal was closely acquainted and familiar with the dauphin, so
the Ghenters took him as their means to gain access to the latter to win
the dauphin's support, for they knew full well that the dauphin could
obtain anything, and that the duke, their natural lord, would not wish
to refuse him. The duke was fully aware that the Ghenters were seeking

11 On the terms of the Peace of Gavere see M. Boone, '1300–1500: the "city-state dream"',
    in Decavele (ed.), *Ghent: in defence of a rebellious city*, pp. 81–105, at pp. 102–3.

12 Louis, dauphin of France, and king from 1461, in self-imposed exile in the Low Coun-
    tries from 1456 to 1461: Vaughan, *Philip the Good*, pp. 353–4; M.G.A. Vale, *Charles VII*
    (London, 1974), pp. 163–93.

13 Head of Philip the Good's council since 1457, present at Bruges from early January
    to late March 1453: M. Prietzel, *Guillaume Fillastre der jüngere (1400/07–1473)* (Stutt-
    gart, 2001), p. 506.

14 W. Blockmans, 'Patronage, brokerage and corruption as symptoms of incipient
    state formation in the Burgundian-Habsburg Netherlands', in A. Maczak and E.
    Müller-Luckner (eds), *Klientelsysteme im Europa der frühen Neuzeit* (Munich, 1988),
    pp. 117–26.

15 Vaughan, *Philip the Good*, pp. 326–7.

to reach their ends by these means, and that the heir to the throne of France would be obliged to involve himself in their affairs. For this reason, desiring to have the goodwill of his people before any other, he had it said to the Ghenters that they should not trouble themselves to have anyone make pleas on their behalf, for when he wished to show his kindness and clemency toward them he would do so without the help of a third party, and all in good time; and that by acting otherwise, they would do their cause more harm than good. The Ghenters realised the full significance of these words and gently backed down in the hope that they might still attain the duke's forgiveness.

The Ghenters nonetheless persevered in the pursuit of their goal, and instead of bothering their duke and lord, which they no longer dared to do, they approached their mediators and pressed them hard, even though they were often rebuffed by the latter and were told of the great dangers which lay in what they sought, for the mediators had seen their master's resolve in the past, and come what may he had resolved never to set foot in the city, and in this matter he appeared steadfast and unshakeable, as far as could be told ...

[The Ghenters insist, arguing that the city was loyal ('there is not a man, child or woman who would not open his or her belly for the duke to place his feet inside') and desperate for a reconciliation; unlike Bruges, the city had never laid a hand on the duke, and had fully repaid 300,000 gold crowns it owed in war reparations.[16] The Bishop of Toul was sympathetic, but not optimistic ...]

> Heavens, we truly hope that you and the people of the city have no inten- tions other than loyal ones and that you only wish for the best, but what trust can one place in the infinite number of other rough and wicked folk, evil youths with no honour among them, nor love, but who have perhaps fought against my lord in battle where, defeated and in flight, their fathers, brothers, uncles, close friends and relatives were killed, and in which they lost barns and had their houses burned and were thus impoverished, and lost their beasts and chattels; and now, perchance, when they see the man for whom all this was done in their snare and stronghold, thinking of revenge for their troubles, they might assemble in the night and while he and we his servants are sleeping they might fall upon us and attempt to kill us all, master and household together?

The bishop of Toul argued well and his allegations were well founded, but it seemed to the Ghenters that it was not difficult to meet his objec- tions. Among them were two principals who knew the city and its affairs profoundly, one of whom was the advocate retained by the city,

---

16 M. Boone, *Geld en macht: De Gentse stadsfinanciën en de Bourgondische staatsvorming (1384–1453)* (Ghent, 1990), pp. 60–1.

a notable and learned man named Matthijs de Grootheere who was of
high standing in Ghent, and another named Jan de Stoppelaere, *bailli*
of the Oudburg and a notable as well.[17] These two, knowing the fears
and wariness of the duke's men to be ill-founded, and that many of the
things they were afraid of would never happen, such was their knowledge of the common people, replied:

> My lords, although there is an infinite multitude of people in Ghent and
> although because of its size the city's affairs are very hard to investigate
> for those who are not accustomed to it, this is not the case for us, nor is
> it an obscure matter to know how to do so, but rather through the most
> expert handling it is possible to know those who are good and those who
> are wicked, and who could start something and who would not, for while
> the number of people is very great, the multitude itself does not give rise to
> confusion, for they are all numbered and known in their innermost thoughts
> by those whose task it is to govern and lead them, such as the deans and
> the aldermen, the merchants, the constables and the men responsible for
> the hundreds and tens[18] in the various parishes and streets, in the member
> of the small guilds as in that of the weavers. As for the bourgeoisie, and the
> suggestion that the powers of its members are unknown, quite the opposite
> is true; for the notables pull together all those of this member because they
> are feared and redoubtable, and are powerful and of good lineage, and the
> rest of the lesser folk who make up this group would not dare oppose their
> will or edict, and this is something we are sufficiently expert in to know how
> things stand. And for these reasons we, with our experience of the city and
> its people through the reports of its leaders, each in his place right down to
> individuals by name and surname indicating who is who, and through our
> experience of the laments and cries we witness with our own eyes everyday
> by everyone wishing to have among them just once before they die the
> person of this noble prince to whom they feel they have done such wrong,
> we, for sure, can speak for them with confidence ...

Then the Marshal of Burgundy said:

> Truly, gentlemen, I have been your harshest enemy in the past and would
> have caused you a great deal of damage had it been in my power; but I was
> never as keen to make war on you then as I am today to advance your cause,

17 Many cities retained one or more learned jurists like de Groothere to represent
their interests in courts or on occasions such as this Entry: P. Rogghé, 'De Gentse
klerken in de XIVe en XVe eeuw: Trouw en verraad', in *Appeltjes van het Meetjesland*
11 (1960), pp. 5–142, esp. pp. 105–13; M. Boone, 'Les Juristes et la construction de l'Etat
bourguignon aux Pays-Bas: État de la question, pistes de recherches', in Duvosquel
et al. (eds), *Les Pays-Bas bourguignons*, pp. 105–120. The Oudburg was a district to the
north-east of Ghent over which the duke had jurisdiction. Occupants of the office of
bailli were commonly notables of Ghent.

18 A reference to the practice of dividing the population into units of ten and one
hundred households for military and other purposes.

and I would dearly love your wishes to chime henceforth with the honour and well-being of my lord. However, you know that formerly you pressed him on this matter and had humble requests made to him, yet we never felt he was disposed to accept; instead, we found him cold, and for that reason it is highly dangerous for us to labour the matter if the willingness does not come from his own heart. Nonetheless, you have asked my lord the dauphin if he is prepared to act as your advocate, and he can achieve a great deal. As for us, we are willing to help you in whatever way we can.

And so it happened that the duke was lobbied from all sides to such an extent that finally he agreed, and the dauphin, who had never visited the city, even offered to go in person with him to make his Entry. The duke raised objections to this on the grounds that evil tongues might say he had endangered the dauphin's life by taking him to a city of such ill-repute, even though it would have greatly pleased the duke to see the dauphin there and to show him such a jewel of a city. Wishing to act wisely in all things, however, the duke sent the bishop of Toul and his marshal of Burgundy to negotiate with the Ghenters over the venue and even the proceedings; to propose all the measures necessary for the security of the two princes; and to deal with certain conditions relating to matters of finance. The two lords went there and stayed for a number of days, and found everything to be in such good order that they saw no defiance there, and no cause whatsoever to quibble. In addition the city offered 20,000 gold *lyons* to the duke, and another great sum to the dauphin, without counting the precious stones prepared for him, for the bishop, for the lord of Croy[19] and the marshal of Burgundy, each with his own share, which all together amounted to such a huge sum that it is a wonder the money was raised at all, considering the ruin that been visited upon the Ghenters and the 300,000 *écus* which they had paid to the duke by the terms of the peace treaty. However, everything was there and even more since.

And the duke gave in to the Ghenters, and it might seem that he did so because of the entreaties of the dauphin, or out of greed; but with due respect to those who might think this, he did so for neither cause, but rather out of one concern alone, which was that it seemed possible the French might visit war and tribulation upon him,[20] and before such a thing could happen the duke deemed it useful to see his people and to have their loyalty and their love behind him, above all the people of this city, chief of them all, and from which one can call upon more counsel,

19 Antoine, lord of Croy, Philip the Good's first chamberlain.
20 Vaughan, *Philip the Good*, p. 346 ff.

succour and mighty feats than from any other. Since the best way of
winning the people's hearts is to be seen by them and to go among them
(and yet also feeling in himself that the time was now right to do so), he
gladly decided to go there; for he had always loved the Ghenters above
all others and still loved them, despite the war he had fought against
them, for he had been raised there as a young child and had grown to
manhood in the city, and he had received many particular signs of love
and favour there.[21]

It was in the month of March in the season of Lent that this arrangement was struck between the duke and his good town of Ghent, and his
Entry into the city was set for the first Thursday after Easter, 6 April.
The arrangement was considered a firm one by all. The Ghenters made
sumptuous and rich preparations for their magnificent reception, for
they are a people of great resolve and ability. And so it happened that
after this agreement had been reached and the Ghenters were making
their great preparations, on 27 March, during Holy Week, in Ghent
and all around the city (but not elsewhere) there was a great earth
tremor which struck fear into the hearts of men and gave rise to many
thoughts; and on top of that, to further increase their fears, St Bertoul
deafened the whole convent by the force of his banging in his reliquary
in the abbey of St Peter, and it is said that this saint only does this when
he is announcing some great event in the future.[22] The saint banged
fiercely and heavily throughout the duration of the earth tremor, so
that if the latter gave cause for concern, so too did this saint, and news
of these events spread far and wide, all the more so because the duke
was due to make his Entry there in a short time. It would be impossible
to give all the various interpretations which were made of this. Some
said 'It's a bad sign and we should be afraid of the coincidence of these
two things occurring at the time of the Entry'. Others said 'It's hardly
surprising that objections have been raised against him going there,
and I consider those who were against it to have been wiser than those

21 In 1411, Philip, then count of Charolais and aged 15, was appointed as his father's
   representative in Flanders in response to Flemish requests. Save for a few months, he
   is thought to have resided in Flanders almost continuously until his father's violent
   death, news of which was conveyed to him in Ghent in September 1419: Vaughan,
   John the Fearless, pp. 153–4. The desire of the Flemish to keep the dynastic heir among
   them was manifest during the youth of Mary of Burgundy and the childhood of
   Philip the Fair.

22 Jean Lemaire de Belges, one of Chastelain's successors as official historian, independ-
   ently described hearing how the saint 'banged and hammered terribly' inside his
   reliquary when any 'mischief or change' was about to befall Ghent: J. Lemaire de
   Belges, *Oeuvres*, ed. J. Stecher, 4 vols (Louvain, 1882–5), iv, pp. 500–1.

who sought it'. Others said 'Look at the danger in taking these two princes among these villainous rebels where they might both be killed, and all of us with them. Upon my death, if I were they I would never set foot in the place'. Others said a thousand other things, each according to his own thoughts.

And so the day of the Entry was approaching. The Ghenters were still making their preparations, and several courtiers went to see the arrangements. Among these men were some from the dauphin's household. The Ghenters had barred off all the roads with double barriers on both sides, from the city gate to the entrance of the duke's residence, so that there would be no access for horses to side streets and crossroads and only to the decorated thoroughfares. The dauphin's men did not understand the mysterious nature of this arrangement and, imagining there to be some wicked and cunning motive behind it, returned at the gallop to their master at Bruges. Having announced to him what they had seen, they counselled him never to go to Ghent, for they feared that some wicked plan might be afoot, and that his life would be in peril if he were to go. This, combined with the earth tremor, the great blows of the saint and the barring of the streets with sturdy timber struck such a fear into the dauphin's mind that he would not have gone to Ghent for the whole world. He even pressed his uncle closely on the matter and advised him not to go, saying that his life and the lives of all his men depended on it …

[The duke agrees to postpone his Entry, originally scheduled for 6 April. News of the delay causes consternation in Ghent, and deputies from the civic elite rush to reassure Philip. The marshal of Burgundy inspects Ghent's preparations and reports back to the duke that all is well. A new Entry date of 23 April (St George's Day) is set, leaving the Ghenters further time 'to do great things'.[23] The dauphin refuses to go, however.]

And so the appointed day arrived, and the duke left Bruges on a Saturday to reside at Eekloo, halfway to Ghent. The following day – which was a fine Sunday, clear and mild – the duke, having heard mass and eaten a light meal, mounted his horse and set off on the road to his city, his route lined by great crowds at the roadside and in the fields. The valets and baggage-carriers went on ahead to ready the lodgings for their masters, and the prince's person was surrounded only by noblemen and

23 The saint was venerated by the duke as a crusading figure, and his son adopted the saint for his war cry. But St George was also important to urban elites, particularly as the patron of many archery and crossbow confraternities, not least that of Ghent itself. D.A.L. Morgan, 'The cult of St George, c.1500: national and international connotations', *PCEEB* 35 (1995), pp. 151–62.

about two hundred archers wearing jackets, some wearing brigandine armour, others not, but all with helmets, bows and quivers in fine order … The notables and nobles of the city came forth from the city in great number, all dressed in black as men who humbled themselves before him and recognised their previous misdeeds. Coming before him in the open fields, the appointed men dismounted, paid reverence to their prince, and presented him with the keys to all the city gates. This done, they placed themselves at the front and led the duke into the city where, at the first gate, he found fine dumb shows of great significance, all very much to the point. The duke also found the gate completely and richly covered from top to bottom in woollen cloths that were decorated in many beautiful ways. From that point on all the streets were draped with red cloth on both sides,[24] with rows of torches set on top of timber barriers all the way to the entrance of the duke's palace, which is fully a good quarter league or more in distance. On the cloths in great silver letters were written the words: *'Veni nobis pacificus dominus; utere servitio nostro, sicut placuerit tibi,* etc.', which in French means 'Come to us, lord of peace, and make such use of us and our service as you please'. These are the words which the peoples of many lands and cities said to Holofernes when, sent from the great king Nebuchadnezzar, he trampled the earth before him. Through crossroads and streets there was an array of dumb shows, each one finer and more splendid than the last, and all appropriate to the occasion, based as they were on matters relating to the city, to Roman and other histories, and some wholly novel in meaning, so that all who beheld them considered them a marvel. Then came the second gate where a great heaven was hung, and from the top of the roof to the ground this bore the arms of all the knights of the Order – a fine sight and the result of a great deal of careful work. Still further on the dumb shows and solemnities grew ever more impressive, so much so that justice could not be done to them without a lengthy and elaborate description, for there were many marvellous things which had never been seen before – although it goes without saying that at all the windows there was a press of fine ladies and damsels in such great number and of such beauty that one could scarcely choose among them. Then came a great bridge across the River Leie near the butcher's hall where mermen were to be found swimming in the water and fighting one another, along with mermaids, quite naked with tousled hair as they are commonly depicted in painting, and right in the middle of the river there was a great ship richly furnished inside with tapestries and

---

24 Cf. [14] which states the cloth was black, grey and red. Different spectators recalled different aspects of the ceremony, as the following makes clear.

all finery of the household, with a great dresser on the poop deck laden with expensive plate, and in front of this ship there were a number of beautiful maidens who acted out their show for the passers-by. On the outside the ship was entirely covered in green cloth, and at the bottom all around burning in the water there were two hundred lit torches, with as many as could be placed on the deck as well. The topmast was raised in the centre with its crow's-nest and the rigging was covered in torches, as was the crow's-nest which was so full of torches that they resembled stars in the heavens, and in the middle of the mast there hung the duke's coat of arms: this too was surrounded by torches, so that the whole boat seemed to be on fire. There were trumpeters and buglers inside the ship who made the river resound with a marvellous melody. In short, never had such a ship been seen, nor one so well executed or so rich.[25] Close by there was a house entirely covered – the roof, walls, door and windows – in lustrous gold, hung from top to bottom with green torches. The butcher's hall, which is large and spacious, was so full of torches that no one had ever seen such a sight; the fishmarket so full of decorations, dumb shows and torches that it could hardly be described, unless at great length; likewise the Friday Market, which was as finely decorated in parts where one could walk by as it was in places where one could not; the belfry, so full of illuminated torches that it could be seen at night from certain vantage points from a distance of five or six leagues, and it seemed to be on fire all around and from top to bottom, for it is a great and ancient edifice, and it was lit up all night and for the three following days; and thus there were more and more marvellous sights which cannot be described lightly, until the duke reached his palace where he dismounted to relax and make good cheer that evening, and where the lords of the town came back to offer him presents of wine and other worthy gifts. That night the greatest bonfires the city had ever witnessed were lit all around, and the torch illuminations were kept until daylight, and again in the same manner the following day by renewed invitation, and then the third and the fourth day to the Friday, when the trades continued to vie with one another in holding feasts and illuminations, as did the street and neighbourhood groups who vied with one another with tables laid out in the streets with wine and food for passers-by with no heed to cost, and men and women sang and

---

25 This scene is entirely absent from [14] because the pageant described was performed the day after the Entry. Chastelain has telescoped the events of the duke's sojourn in the town: Chipps-Smith, *'Venit nobis pacificus Dominus'*, pp. 264–5. It is revealing that the particular pageant the chronicler decided to focus on was performed by the shippers of Ghent, the milieu he originally came from (see general introduction to the present volume).

danced and turned night into day, and then carried on into the daylight
hours. All foodstuffs were sold at the lowest prices and no one dared
to raise them a single penny, nor did anyone dare to cause trouble –
on pain of death – for a single man who belonged to the court. Such
was the treason and malice the Ghenters planned against their prince,
which turned instead into such delight, such love and such honour. The
marshal of the dauphin [Jean de Lescun], known as the Bastard of
Armagnac, was still with the duke when he made his Entry, for his
master had sent him there along with some other lords and noblemen of
his household to see everything. These men were astounded and made
the sign of the cross upon themselves in amazement at the great and
marvellous feat which this Entry truly was, and at the most wonderful
wealth and power of this city, and stated that never had such an event
been witnessed in the world, nor such pomp or excellence as this town,
supreme among all, had exhibited. The duke was so much at his ease
that night that along with only three or four others he went to visit the
feasts and the bonfires throughout the city, and the people cast themselves down before him in joy and kissed the ground he walked upon,
wishing him with great voice all the joy and prosperity the heavens and
the Lord above could bestow upon a man.

14. Welcoming the prince, Ghent, 1458

Kroniek van Vlaenderen van 580 tot 1467 (Maatschappij der Vlaemsche Biblio-
philen: Ghent, 1840), pp. 212–32.

The Joyous Entry of my most redoubted lord and prince Philip …
which he made into his city of Ghent on the feast of St George, Sunday
23 April 1458, and which was organised by the aldermen and others of
the same city of Ghent in the following manner …

Sir Arnout van Gouy, lord of Auby, knight and high *baljuw* of Ghent,[26]
the under-bailiff, the *baljuw* of the Oudburg, four aldermen of the lower
bench of magistrates and four of the upper, along with Master Mathijs
de Grootheere, their advocate, rode out toward my aforesaid most
redoubted lord accompanied by various notables, and noble citizens
of the city of Ghent, all mounted on horseback and dressed in black.
They rode in well-ordered fashion with fully four hundred horses to the

26 Judicial officer representing the prince's authority, set over other local *baljuws* such as
   that of the Oudburg. Incumbents often came from the Ghent *poorterij*. On van Gouy
   see general introduction.

other side of Mariakerke.[27] There they welcomed my lord most humbly, as they were beholden to do, with gracious words and greetings, and Mathijs de Grootheere spoke on their behalf in French:

> Most high, most powerful and most excellent prince, our redoubted and natural lord, we have long wished for your Joyous Entry in this, your good city of Ghent. Now the long-hoped-for hour is upon us, and we thank the Creator for the blessing he has bestowed on us this day, for without doubt this joyous and most happy arrival removes all doubts and all fears from our hearts that your anger against us had not abated; but since it pleases you to grace us with your visit, we feel reassured and certain that the past is now forgotten and erased from your noble heart, for which we thank you in all humility, and we offer you everything that is in our power – our bodies, our goods, our desires, and anything that you would order us to do – for we are ready to live or die for you. Welcome, most redoubted lord and natural prince, to you and your company.

Thereupon my most redoubted lord replied in kind and friendly fashion, and they all repaired in fine array to the city, until they reached his palace of Ten Walle.[28]

Outside the Walpoort,[29] on the outskirts of the city along both sides of the street to the end of the Waldamme[30] as far as the ramparts the deacons and all the sworn members of the guilds and the sworn members of the weavers were spread as far out as possible, each finely dressed in his long cloak of office down to the ground and as many as 500 in number, each bearing a lit torch in his hand.[31] When they became aware of the approach of my redoubted lord, they fell to their knees and removed their hats in fine and graceful order.

From the aforesaid city gate to the first gate of the Ten Walle palace of my most redoubted lord, the streets on both sides were hung with woollen cloth in black, grey and red, five feet or more from the ground at their lowest point. And as one entered from the Walpoort the cloths

27 Roughly 5 km north-west of the centre of Ghent.

28 Also known as the *Prinsenhof*, this residence was located in the north-west of the city near the Bruges gate, at some remove from the edifices associated with civic authority in the centre. The residence was more luxurious than either the *Posteerne* (also located near a city gate, on the west side) or the *Gravensteen* (the old comital castle located closer to the centre, by then rarely used as a residence but maintained for administrative functions).

29 aka the Bruges gate, located on the north-west side of the city.

30 An area of water located by the Walpoort.

31 The deacons of the 53 small guilds and the representatives of the weavers constituted the second and third elements of the Three members which governed Ghent; the first member consisted of the bourgeoisie (*poorterij*).

on the right-hand side were first red, then grey and finally black, while those on the left-hand side were hung in the opposite order, and so they continued on both sides all the way down to the gate of the palace.

Upon the frames from which the cloths were hung, there were a great many torches sticking out through new tin trays, 760 in total, each set at a distance of four ells[32] from one another.

The cloth was divided up by a large number of golden letters: 'Come unto us, peaceful Lord, and make use of our services as you see fit. Judith 3'.[33] In particular the words 'Come unto us, peaceful Lord' were written on the black cloth; 'Make use of our services' was written on the grey cloth; and 'As you see fit' appeared on the red cloth. Between every two words was depicted the crest of our most redoubted lord along with his device of a flint issuing sparks, each embroidered with 150 stitches.[34] From the Walpoort to the palace on the right-hand side there were 65 cloths, each 30 ells in length, and on the other side there were 63 cloths just the same …

On the cloth of the main gates at the Walpoort were depicted the arms of my most redoubted lord, beautifully adorned with his Order of the Golden Fleece and his battle cry of 'Montjoie' in large gold letters, encircled by his motto, 'I shall have no other'. The cloth was covered with fire-steels and flints, the devices of my Lord.

On the parapet of the gate and on the walls there were as many burning torches as could be placed, 62 in total, each set one foot apart on new tin plates.

Between the crenellations of the gate there were many trumpeters and minstrels who played most agreeably from the arrival of my redoubted lord until he was led far into the city, and they were all richly dressed in the arms of my said lord and of the city as befitted the occasion.[35] All people in Holy Orders either having property in the city or being citizens of it – such as the prelates of St Pieters, St Baafs, Baudeloo, Geraardsbergen, Ninove and Drongen, the provost and chapter of St Veerle, the deans, all of the parish priests and other priests of the city, people in minor orders and the beguines of both the beguinages – were

---

32 A measure of cloth approximately one metre or yard in length, but which varies slightly according to locality.

33 Judith 3:6.

34 Philip the Good's personal emblem.

35 M. Clouzot, 'Le son et le pouvoir en Bourgogne au XVe siècle', *Revue historique* 302 (2000), pp. 53–66.

present within the city close by the gate each in their most precious copes, habits and chasubles of their churches in the manner of a fine procession, the prelates first and the others following, lined along both sides of the streets as was appropriate. When they saw my most redoubted lord approach they paid him all due reverence and devotedly sang *Te deum laudamus.*

Outside the same Walpoort, across the river until the end of the Waldamme, stood two stages, one on each side of the road, and on each stage there was a pavilion in which a prophet stood with a long beard, a rich blue fur-lined vestment and a fur-lined hat, and in his hand each held a parchment scroll. On the first prophet's scroll were written the words 'Behold, the name of the Lord cometh from afar. Isaiah 3'.[36] On seeing my most redoubted lord, the second prophet, who stood on the other side of the street and who was dressed like the other, pointed toward the city and the trumpeters who stood above the crenellations of the Walpoort, and held out the scroll in his hand which said 'Blow the trumpet, that all may be made ready (Ezekiel C. 7)'.[37]

Close by the entrance to the city at the foot of the ramparts of the Walpoort, on the left as one enters, there was a stage set high above the ground containing a beautiful arbour or bower draped with green woollen cloths lined with seats, three steps leading down from it. The bower was entirely decorated with a great number of different beautiful flowers with a sweet and fragrant smell, and enclosing it there were ramparts from which the arms of my redoubted lord and those of the city were hung. Immediately below the arms of the city were written in golden letters 'I came upon him whom my soul loves. Song of Songs 3'.[38] In the bower there knelt a young maiden, ten years old or so, dressed in a white silk corset, a white damask cloak, with beautiful long hair done in the fashion of a bride, wearing a myrtle headdress. Joining her hands together most sweetly in supplication, she descended the three steps toward my most redoubted lord as he approached.

Inside the said Walpoort opposite the house called *De Roze* there was a stage covering the street next to the canal, and upon it stood the figure of the Prodigal Son who had ignobly squandered his portion, finely presented in the following manner. The father wore a long hooded gown and a small hat with a red brim, with three servants dressed in black behind him. The son was poorly dressed, his doublet in tatters, his

36 Isaiah 30:27.
37 Ezekiel 7:14.
38 Song of Solomon 3:4.

stockings rent at the knee, and the father met him in this pitiful state
and pardoned him as a result of the son acknowledging his misdeeds.
Beneath the said stage were written the words 'Father, I have sinned
against Heaven and against you. Luke 14'.[39]

In front of the Hospital of Saint John there was a stage with a pavilion
in which there stood a prophet dressed in a long green gown which was
most wonderfully decorated. Facing toward the Walpoort and pointing
with his hand toward the Peperstraat, he held a scroll which bore the
words 'In her tongue is the law of mercy. Proverbs 3'.[40]

At the end of Peperstraat a stage had been erected bearing the figure
of Julius Caesar, the Roman emperor who first founded Ghent. Caesar
was seated on an imperial throne with a long grey beard wearing a long
lined silk gown, with an imperial crown on his head and a sceptre in his
hand. Beside him stood twelve senators, six on either side, dressed in
long lined gowns and fur hoods and caps. One of the twelve senators,
Marcus Tullius Cicero, knelt before Caesar, his head uncovered and his
hood upon his shoulders, and he praised him for various liberties and
signs of compassion he had shown to the prisoners he had captured
when he took Rome, and in front of the emperor and the other senators
he made an oration which began with the words on the scroll he held in
his hand, and which he pointed to with his fingers: 'This day, O conscript
fathers, has brought with it an end to the long silence in which I have of
late indulged'.[41] On the edge of the stage were written the words 'None
of your virtues is greater than clemency. Cicero, in his Orations'.

Across the Holstraat there stood a stage which bore a great black lion
with its jaws gaping as if it was roaring. In its paw the lion held a fine
standard bearing the arms of our most redoubted lord. Opposite this
lion there was another, a beautiful white female meekly stretched out,
and between them lay three white lion cubs which seemed to be half-
dead. When the black lion roared, they awoke and were brought back
to life. Everything was masterfully crafted and lifelike. On the edge of
this stage was written 'He will roar like a lion and the children will be
afraid. Hosea chp. 2'.[42]

39 Luke 15:21.
40 Proverbs 31:26.
41 The phrase is not from Cicero's oration *For Ligarius* (Chipps-Smith, *'Venit nobis
pacificus dominus'*, p. 262 n. 23) but *For Marcus Claudius Marcellus*. Marcellus was a
consul who had sided with Pompey in the civil war, and who was pardoned by Caesar
at the request of the senate. Cicero praised Caesar's clemency in this oration.
42 Hosea 11:10. The lion was the emblem of the counts of Flanders.

On the walls of the convent of Our Lady of Galilee at the end toward
the Torenpoort there was a stage with a splendid pavilion in which a
prophet stood, richly and curiously attired with a long purple gown in
the Hebrew fashion. In his hand was a scroll on which were written the
words 'Here comes the desire of nations, and I will fill this house with
the glory of the Lord. Haggai chp. 2'.[43]

Close by the Torenpoort there was another magnificently adorned
stage hung inside and out with costly tapestries. Upon it stood the
figures of David and Abigail, the wife of conceited Nabal. King David
stood splendidly attired in the armour of the Hebrews with a shield
bearing his emblem of the harp, a fine helmet and a magnificent crown
on top. Behind him stood three of his knights, all richly dressed in
armour in the Hebrew style with wonderfully strange painted coats of
arms. Before David knelt Abigail, whom he held by the hand. She was
dressed in a corset and cloak of green damask silk. Behind her knelt
two women, one dressed in a corset and cloak of black damask silk, the
other in patterned purple silk. All three were a beautiful sight to behold.
On their heads they wore hats and necklaces in the Hebrew style. The
indignation of King David at the aforementioned stupid and conceited
Nabal was assuaged by the humble entreaties of Abigail. In front of this
stage were written in large letters: 'Blessed be the Lord of Israel who
sent you. Kings chp. 24'.[44]

The little Torenpoort in front of the large Torenpoort was covered
from top to bottom in black and grey woollen cloth, in accordance
with the status of my aforesaid redoubted lord, and in the middle there
hung a fine blazon bearing my most redoubted lord's arms with the
crest of his helmet and the insignia of his Order and with his war cry,
finely painted on a banderole. Further down on the same cloth were
richly emblazoned shields bearing the arms of the lords who were then
members of the Order of the Golden Fleece, as finely adorned as those
which are customarily hung in the churches where my most redoubted
lord celebrates the feast of St Andrew. The arms which hung there were
those of the following lords:

[There follows a long and, save for the unexplained omission of Jean de Lannoy,
accurate, list of the 31 knights of the Golden Fleece ...]

The cloth upon which these coats of arms were hung was decorated
with fire-steels and fire-stones. Beneath these coats of arms and imme-

43 Haggai 2:7.
44 1 Samuel 25:32.

diately above the gate there was a scroll, and on it in golden letters were written: 'You have come, desired one, whom we await in the shadows. Story of the Resurrection. Nicodemus'.[45] Above the gate were six trumpeters from whose instruments hung beautiful and costly pennons of silk emblazoned with the arms of the city. The trumpeters played melodiously as my lord the duke went by. The opening and sides of the aforementioned Torenpoort and the parapet above it were covered, at the sides and in the opening, with blue woollen cloth, and on the inside scattered with suns, moons and stars in the guise of a heaven, and twenty torches were placed therein, giving light and clarity because there was no other source of light. This was indeed a most beautiful thing to behold.

At the Poel a great high stage had been constructed with three levels each fifty feet long and twenty-eight feet wide, all decked out in blue cloth and enclosed at the front with white curtains. The mystery which was enacted on this stage was entitled 'The Choir of the Blessed adoring the sacrifice of the paschal lamb' ...

[What follows is a precise description of a physical re-enactment by over 100 figures of Jan van Eyck's *Adoration of the Mystic Lamb* triptych, commissioned by alderman Joos Vijd for the nearby church of St John's in Ghent, completed in 1432 ...]

The Peinsieders lane off the Drabstraat was closed off at the front by a stage on which there stood a pavilion with a shepherd in it, with his crook and the other implements of his profession. The shepherd was carrying a sheep over his shoulder, and he made the animal bleat as my most redoubted lord came past. In front of the scene was written 'Rejoice with me, for I have found what I had lost. Luke 14.'[46]

In the Hoyaert there was a stage bearing the figure of Pompey, the former captain of Rome, with four knights by his side, all splendidly armed with wonderfully emblazoned shields in the Roman style, and in front of Pompey knelt the King of the Armenians and three of his nobles, also beautifully attired with armour and shields in the style of the Saracens. Pompey had imprisoned the King for his rebellion against Rome, but seeing his dejection and humility Pompey took pity on him and restored him to his former status, returning his crown, his lands and his lordships because Pompey took as much joy and praise from giving as from gaining. In front of the stage was written 'He thought

45 The apocryphal gospel of Nicodemus, recounting Christ's visit to Hell.
46 Luke 15:6.

it equally fine to conquer kings and to make them. Valerius Maximus, Book V chp 1, On clemency'.[47] My redoubted lord passed through the Korte Munt, across the Fishmarket, over the Counts' Bridge, across St Veerle square to the foot of the Hofbrug. Here there stood a stage bearing a prophet who was pointing into the water, dressed like the other prophets described above, holding a scroll in his hand with the words 'Look, O Lord, to your servants. Psalms 89'.[48] In the water beneath the Hofbrug there was a figure represented in the following manner: first, a rope was stretched over the water from which there hung a blue sky which opened up; from the opening there emerged an angel who descended to a pavilion which hung above a green island that had been made in the water. The angel lifted up that pavilion with its hand, and below stood our Lord Jesus Christ dressed in a long grey gown. Not far from our Lord there was a little barge containing St John the Evangelist and St Peter, who appeared to be fishing. St John stood up firmly facing our Lord and held in his hand a scroll bearing the words 'It is the Lord'.[49] St Peter wanted to go toward the Lord, but fell into the water up to his shoulders without sinking any deeper, and he lifted his arms out of the water holding a scroll in his hand bearing the words 'Lord, save me'.[50] Our Lord who looked on also had a scroll in his hand bearing the words 'O ye of little faith, why did you doubt?'[51] Then the angel let the pavilion descend over our Lord.

On the Hofbrug at the little gate to the Counts' Castle there was a stage bearing a prophet dressed like the others who pointed toward the Burgstraat, and he held in his hand a scroll bearing the words 'All the trees of forests shall rejoice before the lord, for he comes. Psalms 14'.[52]

At the end of the Burgstraat in front of the house known as The Dragon there stood a large stage decked in green cloth with white curtains across the front, and on the stage there stood a representation devised in the following manner: on one side there was a splendid castle with fine gates, many towers and battlements from which the arms of all the lands of my most redoubted lord were hung as they should be represented, richly decorated with paintings. The castle seemed all to be

47 The story of Pompey and Tigranes, 66 BC, recounted by Valerius Maximus in his *Factorum et dictorum memorabilium*, Book 5, chp 1.9.

48 Psalms 89:16.

49 John 21:7.

50 Matthew 14:30.

51 Matthew 14:31.

52 Psalms 96:12.

made of brickwork and in front of it were written the words 'Unless the Lord keeps watch over the city, the watchman stands guard in vain. Psalm 126'.[53]

In front of the gate of this castle there stood the figure of a man dressed in the following manner: he wore a gown, the right side of which was made of red cloth embroidered with gold down to the ground, and the left side of which was made of goatswool hitched up to his knee. In his left hand the figure held a spade; in his waistband there was a sheaf of corn; and on his head there was a lined hood of the type worn by the Benedictines. Behind him alongside the gates of the castle were written the words 'I love you, Lord, my strength'.[54] The man was dressed thus in order to represent the three estates: the lined hood signified the clergy; the gold-embroidered cloth represented the nobility; and the goatswool, spade and sheaf of corn represented the commons. In front of this man stood a great giant named Mars with a horrifying weapon in his hand, sumptuously dressed and carrying wonderfully strange weapons in accordance with ancient suits of armour, all from paintings, and by his manner he showed he was the defender and protector of the castle. Beside him there stood a black lion with a man inside who roared and growled like a lion in a manner that suggested he wished to help the giant, and on the other side from this stage there was a dangerous and wonderful wilderness, all green with many trees and hedges containing a great many wild animals, some peering out of mountains, rocks and caves, some apparently standing, such as dragons, giant snakes, bears, wolves, foxes and flying serpents, all expensively made according to paintings from real life; there were also live monkeys, hares, rabbits, squirrels and foxes. All of these animals appeared to be ready to bound to the destruction of the castle. The significance of all this was as follows: the castle signified all the lands of my most redoubted lord, which is why all the emblems of his lands were hung upon it; the man dressed in the manner of the three estates represented the Three Estates of the lands of my redoubted lord; the giant, who defended the castle with the lion against the fierce beasts, signified our most redoubted lord and prince, who devotedly protects his lands and the Three Estates against all enemies who would seek to harm him or his lands.

On the Sanderswal[55] at the end of the street at the house known as the Golden Ring there stood a stage decked out in white, and upon it there

53 Psalms 127:1.

54 Psalms 18:1.

55 The name of the area in which the prince's court of Ten Walle was located.

sat King Solomon on his royal throne in an ivory seat, richly dressed in royal garments with three of his knights standing by him. Queen Sheba knelt before the king with three of her maidens, also richly dressed. Solomon held out his sceptre to Sheba as if to put it into her hand, and in front of this stage was written 'Your glory is even greater than I heard tell.'[56]

On the little square of the Sanderswal there was a stage bearing the figure of Gideon dressed as a captain of the Jewish army, splendidly armed in the Jewish style, who stood by an oak tree under which there lay a fleece. Beside Gideon stood three of his knights beautifully attired in painted armour in the Jewish style, and upon the tree there sat an angel who appeared to have promised something to Gideon. On the other side of the tree four Israelites knelt, all dressed in Jewish clothes. In front of this stage was written 'Rule over us, both you and your son, and your son's son; for you have delivered us. Judges 8',[57] which was thus fulfilled after the angel had given him victory.

In front of the gate of the residence of my redoubted lord there was a stage with a great grey elephant. Above his mouth he had a long trunk from which wine spouted forth as though from a fountain, and he had two long hanging ears, two great shiny eyes, a knobbly nose and two long tusks shaped like a boar's teeth, lifelike in every detail. Two men who had seen such an animal alive were involved in making it. The elephant stood in green grassy pasture, and on its back there was a great castle, as though it were built from tiles, in which there stood four little children and two men all dressed in the Jewish manner, black as Moors and each with a javelin in his hand. The children sweetly sang a new song that had been composed for the Entry of my redoubted lord, and in the song each letter at the beginning of the line was a letter from the name of Ghent:[58]

> Long live Burgundy! that's our cry
> Let us preserve him, by our deeds and in our thoughts.
> 'I shall have no other',[59] for he pleases me;
> And so we wish it always.
>
> Long live Burgundy! that's our cry.
> We sing from the heart. I prithee,

56 1 Kings 10:6.

57 Judges 8:22.

58 The song was in French. We have not attempted to translate the composer's acrostic.

59 Philip the Good's motto.

> On this, his joyous Entry,
> Let us spare no expense.
> Since he has come to his land,
> All our sadness is gone;
> And so we sing in our streets:
> Long live Burgundy! that's our cry.

Right beside the gate of *Ten Walle*, the palace of our redoubted Lord, there was a stage upon which a prophet stood, attired after the fashion of the Old Law, and in his hand there was a scroll with the words 'Here is my rest. Isaiah 10'.[60]

All the aldermen who had not gone out to meet my most redoubted lord – that is to say, the greater part of the bench and both of the chief deacons, namely the chief deacon of the small guilds and the deacon of the weavers in their official robes, along with their sergeants, servants and members of their craft, each according to his estate in notable and worthy order – stood in the court yard of Ten Walle, and there they welcomed my most redoubted lord with similar words and offerings as before, and the speech was given by Master Pieter Bierman, advocate and retainer of the city, in the following fashion in Flemish ...

[The speech that follows is identical to that given in French at the start of the Entry by de Groothere.]

Thereupon the prince made a gracious reply and all returned to their homes or lodgings. It was fully nine in the evening, and my lord had spent more than four hours passing between the gate and his palace.

15. An Entry ceremony goes awry, Ghent, 1467[61]

Chastelain, *Oeuvres*, ed. Kervyn de Lettenhove, v, pp. 249–78.

And so came the time for Duke Charles, his eyes still wet with tears from the burial of noble Duke Philip, to prepare to go to Ghent, the capital of Flanders, to take possession of the land, for it was an ancient custom that the prince should show himself there first. Indeed, some Ghenters had already come to Bruges on behalf of their city to present their condolences to the young new duke in his time of sadness, united in their desire to console him and to pay reverence to him, and, in addition, to request, if it pleased him, that he might visit his city and his

60 Psalms 131:14; cf. Isaiah 28:12.

61 Arnade, 'Secular charisma', pp. 69–94; Arnade, *Realms of ritual*, pp. 127–58.

humble subjects who held and wished to acknowledge him as their true and natural prince and lord to the exclusion of all others; as such, they would pay him humble and devout reverence and afford him a cordial reception. Because the city of Ghent has always been a dangerous place, and its common people are to be feared due to the natural influences which prevail there, Charles, the new duke, with the advice of his barons and the men of his council, did not forget to question the Ghenters who had come to see him as to the condition of the city, and to ask whether his security could be guaranteed. He also wanted to know in advance of any demands the common people intended to lay before him on the occasion of his new Entry into the city – demands which, if met or refused, might cause trouble to one side or the other … The Ghent deputies were aware of the close questioning on the duke's behalf and resolved to please and flatter the court, for they were astute and knew how to sail with the prevailing wind. They replied craftily that they were well aware the common people might ask for a number of things, but in any event there was no need to accord them very much – at least not anything that might swell their pride, which would be as great as ever if they were given back their castellanies, and if the taxes which had been levied on all sorts of goods as a punishment for their misdeeds were now to be abolished. It was said that through the collection of these taxes the governors of the city, of whom these representatives were the main men, had taken and continued to take for their own purposes an infinite amount, and that although the sums owed to the prince had been amply repaid, the levies continued, much to the detriment of the people and to the benefit of others in the city, some of them governors. For this reason, and because of the profits they were making so craftily, they advised the duke and his men that the taxes should on no account be abolished; for from the great profits which came in every year, various members of the court could be retained and supported, and they received a free share to turn a blind eye. Indeed, some important people, so it was said, had received a lot of money over a great many years, three or four thousand here, a thousand or five hundred there, distributed annually like rents …

How some of the people of Ghent planned their own reception for the duke, and secretly plotted a disturbance

In Bruges, then, discussions took place in the manner you have heard, and the duke had good intentions toward his people of Ghent. But in Ghent itself rather different discussions took place, in secret and by prior arrangement, and these were quite unknown to the envoys who were with the duke at Bruges. Since the people knew full well that the duke would soon make his Entry into Ghent to take possession of the land, they reasoned maliciously that the time had now come to throw into utter confusion their governors and those who, so they said, were robbing the people – against God, against reason and contrary to all laws – with the pitiless taxes they raised. The prince had been paid long ago, so the people said, and the whole city had paid the double of its debts twice over. Although I speak of the people in general, the people were not all of one faction, nor of one evil intent, nor of one secret conspiracy, but were united only in one common and worthy complaint against the taxes which affected them all, so that the common nature of the harm they felt made for a common grievance. But it must be understood that among the great number of people who live in a place such as Ghent, one finds all sorts, some good, some bad; and it is certain that a sufficient number of evil, wicked, proud and mutinous rebels had conspired in secret to prepare an unnatural gathering for the Entry of this duke, hoping thereby to achieve their ends – principally the abolition by force of this tax and the downfall of the collectors – and reasoning among themselves that the new duke would be forced to consent to their demands, and would not know how to remedy the situation once he had seen them aroused in anger. And so, it was said (and as it has since been found to be true), they had new banners made in secret, and they kept them hidden away until the day of their undertaking; for their banners had generally been confiscated by the peace of Gavere, and they were not allowed to have any from that time onward, on pain of death and contravention of the peace. But now they outrageously presumed to have new ones made, so that they would be able to rally around them once they had made public and set in motion their outrageous plot.

How in the past the notables of Ghent were accustomed to carry the body of St Lieven, whereas now the common folk carry it

It is fitting at this point to note that a multitude of glorious saints repose in Ghent, and among these there is a saint named Lieven, who, from the earliest times since his martyrdom, has wished to be borne to the very spot where he was martyred, around three leagues from Ghent in a village named Houtem.[62] St Lieven has to be left to repose there for one night until the morning, his feast day, when he wishes to be carried back to St Baafs in Ghent, his resting place. In the beginning, it was

---

62 South-east of Ghent, therefore on the opposite side from the point at which the duke made his Entry.

customary for this noble saintly body to be borne and accompanied throughout this marvellous mystery by a great multitude of people in the noblest fashion, and brought back with due solemnity and reverence. As time goes by, however, good customs and morals diminish, then turn bad and grow cold with the passage of the years; worthy people turn their back on charity; the reverence due to male and female saints falls away, only to be taken over in our own times by lowly and poor folk; and the great and the good no longer trouble themselves with it, through lassitude. And so it has come to pass in Ghent, where worthy and pious creatures used to carry and bring back this glorious saintly body every year to the place mentioned earlier, but where nowadays a multitude of rogues and louts carry him, bawling and yelling, singing and braying, scorning everyone and everything and drunk to the last man. And since they travel in a great crowd, they are all in doublets, without gowns, so that they are more lightly clad, and more or less all of them are armed with hauberks, wearing iron helms and carrying full-length swords and short ones; and they commit a great many outrageous acts along their way, like wild men unbound. To see them one might think the whole world was theirs for a day, by dint of the body they bear. However, out of regard for the evils and dangers which might ensue from all this in the future, after the battle of Gavere Duke Philip restored law and order and established by perpetual edict in Ghent that those whose duty it was to bear this glorious saintly body should never carry iron nor staff, nor wear hauberks or anything else of that nature, to avoid the mischief and scandal that can occur when a multitude of such people gather together, which is truly something to be feared …

[The duke set off for Ghent with his treasury in tow, stopping first at Deinze for the night, then nearer to Ghent 'in a pretty little house of a burgher' where he heard the cases of people exiled from the city, 'for it is the custom for a new prince to free such people from their condition, and to lead them in' …]

And so it came to pass that on the very day Duke Charles was due to make his Entry into Ghent, this crowd of all sorts whom I mentioned above vacated the city from the other side, bearing the body of St Lieven to the customary place. And there was a great number of these people, all young, rough men, wild and hot-headed, menials and workers from various trades such as the masons, blacksmiths, carpenters, cobblers, weavers and fullers, brewers and foundry men, and a great many from other trades; and one can well believe that among them there were some evil mutinous types, as it turned out when they returned the following day, as you will hear. And so on this very day, which was the

eve of the feast of St Lieven, Duke Charles, with his good and noble
intentions toward the Ghenters who had served and loved him well,
entered the city with solemn processions going before him, and scarcely
with any less reverence than might have been paid to God. Welcomed
and worshipped by his people by means of great dumbshows, passing
through streets which were nobly hung with cloth, accompanied by
the melodious ringing of bells, the finest in the world, the duke came
directly to the abbey of St Peter with his nobles to give his first oath.[63]
It was then around the hour of terce, which is a most suitable hour for
breakfast, and the meal was ready, most sumptuous and rich. And so
immediately after the oath was taken and reverence paid to the Lord
God in church, the duke breakfasted very well in the company of a
great multitude of lords and noblemen and others, for all were welcome.
There they made good cheer. No one, neither the duke nor anyone else,
had anything other than good faith and salutary intentions, the duke
toward his people in general, and the generality of the people toward
their prince in all humble reverence, and indeed the duke was loved and
cherished a great deal for he had brought them nothing but comfort
and love. However, it could well have been that the people were vexed
and remorseful because of the taxes which were levied on them. They
did not hold this against the new duke, but rather against some of the
leading men of the city about whom they proposed to lodge complaints
with the duke by means of a fine remonstrance, once he was in the
peace and quiet of his home. There was nothing wrong in this, so long
as worse did not follow – which sadly turned out to be the case, and the
danger was such that it should never be forgotten, for the duke himself
was in mortal peril, along with all his nobles, and in danger too of
losing all his lands by rebellion one after the other.

How the rebellious commoners brought St Lieven back, and the disturbance they caused in Ghent

I move on, then, from the manner of the duke's Entry, which was rich
and joyous in appearance, and leave him at rest with all his chivalry that

63 The form of words used in first oaths is sometimes attested, as at Douai in 1472,
    where Charles the Bold sent a letter to the aldermen the day before his Entry stipu-
    lating the oath he would require of them: 'We swear and promise to be good, loyal
    and obedient subjects, to protect your estate and person, your lands, rights, high-
    ness and lordships, and to serve you against all comers'. In return, according to the
    municipal records of the town, the duke 'also swore his oath to the city of Douai in
    the manner respected by his father, God rest his soul, which was read out to him by
    Pierre de Hauteville, adviser of the town, from the biggest Hall Book with 5 bosses
    on the cover which contains the form of words for such oaths': Lecuppre-Desjardin,
    Ville des cérémonies, pp. 143–4.

night in Ghent, making good cheer without any sense or expectation of evil or mischief of any kind. For I wish now to come to the wicked rabble which had left Ghent with the saintly body, and which, that very night, while they had the run of the fields and no one watching over them, made good cheer too, but with evil intent, drinking, eating and whistling, and swearing abominable oaths to the effect that they would accomplish miracles and make a name for themselves, and that they would turn valleys into mountains and mountains into valleys. And it seemed to them that without too much effort they had it in them to cook up an evil brew which, to the nose or the tongue, would have a bitter taste. Fie! a curse on their plots and their boasts!

It is customary in the village to which this saint's body is carried for a fair to be held, and from all the surrounding country the people come with the result that, with the cabarets and taverns which are there in great number, many male and female merchants also come to sell haberdashery and fancy goods and lay out among their wares various objects made of lead which can be used to keep children happy. And so it was that on this occasion, although I do not know whether it was by chance or on purpose, among these lead objects there was a remarkable number of toy hauberks in the form of brooches for attaching to one's sleeves or anywhere else one wanted. And so of all those Ghenters who had come, everyone took and wore about his person a toy hauberk in full view and with great scorn, joking all the while and saying:

> By the blood and wounds of Christ! They banned us from wearing hauberks,[64] but at least we wear them now and for all to see! They will be made of lead, iron and steel later. Let it be done! He who laughs loudly today will pass a bad night with little comfort. Come! Come! let's get back! He who has not tried his hardest has done nothing! Ghent is in the wolves' jaws, in the hands of wicked plundering thieves who consume our very entrails, and in the prince's name they grow fat on our worldly goods and stuff them in their sacks. We are eaten out of house and home, and what's worse, the prince knows nothing of it! But before too long, since he is now in Ghent, he will know all about it, if God permits us to make good our return.

These and similar words were uttered among the rabble on their way back to Ghent, some under their breath, some loud and clear, and a conspiracy was hatched among them in secret, and all was planned out in detail to achieve their ends as it later became apparent. For as soon as they entered the city, and as if acting of one accord, chanting and yelling with the intention of committing some outrage or other,

64 The terms of the peace of Gavere of 1453 were in this respect still in force fourteen years later.

they passed by the Corn Market and there, singing their songs and
fooling about, they waited for each other until all were together in a
great flood of people, and then fell pell-mell upon a little booth there
where the commissioners received the taxes. They smashed it into a
hundred thousand pieces in their rabid, bestial fury, each carrying off
a piece through the town and back to their houses shouting 'I've got a
bit! I've got a bit!' Since they had made such a wicked start they fully
hoped to carry on and win support before anyone could gather to put
up resistance against them, they cried out 'Halt! Halt! Halt!' to one
another and sounded the alarm. Suddenly, from all the surrounding
crossroads, the people arose. In this moment all those with mutiny on
their minds who had previously held themselves back for fear of the law
immediately took up arms, and as though conjured up out of thin air,
banners appeared[65] and people assembled under them to come to the
Corn Market, assembled according to guild (some of which, since time
immemorial, have been naturally mutinous and the first to get up to no
good). And so they came, crying with one horrible voice:

> Kill! Kill these pillaging liver-eaters, these thieving robbers of God and of
> the whole world! Where are they? Let's seek them out and kill them in their
> houses so we can make a great butchery of the men who have lived off us
> and ruined us.

[The crowd decamps to the Friday Market, the site of events of the duke's
Entry the previous day, and continues to grow …]

Now hear a tale which is pitiful and shameful for all Ghenters, especially the good men of the city who suspected nothing of what had
happened. Very soon news of the call to arms reached the duke in his
chambers, just as he was hotly debating with some of his close advisers
what pardons and acts of courtesy he wanted to give to the Ghenters
whom he loved dearly, and upon whom he wished to bestow, so he said,
a number of favours. As the horror of the call to arms rang around the
court and all the duke's servants fled back toward him (partly to guarantee his protection, partly to save themselves), the duke was stupified
and, as if struck between the eyes by a mallet, he was dumbfounded
by this undertaking and could not understand how it had come about,
from outside the city or within, at least on the basis of what he had been
given to understand and what he himself had intended to do. It seemed
to him that in truth this was a strange way of welcoming him and of

---

65 P. Arnade, 'Crowds, banners and the marketplace: symbols of defiance and defeat
   during the Ghent war of 1452–3', *Journal of Medieval and Renaissance Studies* 24
   (1994), pp. 471–97.

marking the beginning of his rule. He reassured himself, however, and fortified himself against the peril like a prince of great courage, and he knew himself to be surrounded by a multitude of great men and valiant knights, together with a great number of well-equipped archers. So the duke called for his steed and immediately ordered that everyone should mount on horseback, for he intended, so he said, to go to see the disturbance. He swore by St George that he would speak to the crowd at close quarters and that he would find out what had moved them to act in this way, and what it was they wanted ...

And so this great crowd of Ghenters remained on the Friday Market, heavily armed and with their newly made banners raised high. From all directions groups of armed men rushed to the gathering and their number increased so greatly that it was a horror to behold. Passing through the streets as they flocked together they encountered courtiers, but they spoke to them gently, saying:

> My lords, have no fear; we wish you well and only seek to serve you. Go where you please, you are in no danger; we are all here for you, to do your will.

And so they would move on, although there was no one who did not tremble with fear and wish he was a hundred leagues away when he heard such words or beheld such upheaval, for never had such dread been felt.

By now the duke was mounted on his steed and in the company of his nobles and archers. He made straight for the market where these rebels were to be found, the lord of Gruuthuse at his side because of his knowledge of the region and the language.[66] And so he reached the market where, at his approach, the great gathering of people began to close ranks and cower before him, each man drawing nearer to the banner of his group shouting 'Halt! Halt!', for they did not know what the duke's intentions were, for good or for ill, and they saw his archers approaching with their brigandine armour and helmets on, and their bows drawn. There was a great many of these fine, strong and unyielding men, and the manner of their approach seemed threatening to the crowd. The people were dismayed as they watched the archers draw near, and they feared the prince's wrath; and from them there arose a great cry as though a dreadful peril was near at hand.

66 According to Chastelain, the duke sent Gruuthuse (Louis of Bruges) to parley with the crowd before going to the Friday Market himself. This account is at variance with other sources which state the duke headed directly for the Friday Market to confront the rebels.

At that point the duke appeared on the market in his black gown with a small baton in his hand. Without further ado he approached the gathering of people and tried to push through them to reach the house where the prince usually goes to when attending events in the square.[67] As he went past he asked them 'What do you want? What is stirring you up, you wicked people?' He treated them angrily and used harsh words, and as he went by he struck one of them with his baton. Immediately he found his life in danger, for the man who had received the blow – so it is said – took it badly and swore on the blood and wounds of Christ, and immediately lunged menacingly after the duke with his pike as if to kill him. He addressed the duke with angry, proud and irreverent words. Indeed, the danger was very great and no one could have done anything about it save God Himself, Who contained the danger. And in that place there was not a single archer or nobleman or man-at-arms, however sure of himself, who did not tremble with fear and wish he could have been in the Orient for his own safety and above all for the safety of the young prince who, they believed, was about to come to a terrible end.

At that point the lord of Gruuthuse, who was beside the duke, saw the error and great recklessness of his master and told him boldly and brusquely:

> Goddam! What are you trying to do? Do you want to get us all killed here by your temper, stupidly and defencelessly? Where do you think you are? Can't you see that your life and ours hang by a thread? You come here and stir up this great crowd with threats and harsh words as if you didn't have the slightest thought or care for the least among us. They are furious beyond all reason or understanding. For the love of Christ! You might be happy to die here, but I'm not; at least not if I can do anything about it: for you can easily treat them differently and calm them with kindness, and thus save your honour and your life... Go on, dismount your horse and get up there, show your worth, make the people admire you for your good sense, and all will be well.

How the shippers and butchers of Ghent came to join the duke, who ascended to address the people on the Friday Market

As the villain who had been beaten stood and cursed his prince through gritted teeth, surrounded by others who may have had a similar wish to commit a great outrage, some of the banner-bearers who stood close by, and who saw and heard the disturbance around their prince, immediately rallied around the duke with all their might to defend him ...

67 The 'high house' mentioned below.

The duke welcomed this assistance with joy and was reassured. Those that joined him were the shippers,[68] butchers,[69] fishmongers[70] and a few other guilds with their banners, and they amounted to a fair number. The duke climbed up into the high house on the Friday Market, and showed himself at the window. Schooled by the lord of Gruuthuse (who stood close by him), the chancellor and others to speak gently and benignly to them, he began in Flemish:

My children, may the Lord save you and keep you! I am your prince and your natural lord and I come to visit you and gladden you with my presence to put you at peace. I pray you, as a favour to me, contain yourselves and be calm. Anything I can do, so long as it is in keeping with my honour, I will accord, so long as it is possible for me to do so.

And at that, with one voice they cried out in Flemish:

Hah! Welcome! Welcome, our lord! We are all your children and we thank you for your kindness toward us!

Then the lord of Gruuthuse, at the duke's command, replied, saying:

Gentlemen, behold your prince, your natural lord by ancient pedigree: not by acquisition, by purchase or through tyranny, but your natural lord by descent through his forefathers for six hundred years, a line which has never failed. He truly believes you will recognise him as your rightful and natural prince, as you did for his predecessors. Thus, if there is anything in him which does not please you, he asks as your prince and lord that you speak to him in terms which good children should use when speaking to their prince; and he desires to be, and will be, amiable and kind in all that you require of him.

And at that they all replied with great voice:

Thank you, thank you my lord! You are our prince and we will have no other, and we are your children. But we beg of you, give us satisfaction against these liver-eaters who are destroying our city and who leave us scrabbling for our bread. They are even of lowly birth and humble origins, for we have

---

68 Ranked sixth of the 53 small guilds in 1356, third by 1540, providing almost twice as many office-holders in the period 1379–1410 as any other small guild: Boone, *Gent en de Bourgondische hertogen*, pp. 76–7. As we have seen, Chastelain's family were shippers.

69 Ranked first of the 53 small guilds in 1356, still first in 1540, providing the second largest number of office-holders in the period 1379–1410 among the small guilds.

70 Ranked second of the 53 small guilds in 1356, still second in 1540, providing the seventh-equal largest number of office-holders in the period 1379–1410 among the small guilds.

seen them as miserable rascals, and now they have become the masters of what is yours, which they steal from us, and they have lands and lordships and live in great estate from your money ...

How a rebellious Ghenter came forward to climb up alongside the duke, holding forth on behalf of his companions

Just as these words were being spoken from below, and as the duke listened with all his heart, a big, rough lout, wild and bold, secretly climbed up and placed himself at the window alongside the duke.[71] Once there he raised his hand, which was clad in a gauntlet of polished black iron, and banged it down heavily on the base of the window frame in front of him to make himself heard. Without paying any reverence to the duke, and without fear, he made so bold as to speak in the following terms:

> – You, my brothers down there, you who seek to make your grievances and complaints known to our prince here about weighty matters that concern you, above all about those who govern this city, who rob the prince and you – you want them punished, right?
> – Yes! cried the others.
> – And you want the levies abolished, don't you?
> – Yes! yes!
> – And you want your sealed gates opened up and your banners restored, just as they were?
> – Yes! Yes!
> – And you would like your castellanies back, and your white bonnets, and the way you used to do things? Isn't that right?
> – Yes! Yes! they replied ...

Now, if confusion reigned among many good and worthy men in Ghent itself, this was even more the case at court, and for many reasons. The duke had Mademoiselle his daughter with him, and he feared he might not be able to get her out of the city because the wicked villeins would not tolerate it if they saw her departure. He had also brought with him from Bruges all the treasure he had found on the death of his father, which amounted to a marvellous sum, and he wished to get this out as well to a more secure place. For if things turned out badly and those wicked people tried to use force against the nobles, all of that great wealth would be scattered and lost, so it seemed to him, and it would be the first thing to be seized. And so it was decided after due deliberation that quietly, and by night, the coffers would be taken away and put on

---

71 Identified as Hoste Bruneel, a 'knecht' (manservant) according to the account given in the *Kroniek van Vlaanderen*: Arnade, 'Secular charisma, sacred power', p. 87 n. 64.

the road to Dendermonde[72] where they would be safe until the duke's arrival. As for Mademoiselle his daughter, as much as possible would be done to secure her departure once the duke had calmed the people somewhat with promises. She would leave with the duke, by consent of the people – for to tell the truth, he feared (as indeed did everyone else) that she would be detained as a hostage until he had consented to everything they wanted. However, good sense and fine words prevailed. After two or three days the duke had them put down their arms and return to their houses, and from that point on negotiations began. The duke assigned his council and the leading men of his household to the task, and he had promises made to the Ghenters that he would give them satisfaction against those with whom they had grievances, and conduct investigations so that justice might be done ... And so by using gentle words, however differently he felt in his heart, the Ghenters were contented and thought they had done a good job. However, this business would cause a great deal of hardship and fear later on, which few of them suspected.[73]

16. Paying for an Entry ceremony, Bruges, 1515

Bruges city archives, expense accounts for the 1515 Entry of Charles, prince of Spain, into Bruges (May 1515). Edited in L.P. Gachard, *Collection des voyages des souverains des Pays-Bas*, ii (Brussels, 1874), pp. 531–42 (from the Bruges town accounts: Stadsarchief, 216, 1515, fos 121r–27v).[74]

---

72 To the east of Ghent between that city and Mechelen.

73 In the summer of 1467 a deputation from Ghent achieved a temporary reconciliation with Charles. The duke was preoccupied with his war against Liège, until his army systematically destroyed that city in October 1468. Realising complete abasement before the duke was now a good idea, the Ghenters submitted. A deputation of leading townsmen was forced to wait for an hour and a half in the snow at Brussels in January 1469 before being admitted to the duke's presence, where the city's charters were torn up before their eyes. Further repressive measures followed before a second Entry ceremony, perhaps intended to cleanse the memory of the first, was held in May 1469: V. Fris, 'La restriction de Gand (13 juillet 1468)', *Bulletijn der Maatschappij voor Geschiedenis en Oudheidkunde te Gent* 31 (1922), pp. 57–142.

74 This Entry was the subject of two early published descriptions, one in French prose by the court historiographer Remy Du Puys, another in Dutch verse by the Bruges rhetorician Jan de Scheerere (Small, 'When *indiciaires* meet *rederijkers*'). Remy Du Puys's account appears in S. Anglo, *La Tryumphante Entrée de Charles prince des espagnes en Bruges 1515* (Amsterdam/New York, 1973). The rhetorician's account is edited in S. Mareel, 'Jan de Scheereres *Triumphe ghedaen te brugghe ter intreye van Caerle*: Teksteditie met inleiding en aantekeningen', *Jaarboek De Fonteine* 55 (2005), pp. 79–143. In what follows, appropriate passages from du Puys's description are translated in the footnotes to clarify the nature of the expenditure.

For carpentry (total: £188 8d)[75] [*Flemish pounds, like all those that follow*]

First, to Cornelis vanden Westhuuse on behalf of Antheunis Pieters for the first item of expenditure: the scaffolds for the model of the forest at the entrance to the Pepper Street (Peperstrate),[76] for the model of the portal of St Donatian's near Red Street (Roo Strate),[77] and for the model of the Town Hall opposite the House of the Mermaid and the Church of the Order of Saint-James,[78] and for the supports holding up the same ... £27 15s.

To the same Master Cornelis, for the second item of expenditure: the hall built on the Mill Bridge,[79] the hills in front of the house of Hanekin in the High Street (Hoochstrate),[80] and the model of the castle by the block house on the corner of St John's Street[81] ... £30 7s 4d.

75 Du Puys (B ii v°) describes the construction of the pageants which follow: 'all the scaffolds were tall and wide, in the form of castles and otherwise, with doors and galleries, constructed with fine carpentry; towers and turrets were ingeniously built and finely decorated with beautiful paintings inside and out, without the use of curtains or tapestries save those required for covering thrones or platforms for the characters (and these coverings were in gold and silver cloth, in velour or other silk)'.

76 In Pepper Street the prince came upon a splendid scaffold 'on which there was a beautifully represented forest which opened in two parts, the first by a wild man. On the front were written two Latin verses which said: "From Liederic the Forester, a man of great age, Gandymede received the city of Bruges". Inside, the origins of the city were acted out by finely decorated characters: how Liederic divided his land of Flanders among his children, and gave his son Ganymede the city of Bruges as his share, making him the first lord and judge of the city. The second part of the forest was opened by a wild woman. Inside, there was a representation of how Joshua left the Promised Land. For alongside each or most of the stages representing some aspect of the history of Bruges there was another depicting a similar story from the Old Testament to signify the prosperity, adversity and conduct of the town' (Du Puys (B ii v°).

77 The miniaturised replication of landmarks of the town was a recurrent theme of the Entry.

78 Built for the first of the Nine Members, the burgesses, this was a model 'in wood and paint of the Bruges town hall with all its gates, doors, windows and tiles, its statues of the counts and countesses of Flanders, the prophets and all the others perfectly replicated ...': Du Puys (B iv v°).

79 Built for the second of the Nine Members, the four cloth guilds, this was 'a perfect copy' of the trading place known as the Old Hall on the market square of Bruges: Du Puys (B v v°).

80 Built for the third of the Nine Members, the butchers and fishmongers, described by Du Puys as 'a very long scaffold on which there had been constructed two great mountains, one covered with cattle and sheep, the other with various other kinds of animals, all of them represented as models or painted flat, as though they were grazing. And on the summit of one mountain there was a golden sheep with horns'.

81 Built for the fourth of the Nine Members, the seventeen building trades, described

To the same Master Cornelis, for the third item of expenditure, namely the ciborium beside the house known as the Crown at the end of the Armourers' Street (Wapenmakers straat),[82] and the bridge on the Square of the Crane,[83] … £23 8s 4d.

To the same Master Cornelis for the fourth item of expenditure: the scaffold on the corner of Fleming Street (Vlamync straat),[84] the pavilion in front of the House of the Bear by the Butter House, and the gallery and gate at the palace of our most redoubted Lord … £19 5s …

To the same, for timbering the Gate of the Holy Cross, the Wooden Hall, and the barrier from the gate up both sides of the street to the palace, on which the cloths were hung and the torches mounted, together with 40 chandeliers for holding the torches, with the delivery and hanging of ropes for the same … £ 40[85] …

[Further carpentry work included 'the scaffold on the bridge by the Crane at the corner of Fleming Street, and the gallery and gate of the palace, as well as a wooden frame from the house of the Easterlings past the St Gillis Bridge up to the Square of the Spaniards.']

---

by Du Puys (C i vᵒ) as 'a mighty castle on and around which there were seventeen towers and turrets. In each of the towers there was a pennon bearing the arms of one of these trades. Two particularly big towers stood out on either side; in the middle of the castle there was a very fine gate with a gold handle which was opened to reveal a great lion holding in one paw a flint and in the other a stone which he struck to produce sparks.' The lion was the symbol of Flanders, the flint the emblem of the Order of the Golden Fleece.

82 Built for the fifth of the Nine Members, the jewellers, described by Du Puys (C ii vᵒ) as 'a great tower built on a round base beautifully carved and painted in the form of a ciborium in a most pleasant and novel fashion, in the middle of which there was a statue of a prophet …'. A ciborium is a cup-shaped vessel in which the bread consecrated at mass is placed.

83 Built for the sixth of the Nine Members, the leatherworkers, described by Du Puys (F ii) as 'a long and wide bridge': in the middle an arch was built to serve as a gate, wide enough for three horses, through which passers-by could proceed. On this arch a great tower was constructed as though from great blocks of stone. Around the tower eleven men played silver trumpets, accompanied by nine characters representing the Nine Members with their coats of arms, each holding a burning torch weighing six pounds.

84 At the end of the street was the spot allocated to the seventh member, the tailors, and 'all who work with the needle'. Here there were 'tabernacles like a fortress, with golden crenellations; on top were three statues of prophets each holding a scroll in his hand …' (Du Puys, F iii vᵒ).

85 According to Du Puys (B i vᵒ), 'From the Entry at the same gate [of the Holy Cross] to the palace there hung at equal distance from one another forty illuminations which were roughly six feet tall, widening toward the base in the form of a papal crown and consisting of three concentric circles, one roughly a foot and a half below the other, and on which there were forty torches placed on pewter plates, making a total of 1,600 torches …'

For painting (total: £135 9s 10d)

To Jan Fabiaen and his companions, for the first item of expenditure, namely the model of the forest, the model of the portal of St Donatian's and everything appropriate to it, according to the pattern and instructions given to him, for £9.

To the same Jan Fabiaen for the second item of expenditure, namely the model of the town hall and the hall with everything pertaining to it, £29 ...

To Lenaert van Cricki and his companions on behalf of Dieric Claerbout for the third item of expenditure: the dunes on the scaffold of the guild of butchers and fishmongers, and the castle built by the blockhouse, according to the instructions received, £19.

To the same, for the fifth item of expenditure and everything related to it: the tabernacle on the corner of Fleming Street, and the pavilion at the House of the Bear by Saint James's Street (Sint-Jacops strate), £8.

To Aernout Zoetaert and his companions, for the fourth item of expenditure: the ciborium by the House of the Crown, and the bridge on the Square of the Crane, £23.

Further, for making nine tunics for the Nine Members, £2 1s 8d and 15s earned by them for undertaking the painting involved.

To Jan vander Strate and his companions for the sixth item of expenditure: the gallery and the gate at the palace and all pertaining to it, £8.

Dieric Claerbout, painter, for having decorated the 40 chandeliers, £5.

For eleven dozen shields with the coat of arms of our most redoubted Lord – £3 16s.

Also, for 41 dozen coats of arms of Flanders, of this city, and also of the burgesses ... £8 4s.

Also, for 30 dozen coats of arms of the guilds of the city ... £4 10s.

Also, for a large shield of the arms of our most redoubted Lord hung in front of the Holy Cross Gate, 6 s; and 26s 8d to the same Dieric for various painting expenses.[86]

86 'In such array the young prince and his entourage rode to the gate of the Holy Cross by which he entered. The gate was covered from top to bottom in white cloth from which there hung several coats of arms bearing the arms of the prince and of the other lands of Flanders, and some of the arms of the town. Above them all there was a greater and richer coat of arms bearing the arms of the prince, below which were written sixteen verses in Latin of which the substance was the following "Charles, prince worthy of long life and all happiness and jubilation/Bruges is comforted by

All of the above items carried out by Dieric, and out of consideration for the slender profit he received from the work, and for certain extra work carried out by him, £2.

To Willem d'Hollandre, for his trouble in drawing up the eleven models for the pageants, 25s [and another 6s 8d; and for two other workers for the same work, 7s 4 and 5s each].

To Dieric Cochuut, for making a great lion and a camel which were used on the scaffolds on the corner of Fleming Street, 25s.

To Donaes Fabiaen, for painting the barrier yellow along both sides of the street from the Holy Cross Gate to the palace, 12s 6d.

To Jan vander Strate, 25s 4d which he earned for the same under-taking.

For illumination (total: £161 6s 5d)[87]

First to Edewaert van Ghysegheem on behalf of various candlemakers, for the fabrication and delivery of 1,700 torches at 7s each, £53 2s 6d.

To Antheunis Rans, for the fabrication and delivery of 600 torches … £18 15s.

To Adriaen van Likerke, for the fabrication and delivery of 100 torches … £3 2s 6d.

To Jan de Smit, for the fabrication and delivery of 2,250 torches £70 6s 3d.

To the same, for 60 lbs of table candles used on the aforementioned eleven scaffolds … £2 15s.

To the same, for nine great torches weighing 40 lbs used on the scaffold on the bridge by the Crane … 23s 4d.

To the same, for three torches weighing ten and a half lbs, used to light the other torches … 6s 1d.

To the same Edewaert on behalf of Christoffels Oosterlync for the

---

your presence, for in you her consolation lies/Alas, it is high time her decline was looked upon with compassion/She who used to be the chief of all honour, of all worldly goods and praise/So her fall is all the harder to bear'": Du Puys B i.

87 According to Du Puys (B i v°) 'it was a pleasure to behold [the torches], for the day was already turning to night. It is above all the custom to hold Entries at night, because of the great light that can be so prodigiously provided. And joined to this reason is the fact that the sight of all the ladies stacked up in all the windows, doors and streets is more becoming by torchlight than by sunlight, just as paintings look more marketable in half-light than they do in broad daylight'.

delivery of ten torches weighing 33lbs, also used to light the torches along the street ... 19s 3d.

To the same Edewaert on behalf of Jooris Cachoore for the delivery of ten torches weighing 30lbs used to light the other torches along the street ... making 17s 6d.

To Pieter Dufour, for fabricating 50 torches of three colours, namely white, red and yellow, which were carried by the swordsmen next to the person of our most redoubted Lord, at 4s per torch ... £10.[88]

Also to Lord Stevin van Praet for six torches which the magistrates had at the reception of our redoubted lord in his palace ... 9s.[89]

For the delivery of canvas used by painters to cover the eleven scaffolds, and also to make certain clothes and related items (Total: £44 8s 1d)

To Symoen de Boot, for delivering 4,477 ells of canvas, namely 1,997 ells of rough white at 21s 6d per hundred ... and 2,480 ells of coarse canvas, at 18s 6d per hundred ...

For the hire and eventual loss of pewter plates (Total: £14 13s 9d 16m)[90]

To Pieter vanden Rade, tinsmith, for the hire of 4,500 pewter plates[91] used everywhere where torches were placed, at a cost of 16 *miten* each, which comes to £12 9s 11d 16m.

To the same, for the loss of 33 of the same plates, each weighing 2 lbs ... £2 1s 3d, and for carrying the said plates back and forth, 2s 7d.

For cloth hanging at the Holy Cross Gate, and from there on both sides of the street to the palace (total: £42 9s 8d)[92]

88 Du Puys (B i v°) noted that 'close by [the young prince] to the right and left there walked 50 young men of the town ... each of whom held in his hand a burning torch of 8lbs most ingeniously formed and painted white, yellow and red, the colours of the prince, which was beautiful to behold.'

89 'Each of the deacons and magistrates ... had a torch weighing 4lbs in his hand to light the darkness and afford a clearer view of the triumphant pomp and solemn plays of all the pageants ...' (ibid.)

90 'The torches were placed on pewter plates to prevent the wax from falling on the passers-by' (ibid.).

91 A figure which corresponds to Du Puys's observation that there were 'large torches in double rows numbering 4,500' (B i v°).

92 'From the Entry at the gate up to the prince's palace, which is a considerable distance, both sides of the street to a height of twelve feet were hung with blue cloths upon wall plates' (ibid.).

As a result of the favour done by this city to the inhabitants of Poperinge,[93] the latter have thus loaned 180 blue cloths to this city on certain conditions previously declared on folio CXV; the said cloths have cost, namely: first, seven people from the city of Poperinge who stayed here, each 32 days at a cost of 2s per day, for the inspection and authentification of these cloths, according to the promise made, which comes to £22 8s [Also small expenses for fullers of Poperinge for mending cloths] ...

To various cloth-dressers, for having stretched, measured, pressed, folded and brushed 169 cloths ... £7 10d ...

For the hire and costs of the actors who were involved twice[94] in the performance on the aforesaid eleven scaffolds, and which were the responsibility of the councillors, clerks and rhetoricians named hereafter, who have signed in their own hands for the costs which they had separately submitted (total: £24 13s 10d)

First, my lord Claeis vanden Bussche, councillor, Joos Scoudharync, clerk, and Guydo vande Riviere, rhetorician, having had all the responsibility for these requirements in three pageants, namely the forest, the portal of Saint Donatian's and the Town Hall: £6 9s 6d.

To my lord Joos Theure, councillor, Jan de Witte, clerk of the orphans, and Cornelis van Wynghene, having had all the responsibility of two pageants, namely that of the Hall and that of the butchers and fishmongers, £4 14s 11d.

To my lord Jooris Janzuene, councillor, Colaert Ghyselin, clerk and Jacop Kempe, rhetorician, having had the responsibility of two pageants, namely the castle and the ciborium, £3 17s 6d.

To my lord Jacop d'Hurtre, councillor, Antheunis Bierman and Andries de Smit, rhetorician, having had responsibility for two other pageants, namely the bridge at the Crane and the pageant on the corner [of Fleming Street], £4 15s 11d.

To my lord Jacop Heyns, councillor, Bossaert Paridaen, clerk and Jan de Scheerere, rhetorician, having had responsibility for the last two pageants, namely the pavilion in front of the House of the Bear and the gallery next to the gate of the palace, £3 16s 9d ...

93 Roughly 50 km south-west of Bruges, therefore not a neighbouring community.
94 At the end of the performance the prince was reportedly so delighted that he asked for an encore the following day.

For the trumpeters who served the Nine Members (the burgesses, the Four Guilds, Butchers' guild, the 17 Members, the Smiths' guild, the Cobblers' guild, the Needlecraft guild, the Bakers' guild and the Brokers' guild) in their pageants .... Total: £31 5s 6d.

For the costs incurred by the rhetoricians and others who conceived the subject matter of the aforementioned eleven pageants, and whose names are set out below; also for several assemblies of members of the magistrates' bench, together with the seven people entrusted with conceiving and carrying out [the Entry] [Total: £5 18s 7d 18m]

First, for certain costs incurred at the aforementioned location of the Blind Ass and elsewhere at various times during the planning of the subject matter of the pageants, £2 17s.

Also in the Blind Ass, the expenses incurred there by the clerks who recorded the instructions for the carpentry and painting, 6s 6d.

For what was consumed by the companions who measured from the gate to the palace to know the distance from one to the other, 2s 6d.[95]

Paid in the treasury, the Monday before Shrove Tuesday, where my lord the mayor of the aldermen was present with some magistrates, as well as the committee organising the Entry, who had all been engaged in matters pertaining to the Entry, 13s 10d.

Paid in the treasury, the first Monday of Lent, where some magistrates were gathered in conference with the organising committee, as well as the rhetoricians, having discussed the matter, and where sustenance consumed came to 11s 5d 18 m.

Paid in Blanckenberge[96] in the afternoon before our redoubted lord's Entry by the organising committee, the rhetoricians, clerks and others charged with matters pertaining to the Entry, 11 s. At the same place, on the afternoon following the Entry of our most redoubted lord, for the expenses of the rhetoricians, the officers of the peace, servants and others involved in the arrangements for the Entry, and particularly for the recovery of the great number of pewter plates which had been lost, in total: 13s 4d.

Paid twice in the Blind Ass for the expenses incurred there by the aldermen and councillors and also some clerks, the day before the Entry,

95 We are grateful to Anna Jane Schnitker for noticing an error in the transcription: 'houc' should be 'hove' (palace).

96 Small town on the coast a few miles north of Bruges.

all having been involved with the Entry, 13s 4d.

For various other matters pertaining to the said Entry [total: £95 16s].

[Small payments for cloth of goat's hair to make certain clothes, some white and red linen for curtains in front of the House of the Bear, 80 balls of wood from which the gilded apples were painted to decorate the 40 chandeliers, 3,000 large pins to keep the coats of arms and cloths in place, and fastening hooks in case pins did not hold ...]

Also, for the six rhetoricians, namely Lord Gillis Ruebs, Jan de Scheerere, Cornelis van Wynghene, Guydo vande Riviere, Andries de Smet and Jacop Kempe, for their trouble and time in creating and planning the aforesaid pageants and for other matters, £36.

To Jan de Scheerere, by order of the chamber, for having written a verse account of the Entry, £2.

To Colaer d'Ault and Jooris Roelants, for having translated the same Entry account from Flemish into French, 20s.[97]

To Jacop de Brouckere, for having fired fifty shots on the road of the New Hall, as well as for the delivery of powder, £8.[98]

To Master Jan de Muelnare, for the fifty companions who carried the torches next to our most redoubted lord and prince, each of whom was helped with the cost of making a red tunic, 4s 2d, which in total makes £10 8s 4d.

To Wulfaert Wulfaerts, for his trouble in constructing the figure of Perseus, which it was hoped would be shown, 3s 4d.[99]

To Pieter Matruut, for his effort and work in having made the said figure operational, 20s.

To Pieter de Brune, painter from Ghent, who was brought here to this city to operate the said figure, for his time, 9s 4d.

For the hire of 20 horses which were used by the clerks and trumpeters for ten journeys for various messages outside the city pertaining to the same Entry ... 13s 4d.

97 On this text, see most recently Mareel, 'Jan de Scheereres *Triumphe*', pp. 92–8.

98 The use of artillery powder in one of the pageants put on by foreign merchants caused an explosion when the Entry was run for a second time the following day at Charles's request. Margaret of Austria was lucky to escape unscathed: Anglo, *La Tryumphante Entrée*, pp. 12–13.

99 Not mentioned by Du Puys, but Jan de Scheerere notes a representation of Perseus at vv. 622 (Mareel, 'Jan de Scheereres *Triumphe*', p. 131).

To the trumpeters who went forth of the city with the clerks who announced the messages and announced the orders, for 20 journeys ... 13s 4d.

To Jan Moscron, for having brought the coat of arms of our redoubted Lord from Ghent, 12 gr.

To Adriaen de Wyntre, clerk of the carpenters' guild, for his efforts in summoning the communality of the carpenters' guild to work on the carpentry, and for having helped to make the supports for the scaffolds, 2s.

To various workers for fetching the torches from Edewaert Ghysegheem's house and from all the other candlemakers, and for having brought them to the usurer's house beside the house of the Order of Saint James, 5s.

To Master Cornelis vanden Westhuuse on behalf of the 17 companion carpenters who had volunteered to light the torches in the forty chandeliers, £31 ...

[Small payments also for poles to light the torches and reeds to prevent them from being set alight if flames fell on them...]

To Anthuenis Vegghelman, for him and his companions, cloth carriers, for the hanging of the cloth from the gate to the palace on both sides of the street, as agreed, 29s 2d.

To various workers, for placing the torches and the pewter plates from the gate to the palace; for hammering in the nails with which the cloth was hung on the eleven scaffolds; for guarding the aforementioned cloth, which remained hanging from Wednesday to the following Monday; for securing the coats of arms and shields; for gathering up the pewter plates and torches; and also to the people who kept watch for eight days at the house of the usurer by day and by night in which all the torches, pewter plates, cloth and other items used in the said Entry were being kept, amounting together, as appears in a letter in which all these various tasks are specified, £5 15s 4d ...

[Small payments to men who placed and lit torches on the Holy Cross gate, in front of the Wooden Hall in the market place, on the hall at the Mill Bridge, on the scaffolds of the butchers and fishmongers ...]

To Donaes Vlamync, for the hire of twelve sets of armour which were hired by my lord the mayor of the aldermen and by Cornelis vanden Leene for £2 12s.

To Adriaen Bosschaert, for having made the scrolls on which the scripts for the pageants were written, 7s.[100]

To Joos Feytins, having written the said scripts, as agreed, 12s 6d.

To the widow of Jan van Hessen, for the delivery of a ream of paper in large format, from which the aforementioned scrolls were made, 7s.

To Aernout de Vos and Claeis, both servants, for the long time they spent gathering together the various people involved in the said Entry, and for the many journeys they made every day between the different people mentioned above, 16s.

To Coppin Minne, for his expenses and trouble in preparing the costume for his character, for his horse and for all pertaining to the same ... 25s.

To Zeghin van Roden, who kept an account of all the aforementioned matters and received all monies given by the Nine Members and all expenses met from that money, for which he is accorded the sum of £6.

To Cornelis vanden Leene, Robert Hellin and the aforementioned Zeghin, for their work and effort in the following matters: to the afore-named Cornelis and Zeghin van Rodin who, from the start worked daily with the rhetoricians to conceive how the Entry could best be done, what pageants could be performed, by what means and how; and further, all together, for having directed the seven people charged with the affairs of the aforesaid Entry. And they conceived and organised the Entry in such ways that it came to a good end and turned out well, to the greater glory of this city; for which they are granted the sum of £7 10s.

To Chaerle Snekant, clerk and servant of Zeghin van Roden, for his effort and work in receiving the torches, pewter plates, shields, paint-ings and all other things used in the Entry in the usurer's house, by the house of the Order of Saint James and elsewhere, and again for having handed them out and distributed them to wherever they were required, 10s.

---

100 Many such scrolls were used. A lion striking a flint had verse written on a scroll by its head ('O Charles, desiring to please you with all my heart/I forge fire and fury to pour on your enemies': fol. C ii vº of Du Puys's account), for instance, while a further inscription was recorded on a nearby tower, also on a scroll.

Other costs incurred as a result of the said Entry

First, because the Land of Flanders granted to our most redoubted lord upon his Entry the sum of 24,000 *guldenen*, each valued at 40 gr, the said money to be employed for redeeming the city of Ninove and the land of Roselaere with everything pertaining to them; of the which 24,000, the city's share amounted to £628 10s, for which the city was granted an exemption to the value of £528 10s; therefore, the rest of the money owed amounts to £100[101] ...

[Smaller payments are made to the prince's household servants and the servants of members of his entourage, including the 'actors of the Lady of Savoy and the footmen of my Lord of Fiennes.[102]]

To Edewaert van Ghysegheem, for the purchase and delivery of a barrel of unprocessed wax weighing 363lbs, at 17 and a half crowns per hundred, making £13 8s 6d.

To the innkeeper at Ypres, for a barrel of Rhine wine holding 12 measures and 4 pitchers ... coming to £6 10s 8d. The aforementioned wine and wax were presented to our redoubted lord, as is the custom, upon his Entry. The last two Entries come to £19 19s 2d.

To my lord the chancellor of Burgundy, My Lord Jan Sauvaige, knight, lord of Escaubeke, the sum of 200 golden *philippus*, which the magistrates ordered to be given to him as the customary gift on the occasion of his inception of the office of chancellor of Burgundy. The 200 *philippus* come to £40 13s 4d.

In payment for a noble banquet held by order of the magistrates in the town hall in this city on the sixth day of May for our most redoubted lord and prince and my lady dowager of Savoy, his aunt, the lords of the Order of the Golden Fleece and many other noblemen and women from his household and in his service. And the cost of the banquet as it is specified in a notebook attached here, including the loss of a silver pitcher, was £60 16s 1d.

To Esquire Jacques of Luxembourg, Lord of Auxy,[103] the sum of 800 golden *philippus*, which the magistrates ordained to be rightfully his,

---

101 Not counting the additional expenses incurred during the stay of the prince's entourage in the town which follow, the costs of the Entry ceremony to the municipality amounted to around £735. The tax reduction received on the occasion of the Entry therefore amounted to around 70% of the cost of the ceremony.

102 Margaret of Austria and Jacques II de Luxembourg, lord of Fiennes, knight of the Golden Fleece, councillor and chamberlain, father of Jacques III below.

103 Jacques III de Luxembourg.

out of consideration and partly in recompense for the great costs incurred by him and by his men in calling the joust which took place here in the month of May last in honour and for the entertainment of our redoubted lord and prince. Thus here by act of the chamber for the aforesaid 800 *philippus*, coming to £166 13s 4d.

To Jooris vander Donc, for the delivery of 19 ells of taffeta of Genoese blue which was used to drape the raised platform set up on the market place during the jousting, at 3s per ell, which comes to £2 17s. Also, for the delivery of two quarters of red velvet with which the keys of the chamber were covered, 6s 6d, ... £4 3s 6d.

To Noël vander Weerde, for his trouble and supervision in making the lists and terrain for the said jousts, which he looked after and maintained... £3 6d.

To Hendric Nieulant, the sum of £8 6s 8d because of the same sum awarded to him by order of the magistrates for the use of two of his houses on the market square, named the Moon and the Crane, for the duration of the jousts. In which house of the Crane our redoubted lord together with my Lady Margaret the dowager of Savoy lodged, and in the house known as the Moon, the magistrates etc.[...]

To Remy du Puys, historiographer of our redoubted lord and prince, the sum of £5 given to him by order of the magistrates for his trouble and work in recording in French the triumphs of the Entry of our redoubted lord and prince in this city.

To Cornelis vanden Westhuuse, carpenter, for having constructed the lists and other items relating to the jousts, as it is specified on a piece of paper which is attached here ... £7 9s 11d.

V: CIVIC SOCIETY AND THE COURT: JOUSTS, SHOOTING FRATERNITIES AND CHAMBERS OF RHETORIC

Introduction

The regular contests of jousters, archers and poets in towns of the Low Countries were among the most distinctive features of festive urban society in the fifteenth century.[1] Most common in the early fifteenth century were those of crossbowmen and archers: guilds may be found in almost every town and even villages across the region.[2] Their origins date back to the late thirteenth or early fourteenth centuries when their military role as part of urban militia was paramount. This role continued into the fifteenth century, and although rulers became less inclined to call upon their military services, regular practising of their skills within towns and in competitions against guilds from other towns, remained central to their activities. But the festive nature of these occasions – the banqueting, selection of new 'kings', and the ludic quality of archery practice (such as toppling wooden popinjays from tall poles) – suggests a social function which went well beyond the basic requirement of military exercise. Regular inter-town competitions could bring together large numbers: 560 crossbowmen with hundreds of retainers at an event in Ghent in 1440, and comparable numbers at Tournai in 1455 [**17b**], while shooting guilds could be large in membership, several hundred-strong in more populous towns.[3]

Archery contests were by no means a purely urban phenomenon. In a region where boundaries between 'aristocrat' and 'burgher' had long been permeable, it is unsurprising to find the aristocracy taking part in the activities of archery guilds [**17a, 17b**]. Local lords might also found such guilds, at least in smaller communities. Creating an archery guild was a means for the local lord to promote martial activities and strengthen ties with those who still looked to him for justice and protection. The creation of an archery guild may also have

1 For a brief overview which includes all these phenomena, see Lecuppre-Desjardin, *La Ville des cérémonies*, pp. 185–97.

2 For shooting guilds, see T. Reintges, *Ursprung und wesen der spätmittelalterlichen schützen-gilden* (Bonn, 1963); E. van Autenboer, *De Kaarten van de schuttersgilden van het hertogdom Brabant (1300–1800)* (Tilburg, 1993–4); M. Carasso-Kok and J. Levy-van Halm, *Schutters in Holland: Kracht en zenuwen van de stad* (Zwolle, 1988); P. Knevel, *Burgers in het geweer: De schutterijen in Holland 1550–1700* (Hilversum. 1994), chap. 1; Arnade, *Realms of ritual*, pp. 65–94.

3 In mid-fifteenth-century Bruges, the St George crossbow guild regularly paid for nearly 200 liveries for its members every year; while the St Sebastian archers' guild had over 300 members (and around 100 attended its annual banquet). SAB, 385, Sint-Joris gilde register; A. Vanhoutryve, *De Brugse kruisbooggilde van Sint-Joris* (Bruges, 1968), p.72; Archief van Sint-Sebastiaansgilde, Bruges, Rekeningenboek 1 (1454–64); H. Godar, *Histoire de la gilde de St Sebastien de la ville de Bruges* (Bruges, 1947), pp. 98–100.

been a source of prestige for the nobleman. Alongside an account of his education, his early career in the service of Simon de Lalaing and the birth of his
children, the Flemish nobleman Jan van Dadizeele noted in his memoirs that
he had succeeded in obtaining a weekly market for those in his charge, and the
creation, in 1463, of a crossbow guild for Dadizeele.[4]

Activities traditionally associated with the nobility also found their place within
an urban context. Jousting events were more exclusive than archery contests,
partly because of the need for horses and more expensive equipment, but many
were staged in towns.[5] Civic accounts from the late thirteenth century, in several
towns in Flanders and northern France, begin to make sporadic payments for
jousting activity on their market places. Some jousting events in the fifteenth
century were still occasionally large: fifty-five jousters at Lille in May 1438
took on more than 100 jousters from Valenciennes, Tournai, Bruges and Ghent
(and from the ducal court)[6]. But by then, there were fewer towns sporting such
occasions: in Flanders the Épinette at Lille and the White Bear of Bruges[7]
were the principal two, and both of them were to disappear during the political
upheaval of the 1480s. Until then, however, their activities, subsidised by civic
funds, continued to weave chivalric culture into the fabric of urban society.
The annual setting up of lists, scaffolding for spectators and breaking of lances
produced the kind of combat which (except for the *pas d'armes* [**2**]) was indis-
tinguishable from that of a more courtly or aristocratic elite.[8]

Rhetoric chambers appear fully fledged only in the third decade of the fifteenth
century, but embryonic forms of their activities are to be found in the 'puys
mariaux' of northern French towns which date back to the thirteenth century
and in the 'ghesellen van de spele' of fourteenth-century Flemish towns.[9] They

---

4 J. Kervyn de Lettenhove (ed.), *Jan van Dadizeele: Mémoires* (Bruges, 1850), p. 3.

5 For Flanders (French-speaking in particular), see Van den Neste, *Tournois*.

6 According to ADN B7662, dossier 9 (L. de Rosny, *L'Épervier d'or* [Paris, 1839], pp.
   29–31, 59–63). The contingent from Valenciennes, dressed as 'wild men', were apparently greeted by the king of the Épinette covered in skins and swan feathers.

7 For the White Bear see A. van den Abeele, *Het ridderlijk gezelschap van de Witte
   Beer* (Bruges, 2000); A. Brown, 'Urban jousts in the Later Middle Ages: The White
   Bear of Bruges', *Revue Belge de philologie et d'histoire* 78 (2000), pp. 315–30. The town
   usually subsidised about six jousters annually for the White Bear jousts, besides the
   'forester' (chief-jouster).

8 For distinctions and overlap between different types of jousting contest, see Van den
   Neste, *Tournois*, pp. 50–54, 140–43.

9 For rhetoric chambers and their origins, see J.J. Mak, *De rederijkers* (Amsterdam,
   1944); H. Liebrecht, *Les Chambres de rhétorique* (Brussels, 1948); E. van Autenboer,
   Volksfeesten en rederijkers te Mechelen, 1400–1600 (Ghent, 1962); Arnade, *Realms of ritual*,
   pp. 159–88; A.-L. van Bruaene, 'Sociabiliteit en competitie. De sociaal-institutionele
   ontwikkeling van de rederijkers kamers in de Zuidelijke Nederlanden (1400–1650)',
   in B.A.M. Ramakers (ed.), *Conformisten en rebellen. Rederijkerscultuur in de Nederlanden
   (1400–1650)* (Amsterdam, 2003), pp. 45–63; A.-L. van Bruaene and L. Derycke,
   'Sociale en literaire dynamiek in het vroeg vijftiende-eeuwse Brugge: de oprichting
   van de rederijkerskamer De Heilige Geest ca. 1428', in Oosterman (ed.) *Stad van
   koopmanschap en vrede*, pp 59–96.

may also have grown out of the tradition of archery events which had often included (and continued to include) contests of a more literary and theatrical sort [19]. At regular meetings of particular guilds or at the grander inter-town events (which mirrored and overlapped with archery events), competitions would usually centre around a theme: prizes were awarded to participants judged to produce the best poetic results [19]. Visual as well as oral display was exhibited and rewarded, for rhetoric chambers also borrowed from the custom of staging plays and *tableaux vivants*, which was certainly current by the late fourteenth century in many town processions [20, 23].[10]

Despite the festive and often secular tone to their proceedings, these social gatherings maintained a religious dimension. Rhetoric chambers often invited participants to discourse on a sacred theme; like shooting guilds they were also set up much as other kinds of devotional fraternity [17a]. The larger ones might maintain their own chapel (with relics) or support priests to say masses for the souls of their members (both men and women); attendance at requiem mass for deceased members might be required of the living. Large proportions of guild entry fees went on the regular support of religious services. Jousting groups do not appear to have the same formal structures as religious fraternities; but their events would invariably involve attendance at a vigil and mass on the eve of jousting.

Whatever the 'secular' or 'religious' dimension of their activities, they all took place within a thoroughly civic context. Their membership demonstrates strong links with the civic government and the upper echelons of civic society.[11] Most exclusive perhaps were the jousters: many of the White Bear of Bruges were landowners outside the city with noble titles, but others were from the capitalist 'elite' (especially brokers and hostellers) who occupied important positions on the two benches of civic magistrates. Archers and rhetoricians often came from a similar background (including richer guildsmen from brewers, bakers, shippers, butchers and weavers), but they could also include others slightly lower down the social ranks. In economically diversified towns, where social competition was intense and hierarchies finely tuned, the act of joining one of these groups announced a certain social standing within the community.

These groups were also 'civic' in the wider functions that they served. Town governing bodies had long sought to regulate the affairs of jousters and archers. Shooting guilds in many towns in the fourteenth century were offi-

---

10 For the overlap in material used by town processions and rhetoric competitions, see B.A.M. Ramakers, *Spelen en figuren: Toneelkunst en processiecultuur in Oudenaarde tussen Middeleeuwsen en Moderne Tijd* (Amsterdam, 1996); A.E. Knight, 'Professional theater in Lille in the fifteenth century', in E. Dubruck and W.C. McDonald (eds), *Le Théâtre et la cité dans l'Europe médiéval*, publ. as *Fifteenth-century studies* 13 (1988), pp. 347–58; M. Smeyers, 'De zeven werken van barmhartigheid en de zeven sacramenten', in M. Smeyers (ed.), *Leuvens palet: Acta Loveniensis,18 Jaarboek 1989* (Leuven, 1989), pp. 143–70.

11 For the following on membership see Arnade, *Realms of ritual*, pp. 71, 164, 168, 173, 192; van Bruaene and Derycke, 'Sociabiliteit en competitie'; Knevel, *Burgers in het geweer*, chp 1; van Autenboer, *Volksfeesten*, pp. 160–207; van de Abeele, *Witte Beer*.

cially granted formal statutes of incorporation; regular subsidies were paid out to them from civic coffers; guild accounts and elections were overseen by civic magistrates. Jousters similarly began to receive regular subsidies from town treasuries; rhetoricians later were subjected to the same civic oversight. All these groups were drawn into the secular and sacred calendar of civic events. At Lille, the archers watched the gates and the jousts at the time of the annual processions of Notre Dame de la Treille (in June) and on Corpus Christi day [22, 18b]; in Bruges, they flanked the relic of the Holy Blood on the main civic procession on 3 May. Most of the jousting of the White Bear by the fifteenth century took place shortly before 3 May, which also synchronised with the beginning of the town's annual May fair. Rhetoricians were also drawn into civic-wide events. Their role as devisers of *tableaux* and plays during town processions seems to have become increasingly formalised in the later fifteenth century.

The civic nature of these festive groups did not lie just in the ceremonial duties required of them within their towns. It is also apparent from the way in which the quality of their activities was deemed to reflect on, and improve, the quality of urban life. Upholding 'the honour of the city' by their efforts, particularly at inter-town competitions, was part of this. Yet honour was to be won not simply through participation and success in occasional contest, but also in more prolonged display of a certain kind of behaviour. The anxiety of town governing bodies to maintain social stability is reflected in a concern, expressed more sharply in the fifteenth century, to develop a sense of public morality among its citizens. Festive groups might serve as exemplary models of ideal civic behaviour. Statutes of shooting guilds often regulated the personal deportment of their members [17a]. Larger towns had shooting guilds for more youthful members, who might thus be schooled in correct public behaviour; their graduation into senior guilds was akin to a rite of passage to an adult world of responsibility in civic affairs.[12] Rhetoric competitions that explored religious themes could also serve as stages for the edification, spiritual and civic, of a wider audience within the town.[13] Suspicion that jousters were no longer fulfilling their role as exemplars of moral behaviour may have contributed to their suppression at Lille in 1487: friars and doctors of theology who were asked to give their opinion suggested that the jousts merely encouraged the vices of vanity, luxury and lechery.[14]

So central were jousting, archery and theatrical events to urban life in the fifteenth century that it comes as no surprise to find them the objects of considerable princely interest. The participation of Burgundian rulers, or high-

12 Arnade, *Realms of ritual*, p.72; Knevel, *Burgers in het geweer*, chp 1.

13 H. Pleij, 'Geladen vermaak: rederijkerstoneel als politiek-instrument van een elite-cultuur', *Jaarboek van De Fonteine* 25 (1975), pp. 75–104; H. Pleij, *De Sneeuwpoppen van 1511: stadscultuur in de late middeleeuwen* (Amsterdam, 1988).

14 The town government of Lille had asked the opinion of friars and doctors in theology about the value of their jousts in 1484 (ADN, B7662). For comment on this document, see Van den Neste, *Tournois*, pp. 169–71; and Brown, 'Urban Jousts'. p. 315. To some extent this criticism was a traditional clerical *topos*.

ranking courtiers, in urban jousts reached a peak in the middle decades of the fifteenth century. Despite an apparent reluctance among courtly chroniclers, such as Chastelain, to record ducal involvement in urban social events – and a preference to report on *pas d'armes* which in theory excluded those of bourgeois birth – the enthusiasm of Charles the Bold and Philip the Good for the Épinette and the White Bear is born out by their support of taxation (at Lille) to fund the events and by their own extravagant outlay when equipping themselves for personal participation [**18a, 18b**].

Ducal willingness to mingle with the urban 'elite' is equally evident in other festive occasions. Archery may not have enjoyed the same chivalric associations as jousting, but Burgundian dukes and courtiers apparently did not find it demeaning to join urban shooting guilds or disport themselves vigorously at archery competitions[15] [**17b**]. Their encouragement of shooting and rhetoric events extended to granting archers and rhetoricians collective privileges, or free passage across their lands to attend inter-town competitions.

Rapprochement with groups of the civic 'elite' was perhaps part of a more calculated policy of extending princely authority. Military need meant that crossbowmen and archers were still demanded by the dukes from towns for campaigns – though less frequently, especially after the contingent from Bruges deserted Philip the Good during his Calais campaign in 1436 and returned to Bruges to seize the city.[16] But it is the key ceremonial roles that archers and other groups played within their cities that best explain ducal interest in them. Rhetoric contests on occasion explicitly focused attention on Burgundian rule: the 1432 competition in Ghent offered prizes for the 'best eulogy on the birth of Josse, the duke's son'. Individual rhetoricians (like Anthonis de Roovere in Bruges) could be rewarded by the dukes – partly for their efforts during the planning of Entry ceremonies.[17] Trans-regional archery or rhetoric competitions were increased from the 1440s, perhaps as a deliberate attempt by Valois and Habsburg rulers to cut across narrower civic and local loyalties, and encourage identification with the wider collection of territories brought together by dynastic union.

Arguably the growing control of rulers over festive events in towns reflects a shift in power toward the state, especially after the mid-fifteenth century. From this perspective it seems ironic that the flourishing of rhetoric chambers, serving to communicate 'civic values', occurred at a time when civic autonomy was being eroded. At Lille, the continuation of the Épinette was more the concern of Valois and Habsburg rulers than it was that of individual citizens: the expense still required of individual jousters had become one less willingly borne [**18b**]. Perhaps by then, service to the state had become a more produc-

---

15 For Duke John the Fearless at the Oudenaarde competition in 1404, and Philip the Good at Ghent in 1440, see Arnade, *Realms of Ritual*, pp. 82, 84–91.

16 Dumolyn, *De Brugse opstand*, pp. 147–57.

17 See above, chapter 1 [**2**]; also J. B. Oosterman, '"Tussen twee wateren zwem ik": Anthonis de Roovere tussen rederijkers en rhétoriqueurs', *Jaarboek van De Fonteine* 39–40 (1999–2000), pp. 11–29.

tive avenue for social advancement for townsmen than indulgence in traditional aristocratic pursuits such as jousting: once the symbols of 'urban autonomy', van den Neste argues, jousts like the Épinette had become symbols of 'urban submission'.[18] Arnade detects a cultural shift by the beginning of the sixteenth century in which urban rhetoricians came to serve state rather than civic power.[19] The shadow of state power was cast more strongly over festive events: arrangements for dramatic spectacles, such as the archery contests at Ghent in 1440, Tournai 1455 [**17b**], or Antwerp 1496 [**19a**], take on a darker aspect when set in the context of recent rebellion and humiliation of civic authority.

Nevertheless, the hold of state power over civic spectacle often remained one of shadow rather than of substance. The involvement of the Valois dukes in urban festivities had generally been subtle and low-key: personal participation in archery or jousting events had been less as a dominating overlord than as a 'first among equals'. Joining an archery guild or developing cordial ties with particular festive groups within a city were uncertain tools of princely authority: the disappearance of jousting groups in Lille and Bruges in the 1480s showed that in times of crisis rulers could not count on the continuation of groups who might be favourably disposed to princely authority. Moreover, 'urban' rhetoricians need not be seen as 'court' ciphers;[20] festive events rarely offered explicit support of Burgundian rule.[21] The focus of rhetoric activities seems to have remained thoroughly civic [**19c**]; and most rhetoric competitions (as at Antwerp in 1496) set themselves religious questions to answer rather than political goals to achieve. In the sixteenth century, these questions might even be troublesome to state authority. The beginning of the Ghent rebellion in 1539 was marked by a rhetoric competition choosing a religious theme which, according to the Habsburg authorities, invited rhetoric that was dangerously Lutheran and politically subversive.[22]

18 For these arguments, see Van den Neste, *Tournois*, pp. 187–208.

19 Arnade, *Realms of ritual*, pp. 190–6.

20 Small, 'When *indiciaires* meet *rederijkers*', pp. 133–61.

21 And rhetoricians in the pay of the duke were inclined to put their poetic skills in the service of peace for their region rather than of military victory for the duke. For Anthonis de Roovere's poem in 1471, bewailing the effects of war, see J.B. Oosterman, 'Oh Flanders Weep! Anthonis de Roovere and Charles the Bold', in M. Gosman, A.J. Vanderjagt and J.R. Veenstra (eds), *The growth of authority in the medieval West* (Groningen, 1999), pp. 257–67.

22 G.K. Waite, 'Reformers on stage: rhetorician drama and Reformation propaganda in the Netherlands of Charles V, 1519–1556', *Archive for Reformation History* 83 (1992), pp. 209–39.

17. Crossbow and archery guilds

(a) Constitution, Béthune, 1413

G. Espinas, *Les origines de l'association. I. Origines du droit d'association dans les villes de la Flandre française jusqu'au début du XVIe siècle. II: Documents* (Lille, 1941), pp. 183–8.

From William of Flanders, count of Namur and lord of Béthune,[23] greetings to all those who read these letters.

We let it be known that for the security and defence of our town of Béthune, by the advice of our beloved friends the *bailli*, aldermen, provost and mayors of the town, we have ordained in response to the request of the archers of the same that henceforward, and for so long as we please, a company of sixty companions and brothers will be elected among the archers of the town and maintained in honour of Our Lord and of Saint Sebastian. This order will have one constable and two mayors who will be elected each year by the brothers or the greater part of them on the last Sunday in April, which is the day the archers will hold their feast. The constable and mayors will henceforward govern and administer the confraternity with the power to investigate, punish and correct all cases of discord, ill-feeling, bitterness and hatred which might arise among the said brothers, and to settle and effect an agreement between all parties concerned as best they see fit, except for criminal cases or cases which result in bloodshed, or cases in which we have a right to levy fines through our own justice. The constable and mayors will swear to uphold this ordinance on pain of being banished from the confraternity for life without leave for appeal. Every companion will be required on joining to swear an oath of obedience to the constable or mayors, and will do whatever they, acting with the counsel of the companions or the greater part of them, should ask of him. No more than sixty members will be admitted to the confraternity unless it be by the authority and permission of our *bailli* and the aldermen of Béthune who may consent to this if necessary. And should anyone of poor conduct or dissolute life seek to join the confraternity, or anyone under sentence of excommunication, he will not be admitted. Should such a person be admitted in error, or as a result of his repeated requests, he will be forced to resign or, if necessary, he will be expelled on the advice of our *bailli* and the aldermen.

We wish the sixty companions and brothers to be organised into six

23 Ruled 1391–1418. His brother, John III, sold the county of Namur to Philip the Good.

groups of ten, each with a reliable chief who will serve as its leader. The groups will be required to go shooting on the days allocated to them in the grounds which were recently given to the confraternity by the *bailli*, aldermen and mayors of the town, and which are situated between the stream running from the meadow ditch and the grounds of the crossbowmen of Béthune. By these letters we confirm the grant of this garden to the confraternity for the practice of archery. We wish the companions to enclose the garden with ditches and fruit trees to make it safe and embellish it, and they may set up as many targets as they like there. Each leader of the groups of ten will have the valet of the confraternity advise its members of the days they are required to shoot, and on such days each group is expected to compete over three rounds for a prize of wine. Anyone who does not attend without good reason will be fined eight *sous*. The fine will be the property of the group of ten who will be shooting that day. And to enable the archers to go to their garden whenever they need to, we grant them the path which the crossbowmen used to use between the said stream and the river.

We wish and ordain that every year on the last Sunday in April the archers will set up a popinjay in the customary place, and whosoever should shoot down the popinjay will be King of the archers for the following year. The King will have his bill paid for him at the annual dinner at the end of each year. All members of the confraternity will attend the annual festival on pain of a fine of twelve *sous* which will be owed to the members, and everyone will wear a suitable and honest hood of a cloth, colour and design chosen by the constable and mayors of the confraternity, on pain of a fine of ten *sous*. Two months before the festival each year the constable and mayors will advise the members of the colour, cloth and design selected, and anyone who has a hood that does not match these requirements can be required to obtain another one … We also permit the constable, mayor and companions of the confraternity to buy a barrel of wine tax-free from whichever tavern they please. They may also assemble in our woods around Béthune to gather the green May branches to decorate the place where they will hold their festival without fear of being fined in our name.[24]

Anyone wishing to join the said confraternity cannot be admitted by the constable and mayors unless it be with the consent and agreement of our *bailli* and aldermen of Béthune. Whoever wishes to join will be tested between two targets in the garden of the confraternity to see if he is sufficiently expert in the sport of archery. If he is admitted, he will

24 Greenery or blossom gathered in honour of May Day.

pay twelve *sous* for his entry to the confraternity and will swear a solemn oath that within the following three months he will acquire two good bows made of yew, three dozen arrows with arrowheads,[25] a hauberk worth at least 32 *sous* and suitable head armour, a sword, and a dagger to be worn as required on pain of a fine of ten *sous*. We permit each of the members of the confraternity to wear his armour and carry one bow with six arrows with heads anywhere in the town or surrounding jurisdictions of our lands, for the purposes of self-defence, without risk of being fined. In return, each archer will be asked every year to swear a solemn oath to serve us and our town, either in Béthune or outside its walls, wherever it should please us or the authorities of the town, so long as they are paid reasonable wages in keeping with those offered to archers from the other good towns of Artois and surrounding areas.

[Resignation on the grounds of old age or illness is permitted on condition of making a gift of one's bow to the guild, and archers are not allowed to pawn or sell their weapons.]

We ordain that the members of the confraternity will have a wax candle made each year to be borne in the procession of the Holy Sacrament. The members of the confraternity are to accompany the candle in the procession, along with their constable and mayors, on pain of a fine of ten *sous*. Should any member of the confraternity die, we ordain that the companions will receive his best bow and three dozen arrows with heads. And if on his death the member is found not to have a bow, the constable and mayors may take from his estate immediately after his death the sum of sixteen *sous*. In return the companions will be obliged to hold a requiem mass for the soul of the deceased, and every member is obliged to attend in person as advised by the varlets of the constable and mayors unless he has good reason not to, on pain of a fine of six *sous*.

The confraternity will have a chest which will be left in the constable's safekeeping, and each of the mayors will have a key. In this chest the entry fines of all new members will be kept, along with the fines and other profits of the confraternity. The constable will be required to give an account of these monies and his expenditure, with receipts, at the end of his term of office on the festival day of the confraternity.

And if it should happen that any town holds a shooting competition and the constable and mayors are advised to participate, we wish them to choose the best archers of the confraternity to go and compete for

---

25 *Flesches a sang*, i.e., an arrow with a head suitable for military or hunting purposes, distinct from an arrow with a simple point used for target practice.

the prizes. The competitors are entitled to the sum of 100 *sous* from the confraternity to meet their expenses and travel costs, on the condition that any prizes they win belong to the confraternity.

[The town of Béthune will give the confraternity six *livres tournois* per year to help it bear its expenses.]

We declare that the constable and mayors of the confraternity will receive the assistance of our ordinary justice in their measures to recover debts arising from any of the fines mentioned above...

[The statutes can only be altered by the sovereign lord with the advice of the municipal officers and his own men. The statutes will be publicly read on market day.]

In support of the present letters we attach our seal on this day, 1 October 1413, in our castle at Namur.

(b) Competition, Tournai, 1455

F. de Reiffenberg, 'La Fête de l'Arbalète et du Prince d'Amour à Tournai en 1455', *Bulletin des séances de la Commission royale d'histoire* 10 (1845), pp. 252–66.

At the beginning of June 1455 the four elected magistrates of Tournai granted permission to the sworn guild of crossbowmen of the town to hold a festival and contest for the crossbow, and promised them, to further the event, the sum of 200 *livres tournois* from the town's funds, and to supply stands for the spectators and targets at their expense on the big market square. These agreements and promises made, the date of 11 August was fixed for the start of the festival, which was to be the same date as the start of the festival of the *Pui* of Love,[26] other-wise known as the king's festival, because the king had appointed one day each year for general processions to be held in all the cathedral churches of his kingdom to give thanks to God for the recovery of his land of Normandy, which had been retaken and had returned to his

---

26 A *puy* is defined in the *New Oxford Companion to Literature in France* (Oxford, 1995), p. 651, as an 'association of medieval and renaissance poets whose president was given the fictitious title of prince (hence the traditional address to a prince at the start of their ballads). They held periodic competitions where lyrics were performed and prizes were awarded. The name may derive from the podium accommodating competitors and judges, or from Le Puy en Velay, where Occitan sources suggest competitions first flourished briefly in the late twelfth century. Later fraternities were mostly in northern and western France, especially Arras (thirteenth century) and Rouen (1486–1654)'.

obedience on the twelfth of the same month.[27] The prince of the *Pui* of
Love that year was the innkeeper Jehan de Courolle, and he was also the
prince of the sworn guild of crossbowmen.

[Four messengers in special green garments are sent around the region to
invite 'free men, great or small, from walled towns or villages' to attend, and
return with 'several fine objects made of precious stones and silver.']

As soon as they had left, work began on the big market square to
build two sturdy, long shooting galleries made of wood, one toward
the belfry, the other toward the House of the Paraclete, along with a
gallery at the same height which connected the two. Both the stands
and the gallery were roofed with planks so people could come and go
while staying dry. This done, on each of the galleries a large fine target
was constructed from straw and covered in green cloth. At the house
on the corner of the street of Our Lady, on the other side from the
platform, a residence for the participants was built. The facade of the
building was painted green, and above the windows there was a roof
made of planks, covered in green drapes on the side facing the market
square. The prizes for the contest were put on display on this roof every
day of the competition. The prizes were: twelve beautifully worked
silver pitchers each weighing thirty-six marks of Troyes;[28] three ewers
also in silver weighing four and a half marks; and nine silver goblets
weighing nine and a half marks. All of these items had gilt edges and
bore the arms of Saint George, of the king and of the city. There were
also two silver arrows which were to be given to the last company to
take their shots and thereby close the competition. The prizes were
to be awarded in the following categories: to the guild which landed
four arrows closest together, three pitchers weighing twelve Troyes
marks; to the guild with the next four arrows closest together, three
pitchers weighing nine marks; to the guild with three arrows closest
together, two pitchers weighing six marks; to the guild with the next
three arrows closest together, two pitchers weighing four marks; to
whoever hit the white, a goblet and lid weighing one mark; to the guild
which made the largest, best presented and most honourable entry into
the town, two ewers weighing three marks; and to the next-best, one
ewer weighing one and a half marks; and to the guild which came the

27 Although surrounded by the Burgundian dominions, Tournai remained a royal town
   throughout our period and celebrated the victories of Charles VII over the English
   which marked the end of the Hundred Years War: Small, 'Centre and periphery in
   late medieval France'.

28 A mark was a quantity of gold or silver weighing eight ounces.

furthest to attend, one goblet with lid weighing one mark; to the guild which put on the best show of torches in the evening, a pitcher weighing three marks; and to the guild which was next-best, a pitcher weighing two marks; to the guild which put on the best plays in French in the evening, a goblet with lid weighing two marks; and to the guild which put on the best plays in Flemish, a goblet with lid weighing two marks; to the guild which processed in the most reverent fashion dressed in the same attire in the procession of 22 August, a goblet with lid weighing one mark; and to the next-best, a goblet without lid weighing half a mark; and to any single crossbowman who landed his quarrel directly in the bullseye, a ring of gilded silver; to the parish or company of the city of Tournai which put on the best plays on the first evening, one goblet weighing seven ounces; and to those who put on the best plays on the next evening, a goblet with lid weighing five ounces; and to best on the third evening, a goblet without lid weighing four ounces. And all those staging plays were to do so every second evening, whether they came from the town or from outside.

On 11 August the crossbowmen of fifty-nine companies made their entries, the finest of which was the Lille guild, all dressed alike and led by Anthony, the Great Bastard of Burgundy, who were presented with two silver ewers. The company from Oudenaarde was also very fine, but in honour of the Bastard of Burgundy they were happy with second place, for which they received their ewer.[29] The Liège company won the prize for the company which travelled furthest to attend. The next morning, which was Tuesday 12 August and therefore the king's festival, a most worthy procession left from the cathedral of Our lady via the *rue des Cannones, rue aux Rates, Puch l'éaue, Croix-St Piat, rue des Alemans, Turé*, up the *rue de Paris*, through the great market square and the *rue Notre Dame*. There was a great crowd of people watching the procession because so many had come to the *Puy* of Love, and even more for the shooting match. The Lille guild processed bearing torches and wearing the same attire, for which they won the silver goblet. The men of Oudenaarde put on the next-best display and won the prize for the most reverent company in the procession, for which they were presented with the goblet mentioned above. Plays were staged on the same day in front of the deacons' hall, which was then being used as the palace of the Prince of Love, from where he and his followers watched the plays. The Prince presented each playwagon with a silver *fleur de*

---

29 Oudenaarde was the next significant town up the Escaut from Tournai en route to Ghent, and the closest Flemish community of note, not to mention the nearest town subject to the duke of Burgundy.

lys weighing eight *esterlins*.[30] And when it was time to dine, the Prince
of Love came down from his palace and went with his entourage to the
great town hall where tables and everything else necessary had been set
out. A rich and noble dinner was served there, for several honourable
and worthy people, both from within the town and beyond, had been
invited. At this meal outsiders ate for free while those of the town were
partly paid for. Once dinner was over, the Prince of Love descended[31]
and went back up to his palace, that is to say the deacons' hall, in front
of which there was a stage in the customary manner on which several
chants royaux[32] were performed on the theme of the great, miraculous
and victorious deeds of the kings of France, especially those which had
come to pass during the recovery of Normandy, Gascony and Bayonne
only recently under the leadership of Charles VII. It was the rhetoricians from outside the town who performed, since those from Tournai
were not allowed to win anything on this occasion. Several *amoureuses*
were also performed by the rhetoricians. Once all the performances
were finished, the composer of the best *chant roial* was called upon to
read the first line of the work again, then he was presented with the
customary prize, which is a silver royal *écu* weighing two ounces. Then
the next-best composer read his work and was given a *dolphin* weighing
one ounce. Both coins bore crowns of gilded silver on their face. Afterward, the poet who had composed the best *amoureuse* was called upon
to deliver the first line of his work, for which he was presented with a
silver crown weighing two ounces, and the next-best received a silver
chaplet weighing one ounce. Several joyous plays were performed to
finish, then all went home or back to their lodgings for the night.

The next day was Wednesday 13 August. The heads of the fifty-nine
companies went up to the town hall to draw lots to see which order they
would be shooting in. A portable meadow had been installed in the town
hall, complete with bushes and flowers ingeniously made from wax, and
in the meadow stood wax female figures representing the companies in
attendance. To the heads of these female figures were attached missals
bearing the names of the cities and towns which had sent companies to
the contest. A beautiful young girl dressed in a bright red tunic embroidered with the emblem of the Tournai crossbowmen stood beside the

---

30 A Hanseatic measure.

31 That is to say, the diners – or at least the prince – were above ground level and were
    therefore on display.

32 '[A] relatively fixed verse form standardized by the Puys, early fourteenth to
    sixteenth centuries, revived in the nineteenth century': *New Oxford Companion to
    Literature in French*, p. 151.

meadow. The girl held a little rod in her hand which she used to touch each of the wax images in turn. Each time she touched one, the missal was taken from the wax model's head and was given to the leader of the company whose town's name appeared on it. In this way the order in which the guilds would compete was decided peaceably and amicably. The order of the competition was as follows:

[There follows a list of companies in order according to the lot drawn, and the number of men (commonly ten) supplied by each: Soignies, Béthune, Binche, Enghien, Hesdin, Roulers, Mons, Maubeuge, the company of the county of Nevers, Dendermonde, Menen, Montreuil-sur-Mer, Chièvres, Ypres, Arras, Condé, Damme, Tirlemont, Bailleul, Leuze, Liège, Nieuwpoort, Leuven, Oudenaarde, Wervicq, Orchies, Lille, Valenciennes, Ath, Dixmuide, Aalst, Ascq, the company of the sensechal of Hainaut, Douai, Hal, Saint-Trond, Avesnes, the company of the lord of Antoing, Veurne and Sluis, as well as teams from the greater and lesser guilds of Nivelles, Brussels, Kortrijk, Bruges, Saint-Omer, Antwerp, Ghent, Mechelen …]

Each member of each guild fired twelve bolts, as stated in the ordinance and instructions that had been sent out. Throughout the competition only two sworn guilds competed each day, one before lunch and one after, and on Saturdays and Sundays only one company took its shots, after lunch. Throughout the competition only a few goods and foodstuffs were sold on the great market square so as not to hinder proceedings. Herring and other fish were sold from the hut behind the market, while wool, shoes, grain and other goods were sold outside the Maulx Gate and on the Cattle Market. Several other foodstuffs were sold on the Chicken Market and on the *Monchiel* as the city magistrates had decreed,[33] and they also announced that no one should go near the targets while shooting was in progress, unless at their own peril. Were injury or death to ensue, the crossbowmen would not be held responsible in law or in any other way.

[On the Thursday, 14 August, at around 8am, the crossbowmen of Tournai competed against those of Soignies, each member of the team firing twelve bolts. They then returned to their lodgings to take wine together. Wine was presented by the city magistrates to the lodgings of the Soignies crossbowmen. The procedure was repeated for the crossbowmen of Béthune who were drawn second; and then for every day of the competition. Details on the measurements of shots were noted down and kept in a locked chest …]

33 The measures taken by the magistrates of Tournai in a meeting on 6 August 1455 can be read in A. de La Grange (ed.), *Extraits analytiques des anciens registres des consaux de la ville de Tournai, 1431–76* (publ. as *Mémoires de la Société historique et littéraire de Tournai 23*, [1893]), pp. 210–14.

This marked the close of the competition on 18 September. Throughout a total of 553 crossbowmen took part, a figure which can be easily verified from what has been noted above.

Once the contest was over the measures were examined and the greater guild of Mechelen was found to have four shots by a single hand which were one and three-quarter inches apart. Since this was the closest, they won the main prize of three pitchers of twelve marks mentioned above. The same inspection revealed that the lesser guild of Mechelen was next with four shots by a single hand which were one and seven-eighths of an inch apart, for which they won the three pitchers of nine marks. The guild of Saint Trond was found to have three shots by a single hand which were three-quarters of an inch apart, for which they were presented with the two pitchers of six marks. The guild of the town of Avesnes were next with three shots that were seven-eighths of an inch apart, for which they won the two pitchers of four marks. The guild of Valenciennes was found to have had eight shots clearly in the white, for which they won the goblet with lid weighing one mark. The guild of Sluis drew the last slot in the competition and so were presented with the silver arrows and the green cloth which had been used to cover the targets. The Lille guild was decreed to have had the best display of torches by night, although the companies from Mechelen, Ghent and Bruges had also made fine displays outside their lodgings, and for this they were presented with the pitcher weighing three marks. Those from Mechelen were found to have the next-best display, for which they received the pitcher weighing two marks. The Lille men acquitted themselves well in the evening plays, as did those from Ypres, the first in French, the latter in Flemish, so they were each presented the prize for the best play in their respective languages ...

The prizes were brought to the lodgings of the companies that had won them on Friday 19 September by the king, constable and several other members of the crossbowmen's guild, accompanied by the minstrels and trumpeters of the city of Tournai. The Tournai crossbowmen brought with them three lithe and gracious virgins in a fine garden who presented the guilds with their prizes. The crossbowmen had draped the facade of their lodgings with tapestries and other hangings and had arrayed a great display of silver plate on richly decorated and well-guarded dressers, as indeed several companies had also done on the days allocated to them to compete. Once all the prizes had been presented, all the companies left the city of Tournai and returned home. On the following day, 20 September, a jury of five considered the parishes and companies of the city of Tournai which had continued to perform plays throughout the competition. It was found that the company of the Prince of Love, which was the company of the rhetoricians, had done best, for which they won the prize of a goblet of seven ounces. Next-best was the company of the parish of Saint-Margaret, for which they were presented with the goblet with lid of five ounces. The players of the parish of Saint-Nicholas received the goblet without lid of four ounces for third prize. Once this was done, the festival and competition came to a close.

18. Jousts

(a) The jousts of the White Bear, Bruges, 1457

[On 14 April 1457, Duke Philip the Good and his son Charles entered Bruges with the Dauphin Louis who was in rebellion against his father Charles VII. Chastelain describes the event as one of tension – partly because of the Dauphin's cowardly behaviour when he mistook a welcoming party of foreign merchants for a hostile force.[34] But once inside the town, the Dauphin was made to wonder at the ceremonies that he saw in Bruges. Charles personally prepared and equipped himself for the jousts of the White Bear (which Chastelain misleadingly considered to be the consequence of Charles's own initiative). The jousts had been an annual event since the fourteenth century. Charles's total outlay was about £418, not far short of the town's.]

Expenses of Charles, count of Charolais

Account by the receiver general of finances of Charles, count of Charolais January to December 1457 (ADN, B3661, fos 34v–5r, 38r–40v, 44v, 68r).

£8 5s to Gérard Pietresoone, rocket[35] worker at Leuven, for 21 rockets and two iron lance tips with square ends delivered by him to the counts at the jousts of the Forester at Bruges in April; ...

12s to Jaquemin Farel, paid out by him at Bruges on a house where the count armed up the day he went to try out a war horse outside the town to joust on the following Sunday; 112s to Pietre Daneman, cooper in Bruges, for a dozen thick lances and three dozen smaller ones, delivered by him to the count when he jousted at the jousts of the Forester at Bruges, with four batons for the foot-valets who followed the count; ...

34 Chastelain, *Oeuvres*, ed. Kervyn de Lettenhove, iii, pp. 301–6, 309–10.
35 Blunt-ended lance.

53s to Jeanin Picquart, armourer for decorating the helm of my lord and putting on it a new *bourlet*,[36] for six clasps for the jousting saddle; ...

£8 14s to Jeannin Sagniel, assistant groom of the count, paid out by him at the jousts in the following way: 7 hats of black beaver, for my lords of Étampes, Auxy, Fromelles and Contay, and other knights and gentlemen who followed the count to the jousts, 12 other felt hats, black and short-haired, for the foot-valets and other companions of the stable who went around the warhorse of the count; ...

£19 9s to Gerard van Benthem, saddler at Bruges for several items delivered for the jousts [including a red velvet covering, and new saddles]; ...

£6 to Jean de Villetart, groom of the duke of Burgundy, who presented a roan warhorse to the count from the duke, on which the count jousted at the jousts of Bruges; ...

£58 4s to Zegher Noppe merchant draper of Bruges for [a total of] 106 ells of black cloth [for clothing of the count's gentlemen and valets at the jousts]; ...

£6 to Roland Ghys, to Ghiselin de Keyser and their companions, trumpeters of Ghent, for their wine when they came to play at Bruges during the jousts;

£20 to Brabant and Hainaut, heralds of arms and their companions, heralds of the duke, which the count gave to them out of courtesy for a prize he won at the jousts;

£4 to minstrels of Bruges for their wine for playing at the jousts; ...

£244 16s to Baudouin Heindricxzoone, jeweller at Bruges for a gold cross garnished with five tablets of diamond and three good pearls, another gold cross similarly garnished, 2 gold batons, each garnished with a diamond, 2 other batons, ... a gold goblet ... which were bought by the count and given by him to madame de Bèvre, madame de Gruuthuse and mademoiselle Estavère and other ladies for the festival of Bruges;

£12 for two small gold batons given by the count as prize for the jousts; ...

£21 33s in cloth for two bottles ... which the count gave to the dauphin during the fair of Bruges; ...

36 Liveried adornment on the helmet.

£20 10s to Aloyet de Destringhes, tailor and chamber valet, for a capar-
ison of blue velvet on the warhorse of the count at the jousts in Bruges,
for making nine surcoats of velvet and black damask worn by knights
and gentlemen following my lord at the jousts, for nine beaver hats, a
mantle of black cloth for my lord [and other items for the jousts]; ...

8s for four lances painted black for the jousts at the Bruges fair and for
twelve black batons carried by the count's men at the jousts ...

Expenses of the town

SAB, 216, Stadsrekeningen, 1456/7, fos 50r, 52r.

[Expenditure by the town on the annual White Bear was heavier in this year
than in previous years (usually around 600 *livres parisis*), and seems to have
included more jousters. Besides these expenses there was also an additional
banquet for the White Bear in the Poorters Loge (which included the burgomaster and 'notables of the Bear' at a cost of more than 19 *livres parisis*, and a
banquet for nobles, including the lord chancellor (Nicolas Rolin) and Antoine,
lord of Croy, which cost almost 720 *livres parisis*. That year the 'forester' (Ogier
Hoonin) was also paid the usual subsidy of 400 *livres parisis*, and a further 26
livres parisis for his journey to the Lille jousts].

[Total costs of the Bear and jousts of May; £745 6s *livres parisis*]:
for 'Beerkin' the herald ... [20s], to the same for his cloth [8s]; for
the fellows who carried the wine to the jousters [3s 4d]; to cover the
jousting areas with straw and dung [20s]; for the sand and 2 lists
[30s]; for straw [32s]; for hiring 24 tin-plate torch-stands [2s 9d];
for 12 jousters' equipment and clothing [£34]; for hiring Coolkerke
house [20s]; for work in the town hall and *Cranenburch* [£4 3s 3d];
for work in the *ghiselhuis* [15s]; for hiring cloth to work on and to sew
[12s]; for the pipers [£2]; for hiring the house in the *mane* [30s]; costs
of my lord Christopher [£2 9s]; for hiring the house of *Bochoute* [£2
12s]; for hiring two rooms in the *Cranenburch* where the burgomasters, treasurers and young ladies were [12s]; for costs on parade and
meal, the evening before the jousts, when the aldermen, *baillis*, burgomasters, former foresters and other notables of the Bear gathered [28s
10d]; for costs of the forester when the burgomasters and young ladies
were gathered [30s]; to Hector van Houdenarde for wax [£2 5s]; for
seats in the jousting area and *Cranenburch* [20s]; to make 2 lists in the
jousting area ...; for 4 openings into the jousting area, and the new
seats to make in wood where the town magistrates and notables sat
[£8 18s 4d]; for a horn decorated with gold [30s 9d].

(b) The joust of the Épinette, Lille, 1486

Archives municipales de Lille, comptes, 16225, fols. 103v-105v: cited in Van den Neste, *Tournois*, pp. 346–50. Date: 1486.

For the expenses due for the jousts [all in *livres parisis*]

To the constables of the crossbowmen, for 30 crossbowmen of the Thirtieth of this town, for having surcoats with the arms of the town, to serve as the tournament and the festival of Lille… £108.

To the constables of the crossbowmen, for their salary and that of 16 crossbowmen of the Thirtieth who, during two days and two nights, carried out the watch at the tournament in 1486 … £20 …

To the constables of the crossbowmen, for their salary and that of 16 crossbowmen of the Thirtieth, who during three days and three nights of the Feast of Lille carried out the watch in the town hall to assist with justice and prevent inconveniences which could happened during the Feast … £30.

On 18 March 1486, following the will and good pleasure of our very redoubtable lord and prince the archduke of Austria, etc. the festival of the Épinette was performed and held in this town. For certain causes the festival had been suspended for several years … which meant that no outgoing king was available; so it was agreed that someone should be found to be the outgoing king in order to accompany the new king in the jousts and to do the other customary things at the expense of the town. At the same time, because there had been great difficulty before in finding people who wanted to undertake the duty of king and jouster, on account of the great expense that they had to sustain above the subsidy that the town had been accustomed to pay, it had been necessary to use rigorous constraints, etc. to maintain the festival. To avoid this and so that the festival can be put on and performed with good will and in the spirit of love and union, and that also the bourgeois of the town capable of carrying out the festival should not be charged with excessive expense, the aldermen, the council of eight men in deliberation and acting on the advice of the treasurers and several former kings of the Épinette, have ordered that for the festival this year the town should pay the necessary sums to the people … for which they have obtained letters of authorisation for this expense from our very redoubtable lord …

To Jacques de Landas, who paid for expenses for food sustained in the *maison du seel*,[37] under the conduct of the said Jacques and of Pierre de Lobel counsellor commissioned by the aldermen on the previous Tuesday before Ash Wednesday for the dinner where the governor, *bailli*, provost, several knights, treasurers and also several former kings and other bourgeois of the town were brought together to make the election of the king of the Épinette for this year as it has been accustomed. And this expense of £200 used to be met by the outgoing king of the Épinette on leaving his kingdom, but for the reasons given above, as there was no former king to meet this expense and other expenses, as will be mentioned later, the £200 which was paid to the former king is discharged …

To Master Jehan de Tenremonde, who paid out for other expenses sustained both for the clothing of Henriet de Tenremonde, his son, who at the request of the aldermen took the place of the outgoing king and accompanied the new king during the festival and jousts, and also for the hiring of a horse, jousting harnesses, caparisons, surcoats and other things for the purpose … £127 6d.

To the said Jehan who paid for other expenses sustained by the said Henriet, the Monday following when he jousted again, because on the previous day he had gained the 'home' prize, for the hiring of a horse, jousting harnesses, caparisons, surcoats and other things for the purpose … £23 15s.

To Jacques Ganthois, present king of the Épinette, for his entry into the festival, the accustomed £200, and also above this for the support of the banquet expenses this year, another £60 … £260.

As for the sum of £400 that was usually paid to the jousters of the festival, both for their clothings, caparisons, mounting and arming etc. and for the sand in the jousting enclosure, and for the cost of the positioning of the lists and barricades of the enclosure and the seats of the aldermen and queens, and also for the expense of the supper on the Saturday, the dinner and supper on the Sunday before Ash Wednesday, the said town will pay the four jousters – Hubert Gommer, Jehan Gobert, Baudin Hangouart and Jeunet de Le Sauch – £60 each to subsidise their expenses for clothing, etc. … £240.

To Jehan Moriel, supplier of sand, for delivering all the sand needed for the jousts … £70.

---

37 We have been unable to identify this building, which may be the *Maison du sceau* (i.e., municipal building where the town seal was kept), the *maison du sel* (salt), or a hostel.

... To the said Jacques de Landas, who had paid for the expense of the supper on the Saturday, dinner and supper on the Sunday before Ash Wednesday ... £289 10s 6d.

As for the expense for positioning the said barricades and lists, for making the seats of the aldermen and the queens and young ladies, and also for the enclosure before the town hall for which the jousters used to pay £22, for this year is paid by the town, and passes to the accounts of the public works ...

To Jacques de Landas and Pierre de Lobel, for their pain and labour for having conducted the festival of the Épinette, as much for the dinners and suppers as for other things ... £9 12s.

To Jehan de le Fortrye, sub-constable of the crossbow guild, for ... the crossbowmen to be at play together the eve of the Sunday before Ash Wednesday after they had presented themselves in arms before the aldermen as is accustomed ... 48s.

To Jacques de Landas, enjoined by full assembly to render account of the expense made and sustained by Henriet de Tenremonde because of the journey made by him as outgoing king of the Épinette, in the name of the town, to the last jousts of Bruges, in accompanying the new king as is accustomed, etc. which he paid out as much for the clothing of the body of Henriet, liveried clothing for his servants and similarly for those of the new king, as for jousting harnesses, caparisons, hiring of horses, and half of the expenses for food and of horses, salaries of minstrels and servants and other expenses he had to make and sustain in Bruges and in going and returning at the encounter of the said new king. The latter has paid the other half, including the expense made by Henriet for the jousts that he had to perform on the Tuesday, at which he had won the prize, and also for the supper on the Wednesday made in this town on his return from the jousts ... and in this case the town remains quit of the £200 for the half of the £400 which it had been accustomed to pay to the outgoing and new king for the journey to Bruges ... £397 2s 8d ...

To Jehan Bonenfant for 5 shafts of lances carried around the Holy Sacrament and the procession to protect the town legislators and other notable people from the press of the people ...

To Jacques Ganthois present king of the Épinette for his journey to the last jousts in Bruges ... £200.

19. Chambers of rhetoric

(a) Competition, Antwerp, 1496

E. Van Autenboer, 'Een landjuweel te Antwerpen in 1496?', *Jaarboek De Fonteine* 29 (1978–1979), pp. 125–50.

The great, triumphant and noble *Landjuweel*[38] held in Antwerp and organised by De Violieren, at which were gathered twenty-eight chambers of rhetoric from Brabant, Flanders, Holland, Zeeland and the Walloon lands, and where the prizes awarded were all of silver. The entry of the *Landjuweel* was held on 19 June 1496 as is mentioned in the invitation sent out to all the rhetoricians as follows:

Distinguished, wise and most beloved lords, fellow brothers and friends.

We commend ourselves most heartily unto your love and most willingly advise you of the following. We were awarded the main prize at the *Landjuweel* at Leuven in the field of rhetoric some time ago. Since that time the prize has remained in our possession as a result of the lamentable troubles of those days, and we have not had the opportunity to offer it again.[39] Now wishing to restore, cultivate and honour the noble art of rhetoric to the best of our ability, and acting with the knowledge and consent of our well-disposed lord the archduke, as well as of our most esteemed lords, burgomasters and aldermen of our city, we have conceived and put into effect a plan for the love and glory of God and of our patron saint, Saint Luke, to hold a festival of rhetoric in this city.[40] Entries over land will commence on 19 June next, and by water the following day. The entrants must make their way in daylight to the marketplace of the city to present themselves to us. We will be honoured to receive the visit of all art-loving and officially recognised chambers of rhetoric or associations which wish to receive the name of chambers of rhetoric, whether of the Dutch or French tongues, and we write to you with a request in the spirit of brotherly love, and to ask

38 Large-scale festival of poetry and drama often lasting several days in which groups of rhetoricians from the hometown and from other towns participate by invitation, performing a range of works in different genres in competition against one another for prizes according to rules clearly established for the occasion.

39 The prize was won in the 1478 contest held at Leuven. The circumstances referred to are no doubt the troubles of Maximilian I's reign which witnessed a number of uprisings against the new Habsburg ruler. See [26].

40 Saint Luke, patron saint of painters and of the united guilds of Saint Luke and De Violieren.

with great cordiality if you will come to our festival and contribute to a
happy outcome, together with rhetoricians from other cities and jurisdictions from this and other lands whom we are also inviting. Hereafter we describe the valuable prizes and jewels that can be won on the
following preconditions.

First of all, the society of rhetoricians which stages the best, most
readily understood and artistic play on the theme of the most profitable
and inscrutable grace established by God for the salvation of mankind
will receive the top prize of three silver pitchers weighing a total of
six Flemish marks. The prize is awarded on condition that the play
is furnished with biblical, allegorical and natural arguments; that it is
novel in form and content; that it has never been performed before; that
the text is clearly pronounced without mistakes; that it has no fewer
than five characters and no more than eight; that it is no shorter than
five hundred verses and no longer than seven hundred; and that the
prompter is not seen.

The society which performs the next-best play under the same conditions will win two rich silver goblets weighing three marks.

The third prize will be a single silver goblet weighing one and a half
marks.

The actor who creates the best serious character with the most substantial role, which is the most expertly acted, and who knows his lines the
best, will receive for himself a rich silver dish weighing two ounces.

The society which – preceding the aforementioned serious play –
performs the most excellent and most poetic prologue of between 125
and 150 verses in which the city of Antwerp is honoured will win a
precious silver castle of Antwerp with eagle weighing three ounces.[41]

The second prize will be a silver eagle bearing the arms of Antwerp on
a shield, weighing one and a half ounces.

The society which recites the most excellent and most reverent poem in
praise of the Circumcision of Our Lord Jesus Christ in the most skilful
and agreeable manner, containing nine strophes including the prince's
strophe,[42] each strophe containing fifteen verses and performed without

41 The crest of Antwerp, still visible on the town hall.
42 A *refrein* is a poem of four or more strophes, all – except for the last, known as the
   'Prinse', which can be shorter – of the same length and in each case closed by a
   'refrain' of one or two verses. The *Prinsestrofe* contains the 'envoy' or dedication to
   the prince of the chamber of rhetoric, or (more often) to another person who is also
   addressed as the Prince or Princess. The connection between this person, who is
   mentioned in passing, and the rest of the poem is often unclear: G. Degroote, *Oude*

fault, will win the highest prize, namely a silver *St Luke painting a picture of the Virgin* [a medallion or statuette in silver] weighing two ounces.

The second prize will be a silver ox bearing the arms of the painters' guild weighing one ounce.[43]

The society which performs the funniest, most merry and most novel *esbattement*[44] around eight o'clock in the evening, raising the most laughter from the public, containing no abusive, scurrilous or disagreeable language, which is newly written, treats a novel theme and has never been performed before, and which is between four hundred and five hundred lines long and virtually without fault, will receive the top prize of three precious silver dishes together weighing two and a half marks.

The next-best *esbattement* performed in the aforementioned manner will win two precious silver dishes together weighing ten ounces.

The third prize will be one precious silver dish weighing five ounces.

The actor who plays the best and silliest comic role, and makes the most nonsense and pulls the craziest faces during the entertainment, virtually without fault and without coarse language or obscene gestures, will win for himself a precious silver pink flower[45] weighing one ounce.

The society which makes the most beautiful, impressive and honourable entry by land in response to our brotherly and heartfelt invitation and initiative will win the top prize of three precious silver dishes which together weigh two marks, on condition that the society arrives with its prince and parades before the stand with the largest possible suite all dressed in the same costume, which they will not have worn in any previous contest. The society which comes second and enters in a splendid manner will win two silver dishes weighing one mark.

The society which makes its entry by land in the most striking, elegant and beautiful fashion at least cost, but parading all in the same costume with its prince before the stand in a manner that does justice to the art of rhetoric as above, will win a silver dish weighing three ounces.

The society which traverses the greatest distance by land to visit us and which arrives and parades in the manner described above will receive two precious silver dishes which together weigh one mark.

---

klanken, Nieuwe accenten: De kunst van de rederijkers (Leiden, 1969), p. 54. We are grateful to Dr Anna-Jane Schnitker for her advice on this point.

43 The ox was the symbol of Luke the Evangelist, patron saint of painters. An ox figured on the arms of the guild of St Luke.

44 Comical play.

45 *Vijolierblomme*: the emblem of the host chamber.

[Similarly, prizes are awarded for the chambers arriving over water.]

Entries by water will take place the day after entries by land are completed, unless unforeseen circumstances should arise due to the weather, wind or water, in which case the aforenamed entries will take place as conditions allow.

Those who come downstream must present themselves either at the wharf or at the crane and come ashore at the barge house. They should then come to the market place and parade before the stand in the manner described above. Those who come upstream will land at Saint John's water and will parade in the aforementioned fashion before the stand.

Once everyone has paraded, both those who came by water and those who came over land, everyone who has come to compete for a prize will go to the place where the drawing of lots for the competition will take place.

Every society must hand over to us a copy of the prologue, morality play, eulogy, refrain and *esbattement* before the drawing of lots. Those which do not do so will not be able to compete for a prize.

The society which is at pains to provide the most beautiful and costly fireworks every evening during this brotherly and pleasant festival will win a top prize of three precious silver dishes which together weigh one mark. The next-best society will win two silver dishes weighing one mark.

The society which provides the most wonderful and least costly fires and other illuminations during the festival will win a precious dish weighing four ounces.

Disqualified from participation are all those players from the chambers which are used to performing invented or true stories in small venues using painted backdrops.[46] Also disqualified from participating are those who have performed *esbattements* in the same venues for money since the contest at Leuven in 1478, where the organisers of the current competition won first prize. In the same manner all travelling players, singers and similar persons are forbidden from participating, not out of disrespect for them, but to permit fully all amateurs and well-wishers the chance to do their best. Such persons would only have been allowed to join in if they had improved their behaviour since that year.

The society or chamber which draws the first lot will receive a silver dish weighing three ounces, and those drawing the last lot a silver dish of two ounces.

46 An attempt to exclude professional actors.

The person who performs the strangest, amusing and funniest fool with the funniest mien without coarseness of language or otherwise will win a valuable silver fool weighing two ounces, and the person in second place will receive an expensive silver female fool weighing one ounce.

Of all societies which are summoned to perform outdoors in the street in the intervals, the one which recounts the silliest, wittiest and funniest jokes, and which raises the biggest laugh without recourse to vulgarity, will win a silver meerkat weighing two ounces. Second prize will be a costly silver long-tailed monkey weighing one ounce.

Finally, let it be known that all societies paying a visit to our beloved festival will win a precious silver rosary with the castle of the city of Antwerp depicted upon it. We also announce that to facilitate the performance of this festival we will have two play wagons made, uncovered and covered, so that all participants can install whatever they need on the wagons in their own time. We do not undertake to make any further provision. All participants will be allowed to make use of the wagons.

As confirmation of all of the above we have asked our aforementioned burgomasters and aldermen of the city to furnish this letter with the seal of the city, which they have done willingly. We request all of you and every other honourable society of rhetoric to come to this festival and help us celebrate it. Moreover, we declare that our aforementioned merciful lord the archduke has, by means of an act which we append here, granted safe conduct to all who will attend the festival. The safe conduct is valid during their presence here and for their journey back, as can be seen from the original document which the bearer of this letter can display.

Written on 12 March 1496, and signed by the prince, deacons, sworn and ordinary members of the society of *De Violieren* of the city of Antwerp.

(b) Le Puy Notre-Dame, Lille, 1479

Antoine Artus, discourse on the Puy Notre-Dame at Lille, in L. Lefebvre, *Le Puy Notre-Dame de Lille du XIVe au XVe siècle* (Lille, 1902), pp. 13–15.[47]

47 Artus was admitted as a bourgeois of Lille in 1561, and was from a family which included several kings of the Épinette at Lille over the fourteenth and fifteenth centuries. He made a career in the prince's *Chambre des comptes.* The majority of princes of the *Puys* from 1401 to 1540 were holders of municipal office, outnumbering court nobles and princely office-holders by around three-to-one. Clerics formed the smallest group, either local abbots or priests attached to the central church of St Peter.

Around the time Jehan Dablaing held the festival and crown of the
Épinette,[48] which was in 1479, the lord of Fiennes, Jacques [I] de
Luxembourg, captain-general of the province of Lille, was elected as
prince of the *Puy*. He conducted himself with due reverence and showed
solemn affection for this office with the magnificence that befitted the
institution ... The conception of this noble festival was that every year
on the day of the Assumption of our most beloved mother and protector
the Virgin Mary a gathering and festival was held by the elected prince
of the *Puy* for the purpose of modest and spiritual entertainment. The
prince summoned all previous princes of the *Puy* to the gathering and
other men of notable standing, and also the duke of Burgundy, the
natural prince of these lands, if that most illustrious person were in
the city at the time. After the gathering had assembled and refresh-
ments had been taken, the rhetoricians of Lille and its surroundings
were given permission to come and make an offering and a presentation in honour of the Virgin Mary of works of rhetoric which they had
composed beforehand. The verses of these rhetoricians were read aloud
in all decent modesty, holding the public's gaze in all honour and with
due reverence, on the lofty and worthy subject of the commemoration
of the beatitude of the Virgin and her Assumption, to the eternal glory
of God. Once the prince was elected, he and his noble company awarded
the prizes to those who had produced the simplest, best, most worthy
and glorious work for our mother the Virgin Mary. The celebration of
this pious and meritorious festival is still remembered today, given that
– as I understand it – it was discontinued in the time of My Lord Guillaume Le Blancq, knight, lord of Houchin,[49] God rest his soul, master
of the prince's *Chambre des comptes* in this city of Lille and father of
Alexandre Le Blancq, lord of Meurchin, present mayor of the aldermen's bench to whom I dedicate this work ... Still today one can see
the escutcheons bearing the arms of all the princes of the Puys in a
circuit around the choir of the convent of the Cordeliers in this town
of Lille ...

(c) **Organisation, Antwerp, 1522**

T. Donnet, 'Un manuscrit de la chambre de rhétorique anversoise, De *Goudt-
bloemen*', *De Gulden Passer* 2 (1924), pp. 1–15, at pp. 12–13.

The following are certain ordinances and rules drawn up and concluded

48 See above [**18b**].
49 Recorded as prince of the Puys in 1532: Lefebvre, *Le Puy de Notre-Dame*, p. 11.

by the prince, chief, deans, elders and other councillors of the guild of the Golden Tree concerning the office of factor for the said guild.

First, the present and future factor will be required to compose works of rhetoric as proposed and instructed by the prince, chief or deans in the service of the city and of the guild.

Item, the said factor will be obliged, every Sunday and certain feast days from Christmas to Shrove Tuesday inclusive, to provide an entertainment or little play for the brothers of the guild when they gather together. He must give the play to the actors in good time so they can rehearse it, and it can be a play he has thought up himself, or one that the deans have ordered.

Item, whenever the present and future factor needs to meet the guild members who are acting to agree matters between them, he will do so in the chambers of the guild and not elsewhere in the city, especially not in taverns.

Item, the factor will be duty bound to maintain harmony and friendship between the actors in his charge, and any quarrel or dispute which arises among them should be pacified and set aside. In the event that this is not possible, he must notify the deans, prince and chief so that they might settle the matter.

Item, the factor can, with the authority of the deans, dismiss an actor who is not suitable or useful.

The factor will keep all the plays that belong to the guild locked up in safekeeping, and the serving dean will have the key. The factor will note in an inventory any items he takes away. In addition a paper book will be placed at his disposal, on condition that the said factor does not give away morality plays, miracle plays or copies of these plays to others, or keep them for himself. Rather, as soon as a play has been performed, he will be required to hand it over straightaway to the deans so that it can be preserved. And once the paper book has been filled for the good of the guild, the factor will be provided with more paper.

Item, now and in the future the factor will receive for his service on an annual basis the sum of thirty Brabant shillings from the aforementioned guild, which will cover his salary and his robe. And the year will be held to begin on the first feast day of the guild following the factor's appointment.

Item, the factor will be exempt from all annual contributions to the guild.

Item, the factor will also be exempt from the cost of expenses he incurs in the chamber or elsewhere while carrying out his duties by order of the prince, chief or deans.

Item, when the factor is called upon to organise the joyous Entry of a prince or princess, he will receive from the same guild twelve Brabant groats for each day he is retained. The guild will keep any gratuities that arise from any such joyous Entry, and the factor will not have any claim on them.

Item, the aforesaid factor will pay twelve Brabant groats per hundred verses of new morality plays, miracle plays, entertainments, prologues and refrains which he composes at the request of the deans, and he is obliged to present the work in fine copy.

Item, the factor will receive a ha'penny per hundred verses which he is required to copy on a roll for the actors to perform the work.

Item, the responsibilities of the guild and the incumbent in the matter of this office can be terminated by either side, provided that a year's notice is given.

VI: CIVIC RELIGION AND THE COURT

Introduction

The control that late medieval urban authorities sought to exercise over the sacred, particularly over cults of saints – control which might seem the exclusive preserve of Church and clergy – is a phenomenon identified in Italian city states as 'civic religion'.[1] In many ways the term is equally applicable to towns in Northern Europe. From the fourteenth century, if not earlier, official civic interest in acquiring patron saints and managing their public veneration is evident. The assumption of civic control over incipient cults (such as in Tournai or Brussels [**20a, 20b, 22**]), the establishment of annual processions with relics around the entire circuit of city walls, the organising of groups within the city at these events [**20a**], the involvement of urban officials even in authenticating new cults beyond city walls [**21**] all point to a will among urban elites in the Low Countries, much as in North Italian towns, to create a sense of civic order by harnessing the intercessory power of saints. The will to impose order was neither united nor successful in every case. Divisions among Brussels town councillors concerning a new cult at Scheut may have been sharper than one of their number, Adriaan Dullaert, was prepared to admit [**21**]. Official municipal control over the annual procession of St Lieven's relics in Ghent was clearly limited, as Chastelain had cause to lament [**13**]. Nonetheless, the will to control is manifest: public expressions of devotion in these towns were clearly deemed to lie within the remit of civic authority.

They were also of interest to princely rulers. Mass pilgrimage to the shrine at Scheut commanded the attention of ducal officials as quickly as it did the concern of the Brussels town council. Much like other princely rulers, the Burgundian dukes built up their own spiritual arsenal, heavenly and terrestrial, of saints and clergy protecting their souls and bodies: some of this effort is displayed in the accounts of Charles the Bold's almoner [**27**]. But the dukes also sought to draw on the spiritual capital of their urban subjects: the same accounts reveal offerings to churches and relics in every town that Charles visited. The involvement of Burgundian rulers in the religious life of their towns was regular, frequent and varied.

1 A. Vauchez, 'Patronage of saints and civic religion in the Italy of the communes', in A. Vauchez, *The laity in the Middle Ages*, transl. M.J. Scheider (Notre Dame, 1993), pp. 153–68 (where there is a reluctance to apply the term to Northern Europe); A. Vauchez, 'Introduction', in A. Vauchez (ed.), *La Religion civique médiévale et moderne (Chrétienté et Islam): Actes du colloque de Nanterre (21–23 juin 1993)* (*École française de Rome*, 213), pp. 1–12; G. Dickson, 'The 115 cults of saints in later medieval and Renaissance Perugia: a demographic overview of a civic pantheon,' in idem, *Religious enthusiasm in the medieval West* (Aldershot, 2000), pp. 6–25.

How this involvement is best characterised may be debated.[2] At one level it
seems aggressive and interfering. The impact on the urban religious landscape
of the ruler's presence – vicarious or personal, living or dead – must have
been considerable. The numerous images of the duke and his family – in gold,
wax, stone and glass – that were donated to churches all over ducal territories
[**25, 27**],[3] for all their penitential intent, were visible memorials of princely
authority. The funeral arranged for Philip the Good in Bruges in 1467 – with
its impressive cortège filing through the city streets – was a more lavish send-
off than any citizen could have afforded [**27**]. The presence or needs of the
living duke in the city might also mean disruption to the normal rhythms of
urban religious activity. Charles the Bold's desire for intercession seems to
have required, in the first year of his rule, the reliquaries of more than fifty
churches to be hauled from shrines and treasuries for his personal inspection [**27**]. His political needs also required the same relics to be dispatched
around the town on ad hoc or 'general' processions which, combined with the
preaching of sermons, could alert townspeople to specific ducal needs: rulers'
requests to towns and their churches for these processions (already apparent
in the late fourteenth century), was increasing under the last two Burgundian
dukes and was stepped up still further by Charles's Habsburg successor in the
crisis years after 1477.[4]

Moreover, the involvement of the dukes in annual civic processions made clear
that these were not purely 'civic' events. After 1448 the city streets of Brussels during its 'ommegang' were to be decorated with escutcheons depicting
ducal arms, and the craft guilds were to put together what seems to be a living
genealogy, everyone of them preparing a representation of a former Brabantine duke on their processional wagon [**20a**]. In 1457 the procession had to
be rearranged to suit ducal convenience: Philip the Good requested that the
Brussels magistracy should postpone the event by a day to allow the dauphin
Louis time to attend.[5]

But it is misleading to view such involvement in urban religious life exclusively
as one of 'state' interference. The role of the dukes in annual civic processions
was usually as passive spectators. Their joining of guilds and fraternities in

2 For an overview, see Lecuppre-Desjardin, *La ville des cérémonies*, pp. 86–102, where
  the emphasis tends to be on ducal use of (and interference in – p. 101) civic religious
  activity.

3 For gold votive images of the duke, see H. van der Velden, *The donor's image: Gerard
  Loyet and the votive Portraits of Charles the Bold* (Turnhout, 2000).

4 For relics and general processions and the use made of them by the dukes, see A.
  Brown, 'Civic ritual: the counts of Flanders and the city of Bruges in the later Middle
  Ages', *English Historical Review* 112 (1997), pp. 277, 289–90; A. Brown, 'Perceptions of
  relics: civic religion in late medieval Bruges', in D. Strickland (ed.), *Images of Sanctity*
  (forthcoming).

5 Cited in R. Stein, 'Cultuur en politiek in Brussel in de vijftiende euuw: Wat beoogde
  het Brusselse stadsbestuur bij de annexatie van de plaatselijke ommegang?' in H. Pleij
  (ed.), *Op belofte van profijt: Stadsliteratuur en burgermoraal in de Nederlandse letterkunde
  van de middeleeuwen* (Amsterdam, 1991), pp. 233–4, from A. Wauters, *L'Ancien ommeg-
  anck de Bruxelles* (Brussels, 1848), p.11.

towns [**24, 27**] suggests participation (perhaps even piety) that complemented rather than appropriated the religious activities of their urban subjects.[6] Their contact with the cults and processions of their territories was not a departure from 'tradition' by a new 'state-building' dynasty. Processions in Lille or Brussels had enjoyed close links with counts of Flanders and dukes of Brabant [**20, 23**]: the Burgundian dukes were not so much 'interfering' in local traditions as maintaining the links to which they were legitimate heirs.

In any case the initiative to draw rulers into closer participation with urban life came more from local than 'state' pressure. The efforts by members of the Brabant and Brussels elites to encourage Burgundian interest in their region (newly acquired by the dukes in 1430) is revealed by – among other things – the efforts to encourage ducal residency in Brussels at the Coudenberg palace; by the production of histories of the region for ducal perusal[7] (to which Adriaan Dullaert also makes reference in his account of the miraculous image [**21**]); and by the orders of the Brussels magistracy to craft guilds for the 'ommegang' to include living reminders of princely ancestors in Brabant. The prologue to the new plays of the Joys of the Virgin Mary also ordered in 1448 might seem egregiously flattering to the Burgundian ruling family and its wider territorial interests, but it also advertised the glories of Brussels itself [**20b**]. Such efforts helped in the process of legitimising Valois Burgundian rule; but the initiative came from a desire among local elites to acquaint the duke with his responsibility toward their traditions and liberties. And occasionally, as in Bruges 1488, they might use religious ceremony to call their ruler to account [**26**].

The uses to which townsmen and rulers subjected the holy were many. But to concentrate focus solely on 'state' or 'civic' control affords only the narrowest view of religious activity that took place in the period and region. It is easy to overlook other creative (and destructive) forces at work besides city and prince: the bishops who were apparently powerful enough to inspire civic processions at Tournai or Lille, or to contemplate armed expeditions into the Brabantine countryside to torch incipient shrines [**21, 22, 23**]; the variety of religious orders which could attract the pious attention of laymen; the clergy of churches who guarded the relics of saints to which secular powers laid claim; the confessors and almoners who could bend the ducal ear and divert ducal resources toward 'appropriate' ends. Clerics and clerical bodies asserted their own agenda over secular authorities. Moreover, the profusion of relics in towns and villages by the fifteenth century, and the vast number of smaller religious groupings of parishes and guilds[8] – of which the accounts of Charles the Bold's almoner offer only a glimpse – suggests lay activity that secular and clerical authorities could react to but scarcely contain.

---

6 For other examples (including Our Lady of the Snow guild in Bruges which numbered more than 1,000 members at its peak), see Brown, 'Bruges and the "Burgundian theatre-state"', pp. 573–89.

7 See more generally R. Stein, *Politiek en historiografie: het onstaansmilieu van Brabantse kronieken in de eerste helft van de 15de eeuw* (Leuven, 1994).

8 More generally see P. Trio, *Volksreligie als spiegel van een stedelijke samenleving: de broederschappen te Gent in de late middeleeuwen* (Leuven, 1993).

20(a). The Brussels *ommegang*:[9] the civic ordinance of 1448

Stadsarchief, Brussels, cartularium VIII, fos 98v–99r, cited in Stein, 'Cultuur en politiek', pp. 241–3.

[An early legend (which includes traditional elements of cult formation, with relic or image theft) put the origins of the Brussels *ommegang* (procession) back to 1348. At some point in that year, the Virgin Mary appeared in a dream to an old woman, Beatrix Soetkens, and ordered her to bring a miraculous statue of the Virgin from Antwerp to Brussels. Despite opposition in Antwerp, the statue arrived in Brussels, and was met by Duke John of Brabant, the magistracy, craft guilds and crossbowmen and was carried to the archers' chapel on the Sablon (Zavel). But it may be that the event and procession began a little later than legend maintained. The earliest secure reference to the annual *ommegang* is in 1366 (or possibly 1359) which would place the arrival of such a statue within a context which was politically charged: in 1357 Louis de Male of Flanders had secured from the duke of Brabant the cession of Antwerp to Flanders after the battle of Asse the year before,[10] despite – according to Adrian Dullaert in his later account of another miracle story [21] – the heroic opposition of Brabantine duke and townsmen. In this context, the acquisition of the miraculous statue seems to take on the guise of a riposte to Flemish aggression.

Be that as it may, every year the statue was honoured with a procession on the Sunday before Pentecost – also the day for the Brussels fair. The early involvement of the city magistracy is evident by 1366 in an agreement between the archers and chaplains of the Sablon chapel mentioning arrangements for the procession.[11] Civic efforts to manage and add lustre to the event in the fifteenth century are most clearly shown in the ordinance of 1448. As for the rulers of Brabant, their continuing interest is attested by occasional gifts to the event in the fourteenth century.[12] This was an interest that the dukes of Burgundy were to inherit with the duchy after 1430, one which the Brussels magistracy evidently hoped to nurture.]

Here follows the ordinance ordered by the mayors, aldermen, and account masters and the good common people of the council of the town of Brussels, to the honour of the God of Heaven and of his beloved and blessed mother, concerning the procession of the Zavel.

First: that the procession will, from now on, be kept better and more honestly than has been the case up until now; it will be handed over, and

---

9 Stein, 'Cultuur en politiek in Brussel', pp. 228–43; id., 'The "Bliscapen van Maria" and the Brussels policy of annexation', *PCEEB* 31 (1991), pp. 139–51, and references cited there.

10 Antwerp was returned to the dukes of Brabant after 1404: see D. Nicholas, *Medieval Flanders* (London, 1992), p. 226.

11 An earlier reference in 1359 may well show official civic involvement: see Stein, 'Cultuur en politiek', p. 399 n. 14.

12 Henne and Wauters, *Bruxelles*, p. 106.

the town of Brussels shall buy the house of Philips Vylens, situated in Brussels in the Guldestraat, at a price that both can agree on. The town will lend this place to the aforementioned brotherhood to carry out the work of the procession.

The town magistrates shall ask the craft guilds who used to put on representations of dukes, and pull them along on wagons,[13] shall continue to do so to the honour of Our Blessed Lady. And also, that the town magistrates shall ask those guilds who until now have not pulled along a duke, that they, on their own or together with one or two other guilds, will in future dress up and pull along a duke, insofar as their finances allow.

The three upper deans of the three craft guilds, or three other important men from the patrician families in the town, or their representatives, shall direct the procession on horseback, to ensure that those who participate in the procession will proceed properly and promptly. To these three the town will give a measure [*stoop*] of wine for their labour.

The magistrate will no longer entertain the prelates and other lords at the town hall with either a meal or breakfast, so as to avoid the procession being delayed or disrupted. As compensation, in the afternoon, every prelate who attends the procession will be given two more measures of wine than has been the case to date.

Every year a play will take place upon the day of the procession, starting on the second hour after noon, on the lower market square in Brussels. This play will be that of 'The Seven Joys of Our Virgin Mary'. Each year, a new 'Joy' will be performed, until all seven have been played. Then it will commence again at the first 'Joy'. The town of Brussels will make a scaffold on which this play can be performed.

The churchwarden of Our Lady will receive from the town, annually, the sum of £5 *grote oud*,[14] to help pay for the troubles and effort he has to endure on behalf of the procession, and that the same procession will be maintained in a more appropriate, more honest and more frugal fashion than has been the case to date. With the gift of this £5 *grote oud* the town will be discharged from having to pay more to the cost of the procession. And the churchwarden has agreed that he will not claim

---

13 This seems to be what is implied by: 'dat men van der stadt wegen bidden sal den ambachten die ter selver processien hertoghen te hebben plegen, dat zij die voirt ter erren van Onser Liever Vrouwen houden end die voirt uuttouwen, gelijc zij tot hiertoe hebbe gedaen'.

14 That is, 'old money', prior to a revaluation of the Brabant pound.

more money from the town, and that he will organise the procession to Our Lady on the Zavel annually, with honesty and without bad faith.

The churchwarden will provide the town, annually, with a good and lawful account, as those of Our Lady have done to date.

Thus have all these points been concluded and decided upon, namely, that the churchwarden will annually organise the procession honestly, appropriately and frugally, until such time as the law should be amended by the town council.

These points have been agreed in the common council of the town on Tuesday 20 February, 1448.

20(b). The Brussels *ommegang* and The Seven Joys of the Virgin Mary, 1448

W.H. Beuken, *Die eerste bliscap van Maria en die sevenste Bliscap van Onser Vrouwen* (Culemborg, 1978), pp. 54–5 (lines 1–36).

[In 1448 the city council of Brussels stipulated that the plays of the Seven Joys of the Virgin Mary (drawn from the Golden Legend) should be performed in the Grand' Place as the conclusion of the annual procession. The prologue's reference to the Burgundian rulers and to Brussels as a latter-day Troy may be interpreted as the city's attempt to encourage civic pride or unity, as well as to identify itself with its rulers; it may indicate how far Burgundian authority had penetrated civic events.[15] If so, this penetration is brief: such references occupy a tiny fraction of the two plays still extant, and the plays as a whole deal with the theme of Fall and Redemption, from Mary's conception to Her Assumption.]

Prologue of the first play:

> Mary, sparkling and shining light
> Immaculate and pure daisy,
> Guard our prince and his wife too,
> And Charlie, our young lord,
> As well as his wife, against grief.
> And all their friends, young and old,
> That God may protect them against all evil,
> And still more that their land, towns,
> Villages, castles, may God always keep
> In peace from all misfortune;

15   For comments on the plays, see Stein, 'Cultuur en politiek in Brussel', pp. 228–43; id., 'The "Bliscapen van Maria"', pp. 139–51.

And all those, to cut short my prayer,
Who seek the profit of this land.
And for Brussels, I pray above all!
So warm greetings to you young and old:
Be welcome, noblemen and common people,
Who with affection are gathered here
In this beautiful square
Be welcome, noblemen and common people!
The pleasure garden of Troy, the noble seed,
Growing and flourishing, is called Brussels.
We greet you warmly, young and old,
Who are gathered here for our feast day.
Be welcome here, as it should be.
Because that dear praiseworthy image,
Which here on the Zavel still stands.
From Antwerp to Brussels came
By miracle, as many know,
And we should like to show you, and for that purpose it is prepared,
For the praise of the heavenly treasury [Mary]
In the form of play as will be seen
The First Joy which here follows …

21. Scheut: The miraculous image of the Virgin Mary, 1450–1457

Adriaan Dullaert, 'Origo sive exordium monasterii Nostrae Dominiae de
Gratia, ordines Cathusiensium, juxta Bruxellam', in E. Reusens (ed), *Origines
de la chartreuse de Scheut, sous Anderlecht*, in *Analectes pour servir à l'histoire ecclé-
siastique de la Belgique*, iv (Leuven, 1867), pp. 87–122.

[Adrian Dullaert (chronicler and secretary of Brussels) relates how in a certain
place called 'Ten Scheute' (between Molenbeek and Anderlecht) outside the
walls of Brussels, a sixty-year-old shepherd called Peter de Asscha planted an
oak tree on a pleasant green spot, next to the public highway, to afford weary
travellers shade from the sun. Years later he affixed a simple image of the Virgin
Mary to the tree and used to pray there three times a day. In 1450, the year
of the papal jubilee, on the day of Pentecost, the image was seen miraculously
illuminated, and a great multitude of men and women came to visit the image;
and during the following three days visitors came not just from Brabant but
also from neighbouring regions, in search of cures for their infirmities …]

Since the multitude of sick continued to visit the place and find cures, and
their oblations in wax and money, objects and animals began to be freely
offered there, and since a small building was erected to house the image
and receive and protect those oblations, these things were brought to
the attention of the town council of Brussels, by Jean d'Enghien, lord

of Kestergat, *amman* of Brussels,[16] esquire, then a knight, and counsellor of the most illustrious lord and prince Philip, duke of Burgundy and Brabant, and count of Flanders, Holland etc. ... the *Amman* and council agreed and unanimously ordered, in accordance with common ecclesiastical law, that, on behalf of the duke and town, they should depute two prudent and suitable laymen who knew how and would be willing and able to regulate and protect the place and the goods or offerings, and to spend them faithfully on the construction of a chapel; and that the oblations thus freely brought there, on the advice of these men and the *amman*, on behalf of the lord duke and the town, should be disposed of to the honour of God and the Virgin Mary, as should appear best and most seemly to them, until it should be ordered otherwise by consent of an overseer; since free, ordered and distinct oblations to the honour of the Virgin had been given by the faithful at that place. This was done and this was how it was ordered to be carried out. So the two men who assumed this burden were Jan Cambier and Egidius van Dielbeke,[17] citizens and inhabitants of Brussels, from the craft of smiths and guild of St John ...

[So much money came from pilgrims, however, that a dispute arose between Martin Steenberghe, secretary of Duke Philip, as the curate of the parish of St John in Molenbeek, and curate of the chapter of Anderlecht over which parish the place was situated (decided in favour of the latter); and a second dispute over the oblations between chapter and the churchwardens of Anderlecht, which seems to have brought the matter to the attention of the bishop ...]

[The] lord John of Burgundy, bishop of Cambrai, resident in Brussels, and other men, clerical and lay, did not know what lay behind these events; rumour grew on account of the multitude of people frequenting the place, the copious amount of oblations being given, the exaltation and dissemination of diverse miracles or at least signs and prodigies, and most of all because of the apparent and presumed idolatory in a place that had not yet been consecrated. Because of all this, it could not be suffered that such a good pastor should find himself personally in a public and profane place, just as it should not be suffered by law, based on the text of the decretals which say: 'It is written: beware

16 The *amman* was a ducal appointment, dealing with matters pertaining to ducal jurisdiction in Brussels. On Jean, see most recently G. Small, 'Local elites and "national" mythologies in the Burgundian dominions in the fifteenth century', in R. Suntrup and J. Veenstra (eds), *Building the past/Konstruktion der eigenen Vergangenheit (Medieval to Early Modern culture*, vol. 7: Frankfurt, 2006), pp. 229–45.

17 Both men were linked to the city government, Cambier being burgomaster in 1451 (see Stein, 'The "Bliscappen van Maria"', p. 141 note 13).

of offering your burnt-offerings in any place that you come upon; but in all places that your lord God will choose, that is in places consecrated by lord God, or in divine tabernacles with prayers and chosen pontificals'. Nevertheless, it happened that the lord bishop, intending to take precautions against evil reports and mutterings of the people, deliberated and concluded that he himself should go personally to the place with a large and powerful party of horsemen, burn down the small building, and thoroughly forbid and prohibit access, adoration and oblations, and place the miracles of the crowds under ecclesiastical punishment and censure, preventing completely any further visits to the site. So fervently had the lord bishop made up his mind to destroy and weaken the place, that he had all his horses saddled up and placed in great readiness, intending to ride there himself, execute his will, and in procession carry back the image of the Virgin Mary on the tree to the mother church of Anderlecht. But suddenly there came before the lord bishop, by inspiration of the Holy Spirit, it may be supposed, the venerable lord and master Jean Rudolphi alias Flamingi, doctor of law and official of the bishop in Brussels, canon of Cambrai, and a good and just man; and through his counsel and persuasion, lest there should be great tumult among the people, the lord bishop remained at his abode and left the small building alone, with the enclosed image on the tree, unburned and undisturbed ...

[A solemn committee was set up, composed of deputies from the bishop, the lord duke and the town of Brussels (including the alderman and Adriaan Dullaert himself), to inquire into the miracles. The committee had difficulties in finding someone of sufficient credibility and standing to bear proper witness to the miracles, so it remained unsure. But pilgrims, with all kinds of ailments, kept coming, offerings kept being made, and further miracles were reported ...]

Having considered all this, and having held lengthy deliberation over these things, it seemed to the lord *amman* and the town council of Brussels that there should be honest and rational agreement that the oblations already given in that place, and others to be offered in the future in honour of God and the glorious Virgin Mary and to increase divine service, should be spent and used there; and that to this end appropriate lands should be bought with this money, and a beautiful and notable chapel be constructed and built in that place. So with the greatest outlay and expense, with God's help, it was undertaken and fulfilled; since this kind of chapel should be built, from the oblations, with white and cut stones, with a thick and round wall of great circumference, and a roof of stone, and beautiful, high and broad glass windows skilfully painted with images of saints and representations and arms of donors.

One of these, standing behind the altar of the Virgin Mary, the lord
Charles of Burgundy, count of Charolais and lord of Béthune etc., only
son, heir and successor of Lord Philip, the then reigning duke, caused
to be made ...

[Other donors, represented in windows, are then described. Nearest Charles
are Jean d'Enghien; Jean de Poitiers, lord of Arcis, counsellor of Duke Philip;
and a member of duchess Isabella's Portuguese family, Peter de Villa. On the
western part of the choir were the windows of: Master Monfrandus Alaert,
a citizen of Ghent, and the duke's procurator general in Flanders (who also
donated ornaments for the altar); William de Pape, a noble; Jan Blankaert,
merchant and citizen of Brussels. On the southern side of the choir, three
windows from Adriaan Dullaert's own family: Maria de Vorda, his former
wife; Adrian and Katherine Bogaerts; Margaret of Mazenseel, mother of his
wife. Near to these were two windows of Jan de Lovaniio and Jan Mosselman,
butchers, and Joducus Sionis, of the clerks' guild. A round window in the nave
above the main door was that of Jan Cambier, churchwarden of the chapel.

Three roofers met with accidents while the chapel was being built which
caused much lamentation among the common people of Brussels and concerns
about delay in the consecration of the chapel; but after four years and further
tribulation, not helped by wars in Flanders, the chapel was consecrated by the
bishop. After a time the mood within the town council in Brussels was that the
site would be suitable for a religious order, perhaps the Observant friars minor,
or that of St William, or a nunnery of St Bridget. The petition of one Brigittine
to assign the chapel to the order was turned down by the town. It was decided
that a friary was inappropriate because the place was at some distance from
the town and that there had been quarrels and litigation between the friars
minor and those of the Observants in Brussels, to the scandal of the people. So
a Carthusian house was decided upon because of its penitential and contempla-
tive life, and because the Carthusians were not burdened by association with
the mendicants in Brussels. In consultation with the *amman*, this choice was
agreed upon.[18] Arrangements are made by the town council for seven brother
friars of the Sack in Brussels to transfer to the new Carthusian monastery. But
the house of these brothers had been badly in need of reform, so careful moni-
toring of the goods of the new monastery and oblations from pilgrims needed
to be made. Papal and episcopal authority was obtained ...]

From all this not just seven religious brothers and priests, converted and
endowed, should be able and ought to live day and night serving God
and the Virgin Mary, praying assiduously for the town and for living
and dead benefactors, but also travellers, pilgrims and the poor coming

18 Another reason for this choice, not mentioned here by Dullaert, but apparently put
   forward by Peter de Thimo, a city pensionary, was that Philip the Good was especially favourable to the Carthusians, and that Philip would therefore be more inclined
   to spend time in Brussels were a Carthusian house set up. See Stein, 'The "Bliscappen
   van Maria"', p. 142.

to the door of the monastery might enjoy the customary bestowal of alms when goods are sufficient. These goods were ordered and collected for these purposes from the beginning; although it was arranged by the rectors of the town that the seven brothers of the Sack, while they lived, should also be provided from these goods with suitable victuals and clothes and other things necessary for living, and should be placed in appropriate places to serve God, that by these arrangements there should be no just cause for quarrelling. It was also arranged, however, that when those brothers of the Sack died, the other brothers should not be able to be chosen and installed by the others. Thus it was done and observed, and all of this is to be found registered in the town book in the vernacular. When all these things were heard and understood in full by the legislators, notwithstanding three legislators endeavouring to resist (who, however, were overcome by just reasoning), everyone of the town council consented unanimously and in concord and, as if by way of the Holy Spirit, it was drawn up in an ordinance, publicly read out in full by me in that very place in their presence, with no word changed, added or taken away from that ordinance.

[The ordinance was then read out loud before the great council of the town, numbering sixty people, and later inscribed in the town's book of privileges. The monastery's buildings began to be constructed, but alms began to diminish because of plague and famine and the poverty of the people. So the town decided to make a new foundation and build it with their own money. Fifty Rhenish florins were found from 'public money'; and in May 1457 the monastery was formally established and the chapel consecrated by the bishop.

Adriaan Dullaert then relates how he discovered from the histories of Brabant that the date of foundation was the hundredth anniversary of another event which occurred at the place called Ten Scheute before the chapel and monastery had been built. On Wednesday within the octave of St Laurence, a battle had been fought between Lodewijk the count of Flanders and the nobles, commune and people of Brussels, defending the town and the lands of the duchess of Brabant (the battle of Asse, 1356). During the battle a noble with the name of Asscha allowed the ducal standard to fall to the ground, upon which the Brabant army submitted to the count and much blood was shed on the battlefield. Through God's work this place of death became transformed a hundred years later into a place of consolation and grace; and whereas the noble standard-bearer by dropping the ducal standard, out of negligence or arrogance, had led to a time of death, a simple and God-fearing man with the same name, de Asscha, in the same place set up a new standard, with the arms of the Virgin Mary, for eternal salvation.]

22. The procession of Our Lady at Tournai, 1461

ADN B4106 (fo.108r)
Date: 1461

[According to Herman of Tournai in the 1140s, the procession was begun by
Bishop Radbod in 1090 as a liturgical rite against the 'burning plague' (ergotism):
so moved was the bishop by the plague's savage effects that he had the entire
population of the whole province gather for a mass fasting in the church of
the Virgin Mary at Tournai.[19] He established that on the following feast of the
Exaltation of the Holy Cross (14 September) everyone in Tournai should go
barefoot on procession, carrying the reliquaries of their saints, around the entire
circuit of the city walls.[20] Herman was already complaining that in his day people
did not walk in the procession unshod, and that knights and young men were
playing games of 'diverse vanities' during the event. Secular involvement was
probably early; certainly by 1284 that of the city magistracy is made explicit;
an exclusive confraternity supporting the cult had already been founded. In
the fourteenth century, the procession became more formalised, with the city
commune paying for the upkeep of the processional route, and for gifts of wine
and money to the participants. Messengers were sent out and a few towns from
the bishopric (notably Ghent) sent representatives. The day before, a municipal
delegation met with the clergy of St Peter to inspect the processional route
and make other preparations. On the day itself, according to a late medieval
processional, three separate processions were undertaken, the first at midnight,
leaving the cathedral with priests carrying crosses, pilgrims following, and
going around the town; the second making a similar tour, at which representatives from Ghent escorted the reliquary of Our Lady; a third after first mass,
with a larger cortège making a tour of the town. Dumbshows and relics lined
the processional route. The counts of Flanders attended or contributed to the
procession in the fourteenth century; the dukes of Burgundy continued this
tradition. The following is the kind of payment that was regularly made by the
dukes, from at least the 1420s, for the cloak clothing the Marian image.]

To Clais Pagant merchant living in Bruges, for the purchase of an imperial cloth of gold acquired and bought by him, from which was made the
cloak for the image of Our Lady in the cathedral church of Tournai the
eve of Holy Cross day in September 1461 ... in the accustomed manner
...: £42;

To Thierry dele Wingarde living in Ghent for 14 packages of miniver for
the cloak of Our Lady ... and for two and a half packages of threads to

---

19 Herman of Tournai, *The restoration of the monastery of Saint Martin of Tournai.* ed.
   L.H. Nelson (Washington, 1996) esp. 20–1. For the procession generally (and difficulties with dating its foundation) see J. Dumoulin and J. Pycke (eds), *La Grande Procession de Tournai (1090–1992)* (Tournai, 1992).

20 For the liturgical tradition of penitential processions see A. Vauchez, 'Liturgy and
   folk culture in the *Golden Legend*', in his *Laity in the Middle Ages*, pp. 129–39.

border the cloak..; and for a chaplet of felt for the image …: £50 16s;

To Regnault de Wittelbegne, embroiderer, and Jehan le Scult, robe furrier, for their salaries for measuring and making the cloak of the image … £7 4s;

To Lancelot Hanois called de Berchem for his salary for having carried the cloak to Tournai … and for a horse for five days (at 20s a day) … and for paying the minstrels who played when the image was dressed as accustomed … £7.

23. The procession of Our Lady at Lille, 1463

ADN B93
Date: May 1463

[In 1254 a statue of the Virgin called Notre Dame de la Treille in the collegiate church of St Peter survived a fire. Miracles occurred and a fraternity was set up. In 1269 papal indulgences were granted to the pilgrims who were flocking to the place. In the following year, Margaret countess of Flanders, partly to encourage alms for the rebuilding of the church, founded a procession, which was then held every year on the second Sunday in Pentecost. In 1275 the processional route was rerouted at Margaret's behest (because of building work on the Dominican friary) so that it passed outside the city walls (and may then have made a complete circuit around the city walls).[21] Duke Philip the Good continued a tradition of comital involvement in the cult by acquiring papal indulgences in 1433 for pilgrims who came to the procession, and on several occasions personally attended the procession.

By this time, if not well before, it was also a civic event organised by the municipality and the collegiate church of St Peter, held shortly after the feast of Corpus Christi. The town accounts list regular expenses for the two processions, which in 1461 came to more than £124.[22] The procession included members of craft guilds who carried torches; *tableaux vivants* were set up along the route. Later in the day, a competition of short plays was conducted, sometimes by parishes or neighbourhoods who took the name of their principal streets or squares.[23] The dukes of Burgundy attended on several occasions and subsidised

21 H. Platelle, 'La Vie religieuse à Lille', in L. Trenard, *Histoire de Lille: des origines à l'avènement de Charles Quint* (Lille, 1970), esp. pp. 358–61; E. Hautcoeur, *Histoire de Notre-Dame de la Treille* (Lille, 1920); id., *Cartulaire de l'église collégiale St Pierre de Lille* (Lille, 1894), i, pp. 367, 431, 432, 367; ii, pp. 461–2.

22 The largest expenses went on the civic officials who attended the procession of the Sacrament (£5), the cloth of gold bought from Antwerp to cover the shrine of Our Lady (£32), and on torches (£20), and for other subsistence expenses of the civic officials (£34): Van den Neste, *Tournois*, pp. 344–5.

23 Knight, 'Professional theater in Lille'; G.A. Runnalls, 'Civic drama in the Burgundian territories', *Revue Belge de philologie et d'histoire* 78 (2000), pp. 414–16. See also [19].

performances. In 1468 (and in 1470) the company of the Place de la Petit Fret of Lille petitioned the ducal *Chambres des Comptes* to assist them with the heavy costs born by them in their Old Testament play during the procession.]

To the honour of God and the Blessed Virgin Mary and the decoration and enhancement of the procession at Lille, we the prelate of fools[24] out of good will with the deliberation of our council, give prizes and jewels to those who ... come on the day of the procession, on floats, carts, scenes or portable scaffolding, to make a dumb-show in the morning while the procession passes by the places set down by us or our deputies; and after dinner to perform before us, where we please, some stories from the Bible, from the Old Testament as from the New, from the life or passion of a saint approved by Mother Church, or other romances and stories contained in ancient chronicles, to the length of at least 300 lines or more if willing, in good and true rhetoric. These stories have not been performed in this town for sixteen years.

For the first prize: an image of Our Lady surrounded with the sun, and the moon beneath her feet, crowned with twelve stars, worth £12. For the second prize: a silver moon worth £6. And for the float or company best and most richly covered and decorated according to and serving its theme, a crown and 12 stars of silver worth 40s. To the float which after supper or the following day if it seems expedient, will come to perform the most joyous and pleasing game of fools, which has not been performed in this town for ninety-nine years, a silver ducat worth 60s ... All those wishing to win prizes are to come on the day of Sacrament [Corpus Christi] between 3 and 4 o'clock after dinner in our clerk's palace ... and bring in writing the story they want to perform ...

24. Valenciennes: fraternity of St Barbara, 1459

ADN B1689, fos 17r–17v
Date: 8 April 1459

[Valenciennes also had an annual procession, the origins of which are traceable (according to a tradition recorded in the thirteenth century) to another apparition of the Virgin Mary in 1008, delivering the town from plague. In return for deliverance, an expiatory procession was founded, one which followed the route marked out by a thread or cord which had miraculously appeared. The cult may well have enjoyed an early association with the count of Hainaut: a charter of 1086 gave comital confirmation of the building of an oratory in the

24 The canon Jean Waterloos occupied the post of the 'prelate' or 'bishop' of 'fools' – which was elected at Epiphany by the choir of the collegiate church of St Peter, at least until 1469 when the post seems to have been abolished.

church of 'Notre Dame La Grande' which housed the relic of the holy cord.[25]
Valois Burgundian involvement in the religious festivities of Valenciennes may
be found in their interest in rhetoric chambers, but also in the foundation of a
fraternity with its own procession.[26]]

Duke Philip the Good, for the glory of God and St Barbara, virgin and
martyr, and for the increase of divine service, has ordered the foundation of a confraternity in the church of the prior and convent of the
Order of Our Lady of Carmelites [white friars] in Valenciennes, for
vespers, vigils and mass on the day of the feast of St Barbara in a suitable place until a chapel be built in honour, and with a representation, of
St Barbara. Every person, secular and religious, who is received into the
confraternity, whether man or woman, will be required to give [*blank*]
at his reception and entry of his goods according to his ability, devotion
and liberality, and offerings …

25. Ghent: windows in the parish church of St John the Baptist, 1462

ADN B4107, fo.104v.
Date: January to August 1462

[Besides offerings to the church buildings, processions, fraternities and reliquaries of their subjects, the dukes of Burgundy donated images of themselves
which served as more personalised kinds of memorial. Of the many media
chosen, stained glass appears most frequently in the ducal accounts [see also
21]. Motives behind such gifts were multiple. Some were votive, made following
a specific vow to a particular saint out of thanks for saintly intercession.[27] More
generally, the dukes, like other benefactors, sought the prayers of the faithful to
ensure the swift passage of their souls through Purgatory: personalised memorials would ensure that prayers were appropriately directed. But undoubtedly
religious concerns were entwined with political needs.[28] Reminders of ducal
rule might be needed in some places more than others – for example, Duke
Philip the Good made a particular effort to populate the windows of churches

25 H. Lancelin, *Histoire de Valenciennes* (Valenciennes, 1933), pp. 23–33, 92–5, 128, 134; A.
Julien, *Histoire du culte de Notre-Dame du Saint Cordon, patronne de Valenciennes* (Valenciennes, 1886).

26 See also the alms and offerings of Charles the Bold in 1468 for gifts to this confraternity
[**27**].

27 See Velden, *The Donor's Image*, on gold votive images (and for the stock of eight of
such images in the Bruges *prinsenhof*, still awaiting disposal in shrines and churches
at the time of Charles the Bold's death in 1477).

28 M. Damen, 'Vorstelijke vensters: Glasraamschenkingen als instrument van devo-
tie, memorie en representatie (1419–1519)', *Jaarboek voor Middeleeuwse Geschiedenis* 8
(2005), pp. 140–200.

in Holland with his image and coat of arms shortly after his acquisition of the
county in 1433. Here, the gift to a church in Ghent (involving negotiation with
churchwardens who occupied important positions within the city hierarchy)
was part of the ducal assertion of authority over a turbulent city, following the
'reconciliation' of 1458 [13, 14].]

To the churchwardens and governors of the parish church of St John the
Baptist in the town of Ghent, the sum of 225 *escus d'or* (of 48 Flemish
groats each) which the duke by letters patent and for the causes and
considerations declared in them, given at Brussels on 14 July 1462,
verified as appropriate, has, by his special grace, given and donated, on
one occasion, to the churchwardens or representatives of that church ...
to work on and decorate three windows ... that is in the middle window
depicting the tree of Jesse around the prophets belonging to it; in the
second window adjoining, a representation of the most noble persons of
the duke, and of his son the count of Charolais; and in the third window
representations of the duchess and the countess of Charolais. Around
and above these three windows, for glass filled with depictions of arms
and devices of the noble lords and ladies, and the arms of peace of the
duke ... £540.

26. Maximilian in Bruges 1488: oaths and general processions

*Het boeck van al 't gene datter geschiet es binnen Brugge sichent Jaer 1477, 14
Februarii, tot 1491*, ed. C. Carton (Ghent, 1859), pp. 222–4.

[On 31 January 1488, Maximilian entered Bruges and quickly found himself
trapped by the citizens. There he was to remain, under virtual house-arrest, until
May. Animosity in Flanders toward the Habsburg ruler had been increasing
since the death of Mary of Burgundy, Charles the Bold's surviving heir, whom
Maximilian had married in 1477.[29] The Estates-General had accepted their son
Philip as count, but at first refused to recognise Maximilian as his guardian.
In Flanders, Ghent took the lead in opposition to Maximilian; a more radical
government in the city allied with Charles VIII of France, who had been
seeking to reassert French sovereignty over the county. In Bruges, antagonism toward Maximilian had been later in developing, but the city had already
suffered economic setbacks during a blockade of Sluis by Maximilian's troops
in 1485, and resented his demands early in 1488 for subsidies and soldiers. The
capture of Maximilian in the city was followed by a period of blood-letting, in
which the duke's officials and then, as more radical elements in the city took
control, leading citizens were executed, culminating in the beheading of Pieter

29 For overviews on this period in Flanders, see Blockmans, 'Autocratie ou polyarchie?';
     and for Bruges: R. Wellens, 'La révolte brugeoise de 1488', *Handelingen van het genoot-
     schap voor geschiedenis 'société d'émulation' te Brugge* 102 (1965), pp. 5–52.

Lanchals on 22 March.[30] But pressure to release Maximilian was made more intense by the presence of German troops outside the city, and on 16 May, Maximilian swore to renounce the regency of Flanders, agreeing to allow the county to be governed by a council which was to include the Three Members of Flanders and the Estates General.

The formalities observed in the oath were based on precedent. They began with a 'general procession' which involved carrying two of the most important relics in the city. Traces of these ad hoc, relic-carrying processions can be documented in the city from the late fourteenth century: the collegiate church of St Donatian claimed a special role in their organisation. During the fifteenth century, they had been increasingly requested by the city authorities and by the ruling prince, often for the purpose for celebrating or supplicating prayers for princely enterprises.[31] Maximilian had himself made use of these processions during the crisis years of the 1480s. The body of St Donatian was requested for procession more than any other relic. Here, however, the relics and procession were being used to extract promises from the prince.

The following account, written by an anonymous Bruges author differs in certain respects from the account later written up by the court historian Jean Molinet.[32] Molinet's view of the event presents it as a more fraught and emotional occasion, and one in which Bruges citizens were made to repent of the 'rude insolence' toward the dignity of their prince. Princely dignity in any case was quickly reasserted: once released from Bruges, Maximilian renounced his oath on the grounds that it was made under duress.]

On 16 May 1488 a general procession was held and undertaken, in which were carried the honoured and glorious shrine and body of St Donatian, which lies in Bruges in the church of St Donatian; also with these were carried the blessed, honoured and Holy Cross, which rests in Our Lady Church, within the town of Bruges; and the glorious, honoured, blessed Sacrament, from the church of St Donatian; and thus the procession with great reverence and honour moved to the house of Jan de Groos,[33] formerly standing by St James's church, where the king of the Romans[34] had been in good protection and safety,[35] for eleven weeks and one day. And with this procession went the chief magistrates of Bruges, and the deans of the guilds, each dean with his sworn men, and the Four Lands,

30 For the execution of Lanchals (who had been receiver-general of all ducal finances under Charles the Bold), see Boone, 'La Justice en spectacle', pp. 43–65.

31 See Brown, 'Ritual and state-building'.

32 *Chroniques de Jean Molinet*, ed. G. Doutrepont and O. Jodogne, ii (Brussels, 1935), pp. 6–13.

33 Jean Gros: see [7c] above.

34 Maximilian's title as heir of the Holy Roman Emperor. Maximilian became Emperor in 1493.

35 Molinet prefers to describe Maximilian's sojourn in Bruges as an 'imprisonment' (*Chroniques*, ed. Doutrepont and Jodogne, ii, p. 9).

Flanders, Brabant, Holland and Zeeland. They brought the Emperor [Maximilian] out of the house and to the main market place; and he came entirely on foot, wearing a black velvet cloak, and a fine scarlet hat, and in this manner proceeded to the house called the Cranenburch. An enclosed space had been set up there, between a stage and the clock of the Cranenburch house, and there they stood, the magistrates, the deans of the town of Bruges, the deputies of the Four Lands.[36] Then the king came to the window, and many nobles with him, and before all the other deputies, standing in the enclosure, all fell to their knees, with their heads bare. And then the king gestured so that they all stood up,[37] and publicly pardoned everyone for all that had happened, as if it had never happened, and the charter of the true peace was shown sealed and delivered into his hands, and the unity of the three members of Flanders and Four Lands, and the king, confirmed it, and sealed it with his hand, and with his hand he wrote that he would truly keep to the peace steadfastly and truthfully. This done, he came out of the house, up on to the stage, before the altar where lay the glorious body of St Donatian, the holy, blessed Cross from Our Lady Church, and the blessed Holy Sacrament from St Donatian's; then the king placed his hand on each of them, and swore, on his head, breast and nobility, to uphold unity and peace, to hold and keep it truly, surely, steadfastly and honourably; and he went to sit in the kingly chair, clad with good cloth and red velvet, made and ordered for him, and the benches of the stage were bedecked with tapestries. The Four Lands sat on the benches, and the magistrates, deans of Bruges and collegiate clergy, stood around the stage. When this had been all fulfilled and done, the king and procession set out again, and when they left, *Te Deum Laudamus* was sung ... the town players standing in their accustomed place, and played *Ave Regina Celorum*, and other pieces of music. The processors and king came to the church of St Donatian with the relics, and then went for a meal at the house of Jan Caneele, near the Coushalle, while the relics of the Holy Cross from Our Lady Church remained in St Donatian's church.

36 According to Molinet, Maximilian's entry into the Cranenburg house at that moment, instead of mounting the platform, had caused great anxiety: a 'hideous cry went up from the people', one so frightening that it caused the churchmen in the square to scatter. It subsided just before Maximilian appeared at the window (ibid., p. 11).

37 Not before, according to Molinet, they were required to seek clemency from Maximilian. The three members of Flanders were made to listen to Jean Rogier haranguing them about the 'great misuse, rude insolence and horrible excess' that they had inflicted, or had allowed the people to inflict, on the 'noble person of the king'; and most of them having been reduced to tears of repentance, they were required to ask forgiveness of the prince through the intercession of the representatives from the Estates General (ibid. pp. 11–12).

Lord Philip of Ravestein who came from Sluis that day with eighty horses, entering by the Coolskerke gate, went to St Donatian's and laid his hand on the body of St Donatian, the Holy Cross and the Holy Sacrament and swore to be good and true. Then the Holy Cross was taken back to Our Lady's church.

27. Ducal offerings and alms, 1468

ADN, B2068, fos 39r–40r, 43r, 61r–2r, 82v–85r, 102r–106v, 132r–35r, 171r–2r, 203v–4r, 252r–53v, 300r–1r, 325v–8r, 356v–59v; now printed in Greve, Lebailly, and Paravicini (eds), *Comptes de l'argentier de Charles le Téméraire*, i, pp. 70–1, 76–7, 100–2, 130–3, 158–64, 199–203, 255–7, 299–300, 363–6, 425–6, 457–60, 497–500.

[The functions of the ducal almoner are described in the Household ordinances of Charles the Bold [4]. The following show a year of household expenditure on alms, offerings and divine service.]

January

Alms and Offerings: total: £324 17s 6d:

£100 to Innocent de Crecy, counsellor and almoner of my lord, to distribute at his discretion;

£20 to Willequin Couton, footman, to distribute alms at the command and order of the duke;

£10 to Pierre Chastel, groom, to distribute in alms;

£180 to Jehan Gourdin, counsellor and master of petitions to the prince, for a tombstone on the sepulchre of Anthoine de la Platiere, squire cupbearer, and for his perpetual obit in the church of St Peter in Louvain;

£14 17s 6d to brother Jehan Desmarez, priest, for offerings, alms and light paid by order of my lord to the confraternity of St Barbara at Valenciennes,[38] where my lord had sent him on his behalf: for a candle (25 lbs) and 4 torches (3 lbs each) (£6 9s 6d); for placing the arms of the duke on these and other candles (11s); for carrying the candle in procession before St Barbara (3s); to 4 clerks carrying the torches in the procession (4s); for offering a gold *escu*; and for 5 gold *escus* given to the reliquaries of St Barbara (25s).

---

38 See [24].

February

Total in alms: £130 ... [Sums distributed by Innocent de Crecy, Willequin Couton, and Pierre Chastel in January appear here and in subsequent months].

March

Total: £669 6s:

£24 to Innocent de Crecy for 4 low masses for those who died in the last wars from Flanders and others in the company of the late duke;

£6 to Innocent de Crecy for a mass that my lord ordered every day in honour of God and St Sebastian [as in January and February: this daily mass appears regularly in later months];

£360 to Jehan Marchant, embroiderer of the duke at Brussels, for his outlay in making of 7 borders ordered to be given to the church of St Lambert, Liège: 4 borders to put on the 4 cloaks, 3 on the chasuble with the habits for the deacon and subdeacon, and to make all along the borders the life of St Lambert;

£29 6s to Jehan le Tourneur, sommelier, for offerings: Friday 11 March of 4 ob. of Rhenish gold (£4 4s) to St Sebastian of Linkebeek (Brussels); Saturday 12 March to Our Lady of Grace (£4 4s); Friday 18 March to St Sebastian (£4 4s); Saturday 19 March to Our Lady of Grace (£4 4s); and to Patoulet by order of my lord 10 gold *escus* (£12 10s).

April

Total in alms: £925 10s:

... £50 to Enguerram bishop of Salubrye, counsellor and confessor, to distribute in alms at his devotion and according to the command of the duke;[39]

£15 to Innocent de Crecy for 4 trentals of 30 masses ordered by my lord every month (this for March), and for a mass of St Sebastian that the duke wanted celebrating every day (60s) [This sum appears regularly in subsequent months].

£80 to Innocent de Crecy to several poor hospitals and poor people on departing from Bruges for Zeeland in April;

105s to Jehan Blanchot dit Croy, footman, at the command of the duke for offerings to the church of St Nicholas at Mons in Hainaut (21s) and to Master Jehan de Mauberge, Ladre near Lille (£4 4s);

39 Enguerrand Seignart, bishop of Silivri (Selymbria). See [8] above.

105s to Pierre Chastel in alms to the town trumpeter of Maubeuge (21s), 3 chapels between Maubeuge and Le Quesnoy (63s), and to St Geneviere on leaving Le Quesnoy (21s);

£500 to the duke in the month of Easter for Holy Week and for Easter to spend himself upon certain devotions and meritorious works;

£19 19s to Innocent de Crecy on the command of the duke for Maundy Thursday, for 20 ells of white cloth to make 4 cloths, one for my lord and another for his first chaplain, the third for his confessor, the fourth for the said almoner, placed and carried before each of them on Maundy Thursday to wash the feet and hands of 13 poor people, as my lord is accustomed to do every year (£4); for 50 other ells of lesser cloth to make 2 large cloths to place on the laps and feet of the poor, the residue of which to make several other cloths for the officers of my lord serving on Maundy Thursday (£7 10s); for the gift given by my lord to each of the poor, 13s each (£8 9s);

Total in offerings: £272 1s:

£50 to the bishop of Salubrye for the offering on Good Friday to the True Cross and for confessions of the lesser officers of his *hôtel* on Easter day;

£23 13s for offering by order of my lord to St Sebastian, at Our Lady of Riez, and to Our Lady of Alsemberg [Brabant] on his last departure from Brussels, by certification of Olivier de la Marche (in 8 gold *escus* and 13 ob. of Rhenish gold);

£54 to Philippe Siron, counsellor and first chaplain of his domestic chapel for offerings: for mass in the church of St Waudru at Mons (21s) and to the reliquaries there (105s), and to the church of St Vincent, Soignies (21s) and to the reliquaries there (105s), and to the cordeliers of Mons (21s) and to the reliquaries there (105s); 4 April to the church of St Maubeuge (21s) and to the reliquaries there (105s); 5 April to the church of St Quesnoy for the same (£6 6s); 6 April to the church of St Amand, Valenciennes for the same (£6 6s); 9 April to St Donatian's church in Bruges on Palm Sunday and for the reliquaries there, given as offering by the duke in the church (£6 6s); 24 April to the abbey of Middelburg in Zeeland (16s) and reliquaries there (£4 4s); 27 April to the church of St John, Sluis £4 19s;

£10 for the offering of the duke to the church of St Donatian at Bruges when he was received as lord and prince of the county (8 gold *escus*);

£134 8s to Tomasso Portinari, merchant living in Bruges, for a cloth of gold of 8 ells that the duke gave to St Donatian's at his reception and 'joyous Entry'.

May

Total in alms: £295:

... £15 to Innocent de Crecy: for 120 prebends [doles] to the poor that my lord ordered to be distributed on Sunday 8 May when he held the feast of the Golden Fleece in the church of Our Lady in Bruges[40] to 120 poor people, each prebend worth 2s (£12); for 30 masses, 15 of the Holy Ghost, 9 of Our Lady, 6 of St Katherine, which my lord had said and celebrated in the church of Our Lady, at 2s per mass (60s).

Total in offerings: £993 12s 8d:

£36 to Guillaume Doré, clerk of the domestic chapel of my lord, for having a wax model of a man on his knees, weighing 60 lbs, which my lord formerly had presented in his name to St Adrian at Geraardsbergen; and for an offering (£24) which my lord ordered for the reliquaries of St Adrian;

52s to Charles de Visen, esquire, for an offering made by my lord before the image of St Thomas when he last left Bruges to go to Zeeland;

£29 9s to his confessor, bishop of Salubrye, for offerings at Brussels 6 January, day of Kings, (25s) and for a sermon (25s); 16 January to Our Lady of Grace by Brussels (54s); to St Gudule, Brussels, 5 gold *ridders* (£6 15s); 2 February on the Purification of Our Lady (25s) and for a sermon (25s); 2 March Ash Wednesday (25s) and for a sermon (15s); at Annunciation 25 March (25s) and for a sermon (25s); on Palm Sunday 10 April (25s) and for a sermon (25s); on Maundy Thursday (25s), at Easter (25s) and for a sermon 35s; to the church of Our Lady in Bruges 3 May (25s) and for a sermon (25s); day of Ascension for a sermon (25s);

£925 11s 8d on the obsequies of Jacques de Bourbon[41] in the church of St Donatian, Bruges, on 24 and 25 May ...

40 For other expenses connected with the feast: £106 14s for 17 ells of taffeta, inlaid with colours of azure, yellow and black, for *cottes d'armes* and banners; £298 18s for painting a large wooden tableau with the arms of Philip the Good to set above the place where the duke sat in the church (£9 12s); another tableau with the arms of those attending; and one with the arms of dead members; and for offerings at mass for the souls of dead members, for wax, for heralds; also to Tomasso Portinari £8,398 13s for a total of 1857 ells of cloth for harnesses, robes for household staff for the feast; £134 8s for 8 ells of cloth of gold for an altar cloth which the duke had placed in the church on the day of the feast (B2068, fos 102r–2v, 106v–107v, 379r–82r; Greve, *Comptes*, i, pp. 159, 164–5, 528–32).

41 Knight of the Golden Fleece.

June

Total in alms: £333 6s:

... £50 to Master Thibault Barradot, secretary to my lord,[42] during the illness of Jacques de Bourbon to give to the papal legate being then in Ghent so that the said Jacques before his death obtained by the mercy of God the indulgences which the Pope had given and which could be acquired in Ghent;

... 64s to the almoner for 30 requiem masses for the soul of the late Jacques de Bourbon and 2 masses at the devotion of my lord;

60s to the almoner for requiem masses on command of my lord for the soul of the late Henry le Blanc, kitchen boy of my lord, killed in Bruges;

£12 2s to the almoner for 30 masses which my lord had celebrated in Sluis for the soul of Jacques de Bourbon on 19 June (60s) and for having put in holy ground the body of the Bastard of Condé,[43] formerly executed by justice (62s) and for 60 masses celebrated for his soul (£6);

Total in offerings: £854 12s:

£25 4s to Innocent de Crecy, almoner, for offerings made for the duke in the church of Our Lady in Aardenburg 13 June;

£6 6s for the offering my lord made to the church of Our Lady of Goes in Zeeland when he was there;

£19 4s for the offering my lord made to the church of Our Lady in Aardenburg when he was there 11 and 17 June by certification of Olivier de la Marche;

£39 12s for the offering my lord made to the church of the Holy Ghost at Rue, for 180 lbs of wax which my lord out of devotion offered there and was presented by him, including 3 escutcheons with the ducal arms placed on the wax (12s) ...

[There are similar gifts to the churches of Our Lady at Liesse; St Martin of Tours; St Hubert in Ardenne; St Nicholas at Varangéville];

... £580 10s for the annual [anniversary service] of the dead duke celebrated in the church of St Donatian in Bruges on 14 and 15 June 1468

---

42 Later served Maximilian, took a wealthy wife in Bruges and was buried at St Donatian's. His son was an alderman of the town and a member of Holy Blood confraternity.

43 Ernoul, illegitimate son of Ernoul de La Hamaide, lord of Condé. On his controversial execution, see Chastelain, *Oeuvres*, v, pp. 397–405.

... (£105) 700 lbs of wax bought in Bruges for 50 large torches for the church and altar;[44]

£25 to my lord's confessor, the bishop of Salubrye, for offerings and sermons; 5 June, Pentecost, for the offering of my lord in his *hotel* in Bruges (25s) and for a sermon (25s) and to be distributed on the said day by my lord himself and at his pleasure (62s); 12 June, Trinity, for the offering of my lord (25s) and for a sermon before him (25s); in June at the anniversary service of the former duke (25s) and for the buying of a mourning cloak for the service belonging to the confessor which my lord held before him (£12 10s); 16 June offering (25s) and a sermon (25s); 24 June, John the Baptist's day (25s), and sermon (25s).

July

Total in alms: £286 1s:

... £20 to Willequin Couton to distribute in alms on the day of my lord's jousts ...

21s to 2 poor children who sang before my lord, a gift he gave for food and in alms, a florin of Rhenish gold.

Total in offerings: £94 7s:

£2 1s for the offering made by the treasurer, on the command of my lord, to Our Lady of Aardenburg 16 July when my lord put to sea for Holland in 12 gold *escus* (£15) and for 6 candles of 30 lbs (£6); for a low mass (2s);

£13 13s for an offering made by my lord to Our Lady of Gravezande 19 July when he was in Holland;[45]

£10 10s for 4 candles (60 lbs of wax) made by my lord at the tomb of madame of Charolais at Antwerp 1 August;

£10 7s to the bishop of Salubrye, confessor, for offerings: on 16 July for a certain offering my lord made out of devotion (56s); 18 August at Middleburg, Zeeland (24s); and to Our Lady of Gravezande 1 gold *escu* and 5 florins of Rhenish gold (£6 11s)

---

44 Other payments for the funeral of Philip the Good appear elsewhere in the accounts (B2068, fos 175–6; Greve, *Comptes*, pp. 260–1): £1,400 to the dean and chapter of St Donatian, for a mass of requiem at the High Altar, for 1,329 lbs of wax for the service and 4 large candles around the tomb during the service.

45 Innocent de Crecy was also paid £14 for another offering to Our Lady of Gravezande and £9 for 140 images of Our Lady of Gravezande of which 15 were gilded and distributed by my lord to several knights and esquires with him on his voyage to Holland (B2068, fo 176r; Greve, *Comptes*, p. 261).

£21 4s to Philippe Siron for offerings: at Ascension (25s); 12 June for a mass at Our Lady of Aardenburg and for the late Jean Lamirot (£4 6s); for 4 candles (1 lb each) and 2 *philippus clinquars* given by my lord and the duchess on the day of their nuptials (42s); 27 July for the offering my lord made at mass for his first entry into Delft [Holland] and to the relics of St George there (£13 13s).

August[46]

Total in alms: £269 10s:

… £4 4s to Jean le Saige, a poor man, for cloth and lining my lord gave for making a robe in March; and to a man to whom my lord gave alms 16 August (6s).

Total in offerings: £19 16s:

£12 9s to Philippe Siron, first chaplain, on orders of my lord for offerings: 2 August at Antwerp for the mass of requiem of madame de Charolais (25s); to St Sebastian's church, Brussels (£7 7s); 6 August to Our Lady of Grace, Brussels (77s);

£7 7s to Jehan le Tourneur, sommelier, for offerings made by my lord in August at Our Lady of Gommegnies (£4 4s) and for a gift to a poor woman at the Hague in Holland (63s).

September[47]

Total in alms: £571 1s:

… £8 8s to Pierre Chastel, groom, for alms to Ernoulet who was hackney servant of the dowager duchess (21s); to Master Jean le Mauberge, leper, when my lord went from Courtrai to Lille (£6 6s); a poor man living between Cambrai and Le Quesnoy (21s);

£7 10s to Willequin Couton for a person, [upon which amount] my lord does not wish to expand;

£8 8s to the almoner for a poor man between Cambrai and Le Quesnoy in August; and in July to a poor varlet;

£7 10s for certain alms;

£120 to Innocent de Crecy as my lord left Le Quesnoy in August on

46 Also payment of £48 to the church of Our Lady of Roes in Haynin to make a window.
47 See also payments to churches: £21 to chapel of Our Lady of the Garenne at Hesdin for repairs £21; £24 church of Ancre for repairs; £60 to church of St George near Douai for repairs (B2068, fos 232v–33; Greve, *Comptes*, p. 358).

which he wants no further declaration;

£17 5s to Innocent de Crecy for alms to the grey sisters at Aalst (£4); the Carmelite friars at Nielles near Aalst (£6); the church of Our Lady in Courtrai (£4 4s) and to the children of the choir (21s);

£24 to Innocent de Crecy for alms to Our Lady of Galilee at the Hague (£6); sisters of the convents of St Elizabeth (£6) and convents of the order of St Augustine at the Hague (each £6); to the Nazareth convent near Riswijck (£6);

… 78s to Innocent de Crecy for 3 masses of Our Lady, St Clare and St George celebrated on 13 days in September;

£9 to Innocent de Crecy for a spoken mass in the church of Our Lady of Grace near Brussels every Saturday and for an offering there …

£13 10s to Innocent de Crecy for a mass every Friday at St Sebastian's Linkebeek, Brussels, with offerings to the shrine (and 1 lb wax as at the church of Our Lady);

£9 for similar masses and offerings in the chapel of St George near the Hague every Tuesday;

£13 10s for similar masses and offerings every Wednesday at the chapel of St George at Douai;

£80 to the regular churches of Syon and the brothers of the Cross of Schiedam by Delft; each church (£40) to make a window of such personages as the lord lieutenant of Holland and Master Anthoine Michel advise.[48]

Total offerings: £51 1s:

£38 12s to the bishop of Salubrye for offerings: 5 August, day of St Dominic, for the offering of my lord to the friars preacher in Brussels (25s) and to the reliquaries there (£6 6s); 15 August, day of Our lady, for his offering (25s) and sermon (25s); 8 September, day of the Nativity of Our Lady, for his offering to St Fussy at Péronne (25s) and offering to the relics there (£6 6s) and sermon (12s); for a third of the cost of the robes of the confessor for June, July, August and September (£20);

£12 4s to Laurent Bouquery, clerk of the oratory of my lord, for daily offerings paid on my lord's command from 11 January to 31 August 1468 (244 days).

48 Ducal secretary.

October

Total in alms: £468 4s:

... £195 4s to Innocent de Crecy which my lord ordered to be delivered to friars minor and other *hôtels de Dieu* in Péronne and around Lihons-en-Santerre and for several good people at Lihons for great losses suffered under men of war who were lodged in these places and elsewhere;

£8 to Jehan de Bours, curate of St Saviour's in Péronne for obsequies by order of the late duke for the soul of Hugues de Neufville called Le Moisne his servant (13 low masses of requiem and other suffrages);

Total in offerings: £25 4s:

£21 to Guillaume Dore for offerings made by my lord at Bapaume 6 gold florins (£6 6s); in the church of Our Lady Cambrai (£8 8s); in the church of St Albain at Namur (£6 6s)

£4 4s to Innocent de Crecy for offerings of my lord to the reliquaries of the church of St Peter at the castle of Namur.

November

Total in alms: £701 16s:

... £238 to the almoner commanded by my lord for various religious houses, hospitals and other poor in the region of Liège;

£12 10s to Innocent de Crecy for the cordeliers at Huy at the command of my lord ...;

£18 6s to Innocent de Crecy for 3 daily masses of Our Lady, St Clare and St George, October and November;

£40 10s to Innocent de Crecy for a said mass every Saturday before Our Lady of Grace in Brussels and offering of a florin at the altar and 3 florins at the reliquaries, and candle of 1 lb wax;

£36 to Innocent de Crecy for a mass every Friday at the church of St Sebastian at Linkebeek near Brussels and offerings to altars and relics (October and November);

£40 10s to Innocent de Crecy for mass every Tuesday in the chapel of St George near the Hague in Holland (October and November);

£40 10s to Innocent de Crecy for mass every Wednesday in the church of St George of Gouy-sous-Bellonne near Douai;

£10 10 to Guillaume Couters for poor women of Liège.

Total in offerings: £430 4s:

£12 12s to Guillaume Dore, clerk of the oratory, at Maastricht for the offerings of my lord when in Liège, All Saints Day (21s), to the large church (21s) and reliquaries (£10 10s)

£13 15s to Guillaume Dore for offerings to the reliquaries of St Sebastian church of Val Notre-Dame-lèz-Huy [near Liège] the day he arrived (25s); 20 November for the offering of my lord at high mass (25s) and to the relics there (£11 5s);

£26 5s to Guillaume Dore for offering St Katherine's day at Val Notre-Dame-lèz-Huy; 28 November to relics of the church of Our Lady Louvain (£25 4s);

£125 to Guillaume Dore for offering 100 gold *escus* to St Sebastian church at Linkebeek to the altar and relics there where my lord made his pilgrimage 3 December;

£12 12s to Jehan Rochefay dit Le Rosquin[49] for 12 pennies of Rhenish gold offering of my lord to St Croix near the Hague (Holland);

£240 to Jehan de Zeghelbecque, an embroiderer at Maastricht for a piece of very fine embroidery to make an altar cloth or a pennant to carry in procession, on which was embroidered the miracle of the key which Our Lord gave through his angel to St Servaiz; which my lord bought from the said Jehan to give to St Servaiz in Maastricht in honour of God, including certain escutcheons armed with the arms of my lord which the said Jehan had embroidered and placed on the said work.

December

Total in alms: £425 18s:

... £9 6s to Innocent de Crecy for daily masses or Our Lady, St Clare and St George;

[£81 total for masses and offerings on Tuesdays, Wednesdays, Fridays and Saturdays at the churches as in November];

£57 4s to Philippe Siron for two masses celebrated at the command of my lord in St Donatian's church, Bruges, from St John the Baptist's day to the end of December (191 days) for the soul of the late duke ...

£13 8s to Jehan Blanchot dit Croy: to a poor woman who had lost a calf and a quantity of oats on 15 October when my lord left Lihons; to 6 poor women when my lord passed by Miraumont (42s); to gatekeepers of the castle of Péronne in October (10s); 29 December to the gatekeepers of

49 Counsellor and first esquire of the stables.

the castle of Vilvorde [Brabant] (42s) and to workers for cleaning the ditches of the castle (42s).

Total in offerings: £316 8s:

£24 to Innocent de Crecy for offerings: 10 December to Our Lady of Grace, Brussels (£6 3); 17 December to Our Lady of Grace, Brussels 4 ob. of Rhenish gold (£4 4s); for mass in the church of Our Lady of Sablon for the soul of Guillaume de Boschuise, varlet of the bedchamber of my lord and to a poor archer wounded in the hand at the siege of Liège in the company of the lord of Auxy (£10);

£79 10s to the bishop of Salubrye for offerings: 3 December to Our Lady of Grace, Brussels, 1 gold *escu* and 4 ob. of Rhenish gold (109s); 4 December, St Barbara's day, to the Carmelite [white] friars of Brussels (£6 10s); 8 December, day of Conception of Our Lady, to the friars cordeliers of Brussels, for the relics there 4 gold *escus* (100s) and for a sermon (25s); 19 December to the friars preacher, Brussels, 6 gold florins (£6 6s); the offering of my lord at Christmas for distributions 3 gold *escus* (75s) and 3 masses; on Christmas day distributed at the command of my lord in certain ways of which he does not wish further elaboration 40 gold *escus* and for a sermon (25s);

£60 for the offering of my lord on his behalf by the treasurer to the reliquaries of the confraternity of Our Lady of the Dry Tree at Bruges, by certification of Master Pol Deschamps, dean of the confraternity;[50]

£120 for the offering to Our Lady of Grace, Brussels by the treasurer at my lord's command;

£26 16s to Philippe Siron for offerings of my lord: 8 December to the cordeliers of Brussels (25s): 9 December to St Sebastian's church (25s) and its relics (63s); 16 December to St Sebastian's church (25s) and its relics (63s); 23 December to St Sebastian's church (25s) and its relics (59s); 24 December to Our Lady of Grace, Brussels (£4 4s); 30 December to St Sebastian's church (£4 4s); 31 December to Our Lady of Grace, Brussels (£4 4s);

£6 2s to Lewens Bouquery, clerk of the oratory, for the daily offering of 12d at his command from 1 September to the last day of December (122 days).

50 The confraternity of the Dry Tree was well established in Bruges by 1396, in the church of friars minor, and was an exclusive body with an annual membership of about 60, all of high social standing, including townsmen, courtiers and foreign merchants resident in Bruges. Duke Philip the Good had also been a member. See Brown, 'Bruges and the "Burgundian theatre-state"', pp. 578–9 and references cited there.

SELECT BIBLIOGRAPHY

Armstrong, C.A.J., *England, France and Burgundy in the fifteenth century* (London, 1983).

Arnade, P., *Realms of ritual: Burgundian ceremony and civic life in late medieval Ghent* (New York, 1996).

Blockmans, W. and Donckers, E., 'Self-representation of court and city in Flanders and Brabant in the fifteenth and early sixteenth centuries', in W. Blockmans and A. Janse (eds), *Showing status. Representations of social positions in the late Middle Ages* (Turnhout, 1999), pp. 81–111.

Blockmans W. and Prevenier, W., *The Promised Lands. The Low Countries under Burgundian rule, 1369–1530* (Philadelphia, 1999).

Boone, M., *Gent en de Bourgondische hertogen, c. 1384–c. 1453. Een sociaal-politieke studie van een staatsvormingsproces* (Brussels, 1990).

Boone, M. 'Destroying and reconstructing the city. The inculcation and arrogation of princely power in the Burgundian-Habsburg Netherlands (14th to 16th Centuries)', in M. Gosman, A. Vanderjagt and J. Veenstra (eds), *The propagation of power in the medieval West* (Groningen, 1997), pp. 1–33.

Boulton, D'A.J.D., *The knights of the crown: The monarchical orders of knighthood in later medieval Europe, 1325–1520* (2nd edn, Woodbridge/New York, 2000).

Brown, A., 'Civic ritual: the counts of Flanders and the city of Bruges in the later Middle Ages', *English Historical Review* 112 (1997), pp. 277–99.

Brown, A., 'Bruges and the 'Burgundian Theatre-State': Charles the Bold and Our Lady of the Snow', *History* 84 (1999), pp. 573–89.

Brown, A., *The Valois dukes of Burgundy* (Oxford, 2001).

Brown, A., 'Ritual and state-building: ceremonies in late medieval Bruges', in J. van Leeuwen (ed.), *Symbolic communication in late medieval towns* (Leuven, 2006), pp. 1–28.

Caron, M-T. and Clauzel, D. (eds), *Le Banquet du Faisan, 1454: l'Occident face au défi de l'empire ottoman* (Arras, 1997).

Cockshaw, P. and Van den Bergen-Pantens, C. (eds), *L'ordre de la Toison d'or, de Philippe le Bon à Philippe le Beau (1430–1505): idéal ou reflet d'une société?* (Brussels, 1996).

Cools, H., *Mannen met macht. Edellieden en de moderne staat in de Bourgondische-Habsburgse landen (1475–1530)* (Zutphen, 2001).

Damen, M., *De staat van dienst: De gewestelijke ambtenaren van Holland en Zeeland in de Bourgondische periode (1425–82)* (Hilversum, 2000).

Decavele, J. (ed.), *Ghent: In defence of a rebellious city* (Antwerp, 1989).

De Win, P., 'The lesser nobility of the Burgundian Netherlands', in M. Jones (ed.), *Gentry and lesser nobility in late medieval Europe* (Gloucester/New York, 1986), pp. 95–118.

Huizinga, J., *The autumn of the Middle Ages*, transl. R.J. Payton and U. Mammitzsch (Chicago, 1996).

Hurlbut, J.D., 'Ceremonial entries in Burgundy: Philip the Good and Charles the Bold, 1419–1477' (PhD dissertation, Indiana State University, 1990).

Kipling, G., *Enter the king: Theatre, liturgy, and ritual in the medieval civic triumph* (Oxford, 1998).

Lecuppre-Desjardin, E., *La ville des cérémonies: espace public et communication symbolique dans les villes des Pays-Bas bourguignons (XIVe–XVe siècle)* (Turnhout, 2004).

Nicholas, D., 'In the pit of the Burgundian theater state: urban traditions and princely ambitions in Ghent 1360–1420', in B.A. Hanawalt and K.L. Reyerson (eds), *City and spectacle in medieval Europe* (Minneapolis, 1994), pp. 271–95.

Paravacini, W., *Menschen am Hof der Herzöge von Burgund* (Stuttgart, 2002).

Paviot, J., *Les ducs de Bourgogne, la croisade et l'orient (fin XIVe–XVe siècle)* (Paris, 2003).

Peters, E. and Simons, W.P., 'The new Huizinga and the old Middle Ages', *Speculum* 74 (1999), pp. 587–620.

Pleij, H., *De Sneeuwpoppen van 1511: stadscultuur in de late middeleeuwen* (Amsterdam, 1988).

Prevenier, W. and Blockmans, W., *The Burgundian Netherlands* (Cambridge, 1986).

Schnerb, B., 'Burgundy', in C. Allmand (ed.), *New Cambridge medieval history, 7: c.1415–c.1500* (Cambridge, 1998), pp. 431–56.

Small, G., *George Chastelain and the shaping of Valois Burgundy: political and historical culture at court in the fifteenth century* (Woodbridge/Rochester, NY, 1997).

Small, G., 'When *indiciaires* meet *rederijkers*: a contribution to the history of the Burgundian "theatre state"', in J. Oosterman (ed.), *Stad van koopmanschap en vrede: Literatuur in Brugge op de grens van middeleeuwen en rederijkerstijd* (Leuven, 2005), pp. 133–61.

Small, G., 'Of Burgundian dukes, counts, saints and kings, 14 CE–c.1500', in D.J.D. Boulton and J.R. Veenstra (eds), *The ideology of Burgundy: the promotion of a national consciousness, 1364–1565* (Leiden, 2006), pp. 151–94.

Smith, J.C., '*Venit nobis pacificus Dominus*: Philip the Good's triumphal entry into Ghent in 1458', in B. Wisch and S. Munshower (eds), *'All the world's a stage...': art and pageantry in the Renaissance and Baroque. Part 1. Triumphal celebrations and the rituals of statecraft. Papers in Art History from the Pennsylvania State University, VI* (Pennsylvania, 1990), pp. 259–90.

Smolar-Meynart, A. and Vanrie, A. (eds), *Le palais de Bruxelles: huit siècles d'art et d'histoire* (Brussels, 1991), pp. 15–90.

Sommé, M., *Isabelle de Portugal* (Villeneuve-d'Ascq, 1997).

Stein, R. et al. (eds), *Powerbrokers in the late Middle Ages. The Burgundian Low Countries in a European context* (Turnhout, 2001).

Trio, P., *Volksreligie als spiegel van een stedelijke samenleving: de broederschappen te Gent in de late middeleeuwen* (Leuven, 1993).

Van Bruaene, A.-L., 'Sociabiliteit en competitie: De sociaal-institutionele ontwikkeling van de rederijkers kamers in de Zuidelijke Nederlanden (1400–1650)', in B.A.M. Ramakers (ed.), *Conformisten en rebellen. Rederijkscultuur in de Nederlanden (1400–1650)* (Amsterdam, 2003), pp. 45–63.

Van den Neste, E., *Tournois, joutes, pas d'armes dans les villes de Flandre à la fin du Moyen Âge (1300–1486)* (Paris, 1996).

Vanderjagt, A.J., 'The princely culture of the Valois dukes of Burgundy', in M. Gosman, A. MacDonald and A. Vanderjagt (eds), *Princes and princely culture, 1450–1650*, 2 vols (Leiden, 2003–5), 1, pp. 1–29.

Vaughan, R., *Charles the Bold* (2nd edn, introduction W. Paravicini; Woodbridge, 2002).

Vaughan, R., *Philip the Good* (2nd edn, introduction G. Small; Woodbridge, 2002).

Walsh, R.J., *Charles the Bold and Italy 1467–1477: politics and personnel* (Liverpool, 2005).

INDEX